I actually had a cold all throughout January. For the first time in my life I can claim the achievement for being sick a full 1/12th of a year. You've probably already figured this out but my motto for the year is "stay positive."

-Tite Kubo

BLEACH is author Tite Kubo's second title. Kubo made his debut with ZOMBIEPOWDER., a four-volume series for WEEKLY SHONEN JUMP. To date, BLEACH has been translated into numerous languages and has also inspired an animated TV series that began airing in the U.S. in 2006. Beginning its serialization in 2001, BLEACH is still a mainstay in the pages of WEEKLY SHONEN JUMP. In 2005, BLEACH was awarded the prestigious Shogakukan Manga Award in the shonen (boys) category.

BLEACH
VOL. 67: BLACK
SHONEN JUMP Manga Edition

STORY AND ART BY
TITE KUBO

Translation/Joe Yamazaki
Touch-up Art & Lettering/Mark McMurray
Design/Kam Li
Editor/Alexis Kirsch

Printed in the U.S.A.

Published by VIZ Media, LLC
P.O. Box 77010
San Francisco, CA 94107

10 9 8 7 6 5 4 3 2 1
First printing, July 2016

www.viz.com

THE WORLD'S
MOST POPULAR MANGA
www.shonenjump.com

The future, pitch black, upside down

BLEACH 67 | BLACK

ALL STARS ★ AND

アスキン・ナックルヴァール

ASKIN NAKK LE VAAR

OH-ETSU NIMAIYA

二枚屋王悦
ニマイヤオウエツ

黒崎一護
クロサキイチゴ

ICHIGO KUROSAKI

plot

Ichigo Kurosaki meets Soul Reaper Rukia Kuchiki and ends up helping her eradicate Hollows. After developing his powers as a Soul Reaper, Ichigo befriends many humans and Soul Reapers and grows as a person...

Yhwach leads his Quincy army, the Stern Ritters, into the royal palace of the Soul Society. With Urahara's help, Ichigo and company follow closely behind, hoping to retrieve their friend Uryu. Meanwhile, Squad Zero reveals their true powers in an attempt to protect the palace. Yhwach assembles his strongest warriors and the two clash. Squad Zero seems to have the advantage but Oh-Etsu suddenly seems faint. What exactly is Nakk Le Vaar's power...?

BLEACH

YHWACH

ユーハバッハ

兵主部一兵衛
ヒョウスベイチベエ

ICHIBE HYOSUBE

KISUKE URAHARA

浦原喜助
ウラハラキスケ

STORIES

BLEACH 67

BLACK

CONTENTS

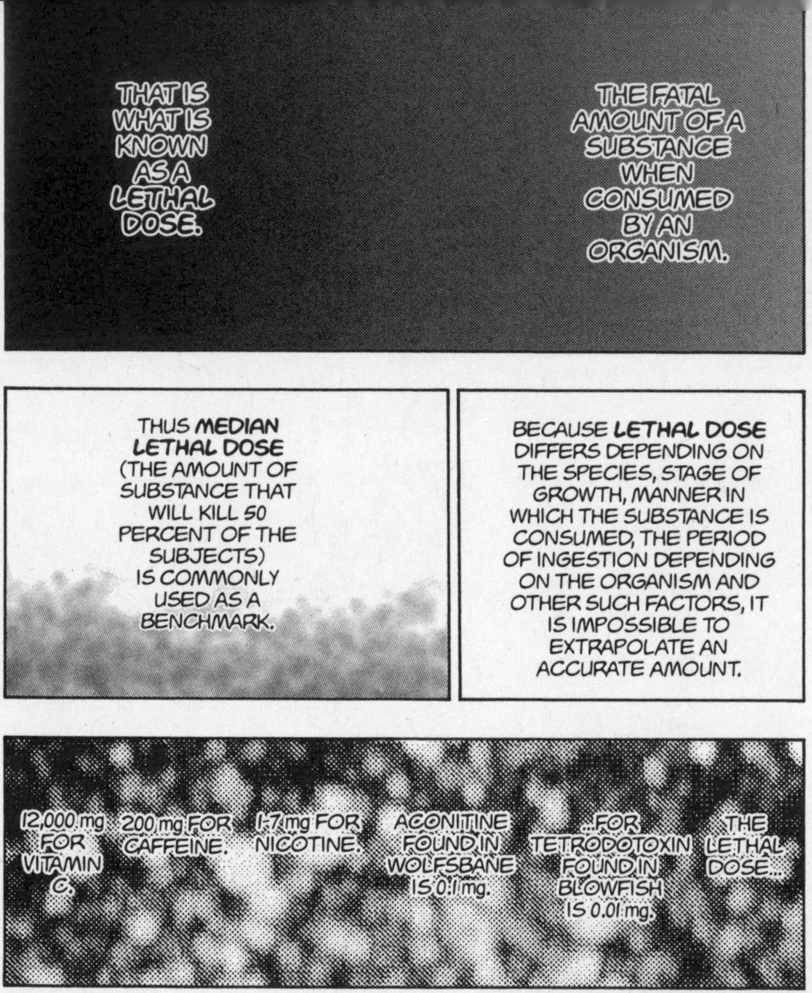
THE FATAL AMOUNT OF A SUBSTANCE WHEN CONSUMED BY AN ORGANISM.
THAT IS WHAT IS KNOWN AS A LETHAL DOSE.
BECAUSE LETHAL DOSE DIFFERS DEPENDING ON THE SPECIES, STAGE OF GROWTH, MANNER IN WHICH THE SUBSTANCE IS CONSUMED, THE PERIOD OF INGESTION DEPENDING ON THE ORGANISM AND OTHER SUCH FACTORS, IT IS IMPOSSIBLE TO EXTRAPOLATE AN ACCURATE AMOUNT.
THUS MEDIAN LETHAL DOSE (THE AMOUNT OF SUBSTANCE THAT WILL KILL 50 PERCENT OF THE SUBJECTS) IS COMMONLY USED AS A BENCHMARK.
THE LETHAL DOSE...
...FOR TETRODOTOXIN FOUND IN BLOWFISH IS 0.01 mg.
ACONITINE FOUND IN WOLFSBANE IS 0.1 mg.
1-7 mg FOR NICOTINE.
200 mg FOR CAFFEINE.
12,000 mg FOR VITAMIN C.

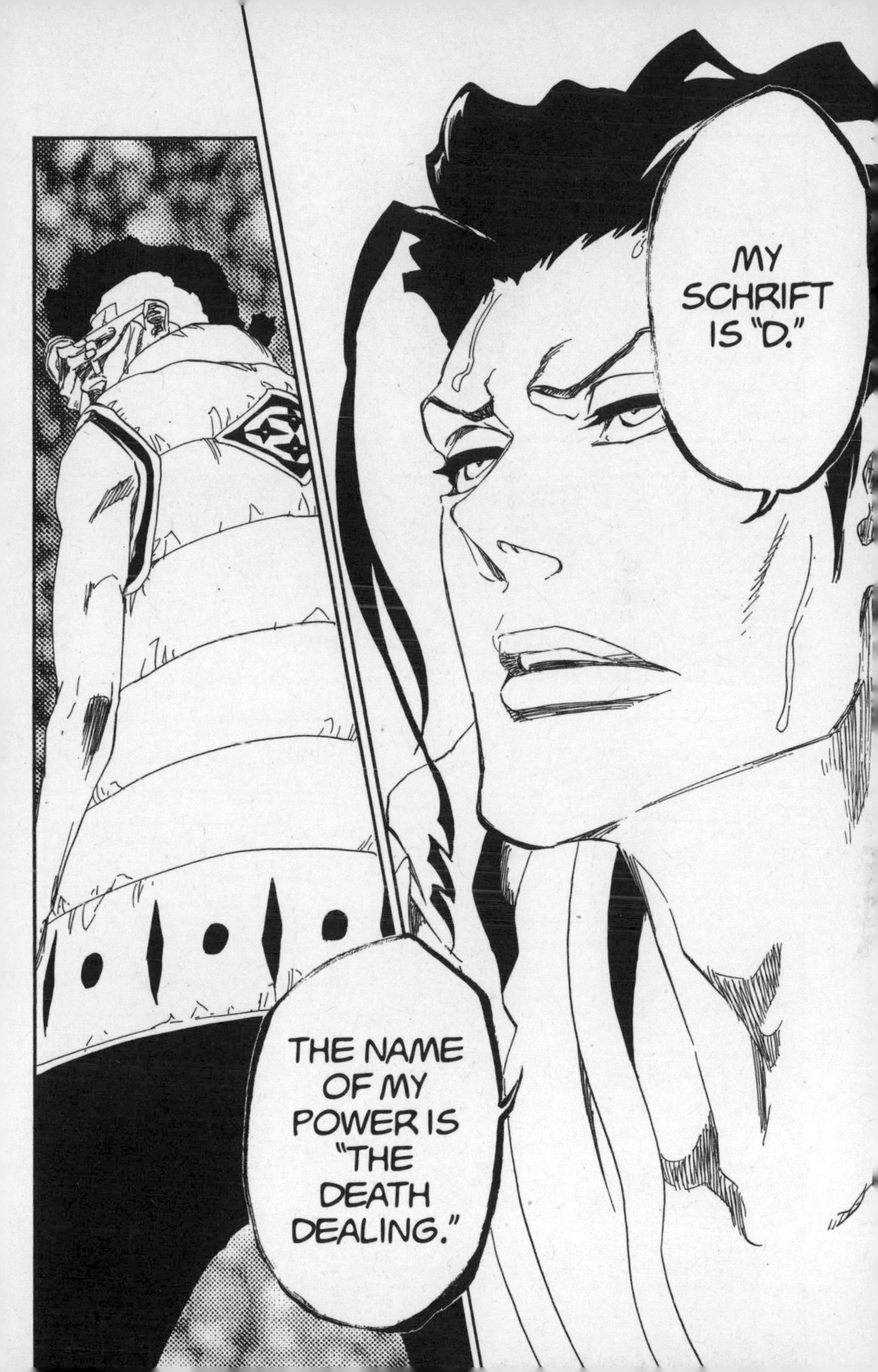
MY SCHRIFT IS "D."
THE NAME OF MY POWER IS "THE DEATH DEALING."

READ THIS WAY

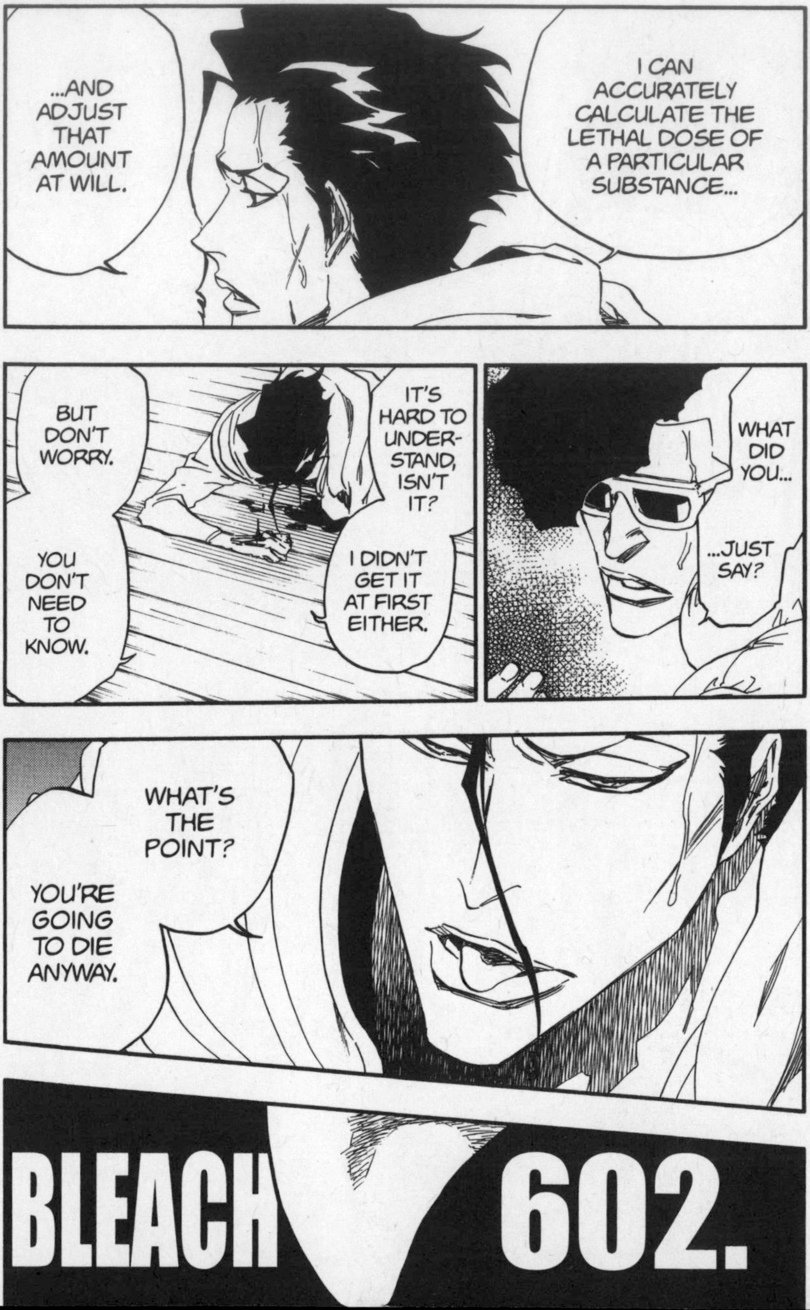
I CAN ACCURATELY CALCULATE THE LETHAL DOSE OF A PARTICULAR SUBSTANCE...
...AND ADJUST THAT AMOUNT AT WILL.
WHAT DID YOU...
...JUST SAY?
IT'S HARD TO UNDERSTAND, ISN'T IT?
I DIDN'T GET IT AT FIRST EITHER.
BUT DON'T WORRY.
YOU DON'T NEED TO KNOW.
WHAT'S THE POINT?
YOU'RE GOING TO DIE ANYWAY.
BLEACH 602.

Bane Licking Good

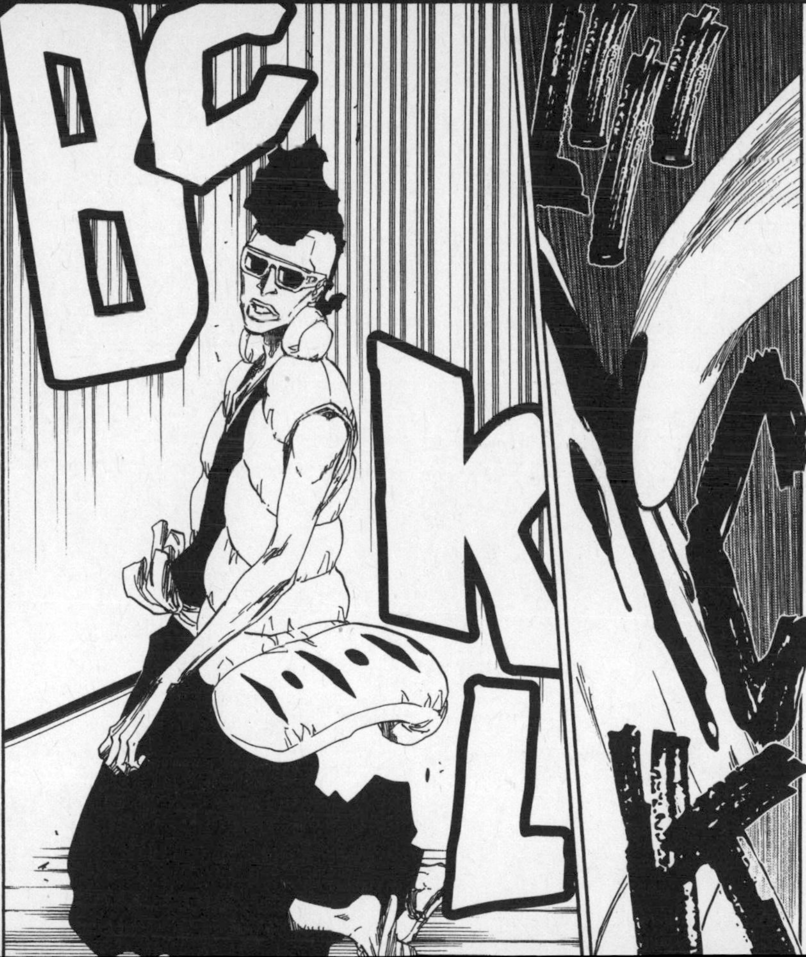

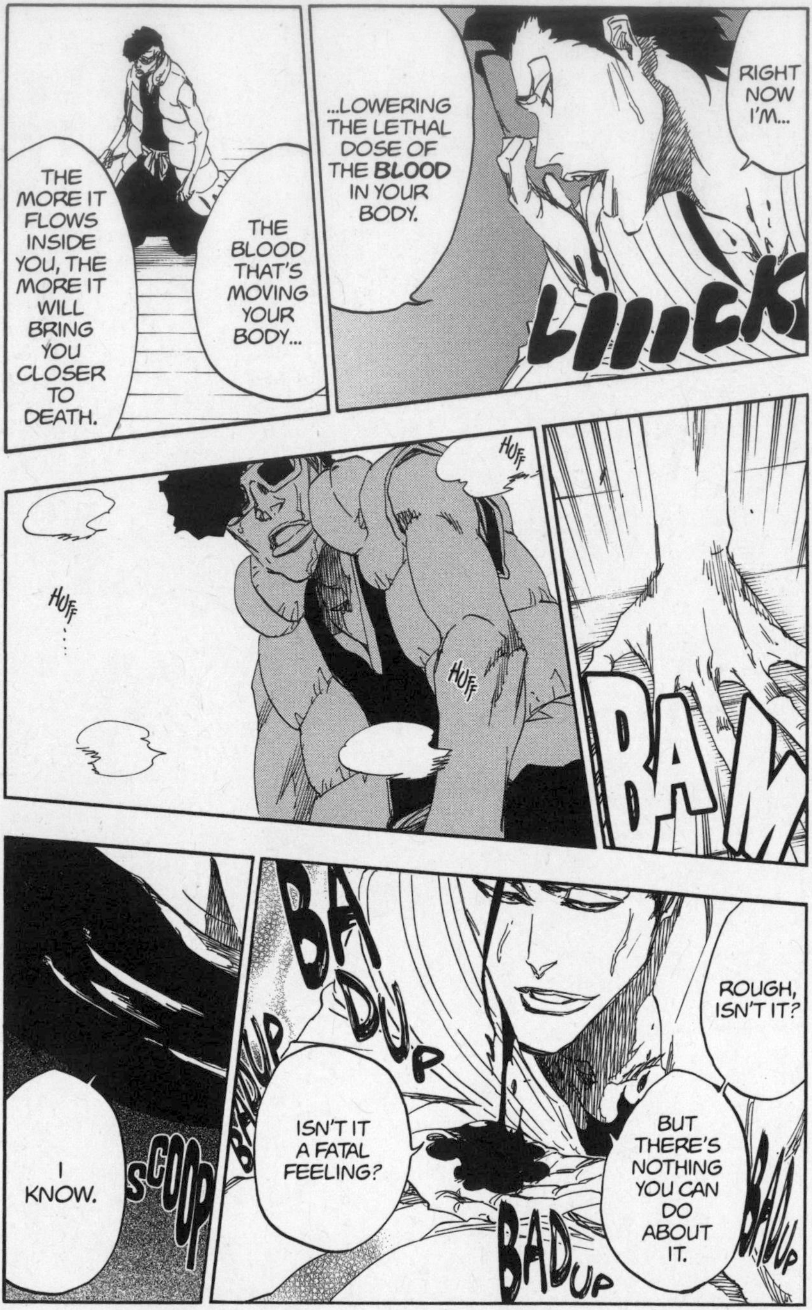
RIGHT NOW I'M...
...LOWERING THE LETHAL DOSE OF THE BLOOD IN YOUR BODY.
LIIICK
THE BLOOD THAT'S MOVING YOUR BODY...
THE MORE IT FLOWS INSIDE YOU, THE MORE IT WILL BRING YOU CLOSER TO DEATH.
BAM
HUFF
HUFF...
HUFF
ROUGH, ISN'T IT?
BADUP
BUT THERE'S NOTHING YOU CAN DO ABOUT IT.
BADUP
BADUP
ISN'T IT A FATAL FEELING?
BADUP
I KNOW.
SCOOP

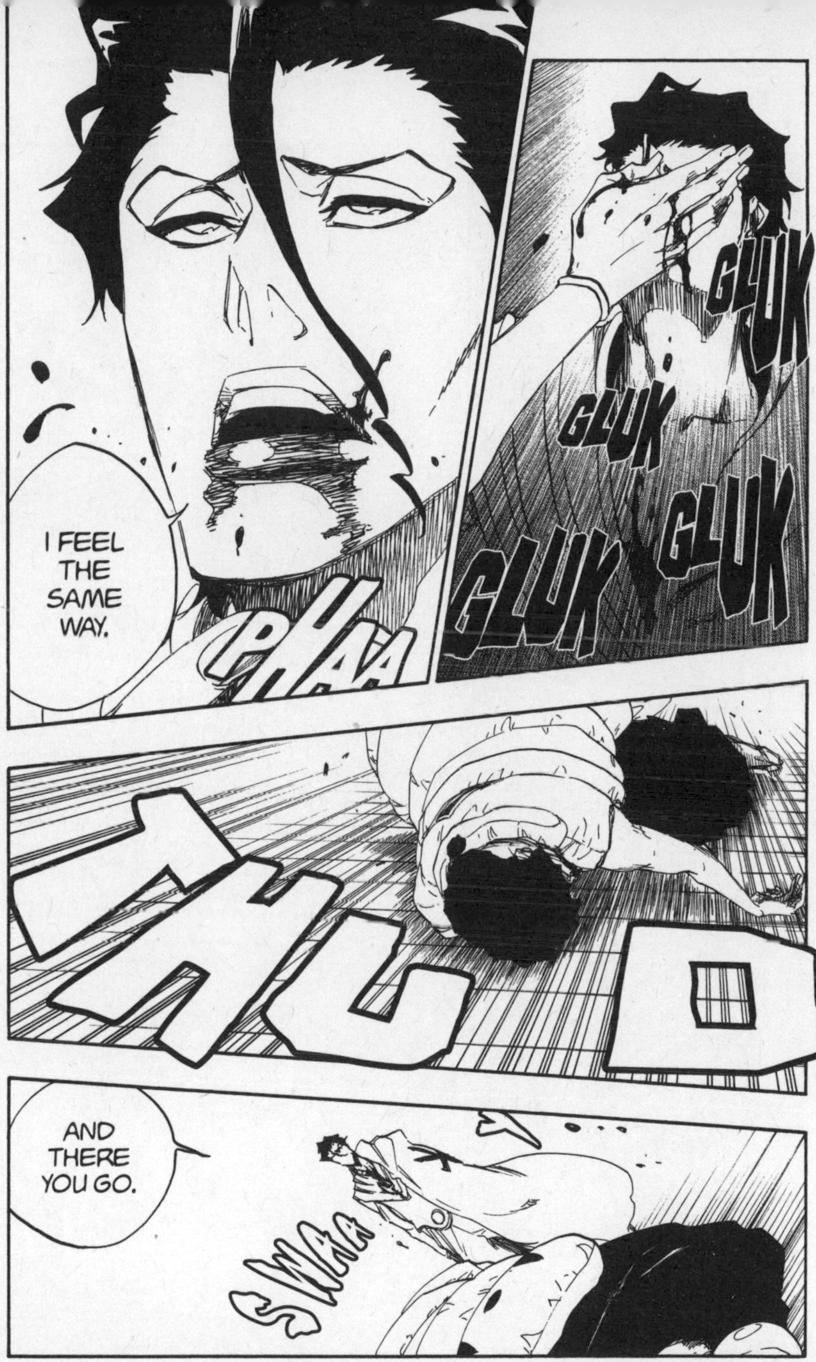
GLUK
GLUK
GLUK
GLUK
I FEEL THE SAME WAY.
PHAA
AND THERE YOU GO.
SWAA

READ THIS WAY

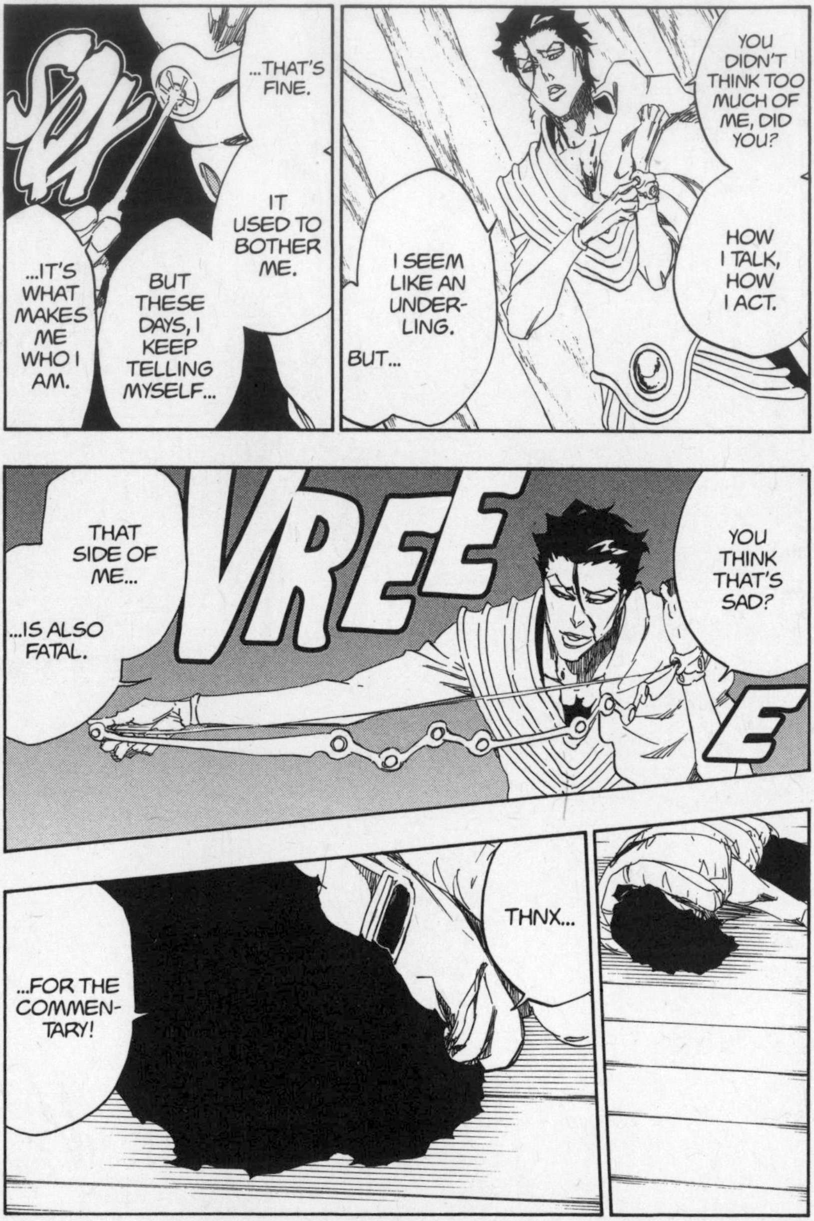

YOU DIDN'T THINK TOO MUCH OF ME, DID YOU?
HOW I TALK, HOW I ACT.
I SEEM LIKE AN UNDER-LING.
BUT...
...THAT'S FINE.
IT USED TO BOTHER ME.
BUT THESE DAYS, I KEEP TELLING MYSELF...
...IT'S WHAT MAKES ME WHO I AM.
VREE
E
YOU THINK THAT'S SAD?
THAT SIDE OF ME...
...IS ALSO FATAL.
THNX...
...FOR THE COMMEN-TARY!

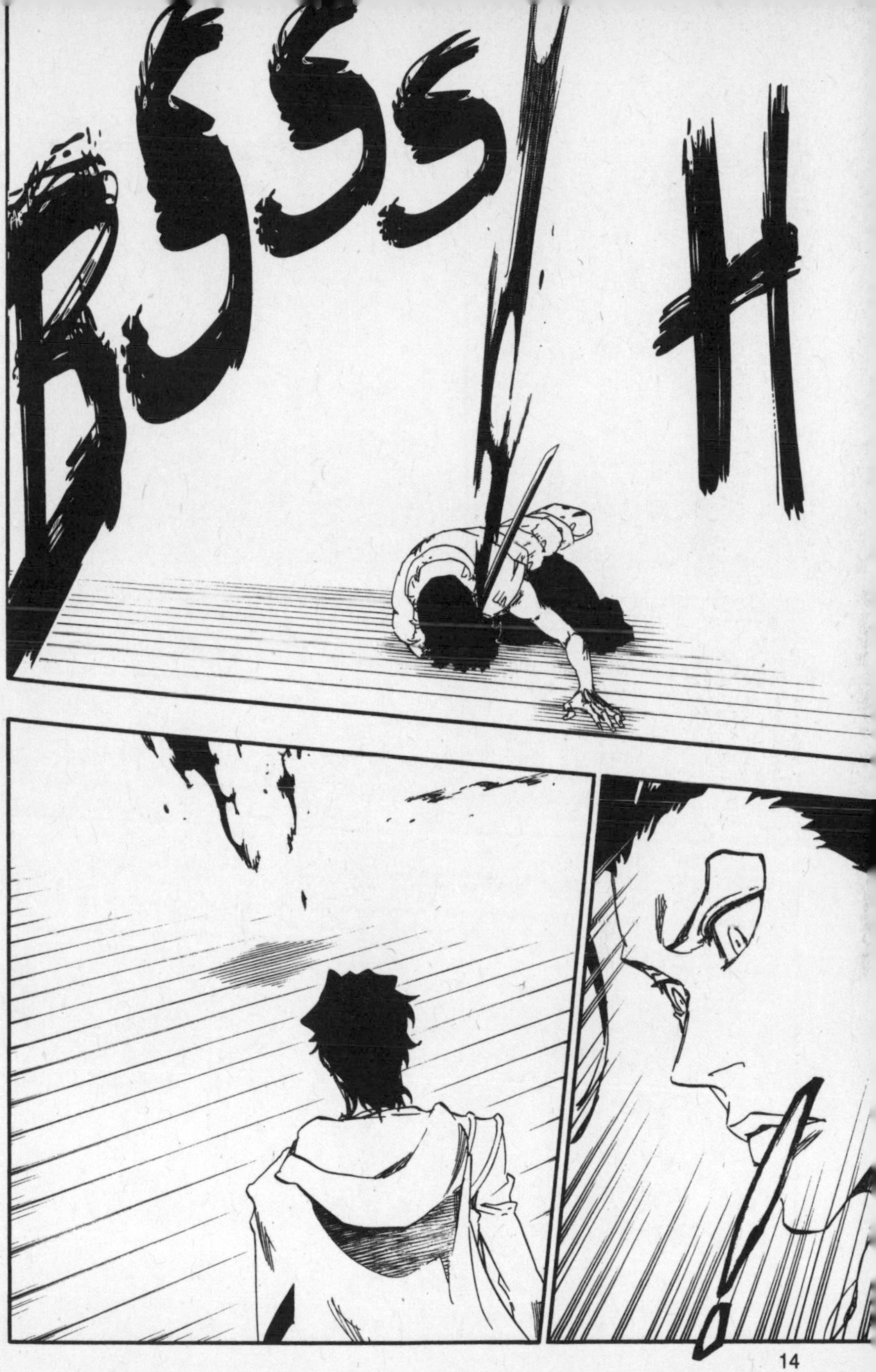
BSSSH

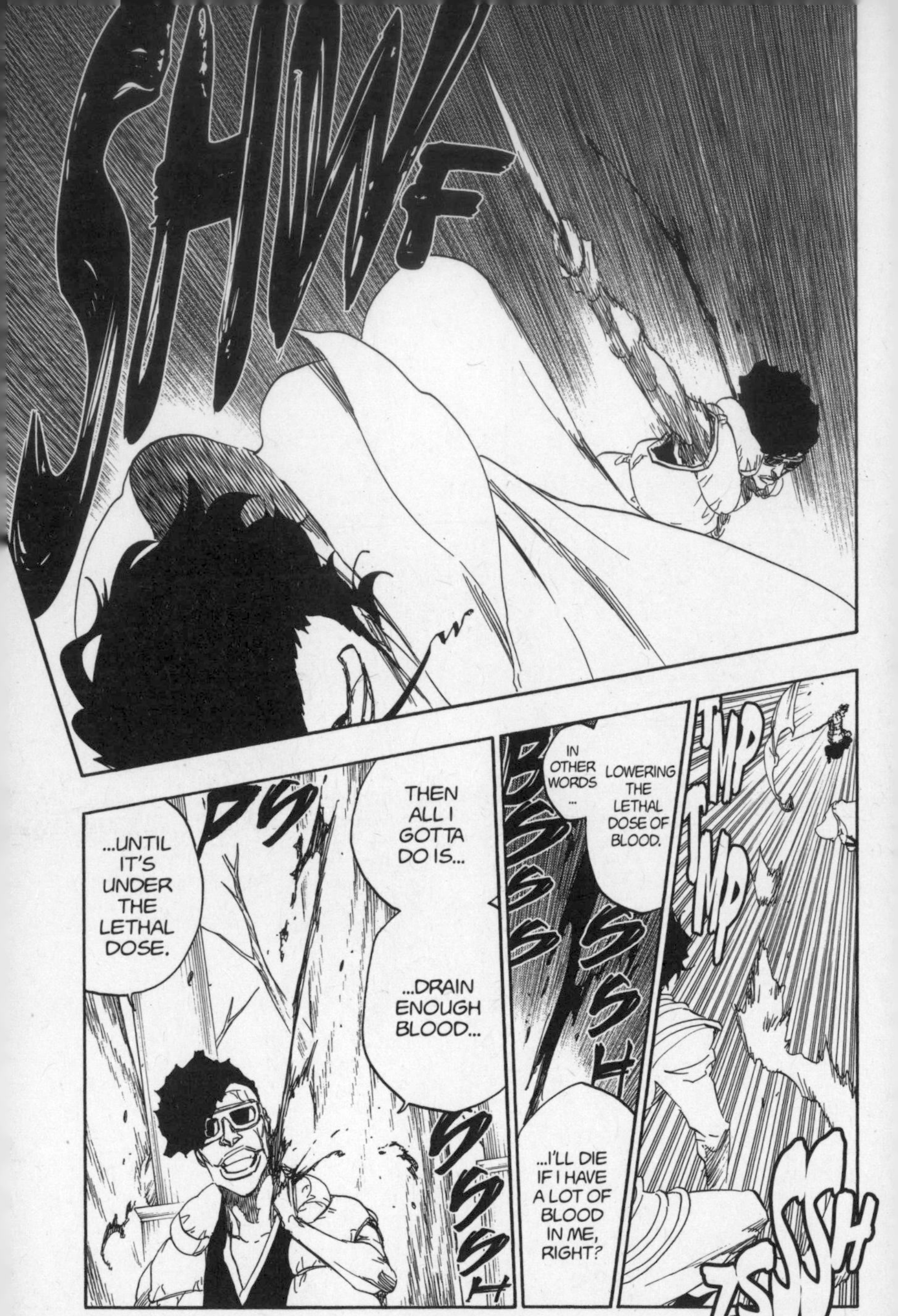
SHWF
TMP
TMP
ZSSSH
LOWERING THE LETHAL DOSE OF BLOOD.
IN OTHER WORDS...
...I'LL DIE IF I HAVE A LOT OF BLOOD IN ME, RIGHT?
THEN ALL I GOTTA DO IS...
...DRAIN ENOUGH BLOOD...
...UNTIL IT'S UNDER THE LETHAL DOSE.

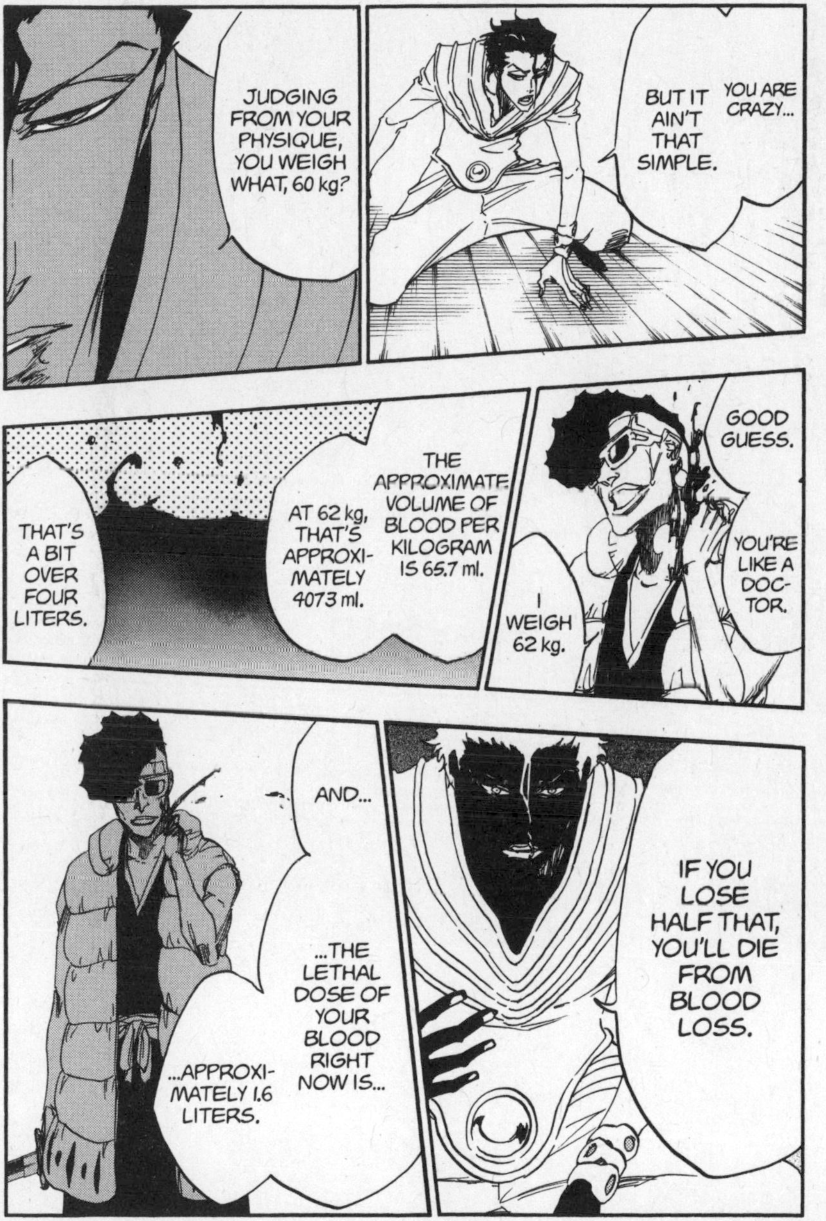
YOU ARE CRAZY...
BUT IT AIN'T THAT SIMPLE.
JUDGING FROM YOUR PHYSIQUE, YOU WEIGH WHAT, 60 kg?
GOOD GUESS.
YOU'RE LIKE A DOCTOR.
I WEIGH 62 kg.
THE APPROXIMATE VOLUME OF BLOOD PER KILOGRAM IS 65.7 ml.
AT 62 kg, THAT'S APPROXIMATELY 4073 ml.
THAT'S A BIT OVER FOUR LITERS.
IF YOU LOSE HALF THAT, YOU'LL DIE FROM BLOOD LOSS.
AND...
...THE LETHAL DOSE OF YOUR BLOOD RIGHT NOW IS...
...APPROXIMATELY 1.6 LITERS.

READ THIS WAY

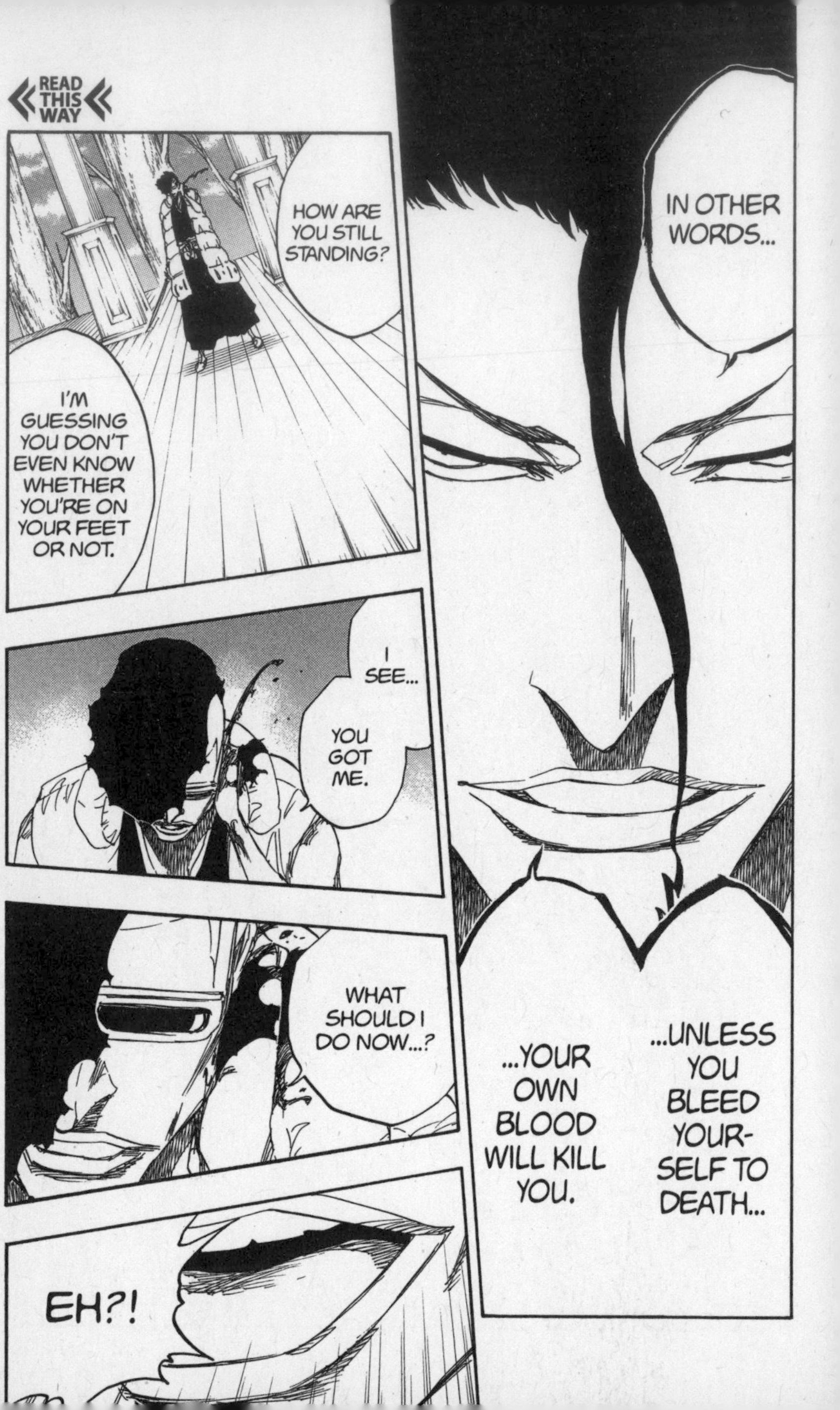
IN OTHER WORDS...
...UNLESS YOU BLEED YOUR-SELF TO DEATH...
...YOUR OWN BLOOD WILL KILL YOU.
HOW ARE YOU STILL STANDING?
I'M GUESSING YOU DON'T EVEN KNOW WHETHER YOU'RE ON YOUR FEET OR NOT.
I SEE...
YOU GOT ME.
WHAT SHOULD I DO NOW...?
EH?!

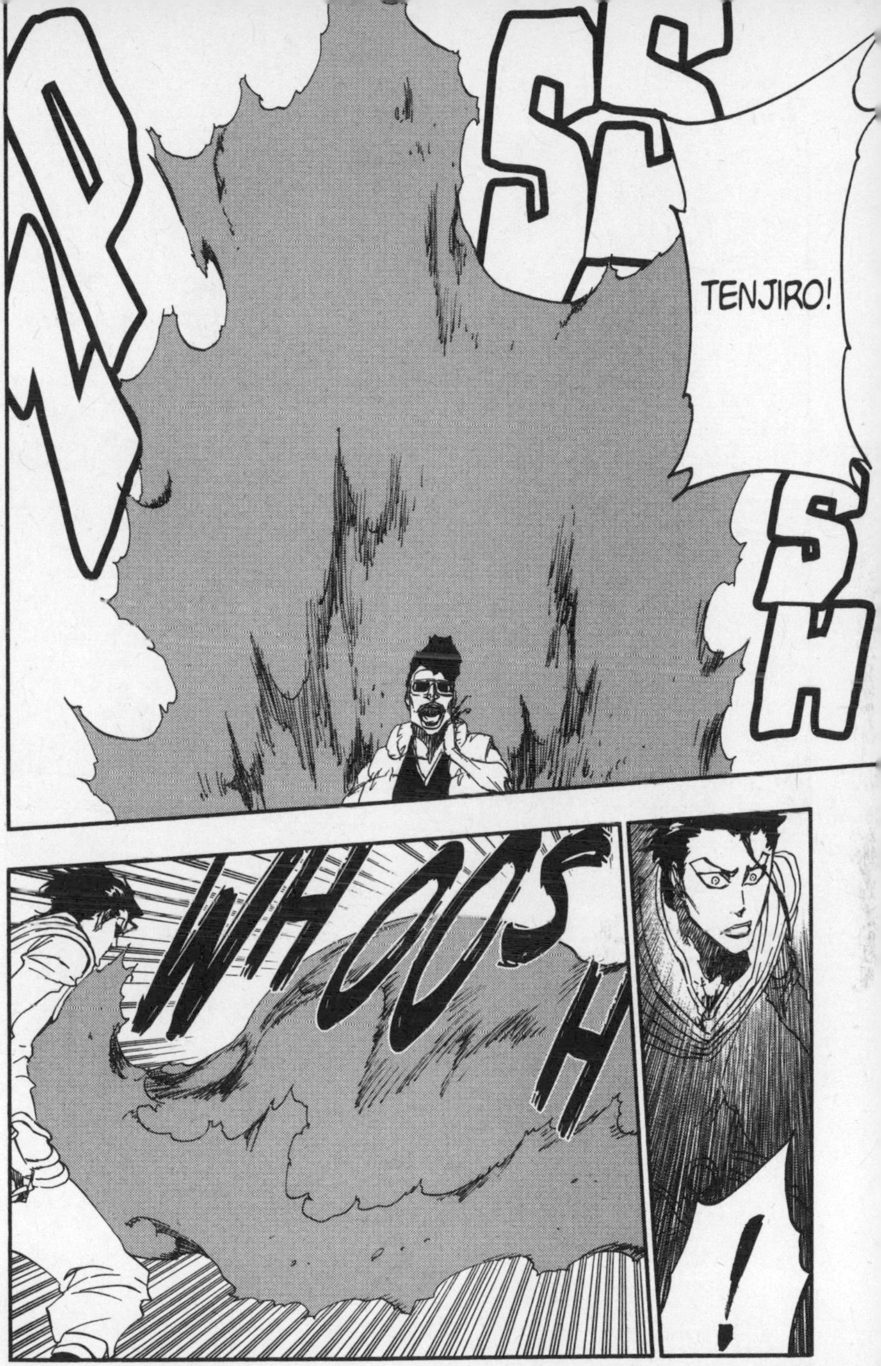
TENJIRO!
!
WHOOSH

READ THIS WAY

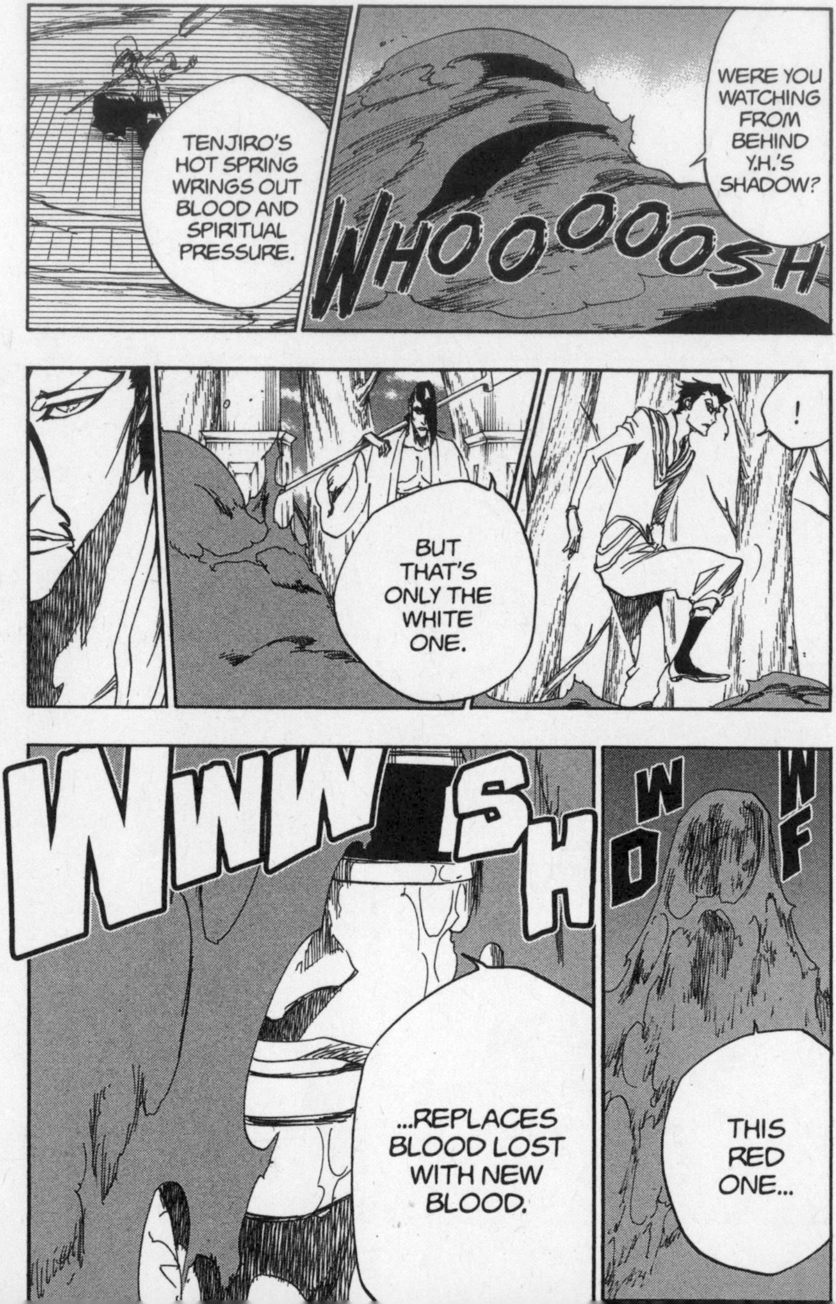
WERE YOU WATCHING FROM BEHIND Y.H.'S SHADOW?
WHOOOOOSH
TENJIRO'S HOT SPRING WRINGS OUT BLOOD AND SPIRITUAL PRESSURE.
!
BUT THAT'S ONLY THE WHITE ONE.
THIS RED ONE...
...REPLACES BLOOD LOST WITH NEW BLOOD.

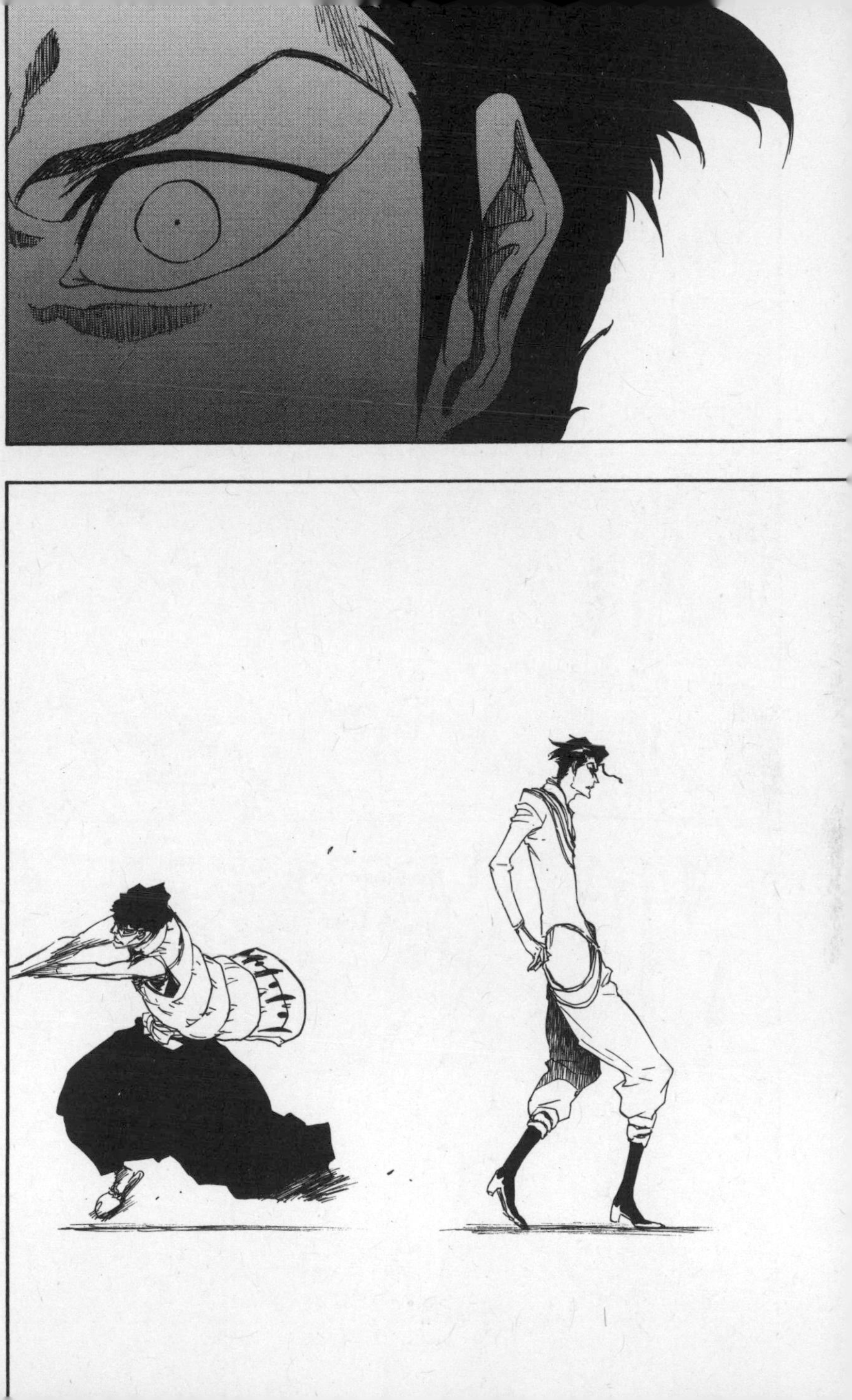

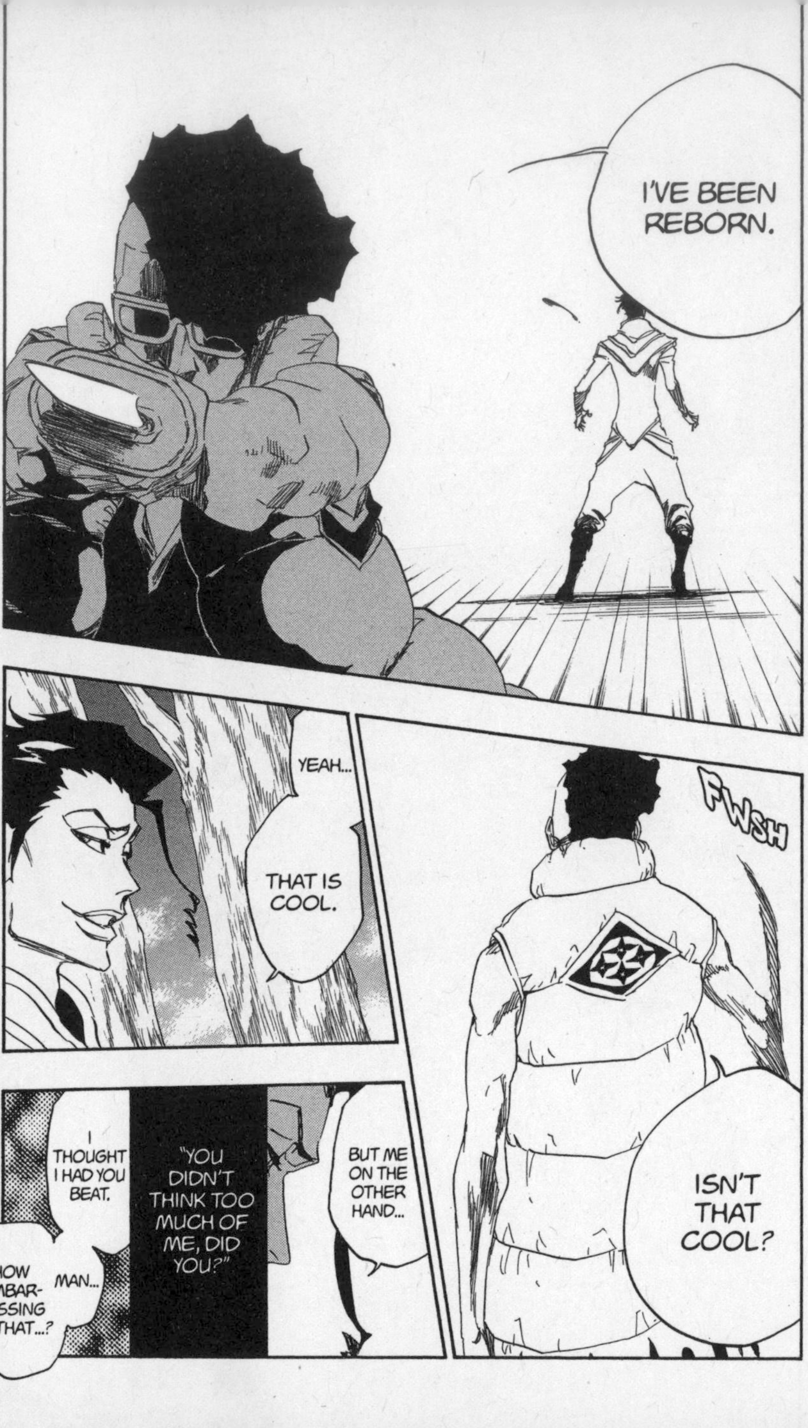
I'VE BEEN REBORN.
FWSH
ISN'T THAT COOL?
YEAH...
THAT IS COOL.
BUT ME ON THE OTHER HAND...
"YOU DIDN'T THINK TOO MUCH OF ME, DID YOU?"
I THOUGHT I HAD YOU BEAT.
MAN...
HOW EMBAR-RASSING IS THAT...?

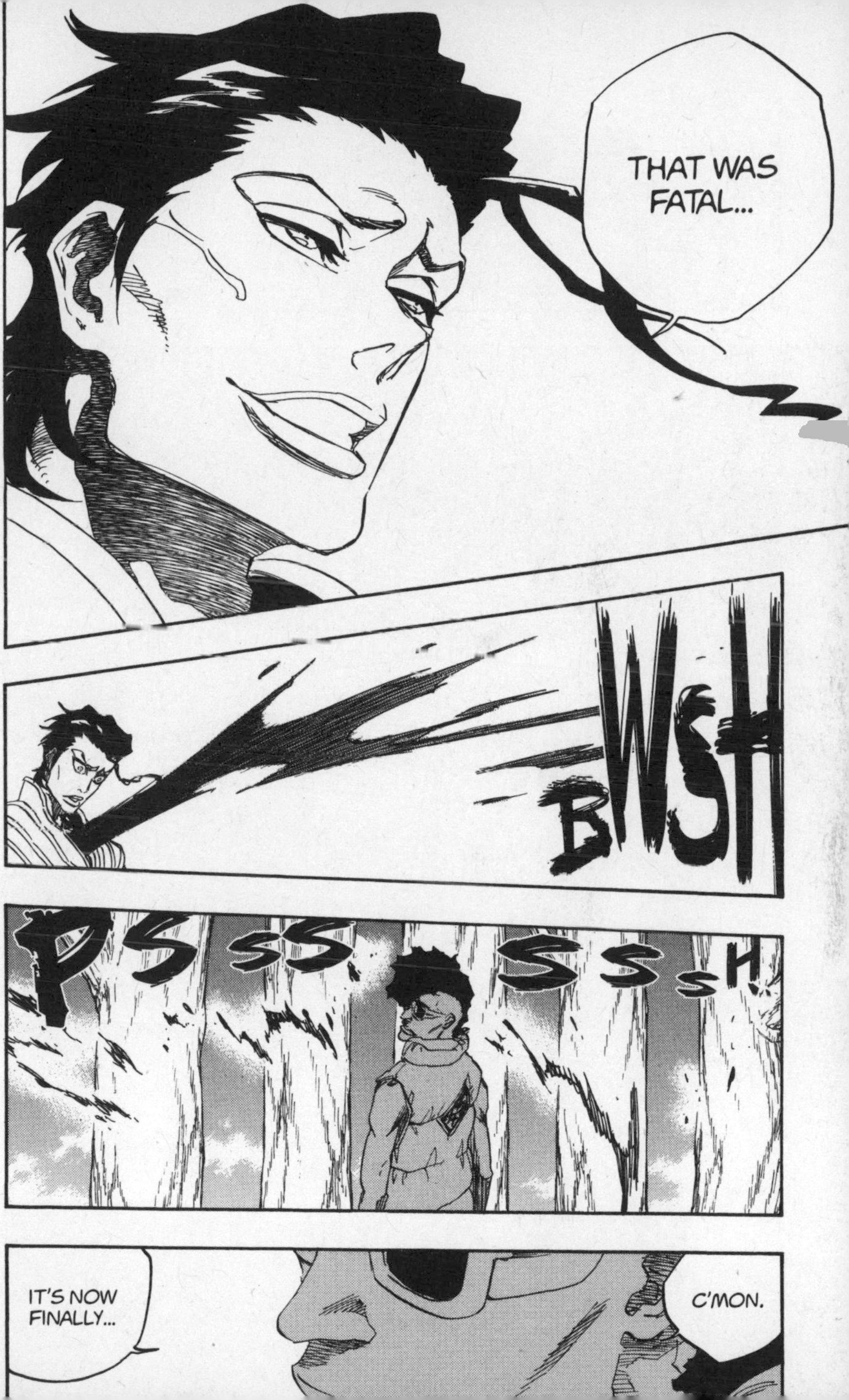
THAT WAS FATAL...
BWSH
PSSSSSSH
C'MON.
IT'S NOW FINALLY...

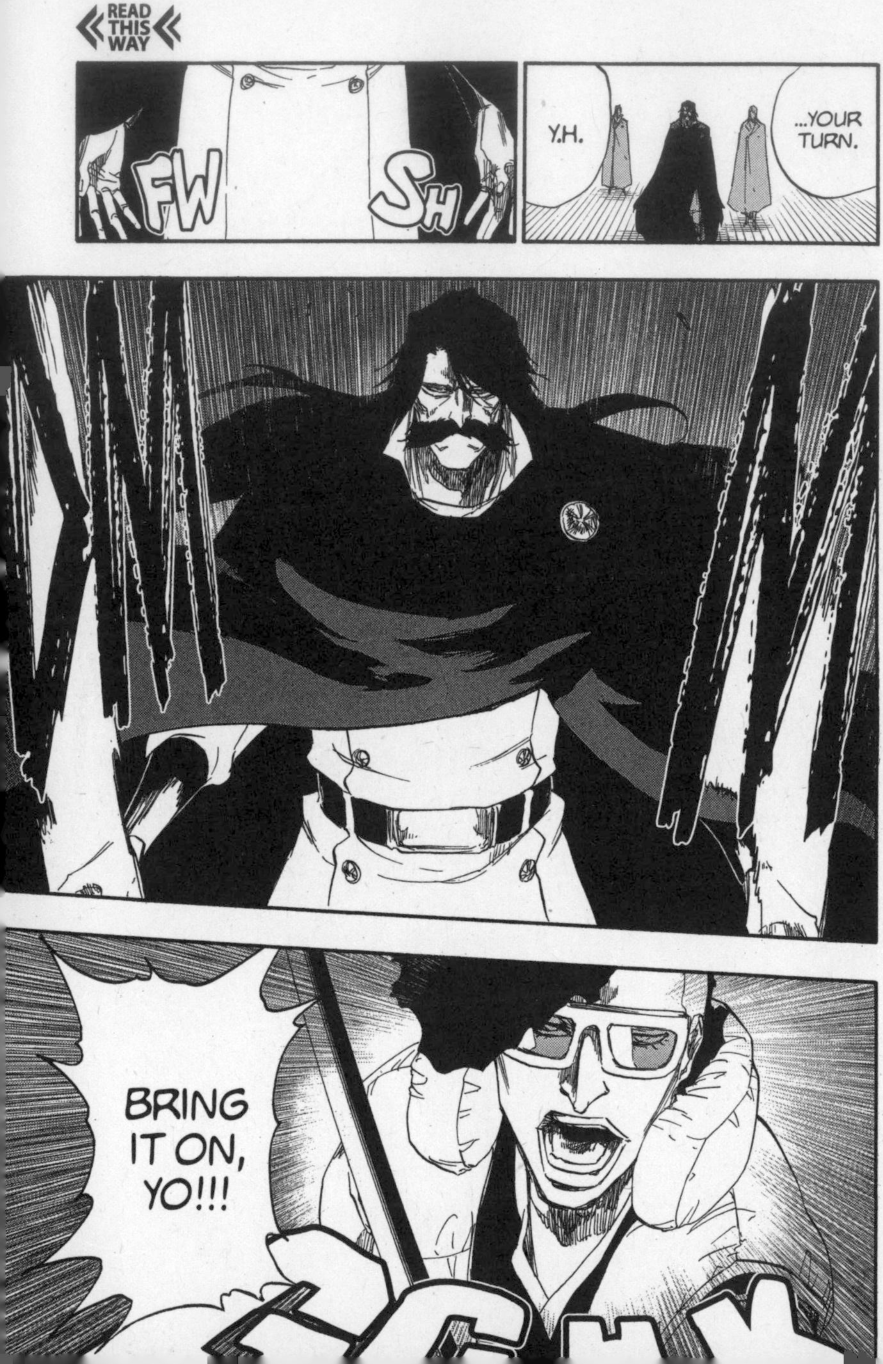
READ THIS WAY
...YOUR TURN.
Y.H.
SH
FW
BRING IT ON, YO!!!

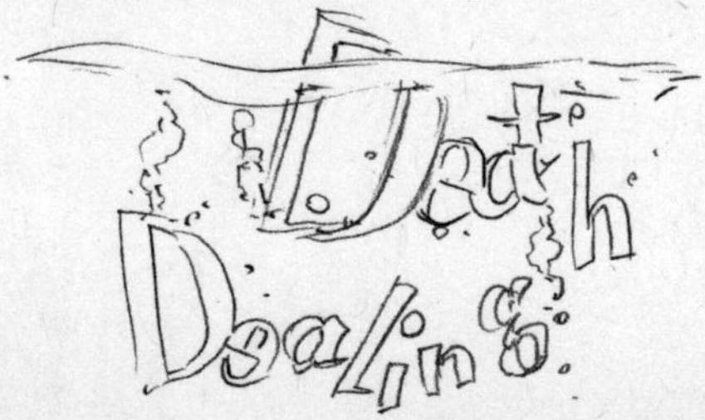
the
Death
Dealing

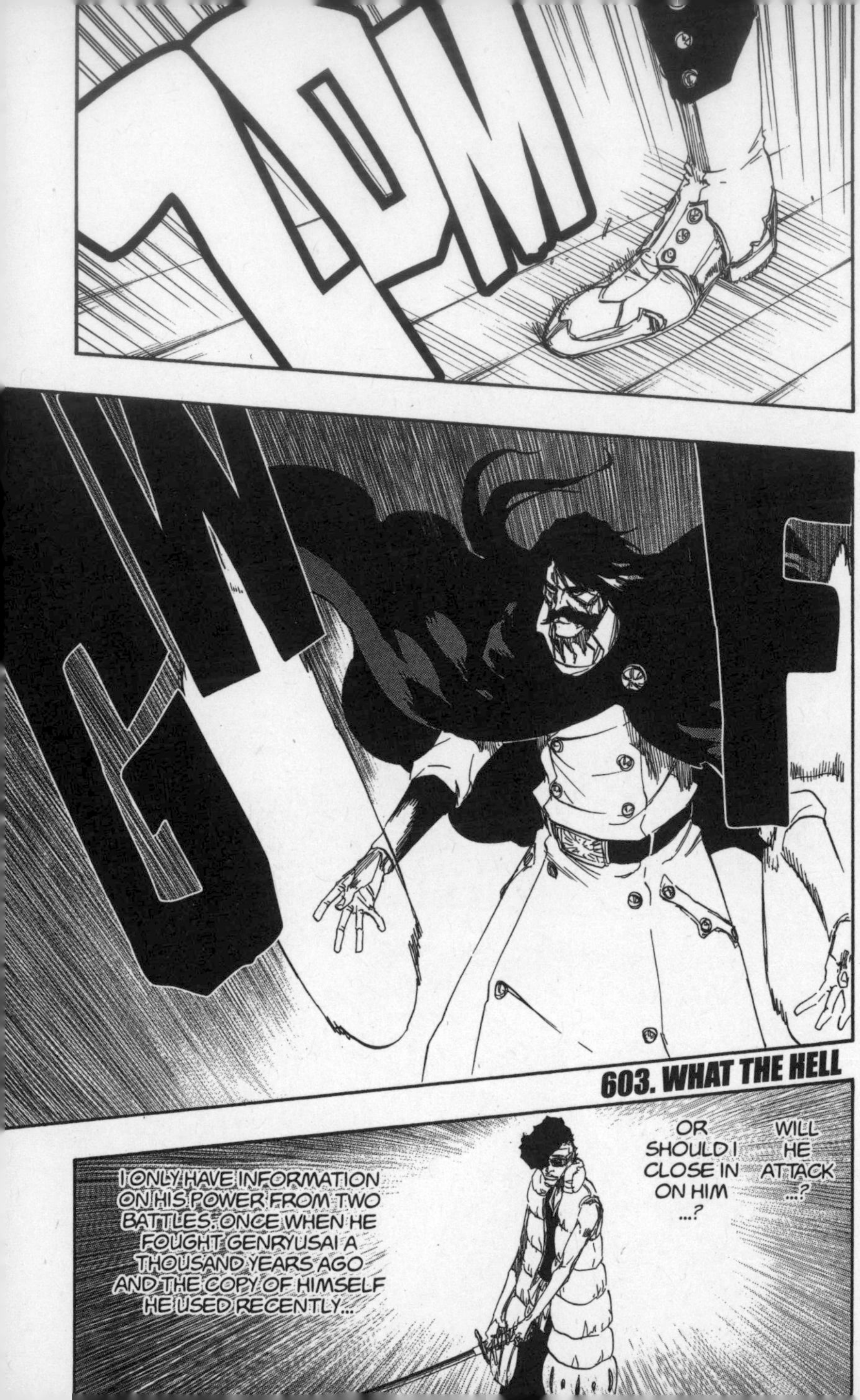
603. WHAT THE HELL
WILL HE ATTACK ...?
OR SHOULD I CLOSE IN ON HIM ...?
I ONLY HAVE INFORMATION ON HIS POWER FROM TWO BATTLES. ONCE WHEN HE FOUGHT GENRYUSAI A THOUSAND YEARS AGO AND THE COPY OF HIMSELF HE USED RECENTLY...

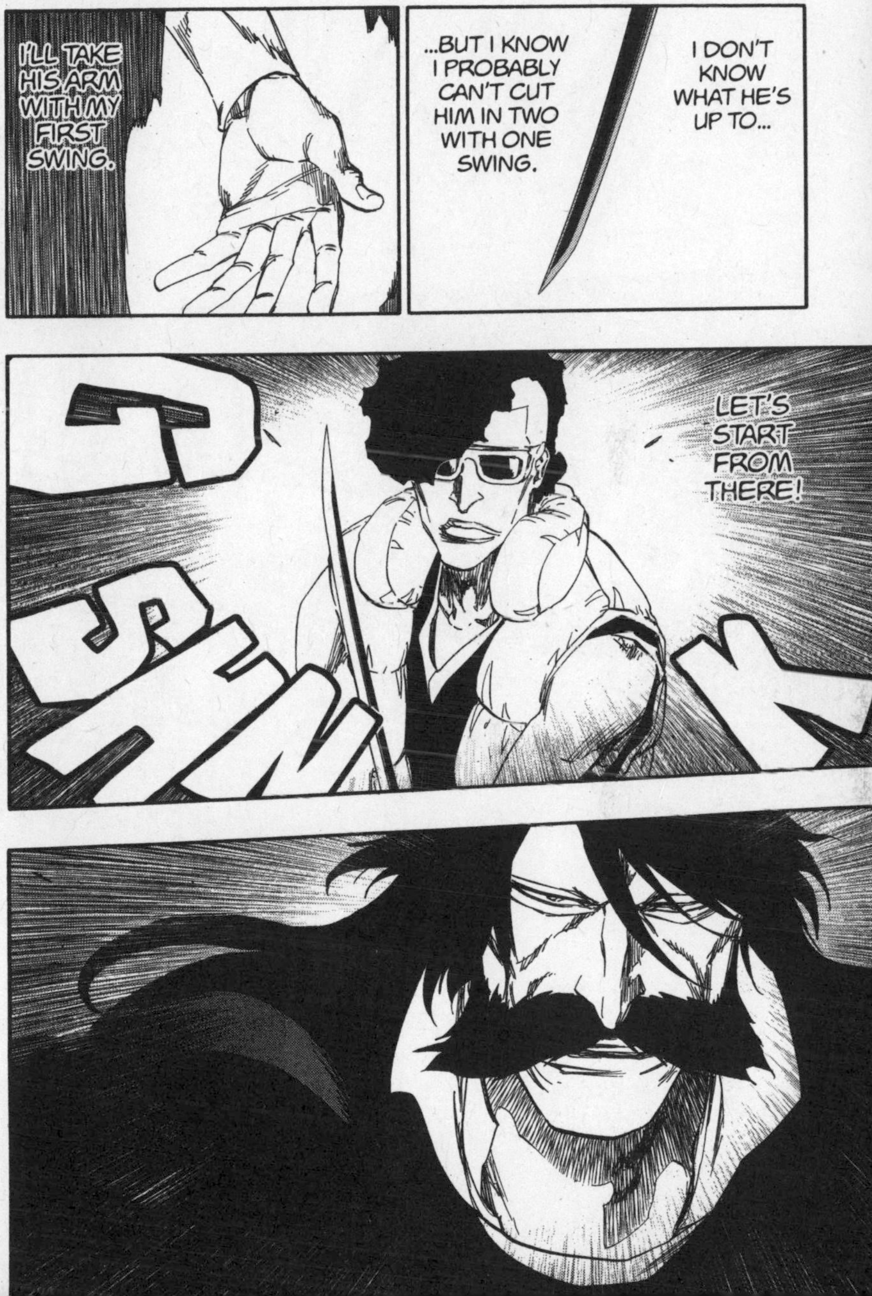
I DON'T KNOW WHAT HE'S UP TO...
...BUT I KNOW I PROBABLY CAN'T CUT HIM IN TWO WITH ONE SWING.
I'LL TAKE HIS ARM WITH MY FIRST SWING.
LET'S START FROM THERE!

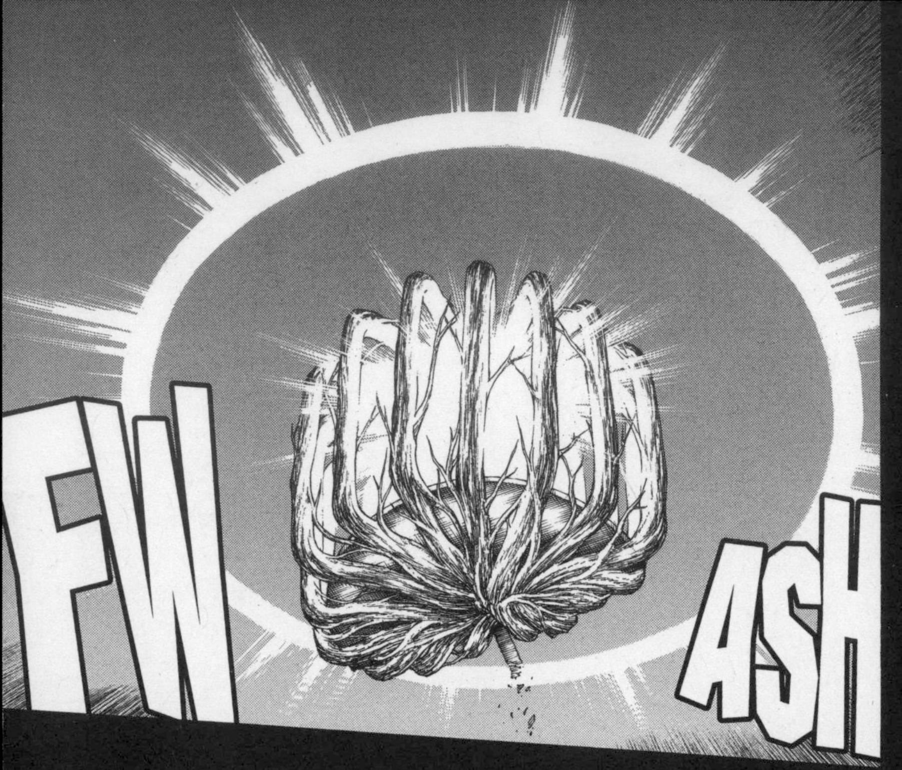
FWASH

BLEACH 603.

What The Hell

PLIP
PLIP
PLIP
ZSAAAAA
HUFF
HUFF
HUFF

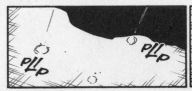

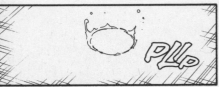

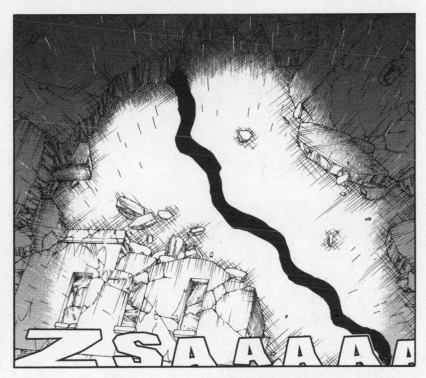

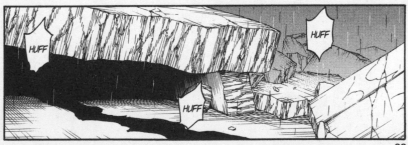

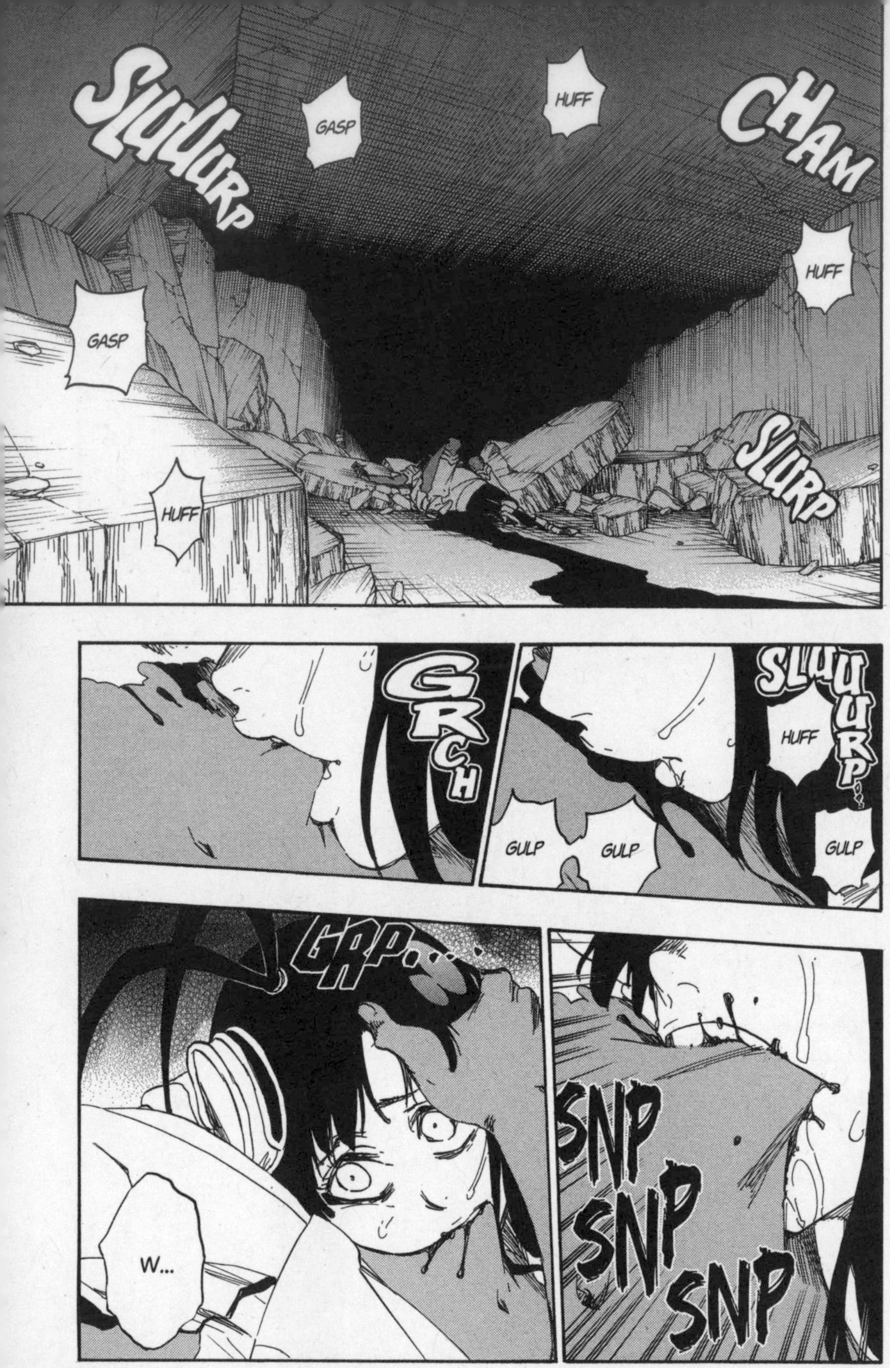
CHAM
HUFF
HUFF
GASP
SLUUURP
SLURP
GASP
HUFF
SLUUURP...
HUFF
GULP
GULP
GULP
GRCH
SNP
SNP
SNP
SNP
GRP...
W...

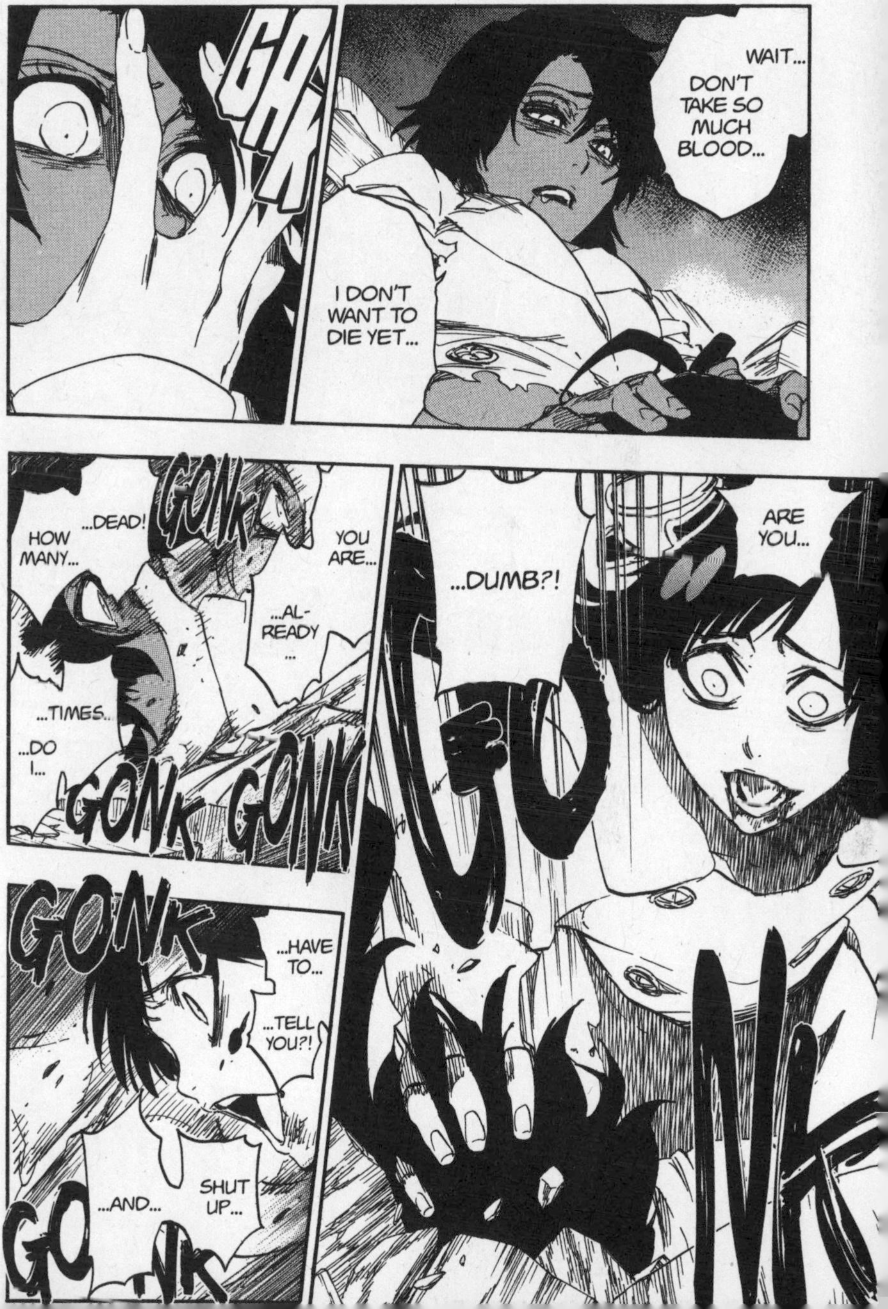
WAIT...
DON'T TAKE SO MUCH BLOOD...
I DON'T WANT TO DIE YET...
GAK
ARE YOU...
...DUMB?!
GONK
GONK
YOU ARE...
...AL-READY...
...DEAD!
HOW MANY...
...TIMES...
...DO I...
GONK GONK
GONK
...HAVE TO...
...TELL YOU?!
SHUT UP...
...AND...
GONK

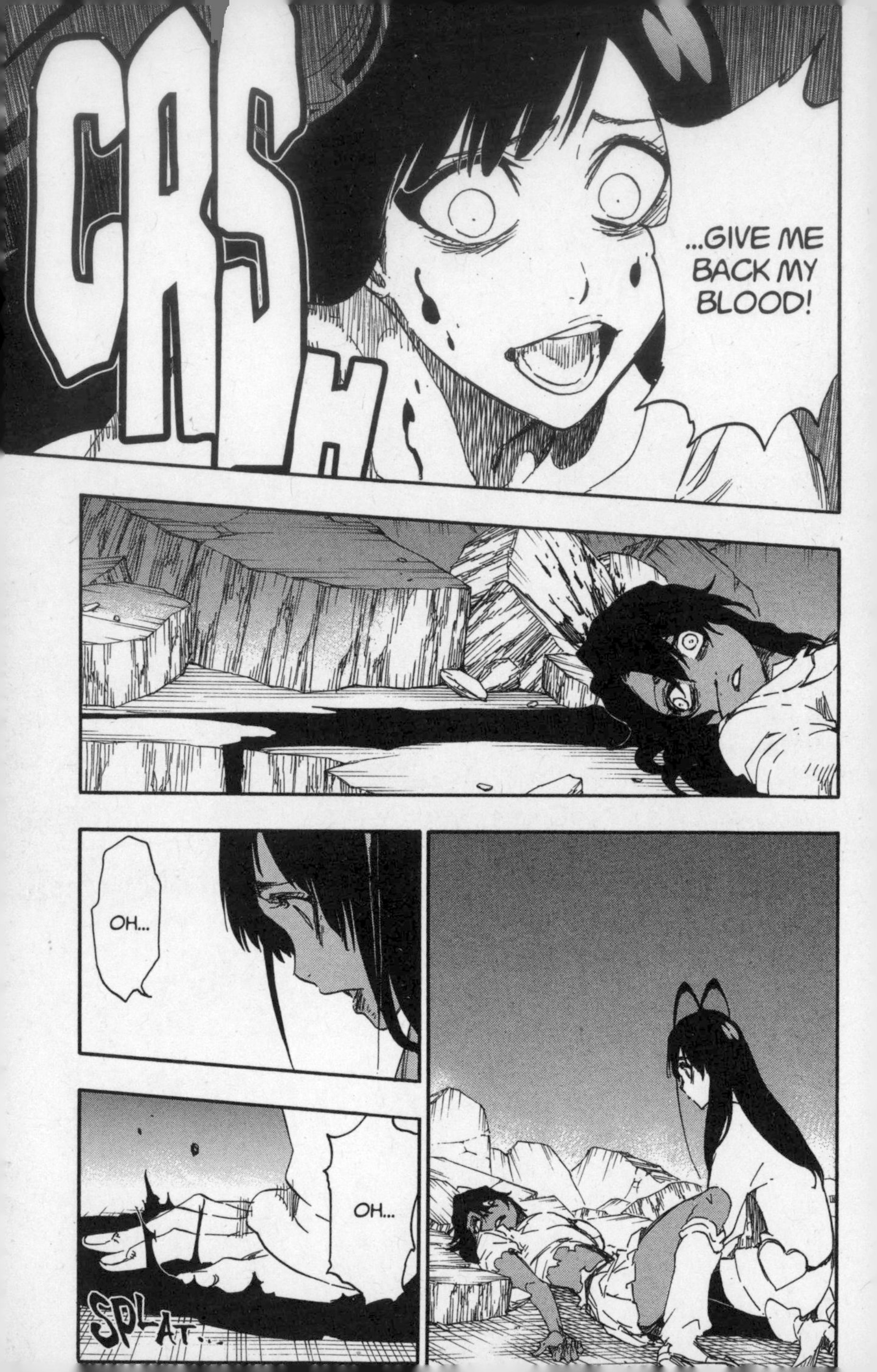
...GIVE ME BACK MY BLOOD!
CRASH
OH...
OH...
SPLAT...

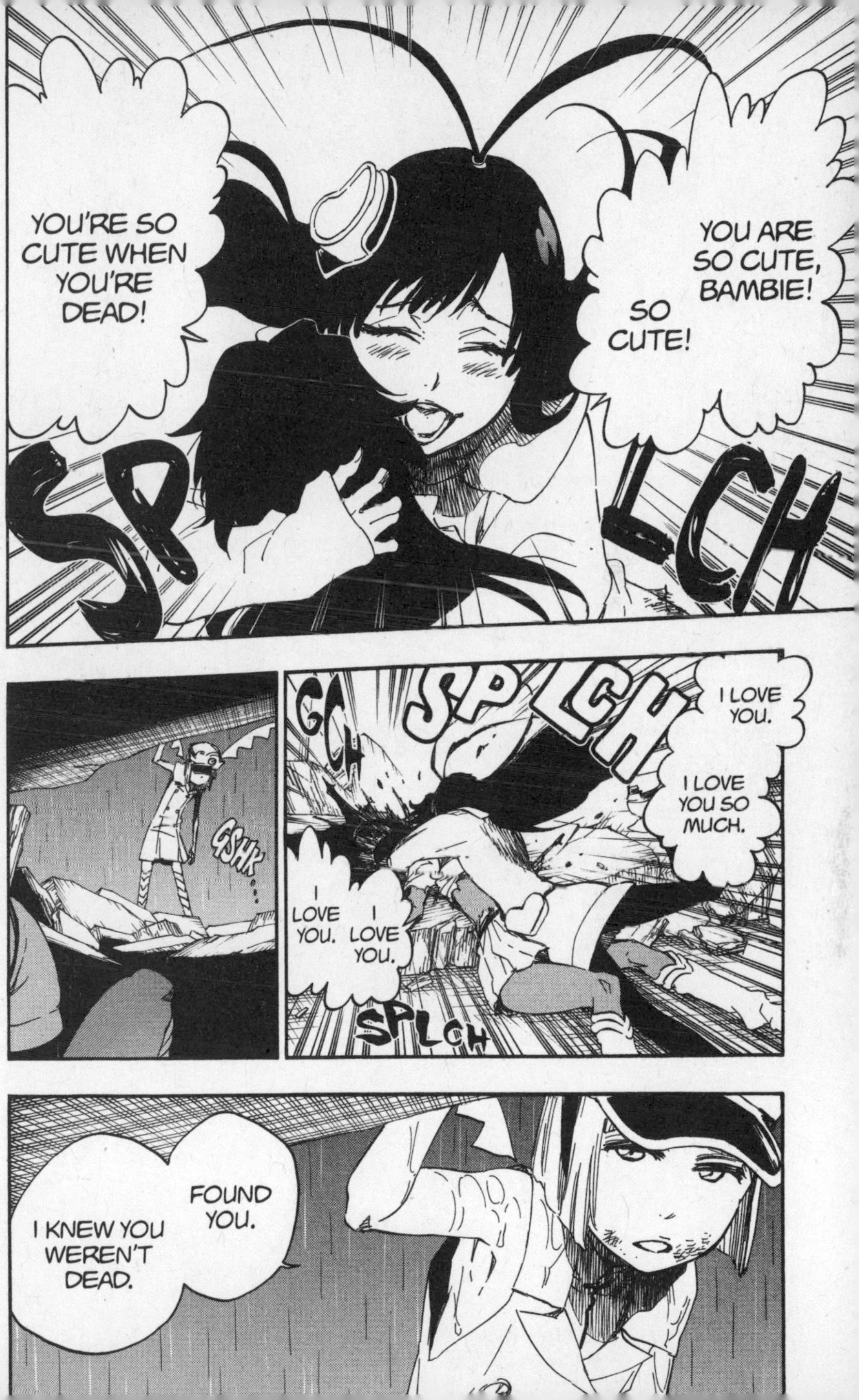
YOU ARE SO CUTE, BAMBIE!
SO CUTE!
YOU'RE SO CUTE WHEN YOU'RE DEAD!
SPLCH
SPLCH
GG
I LOVE YOU.
I LOVE YOU SO MUCH.
I LOVE YOU.
I LOVE YOU.
SPLCH
GSHK
FOUND YOU.
I KNEW YOU WEREN'T DEAD.

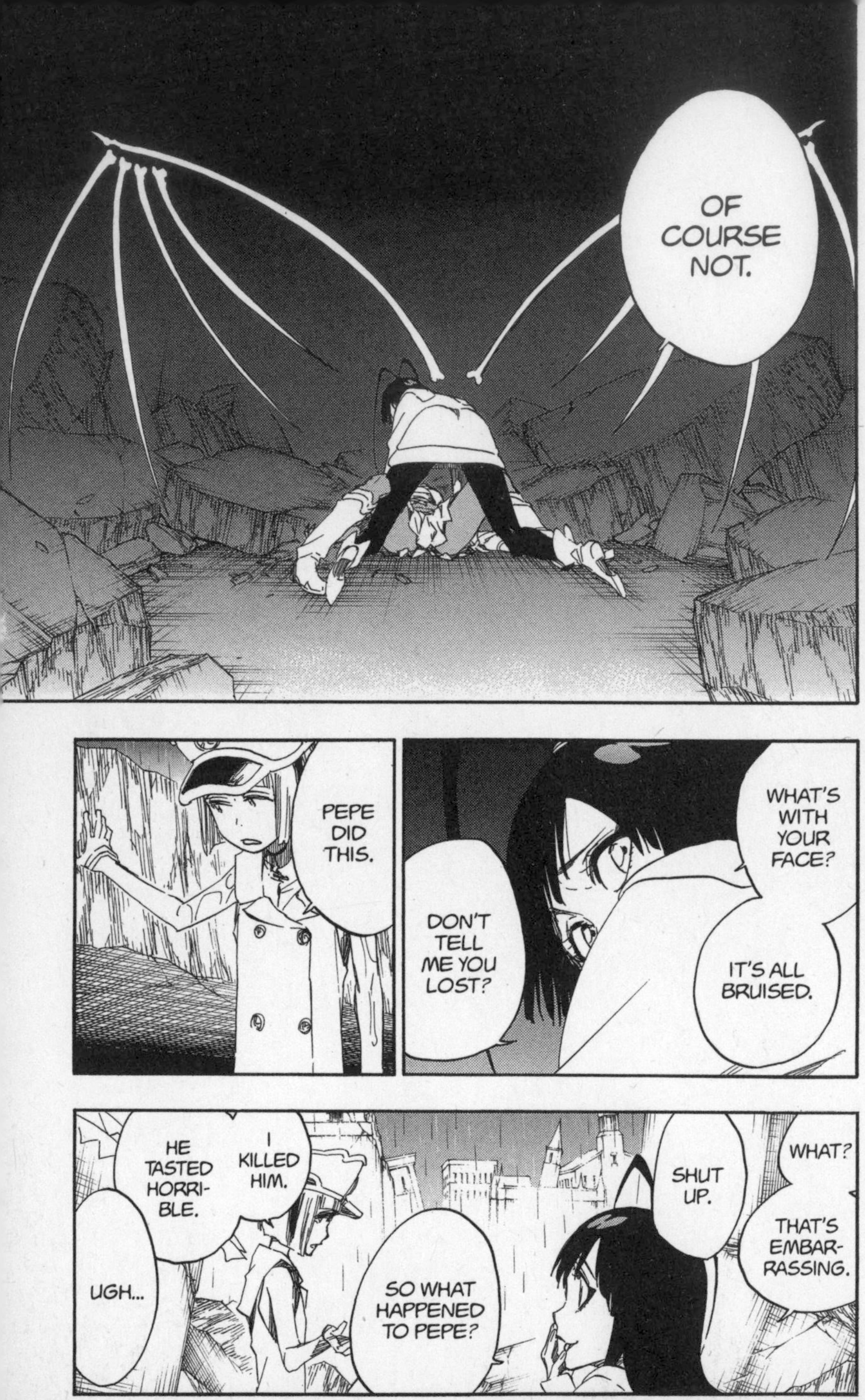
OF COURSE NOT.
WHAT'S WITH YOUR FACE?
IT'S ALL BRUISED.
DON'T TELL ME YOU LOST?
PEPE DID THIS.
WHAT?
THAT'S EMBAR-RASSING.
SHUT UP.
SO WHAT HAPPENED TO PEPE?
I KILLED HIM.
HE TASTED HORRI-BLE.
UGH...

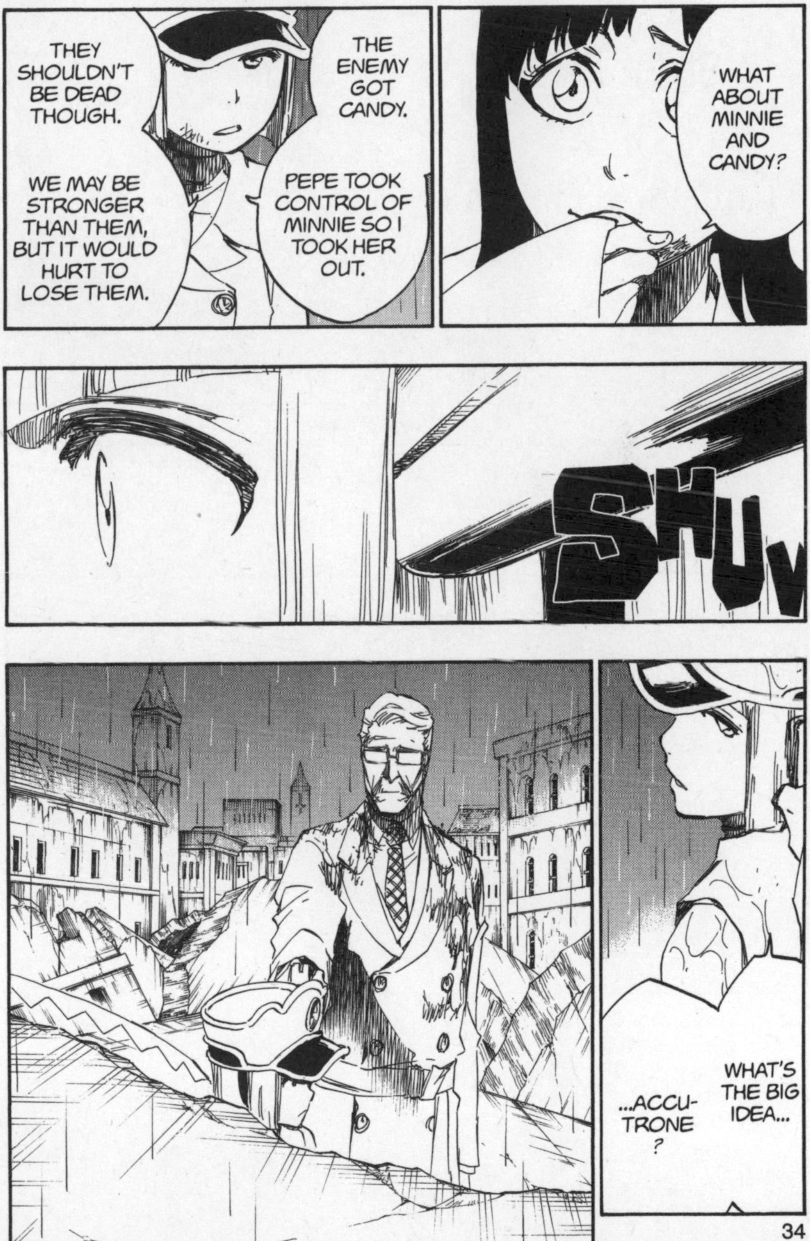
WHAT ABOUT MINNIE AND CANDY?
THE ENEMY GOT CANDY.
THEY SHOULDN'T BE DEAD THOUGH.
PEPE TOOK CONTROL OF MINNIE SO I TOOK HER OUT.
WE MAY BE STRONGER THAN THEM, BUT IT WOULD HURT TO LOSE THEM.
SHUV
WHAT'S THE BIG IDEA...
...ACCU-TRONE ?

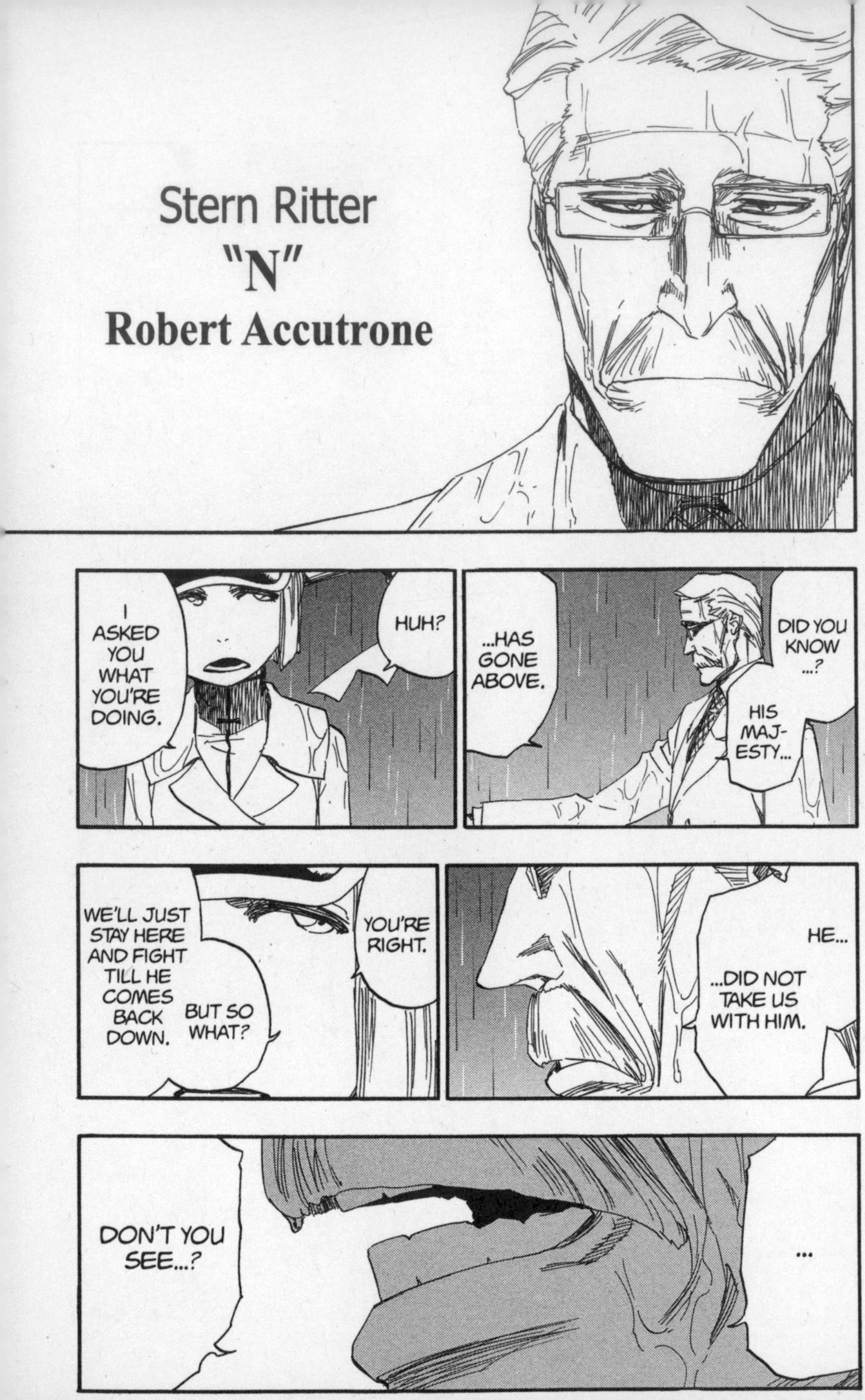
Stern Ritter
"N"
Robert Accutrone
DID YOU KNOW ...?
HIS MAJ-ESTY...
...HAS GONE ABOVE.
HUH?
I ASKED YOU WHAT YOU'RE DOING.
HE...
...DID NOT TAKE US WITH HIM.
YOU'RE RIGHT.
BUT SO WHAT?
WE'LL JUST STAY HERE AND FIGHT TILL HE COMES BACK DOWN.
...
DON'T YOU SEE...?

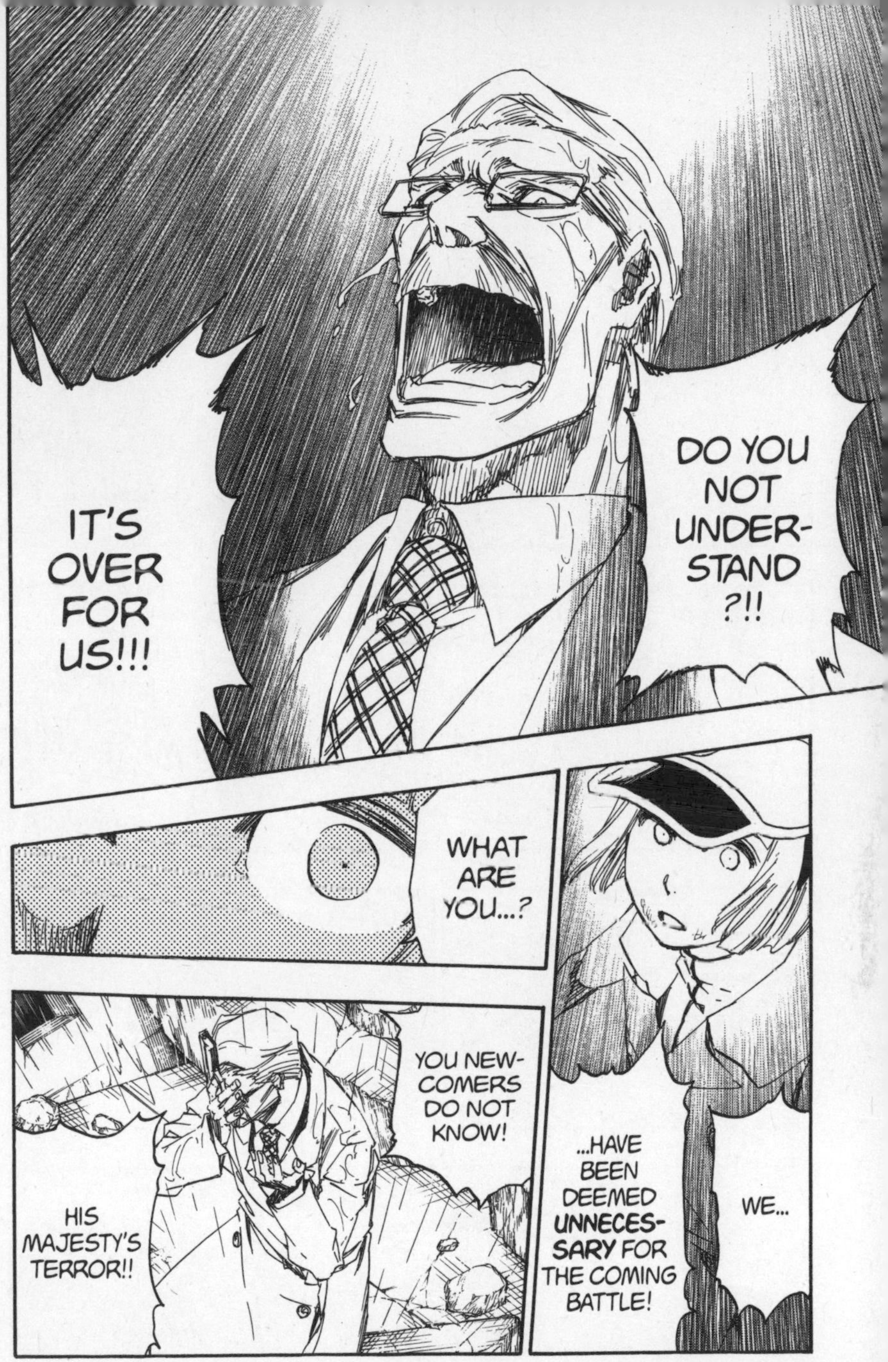
DO YOU NOT UNDER-STAND?!!
IT'S OVER FOR US!!!
WE...
...HAVE BEEN DEEMED **UNNECES-SARY** FOR THE COMING BATTLE!
WHAT ARE YOU...?
YOU NEW-COMERS DO NOT KNOW!
HIS MAJESTY'S TERROR!!

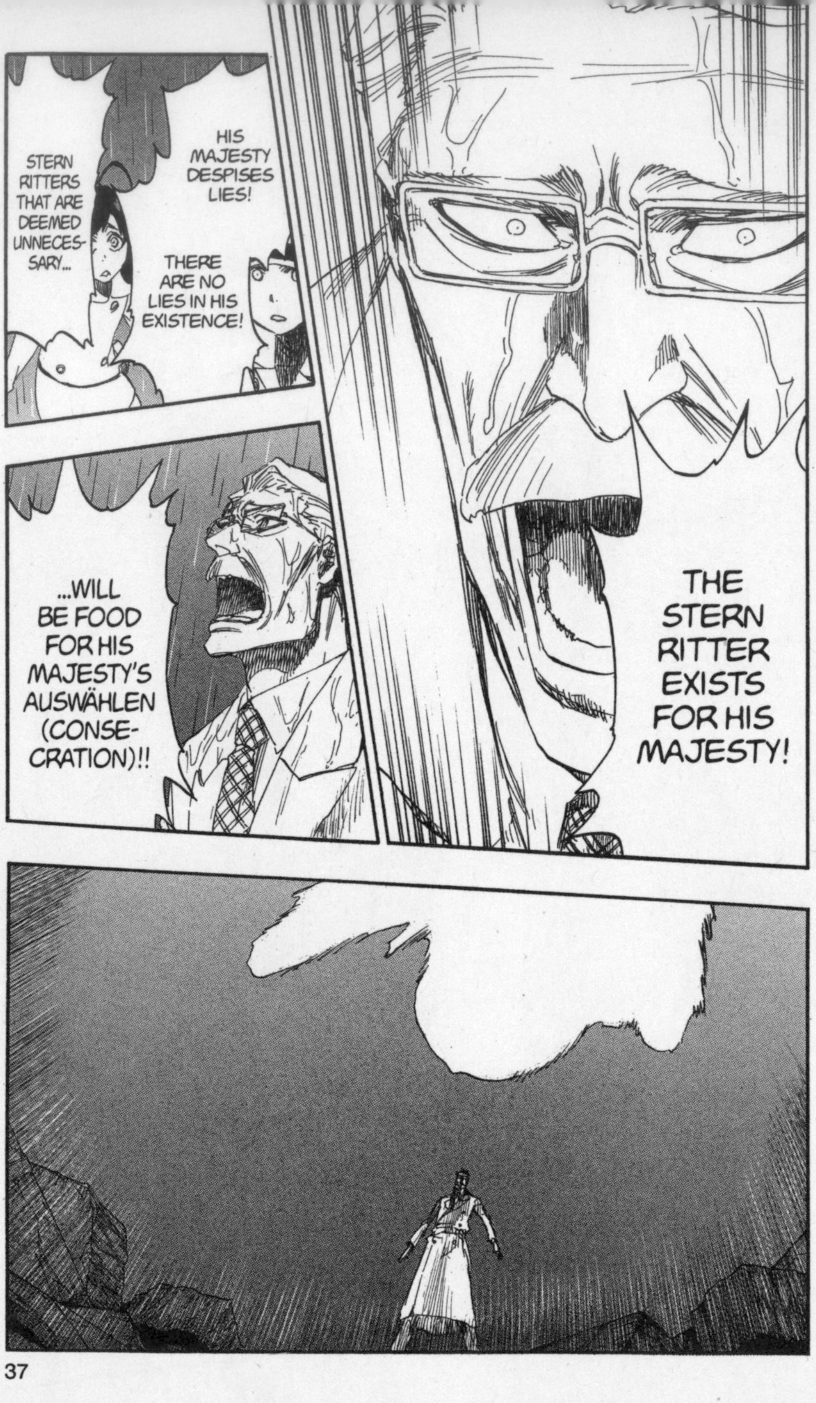
THE STERN RITTER EXISTS FOR HIS MAJESTY!
HIS MAJESTY DESPISES LIES!
THERE ARE NO LIES IN HIS EXISTENCE!
STERN RITTERS THAT ARE DEEMED UNNECES-SARY...
...WILL BE FOOD FOR HIS MAJESTY'S AUSWÄHLEN (CONSE-CRATION)!!

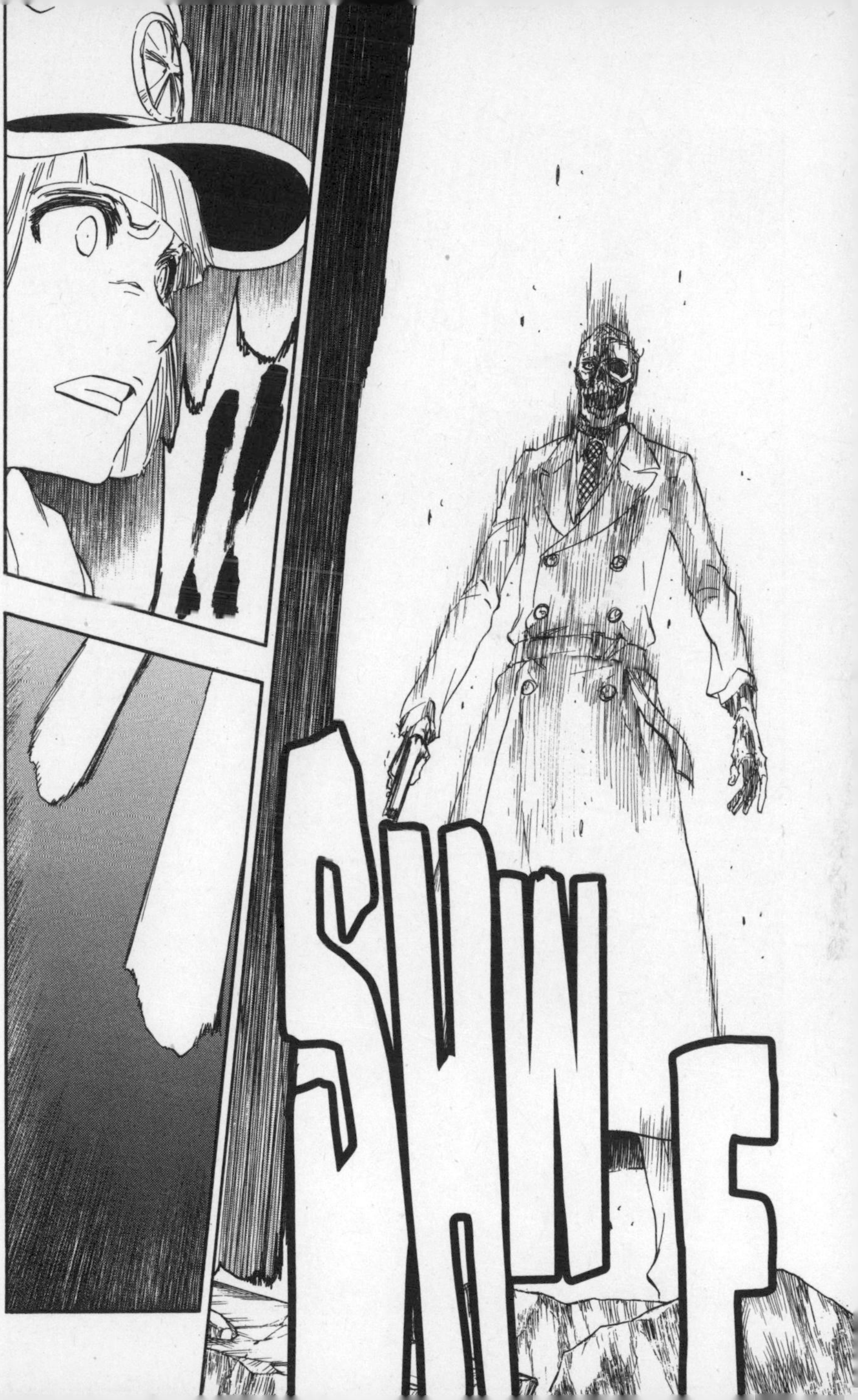

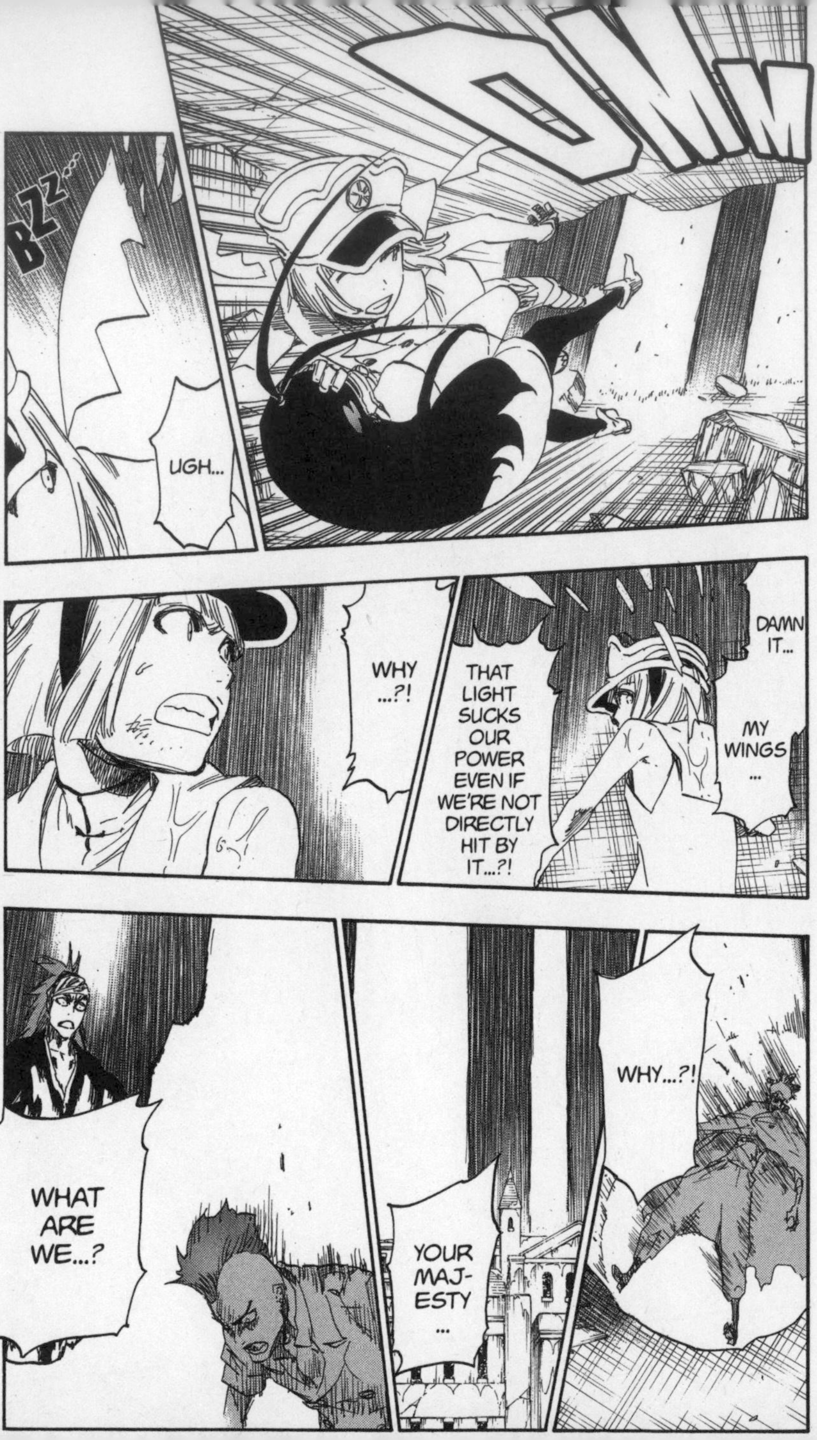
DOMM
BZZ...
UGH...
DAMN IT...
MY WINGS...
THAT LIGHT SUCKS OUR POWER EVEN IF WE'RE NOT DIRECTLY HIT BY IT...?!
WHY...?!
WHY...?!
YOUR MAJ-ESTY...
WHAT ARE WE...?

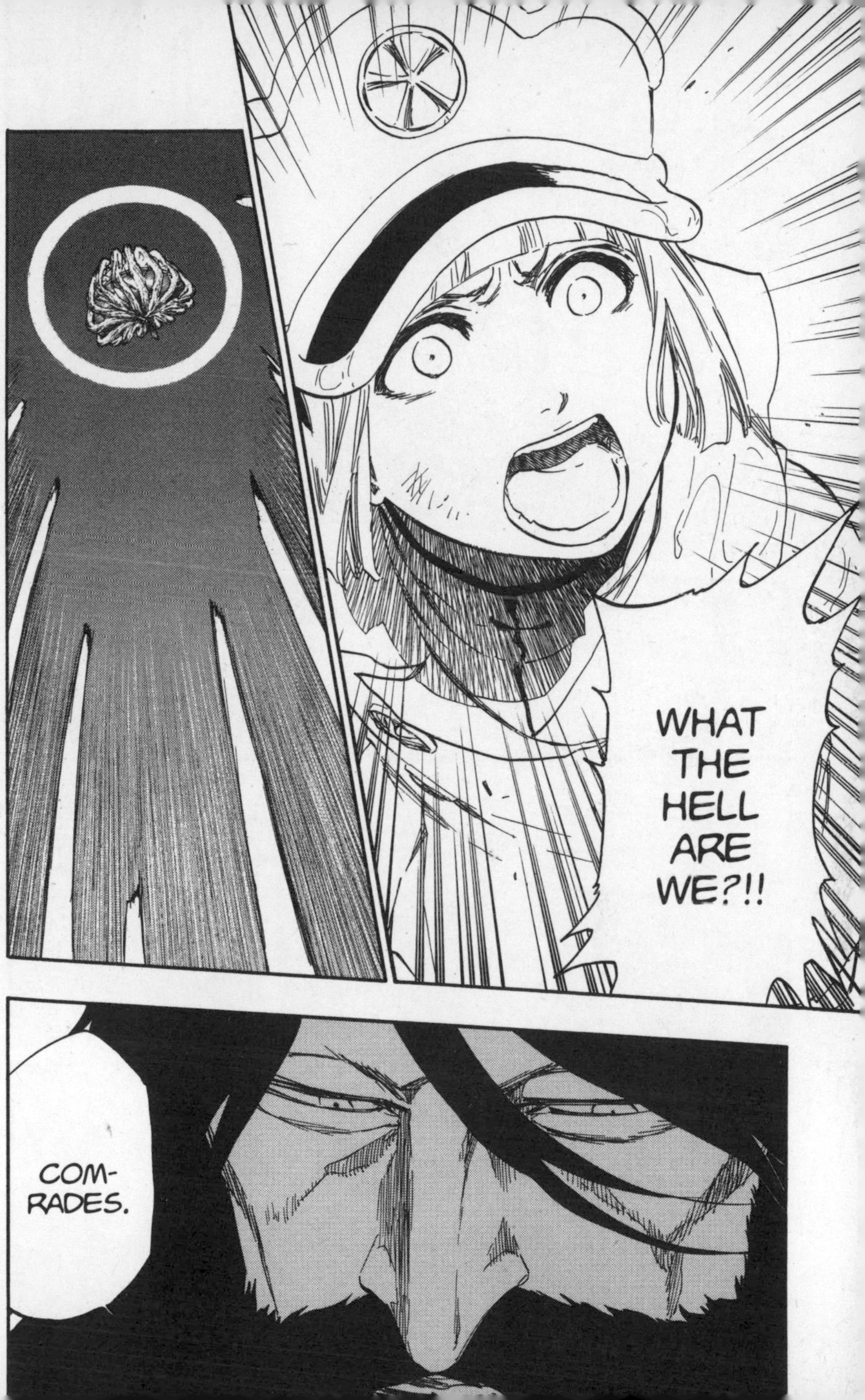
WHAT THE HELL ARE WE?!!
COM-RADES.

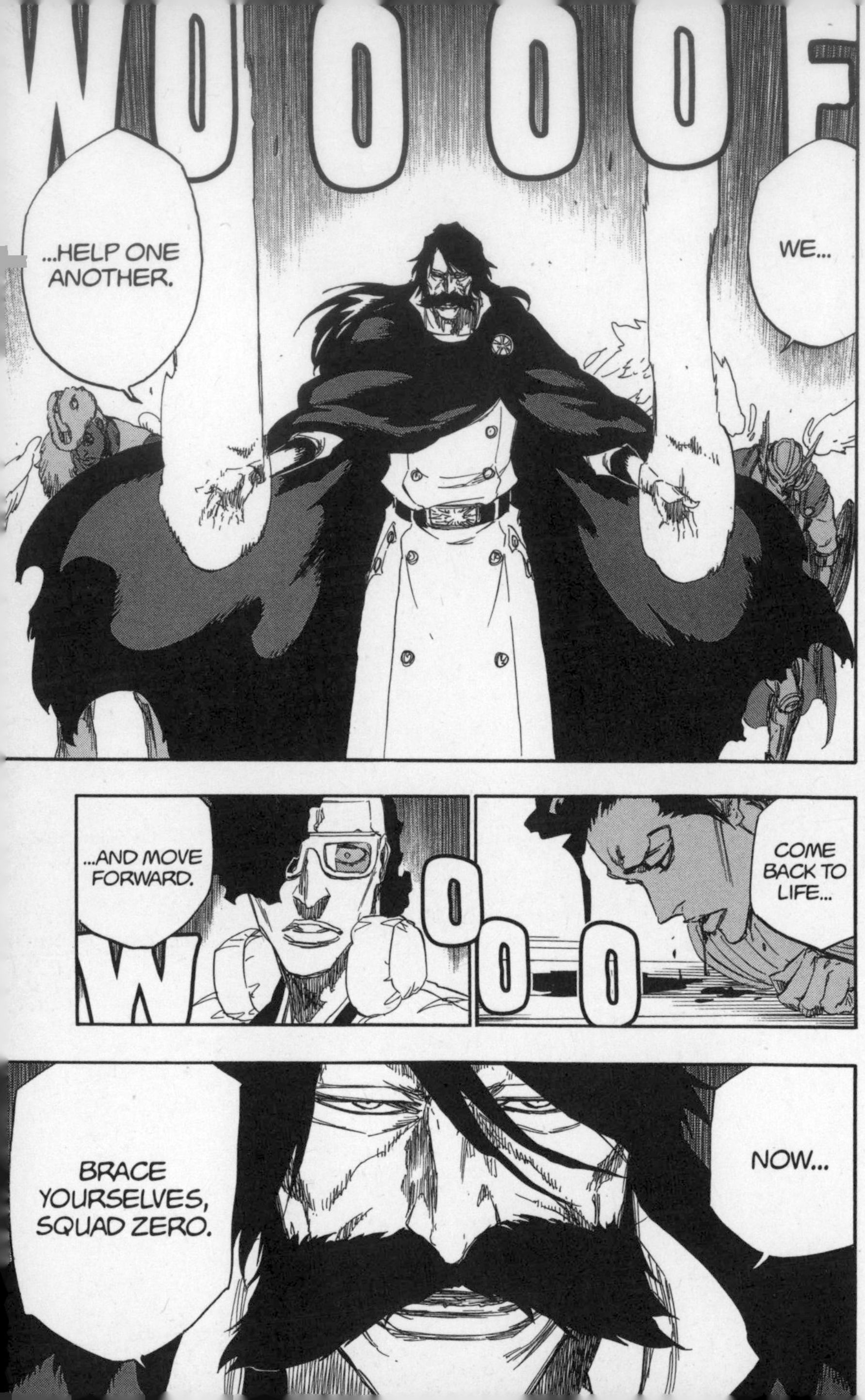
WOOOF
WE...
...HELP ONE ANOTHER.
COME BACK TO LIFE...
...AND MOVE FORWARD.
WOOO
NOW...
BRACE YOURSELVES, SQUAD ZERO.

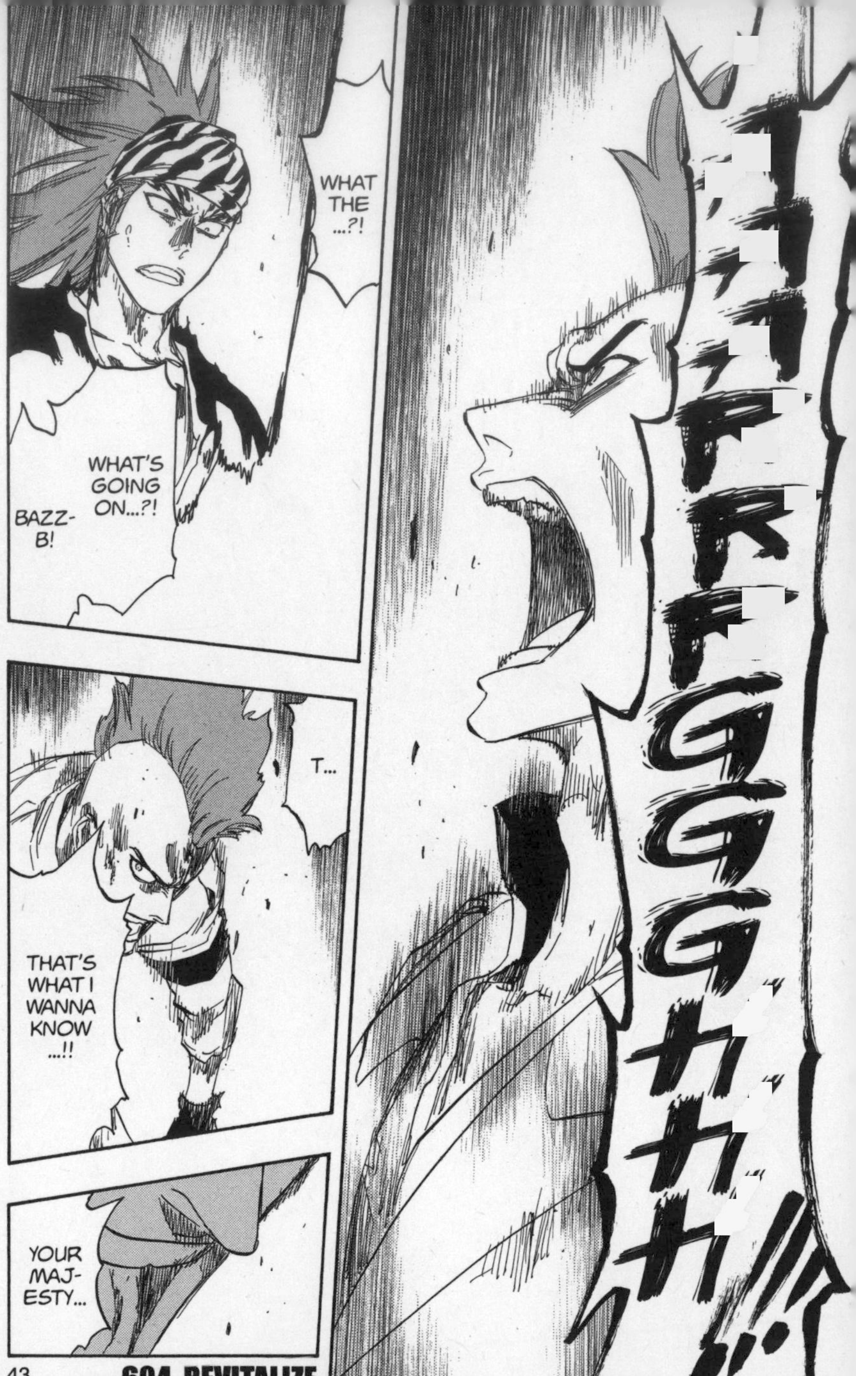
RRRGGGHHH!!
WHAT THE ...?!
WHAT'S GOING ON...?!
BAZZ-B!
T...
THAT'S WHAT I WANNA KNOW ...!!
YOUR MAJ-ESTY...

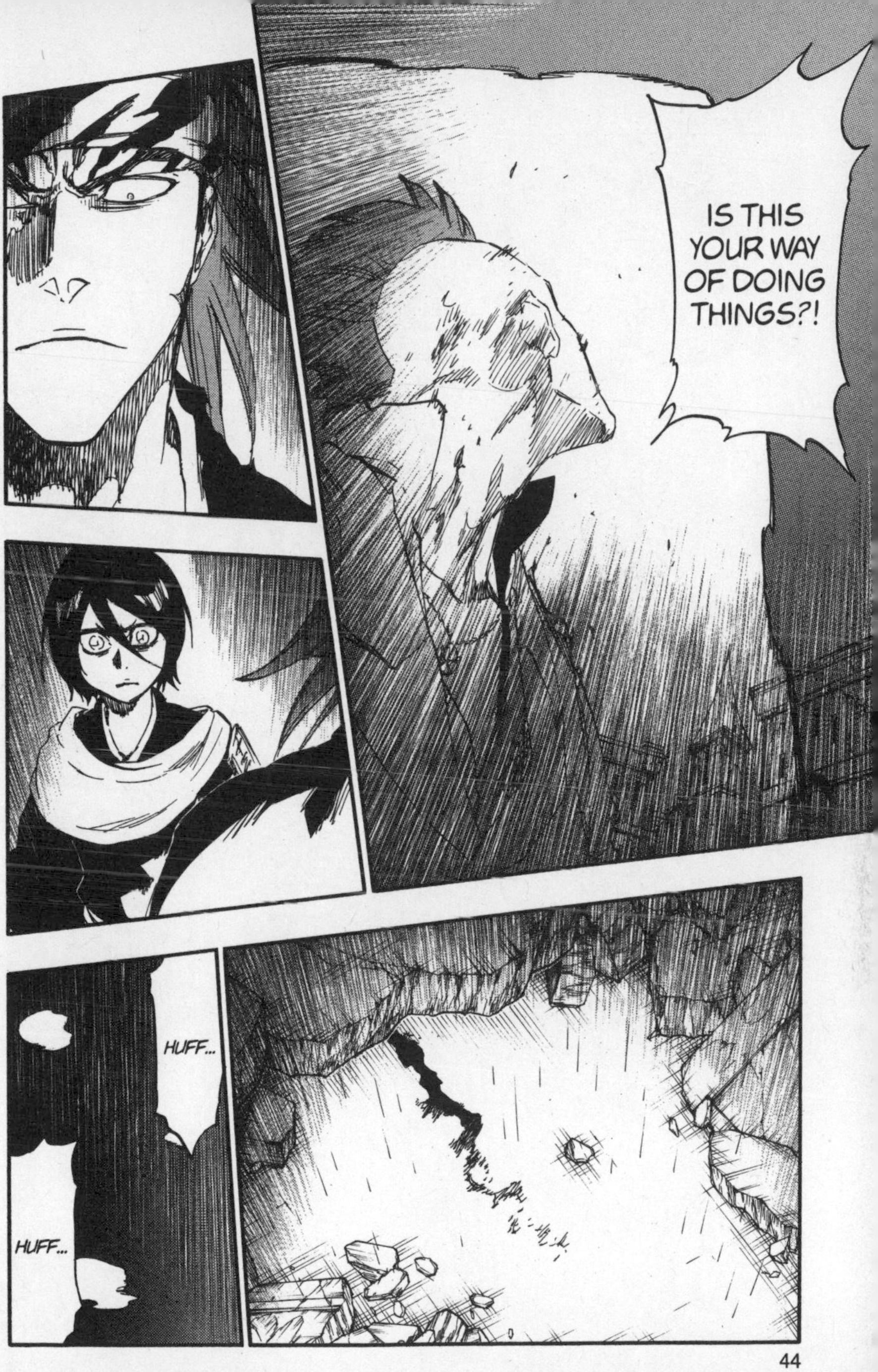
IS THIS YOUR WAY OF DOING THINGS?!
HUFF...
HUFF...

READ THIS WAY

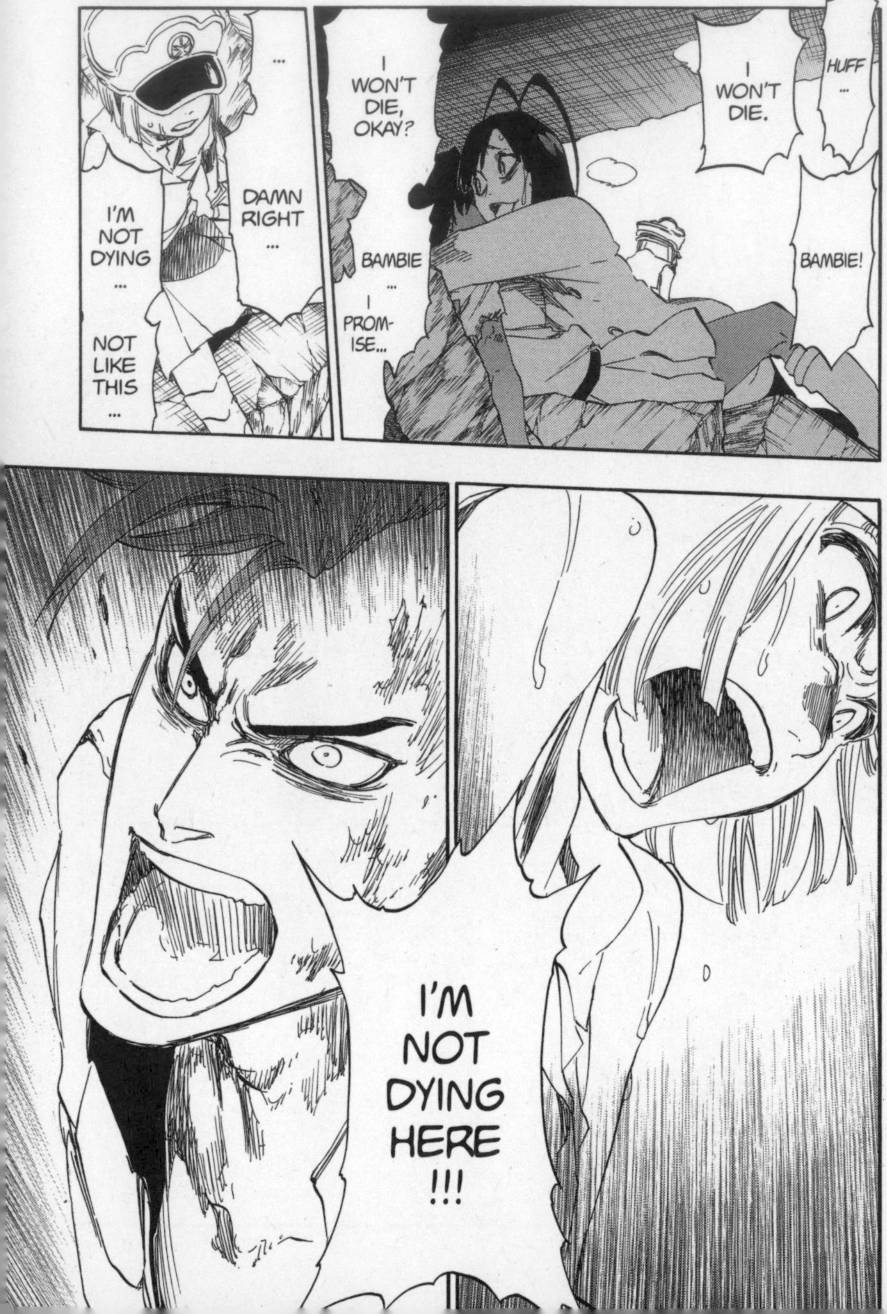
HUFF ...
I WON'T DIE.
BAMBIE!
I WON'T DIE, OKAY?
BAMBIE ... I PROMISE...
...
DAMN RIGHT ...
I'M NOT DYING ...
NOT LIKE THIS ...
I'M NOT DYING HERE !!!

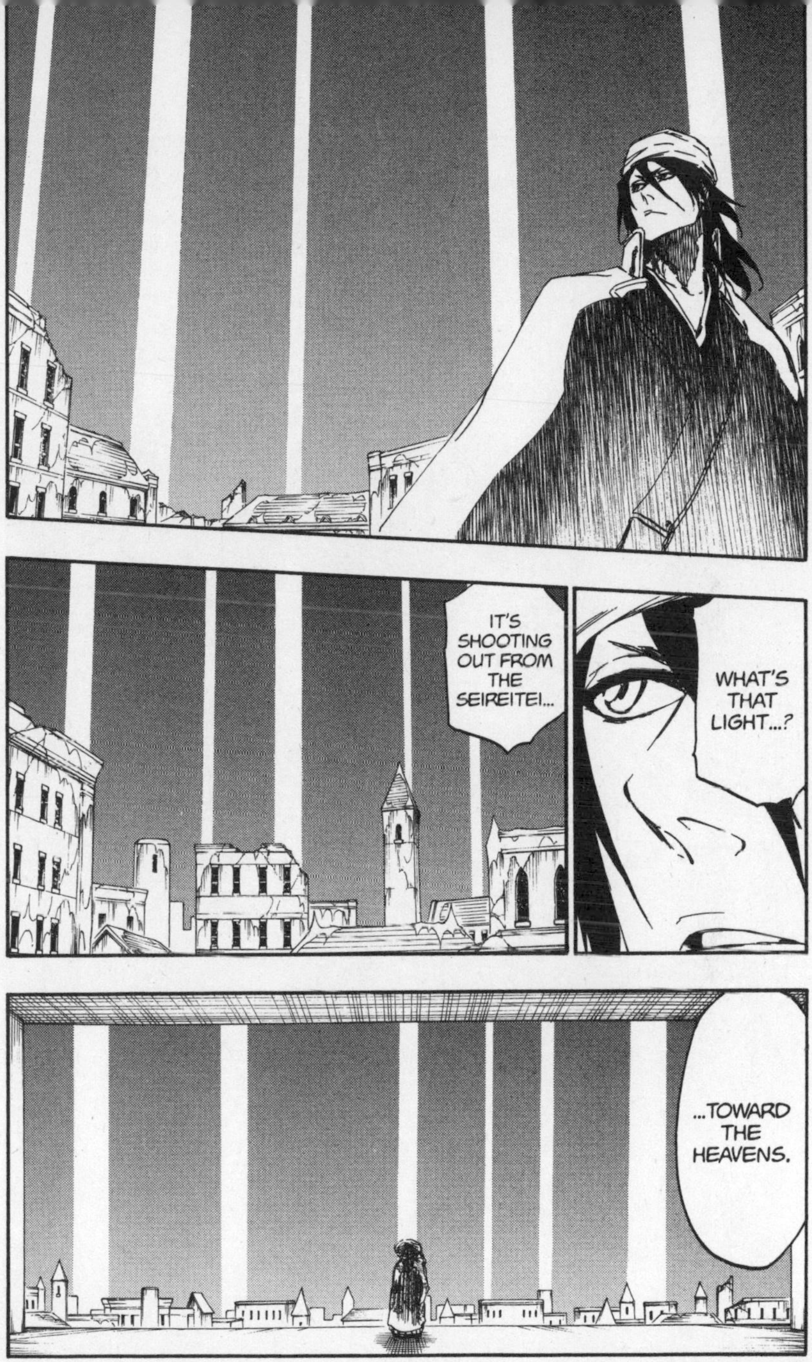
WHAT'S THAT LIGHT...?
IT'S SHOOTING OUT FROM THE SEIREITEI...
...TOWARD THE HEAVENS.

READ THIS WAY

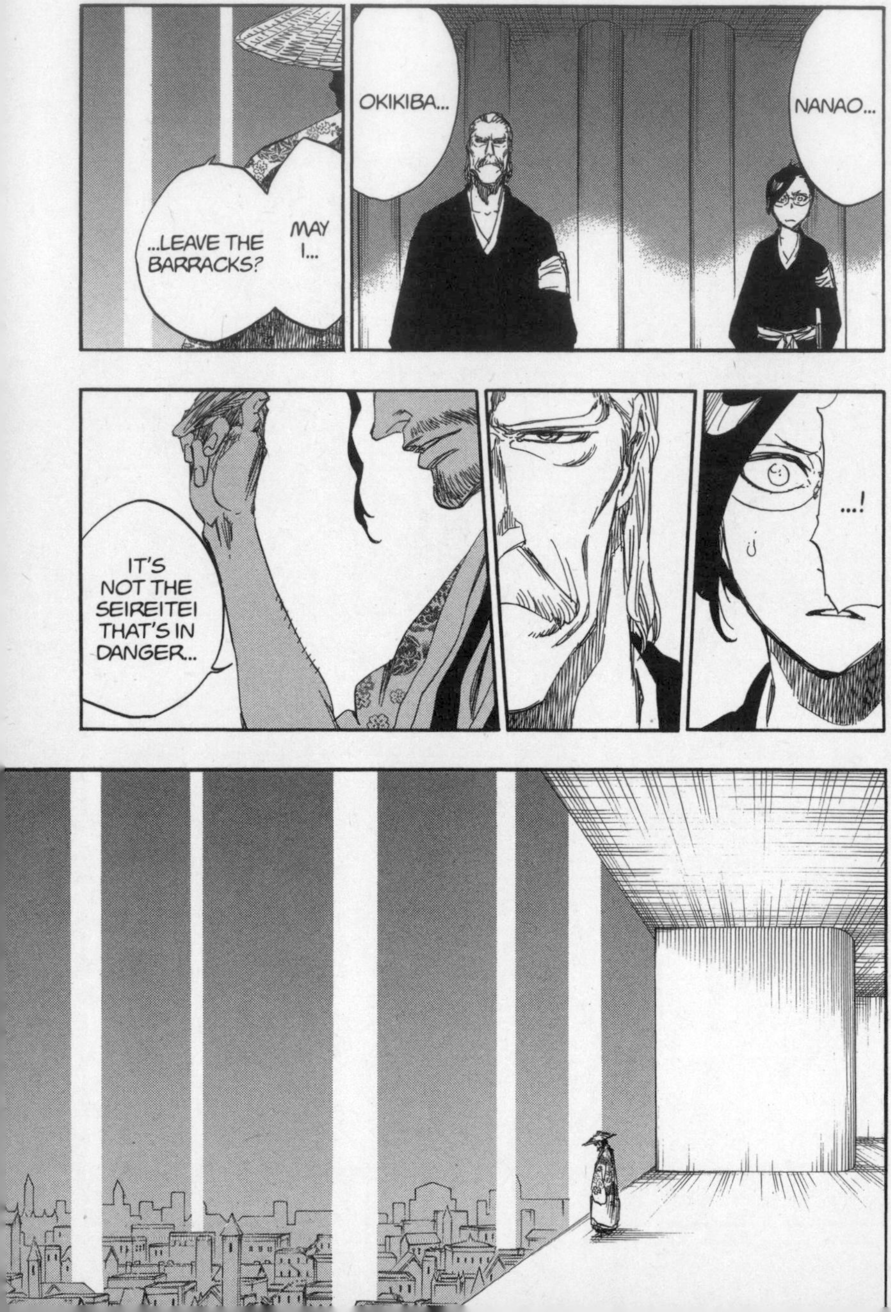
NANAO...
OKIKIBA...
MAY I...
...LEAVE THE BARRACKS?
...!
IT'S NOT THE SEIREITEI THAT'S IN DANGER...

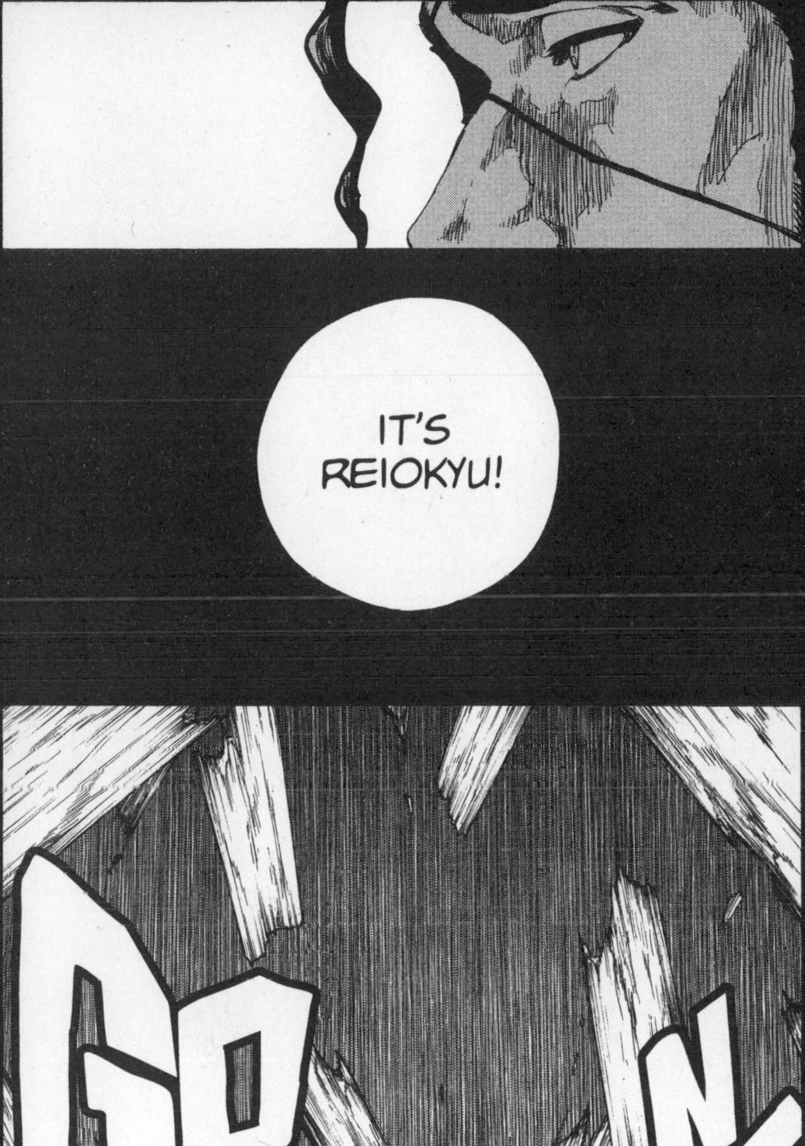
IT'S REIOKYU!
GONK

BLEACH 604.

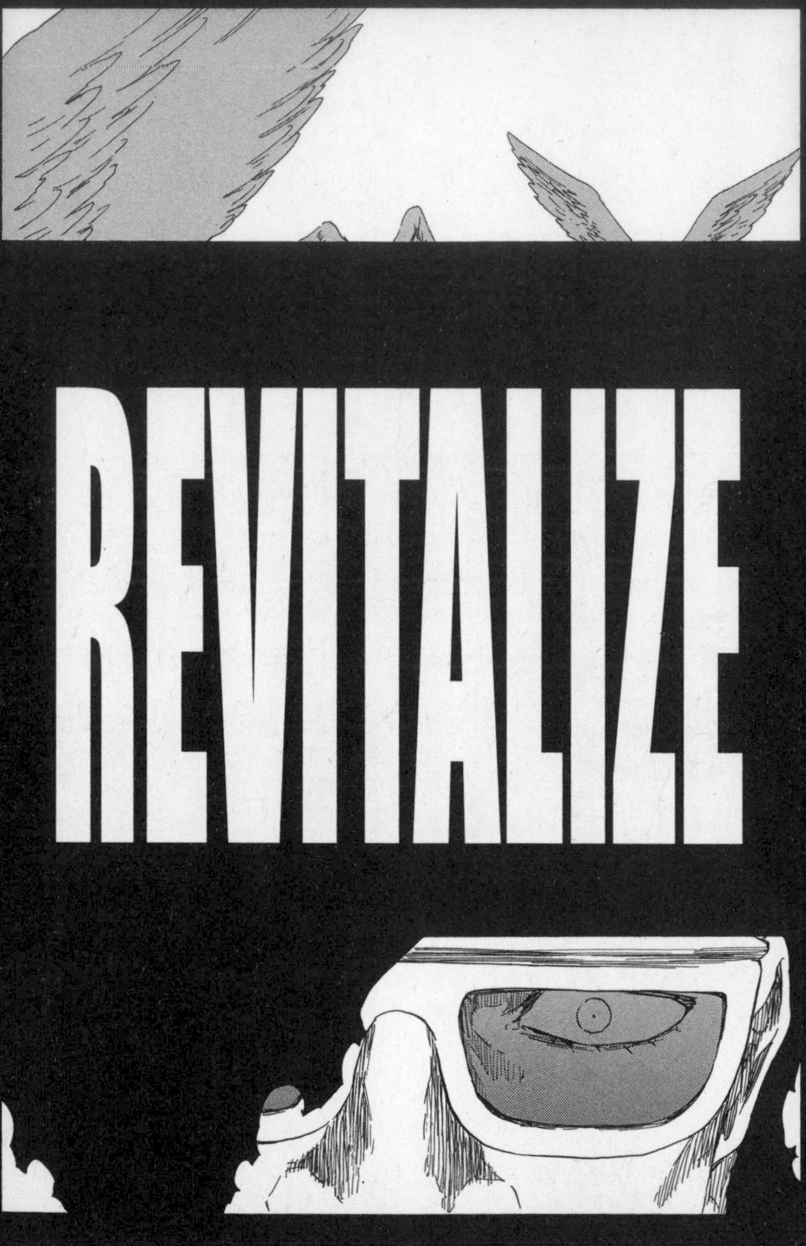
REVITALIZE

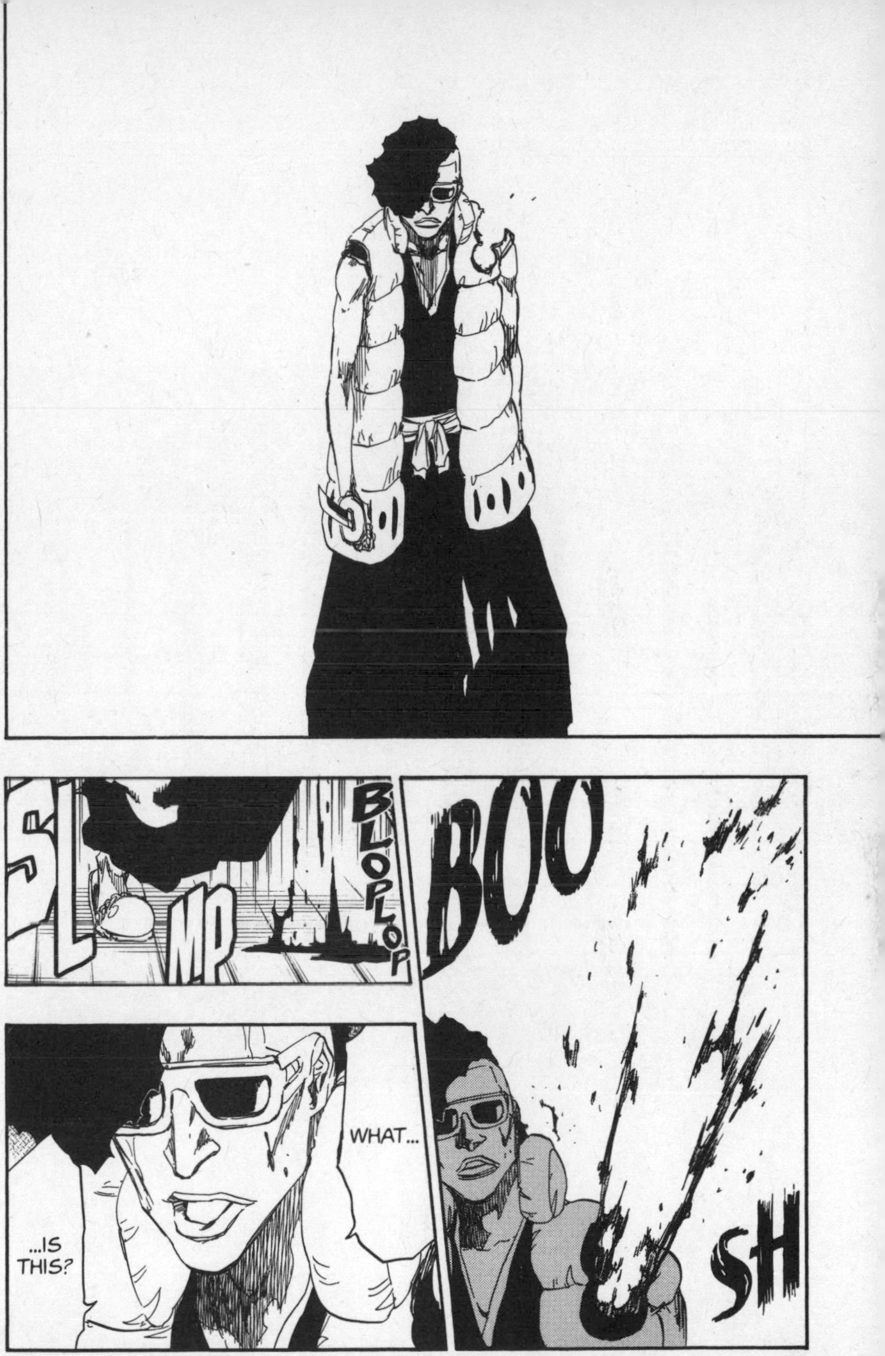

BOO
SH
SL
MP
BLOPLOP
WHAT...
...IS THIS?

READ THIS WAY

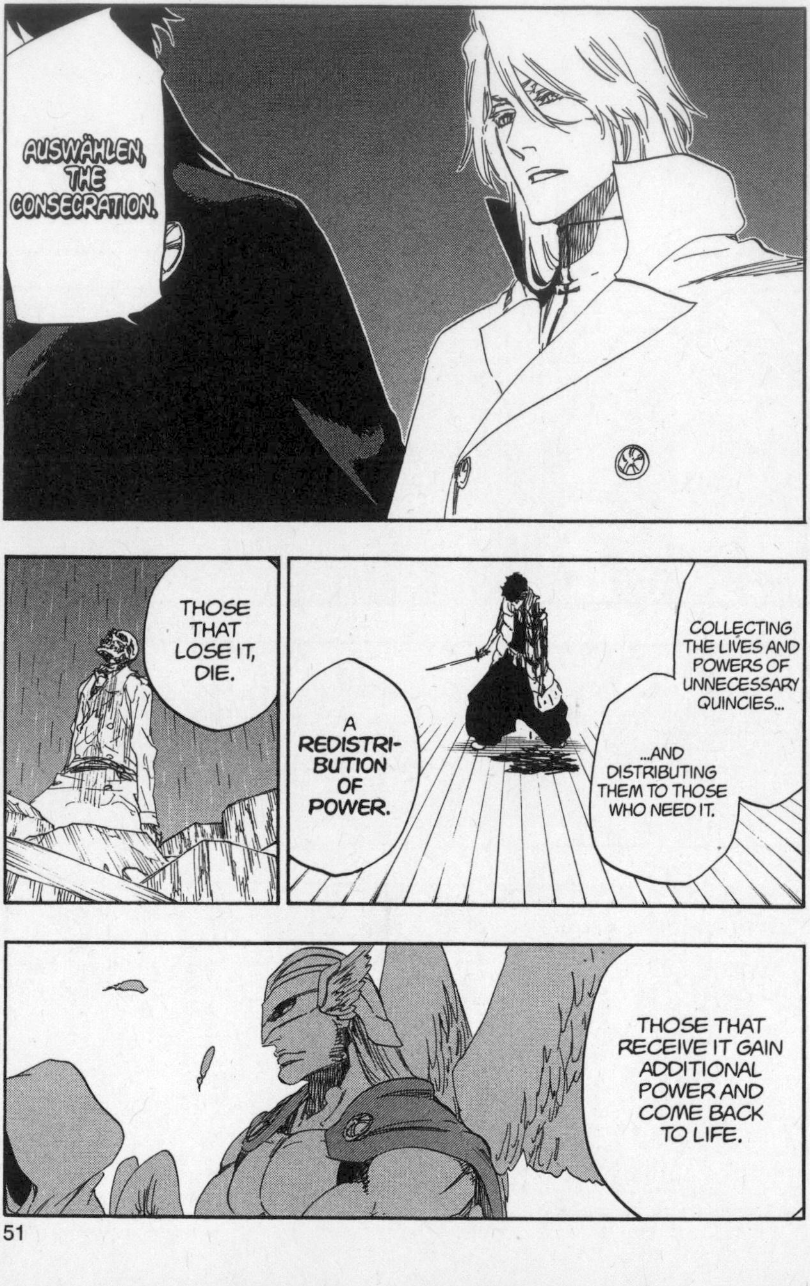
AUSWÄHLEN, THE CONSECRATION.
COLLECTING THE LIVES AND POWERS OF UNNECESSARY QUINCIES...
...AND DISTRIBUTING THEM TO THOSE WHO NEED IT.
A REDISTRI-BUTION OF POWER.
THOSE THAT LOSE IT, DIE.
THOSE THAT RECEIVE IT GAIN ADDITIONAL POWER AND COME BACK TO LIFE.

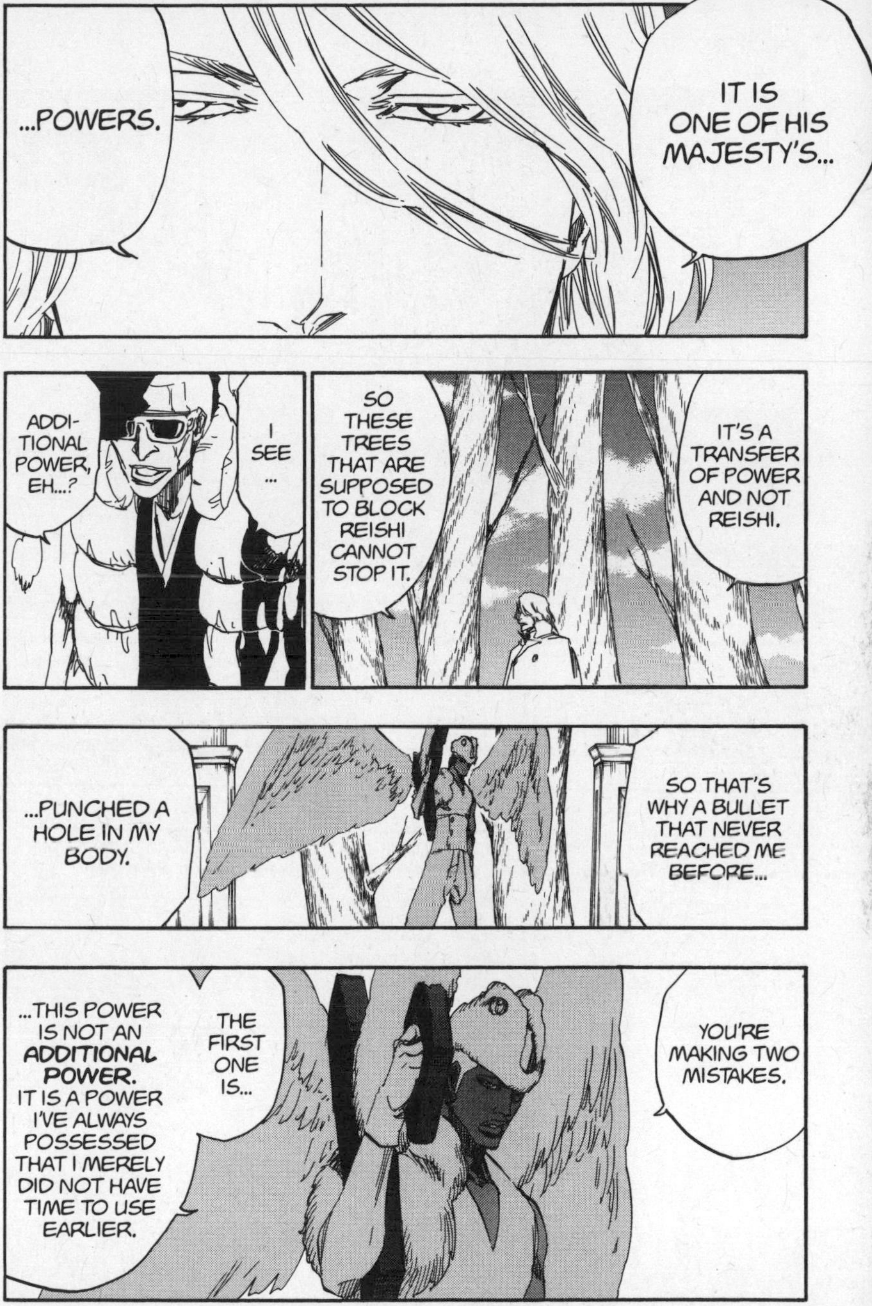
IT IS ONE OF HIS MAJESTY'S...
...POWERS.
IT'S A TRANSFER OF POWER AND NOT REISHI.
SO THESE TREES THAT ARE SUPPOSED TO BLOCK REISHI CANNOT STOP IT.
I SEE ...
ADDI-TIONAL POWER, EH...?
SO THAT'S WHY A BULLET THAT NEVER REACHED ME BEFORE...
...PUNCHED A HOLE IN MY BODY.
YOU'RE MAKING TWO MISTAKES.
THE FIRST ONE IS...
...THIS POWER IS NOT AN **ADDITIONAL POWER.** IT IS A POWER I'VE ALWAYS POSSESSED THAT I MERELY DID NOT HAVE TIME TO USE EARLIER.

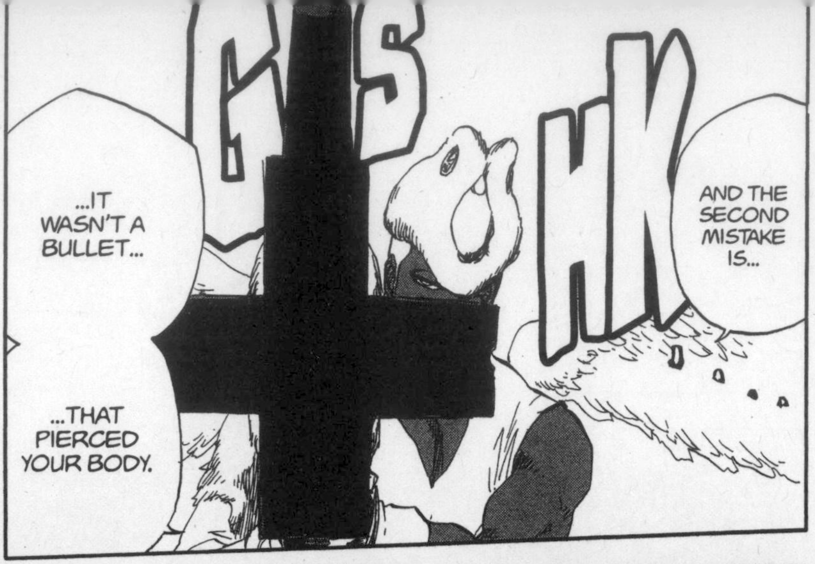
AND THE SECOND MISTAKE IS...
HK
...IT WASN'T A BULLET...
...THAT PIERCED YOUR BODY.

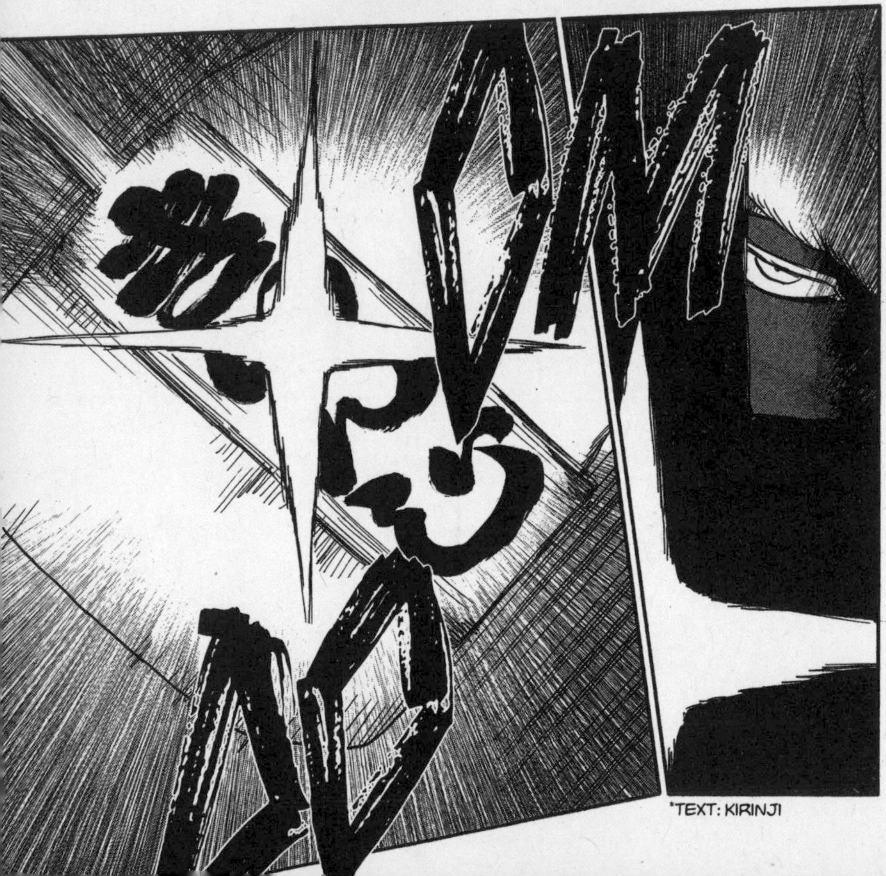

*TEXT: KIRINJI

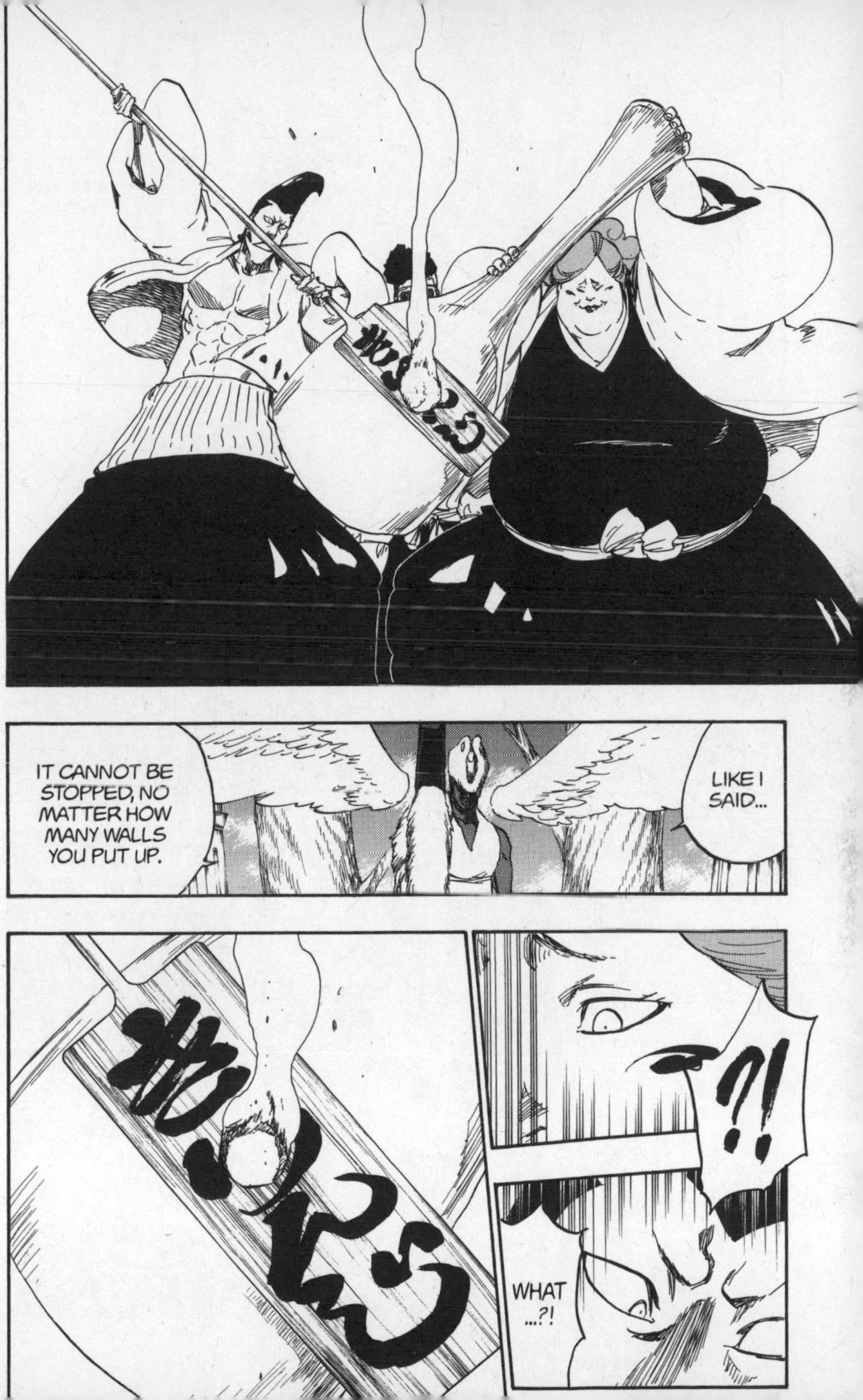
LIKE I SAID...
IT CANNOT BE STOPPED, NO MATTER HOW MANY WALLS YOU PUT UP.
?!
WHAT ...?!

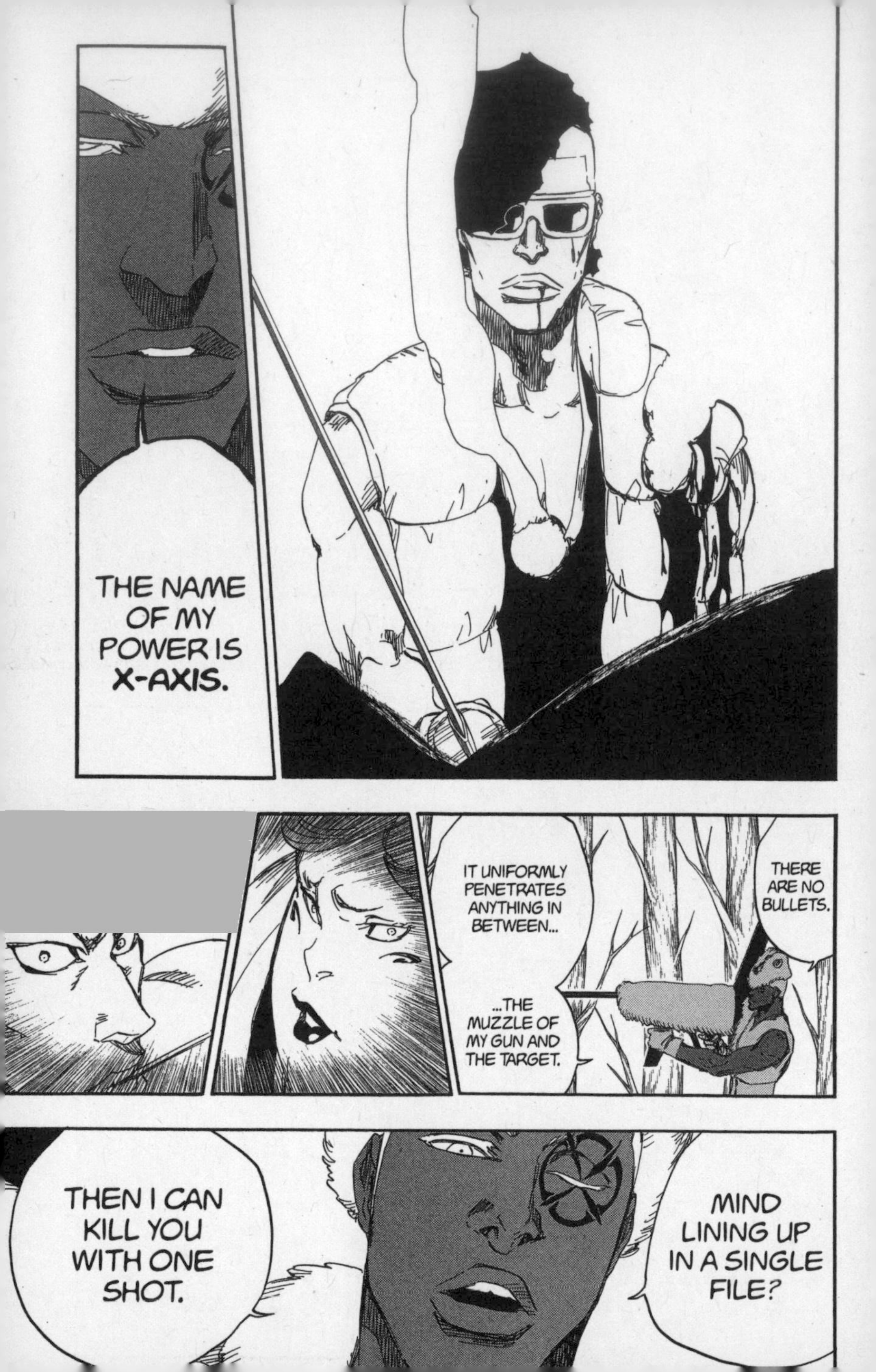
THE NAME OF MY POWER IS **X-AXIS.**
THERE ARE NO BULLETS.
IT UNIFORMLY PENETRATES ANYTHING IN BETWEEN...
...THE MUZZLE OF MY GUN AND THE TARGET.
MIND LINING UP IN A SINGLE FILE?
THEN I CAN KILL YOU WITH ONE SHOT.

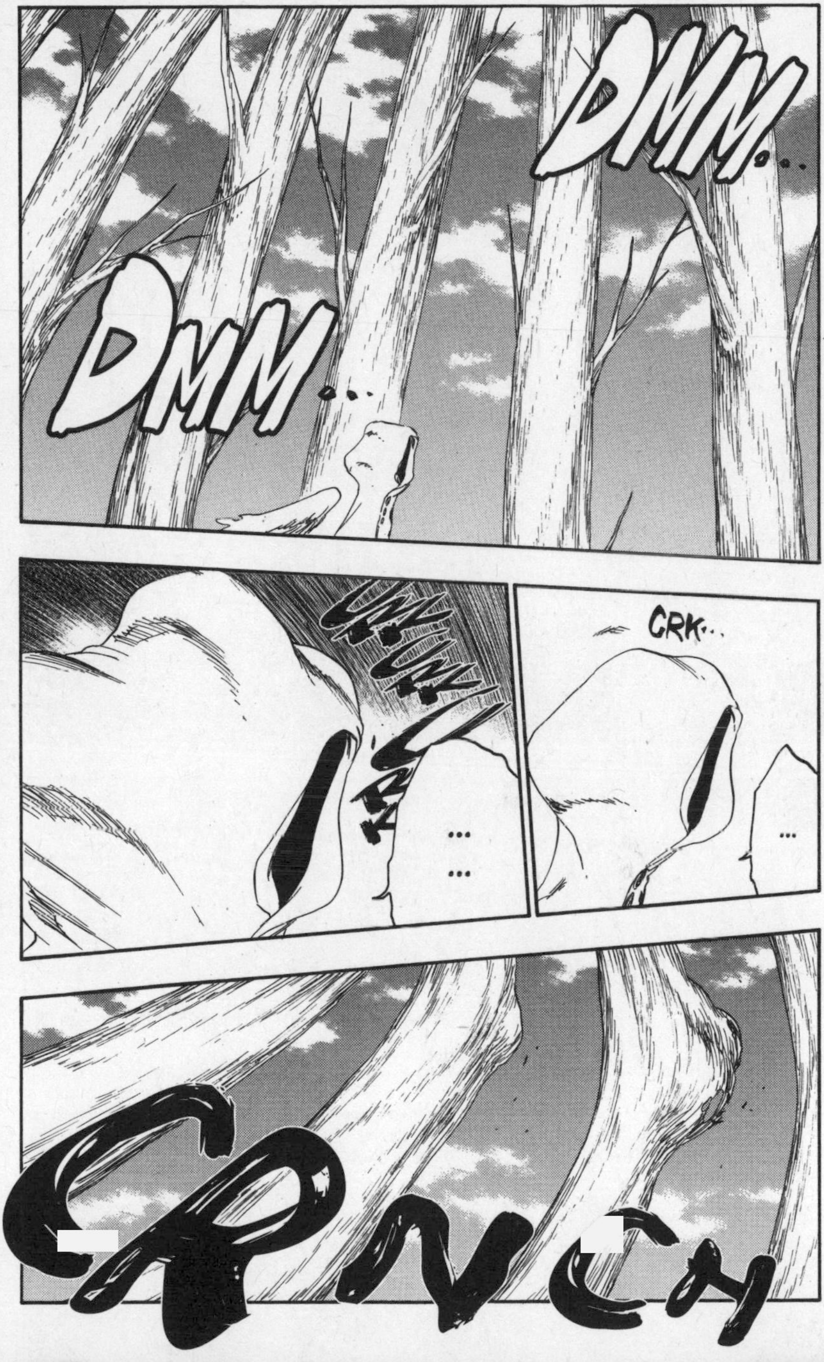
DMM...
DMM...
CRK...
...
...
...

SNP SNP SNP

FWAS...H

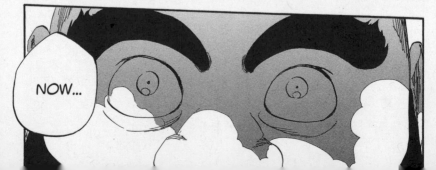

NOW...

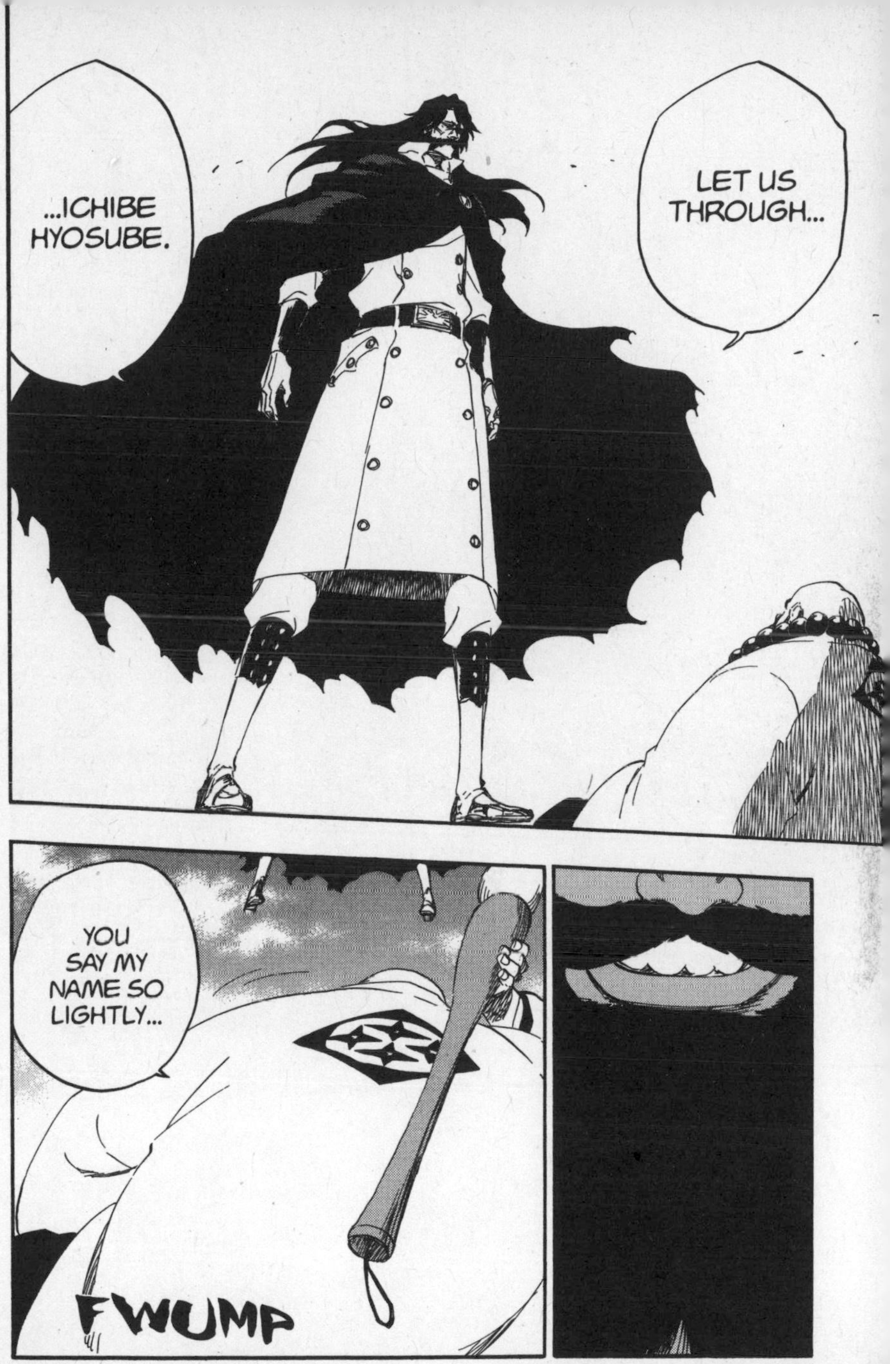
LET US THROUGH...
...ICHIBE HYOSUBE.
YOU SAY MY NAME SO LIGHTLY...
FWUMP

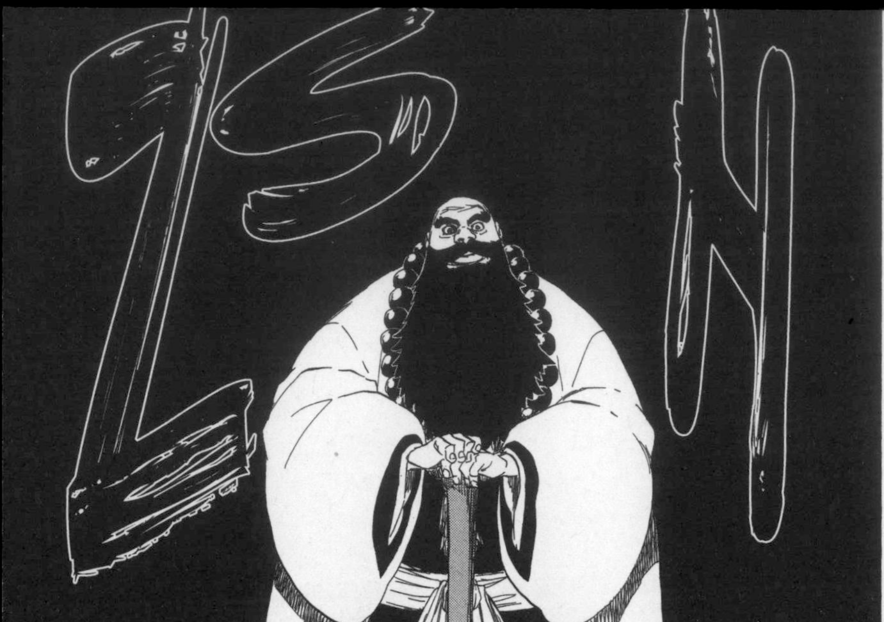
DON'T BLAME ME IF YOU LOSE YOUR VOICE.

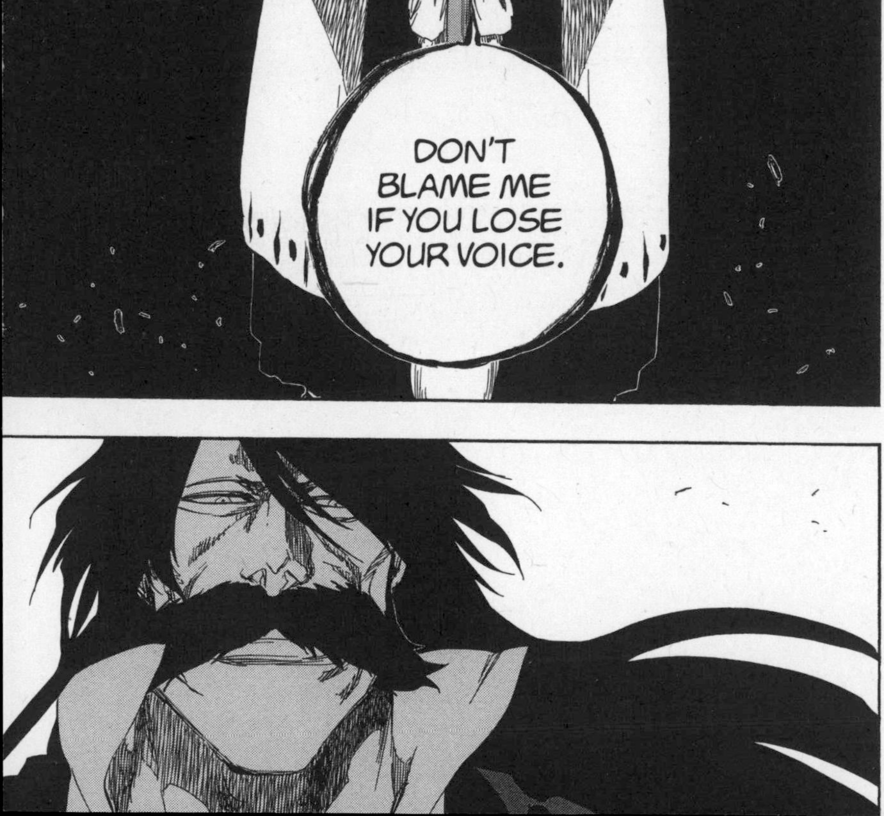

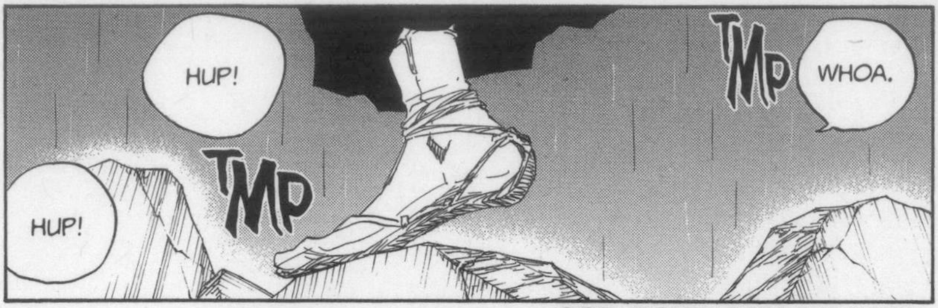
TMP
WHOA.
HUP!
TMP
HUP!

605. DON'T CALL MY NAME

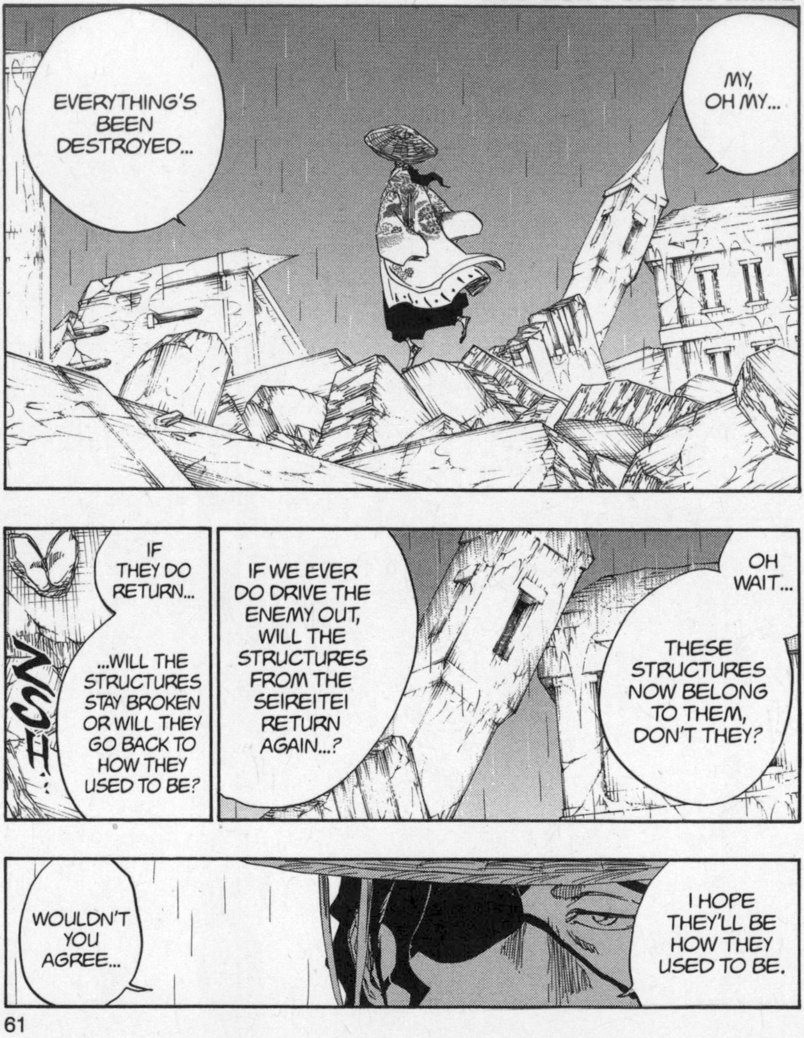
MY, OH MY...
EVERYTHING'S BEEN DESTROYED...
OH WAIT...
THESE STRUCTURES NOW BELONG TO THEM, DON'T THEY?
IF WE EVER DO DRIVE THE ENEMY OUT, WILL THE STRUCTURES FROM THE SEIREITEI RETURN AGAIN...?
IF THEY DO RETURN...
...WILL THE STRUCTURES STAY BROKEN OR WILL THEY GO BACK TO HOW THEY USED TO BE?
I HOPE THEY'LL BE HOW THEY USED TO BE.
WOULDN'T YOU AGREE...

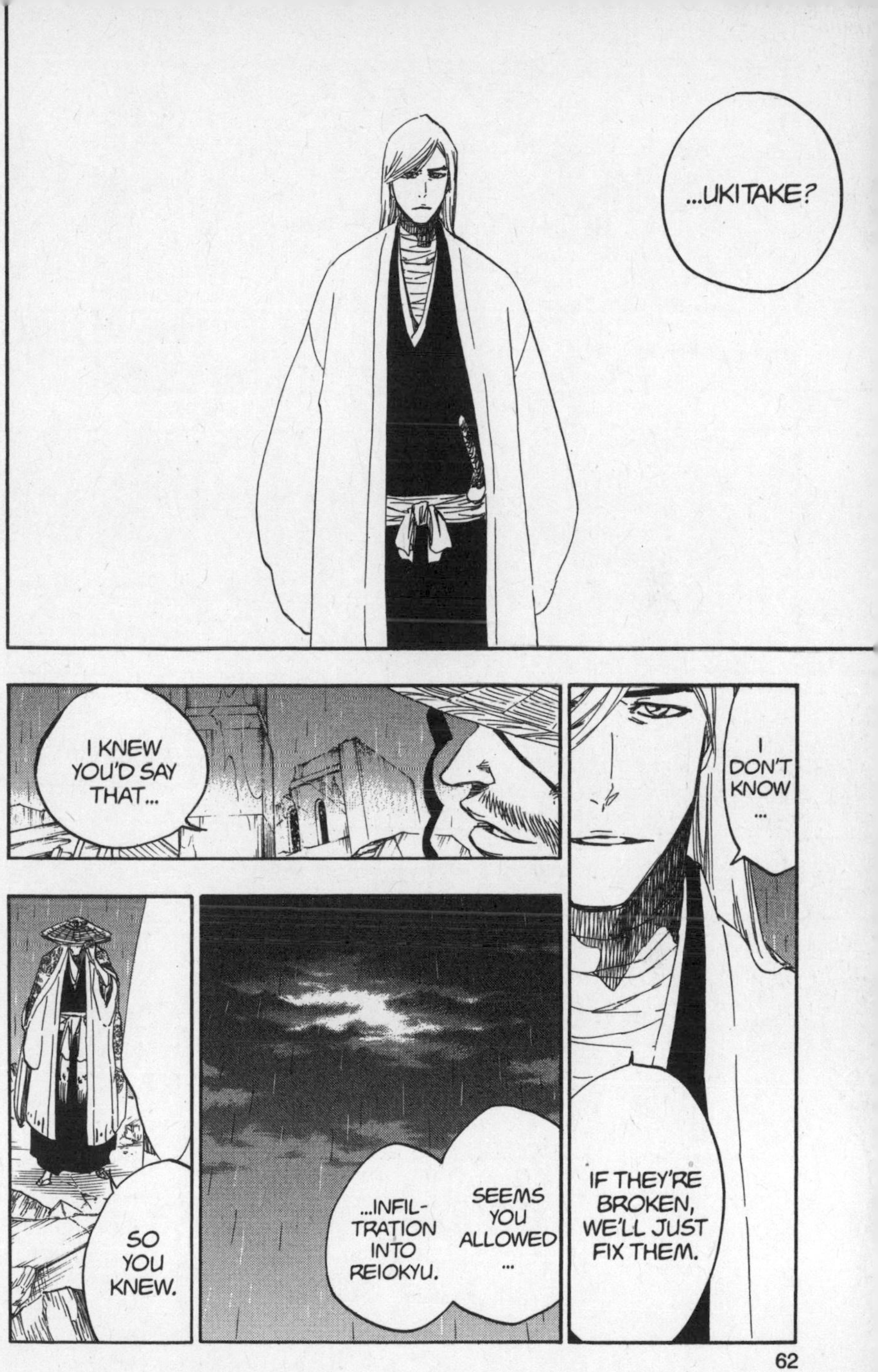
...UKITAKE?
I DON'T KNOW ...
IF THEY'RE BROKEN, WE'LL JUST FIX THEM.
I KNEW YOU'D SAY THAT...
SEEMS YOU ALLOWED ...
...INFIL-TRATION INTO REIOKYU.
SO YOU KNEW.

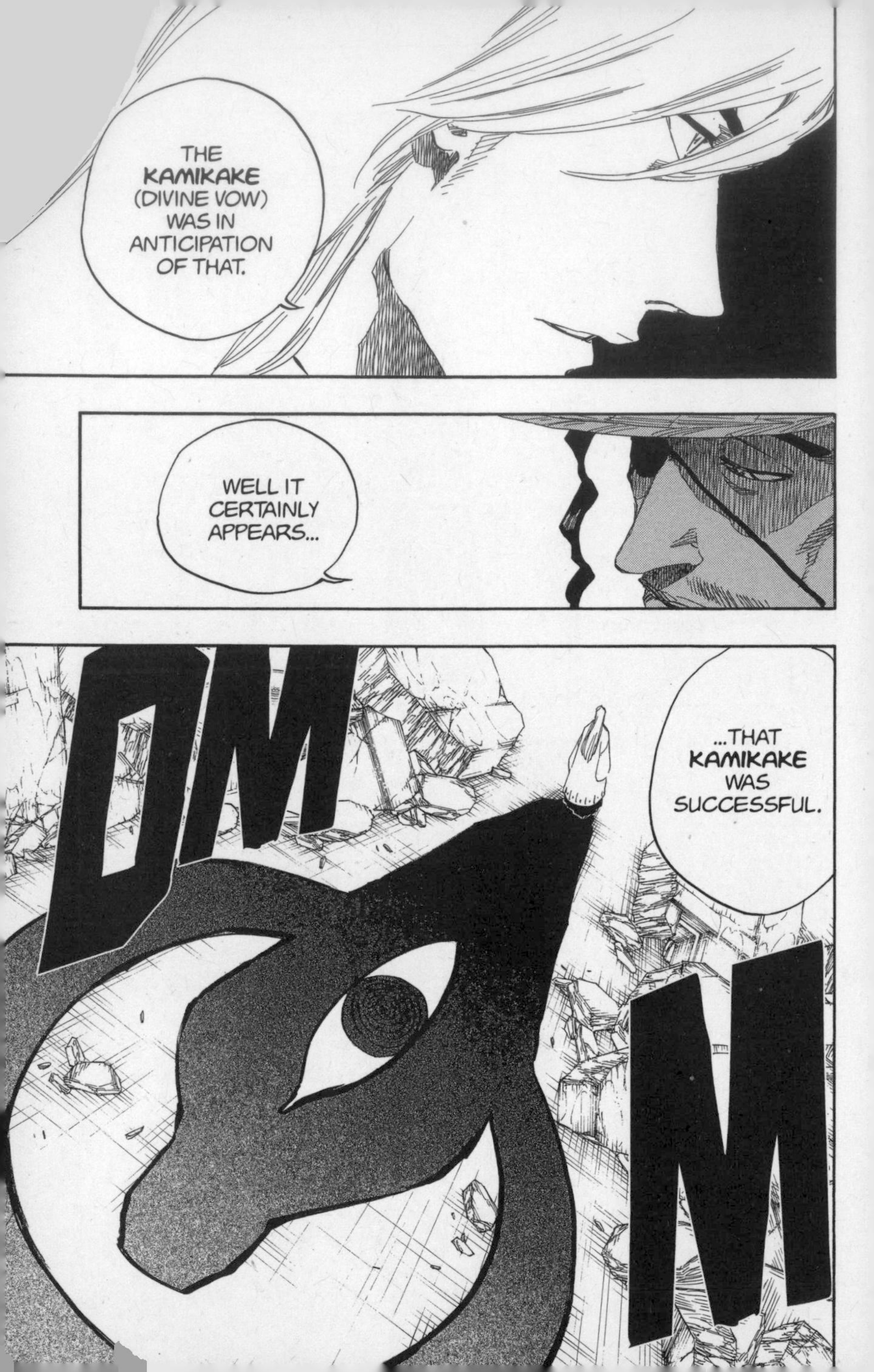
THE **KAMIKAKE** (DIVINE VOW) WAS IN ANTICIPATION OF THAT.
WELL IT CERTAINLY APPEARS...
...THAT **KAMIKAKE** WAS SUCCESSFUL.
DM
M

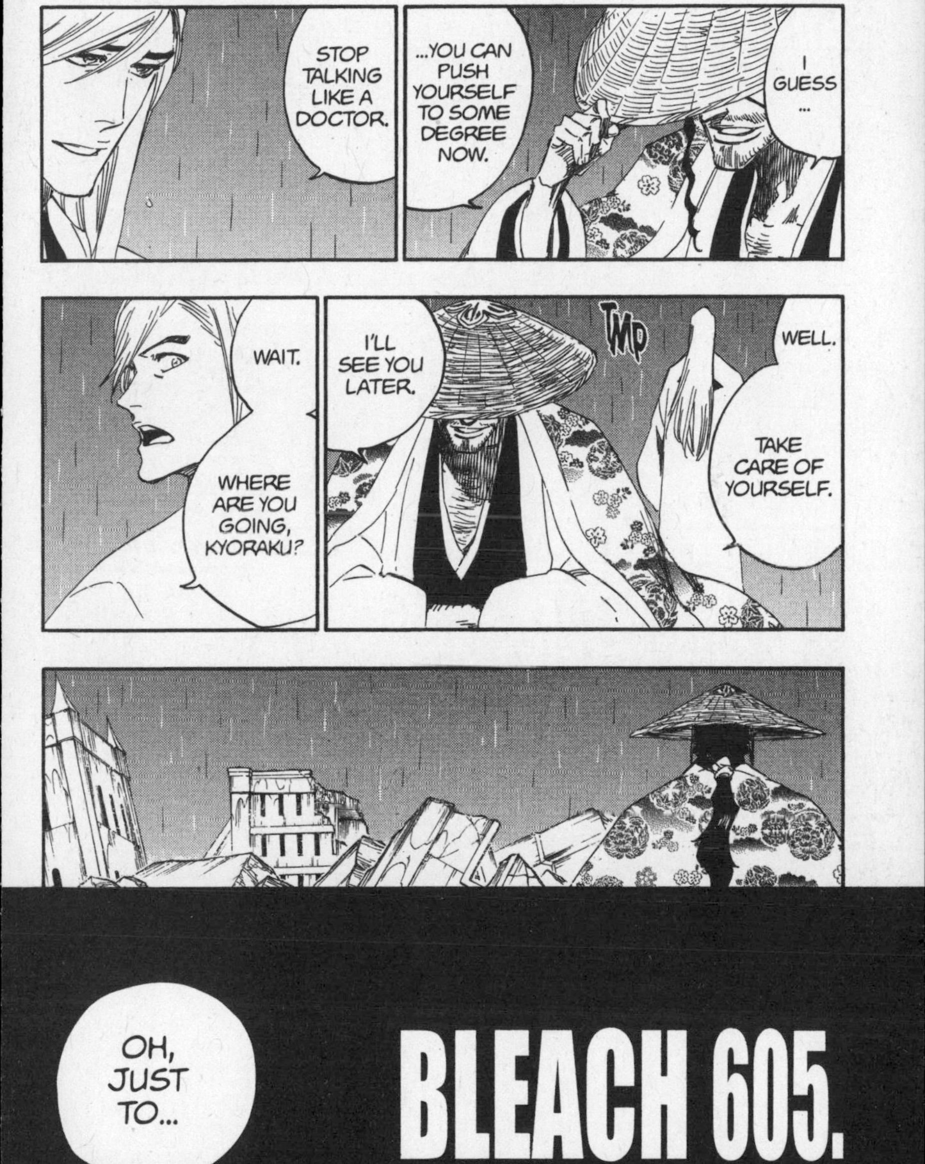
I GUESS ...
...YOU CAN PUSH YOURSELF TO SOME DEGREE NOW.
STOP TALKING LIKE A DOCTOR.
WELL.
TAKE CARE OF YOURSELF.
TMP
I'LL SEE YOU LATER.
WAIT.
WHERE ARE YOU GOING, KYORAKU?
OH, JUST TO...
BLEACH 605.

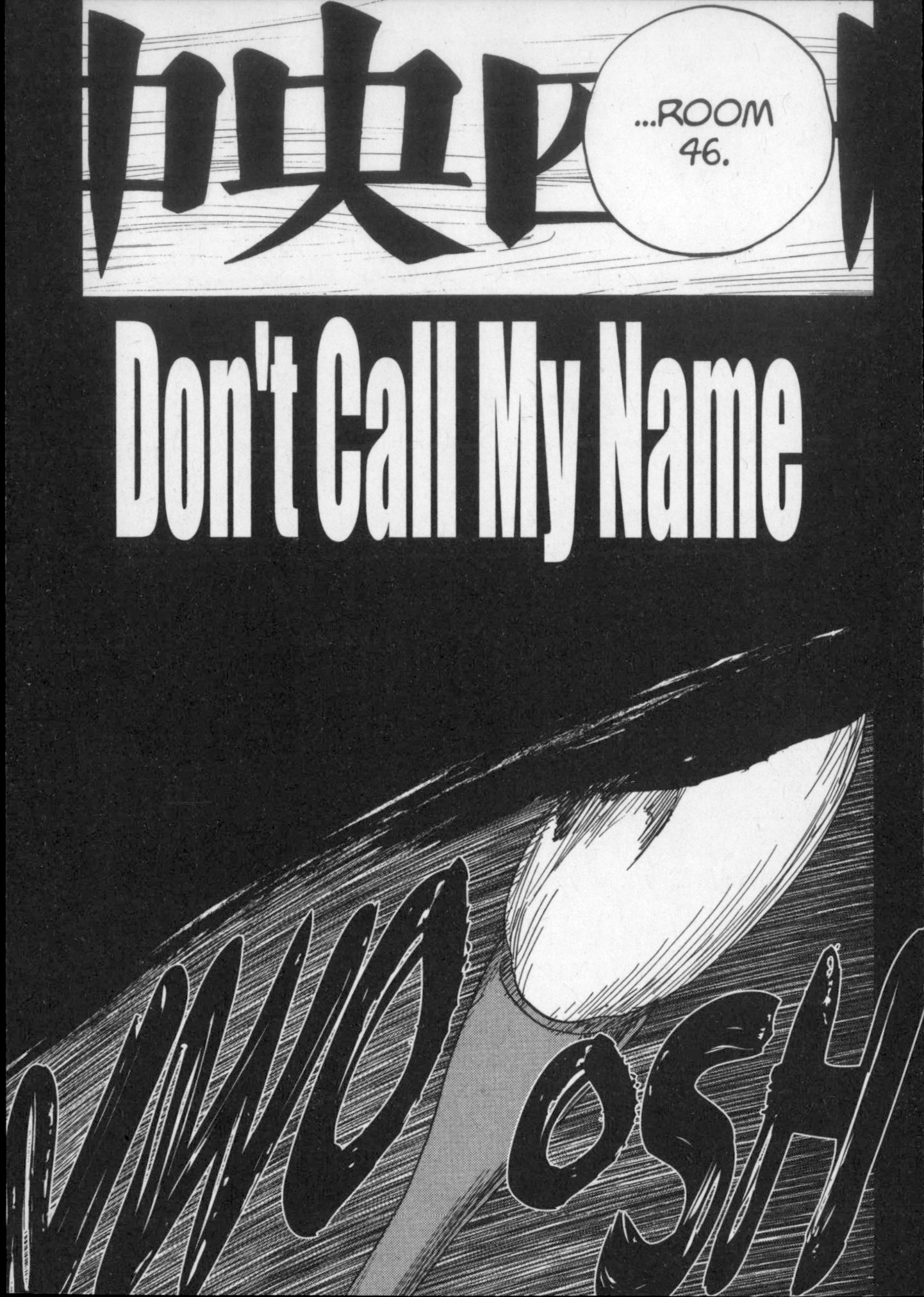
...ROOM 46.
Don't Call My Name

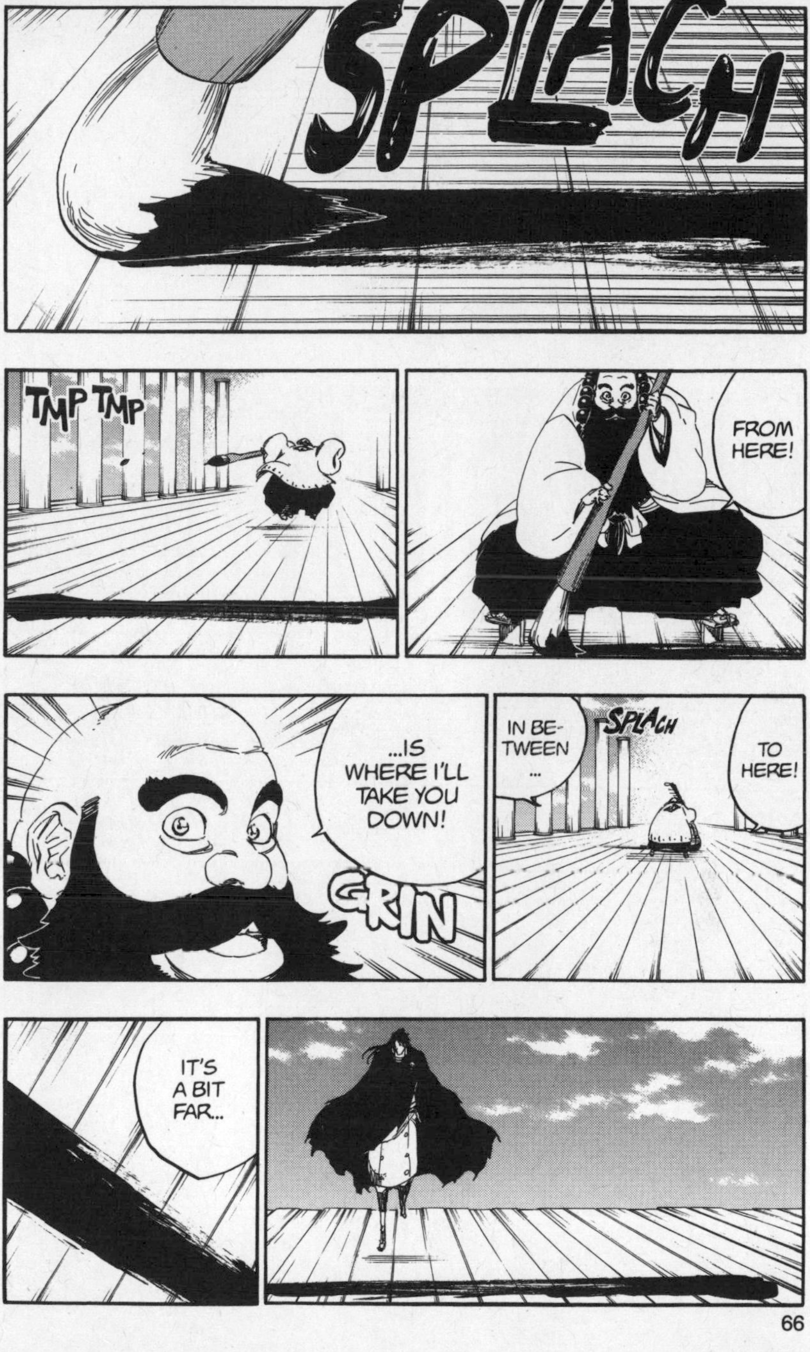
SPLACH
FROM HERE!
TMP TMP
TO HERE!
SPLACH
IN BE-TWEEN ...
...IS WHERE I'LL TAKE YOU DOWN!
GRIN
IT'S A BIT FAR...

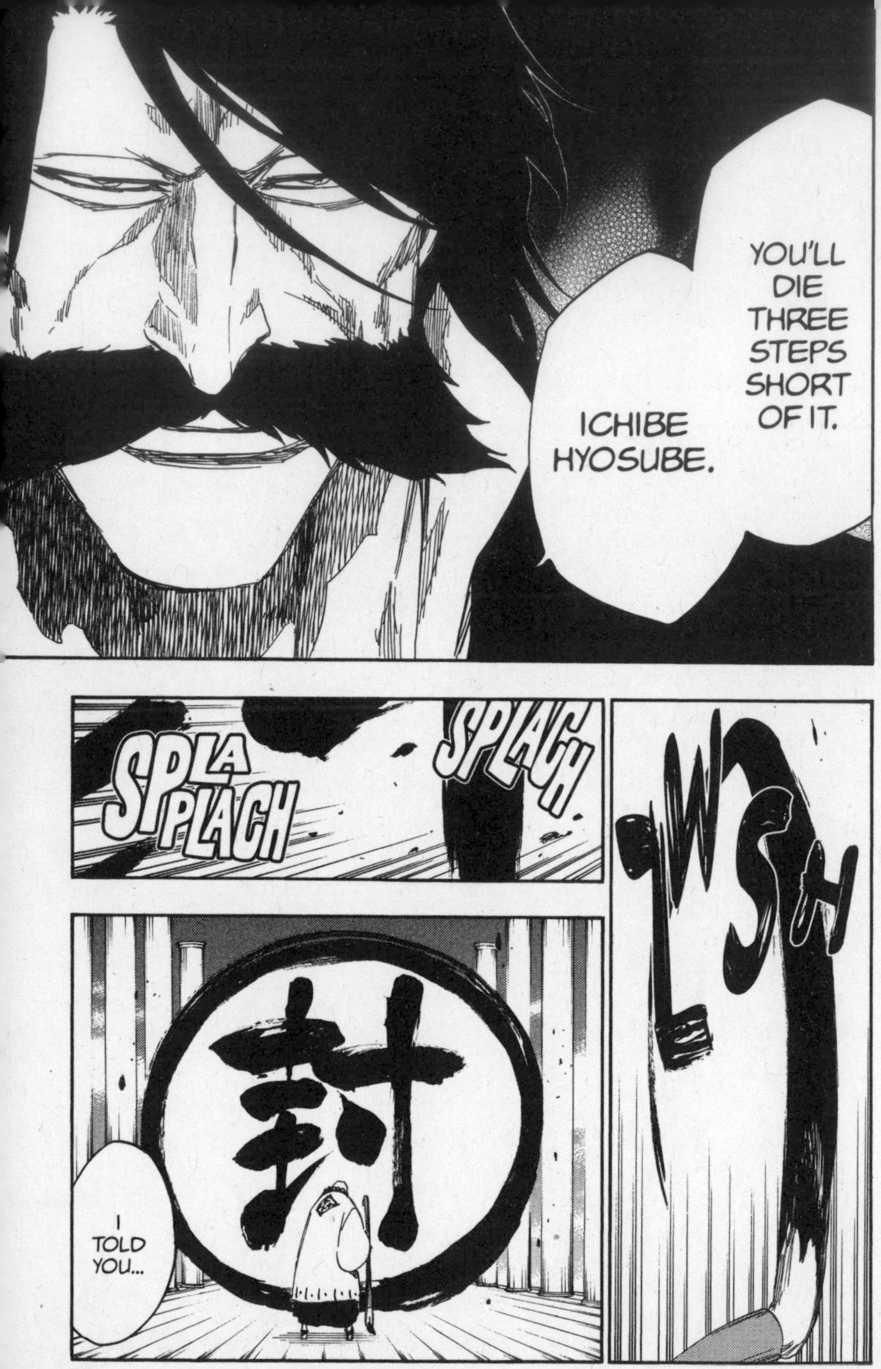
YOU'LL DIE THREE STEPS SHORT OF IT.
ICHIBE HYOSUBE.
WSH
SPLACH
SPLA SPLACH
封
I TOLD YOU...

*TEXT: SEAL

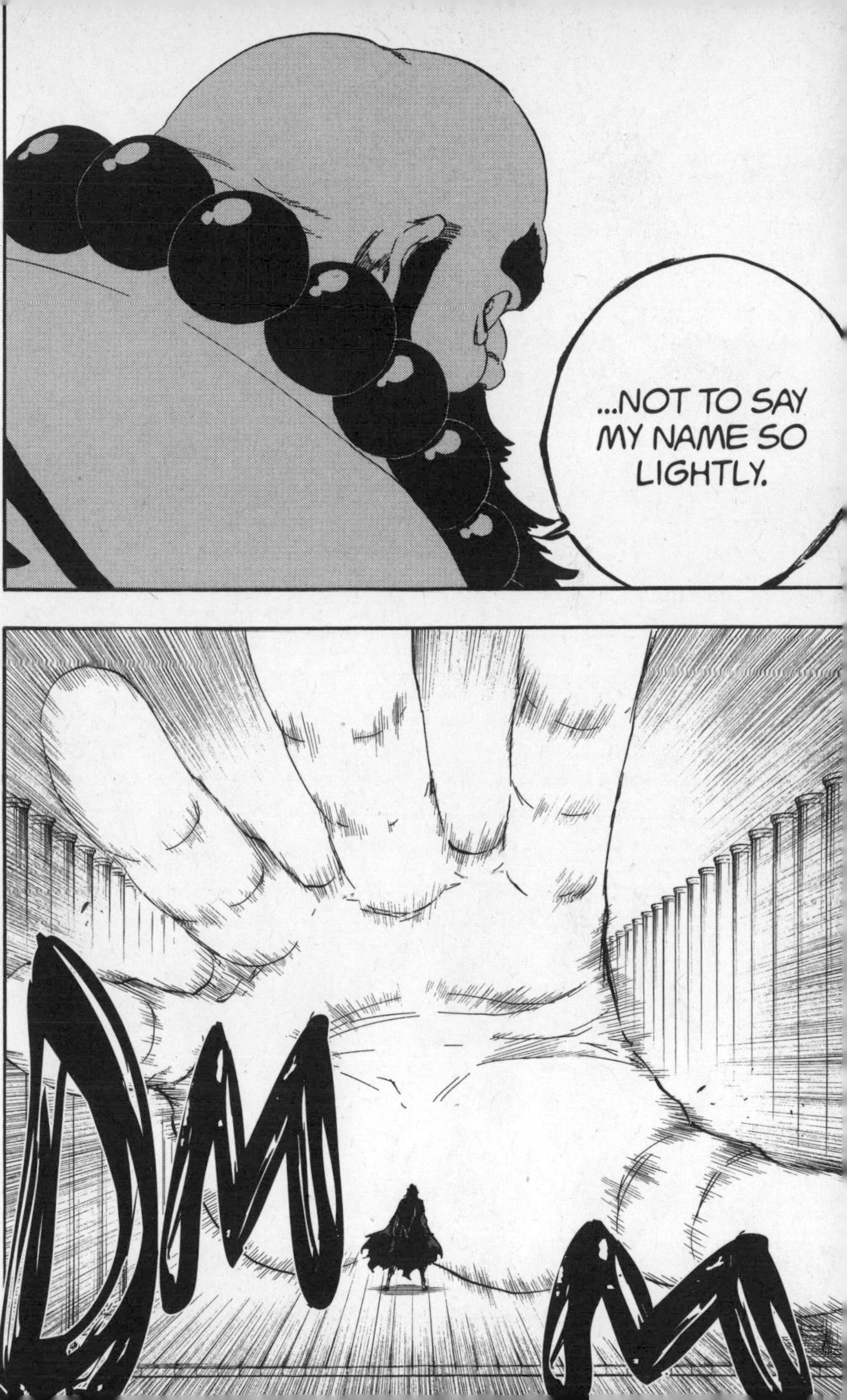
...NOT TO SAY MY NAME SO LIGHTLY.

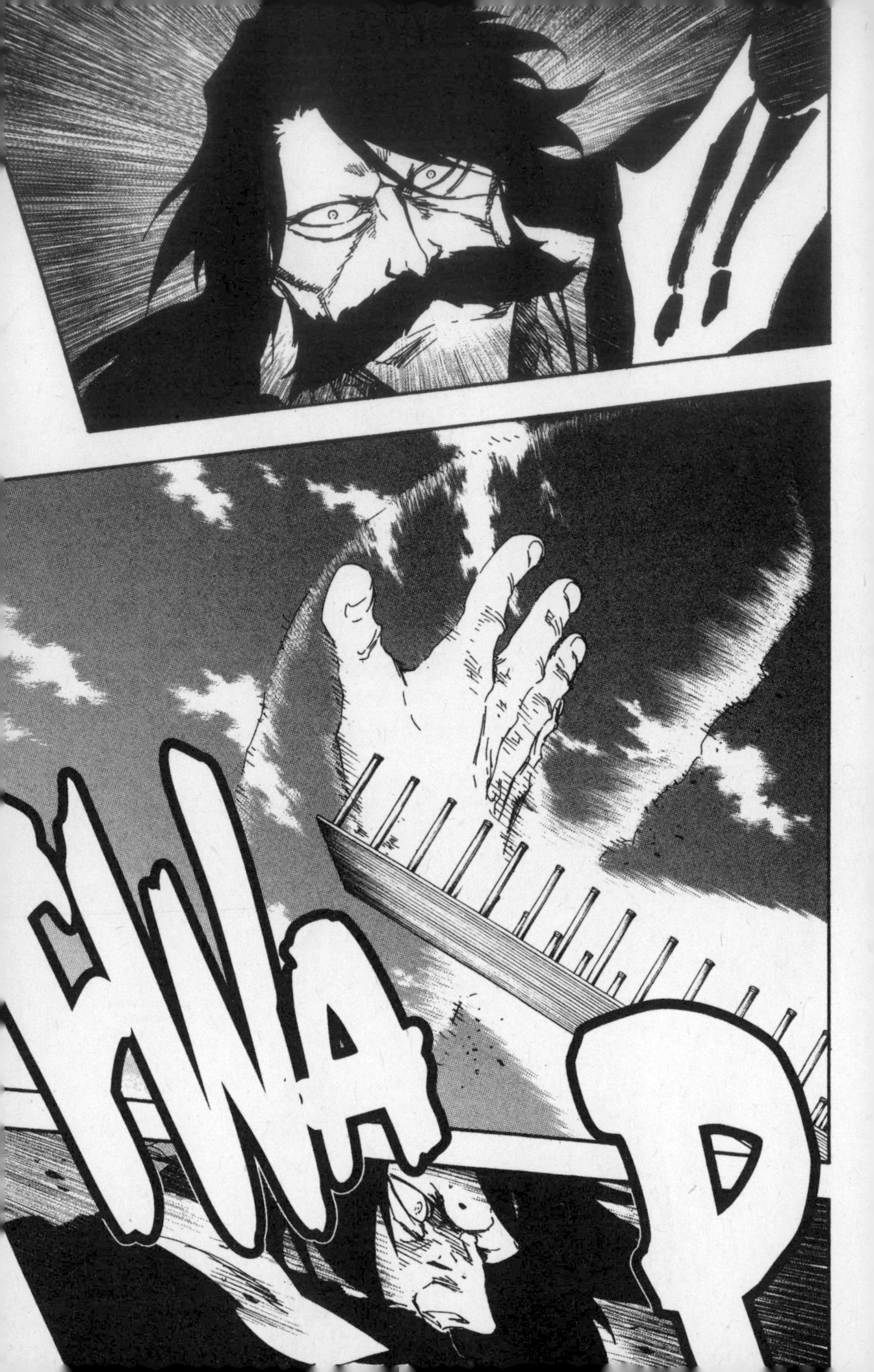
!!
HAP

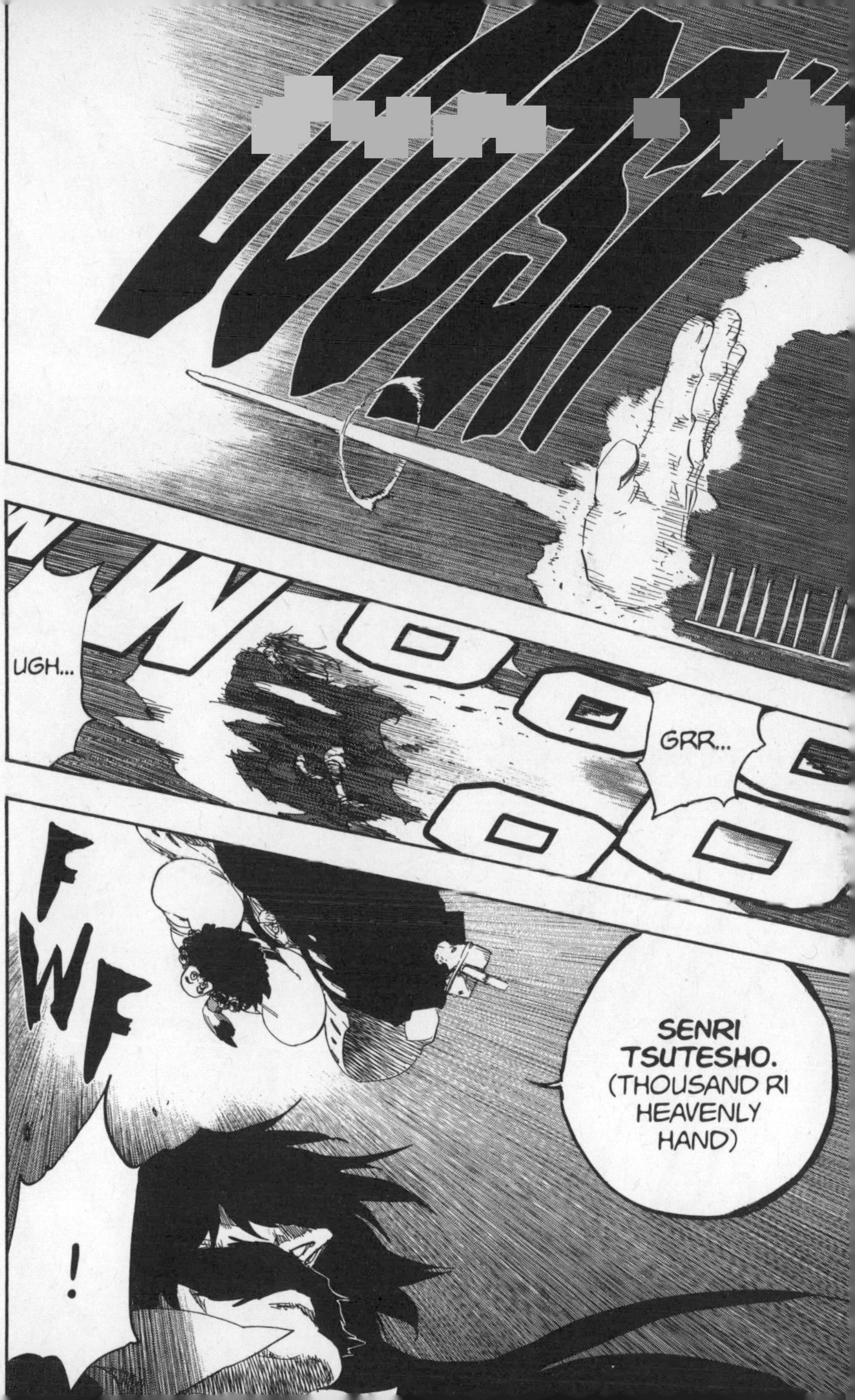
GRR...
UGH...
SENRI TSUTESHO. (THOUSAND RI HEAVENLY HAND)
FWF
!

READ THIS WAY

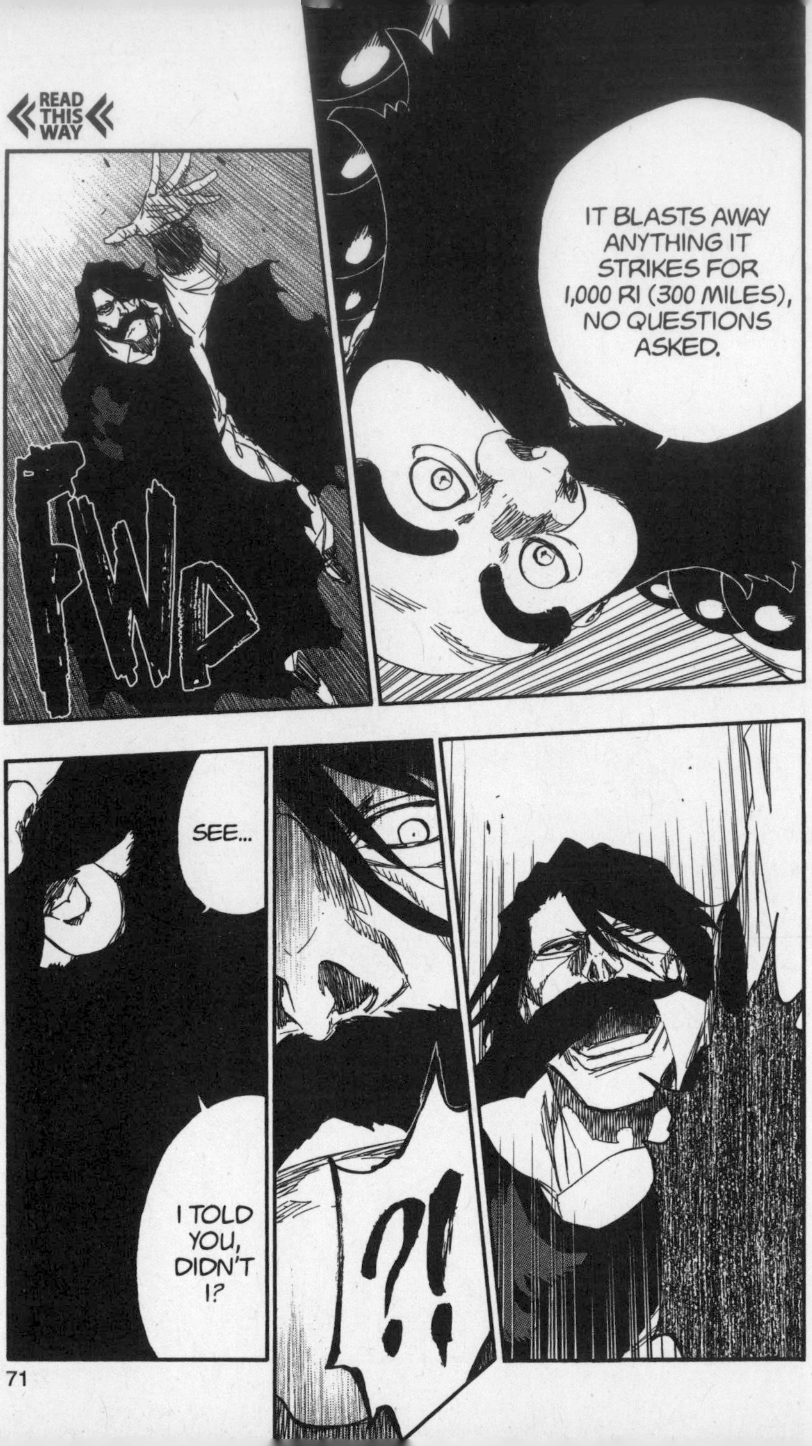

IT BLASTS AWAY ANYTHING IT STRIKES FOR 1,000 RI (300 MILES), NO QUESTIONS ASKED.
FWD
?!
SEE...
I TOLD YOU, DIDN'T I?

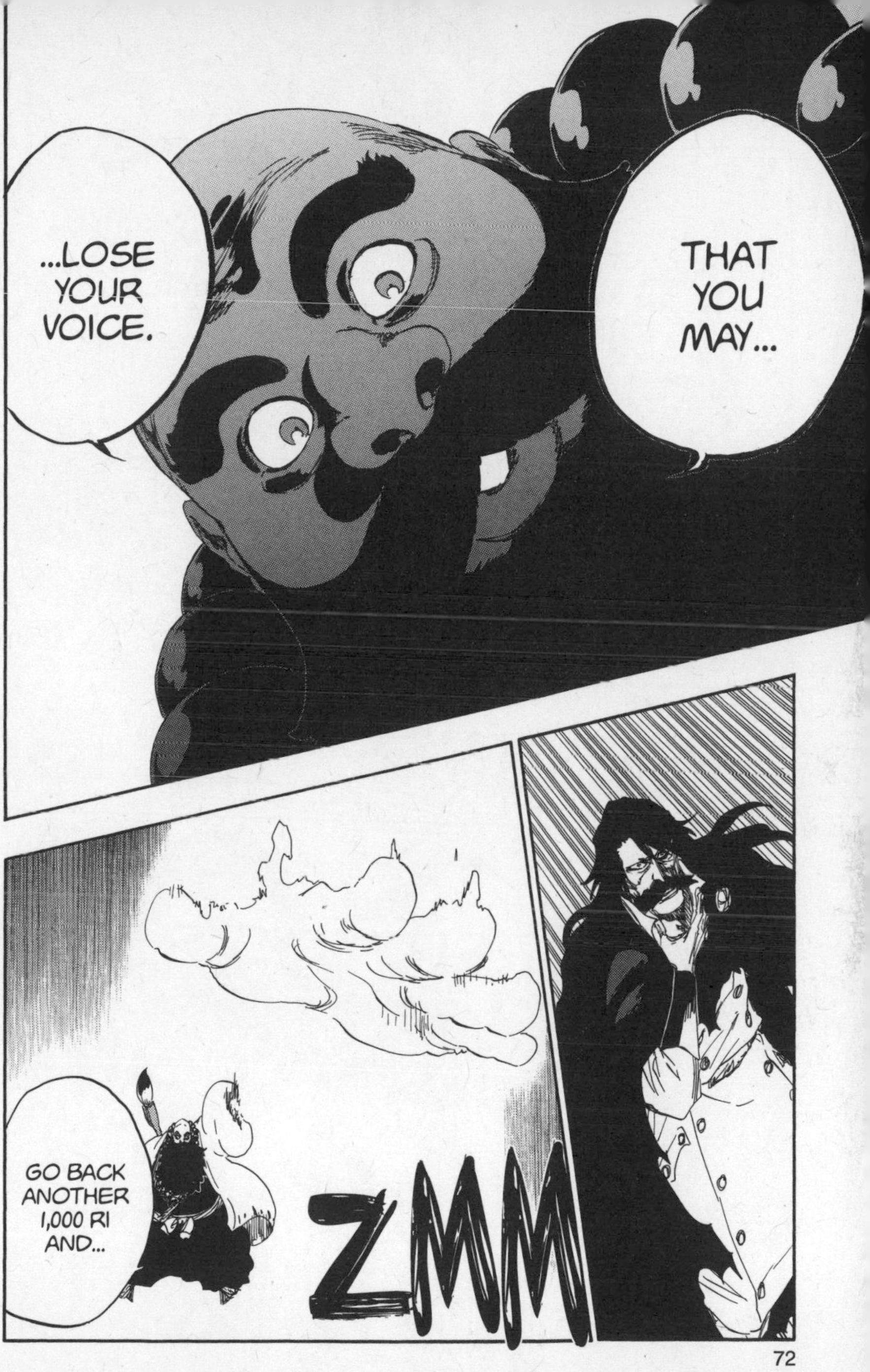
THAT YOU MAY...
...LOSE YOUR VOICE.
GO BACK ANOTHER 1,000 RI AND...
ZMM

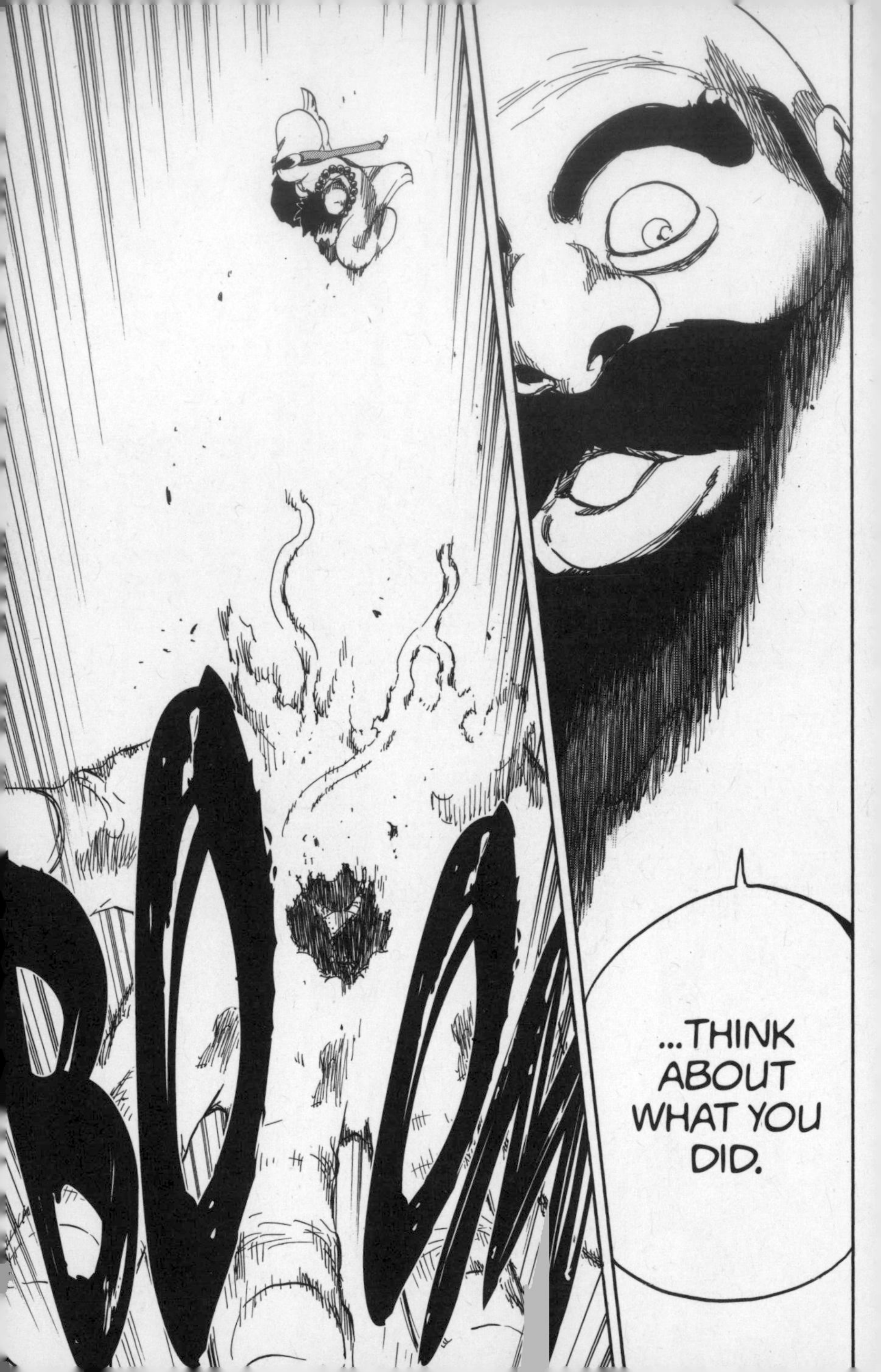
...THINK ABOUT WHAT YOU DID.
BOOM

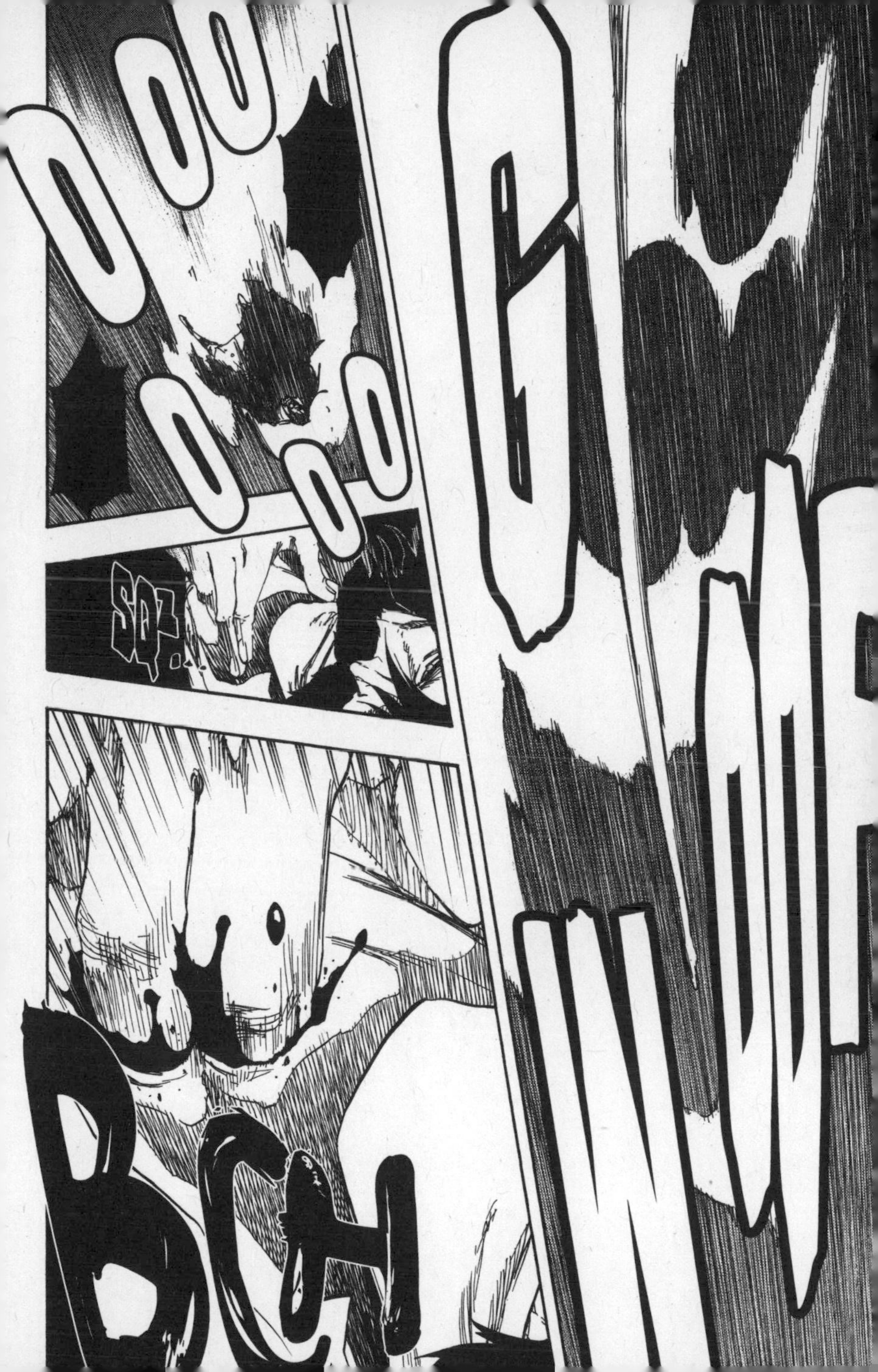
SQZ...

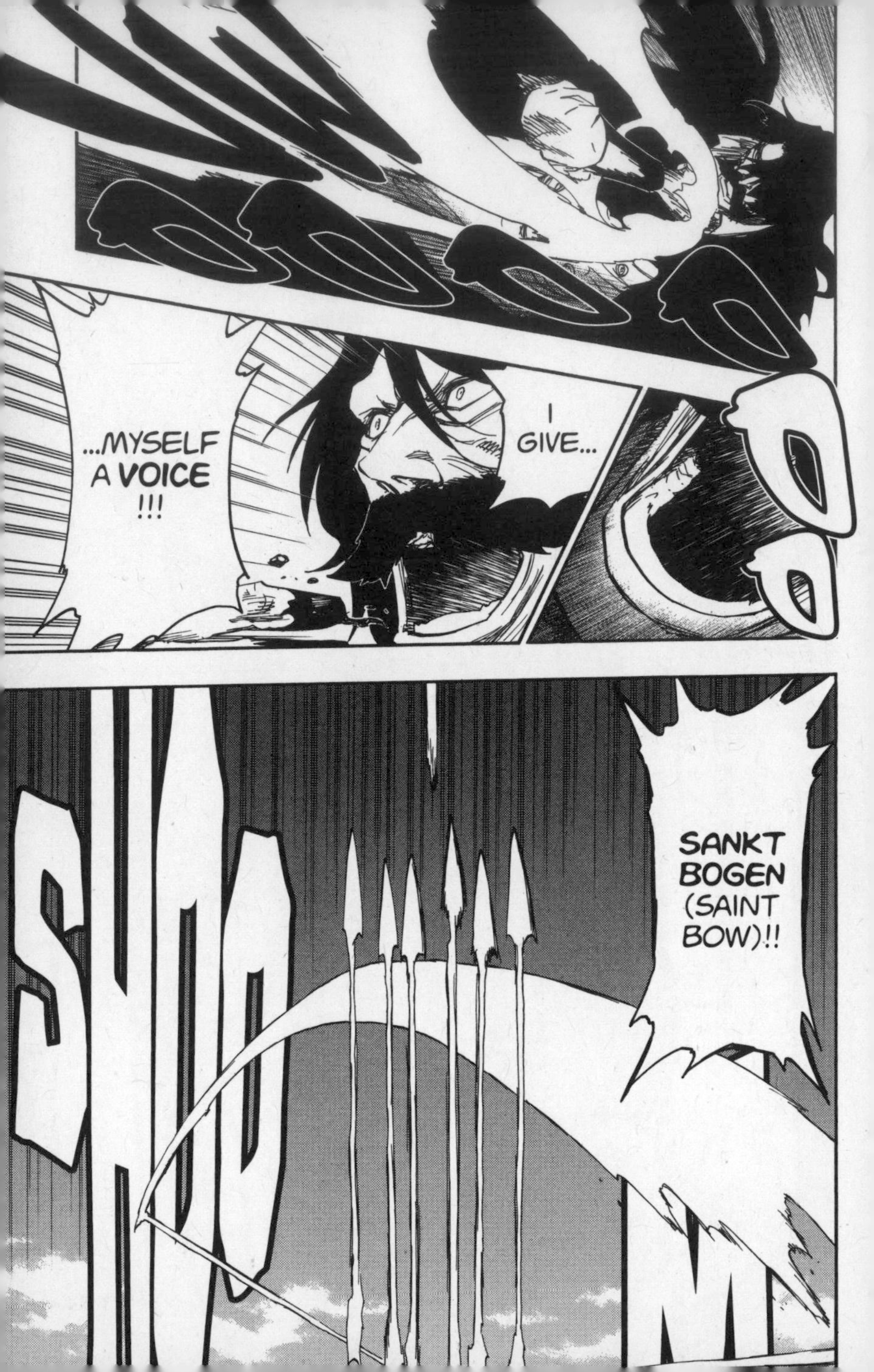
I GIVE...
...MYSELF A VOICE !!!
SANKT BOGEN (SAINT BOW)!!
SHOOM

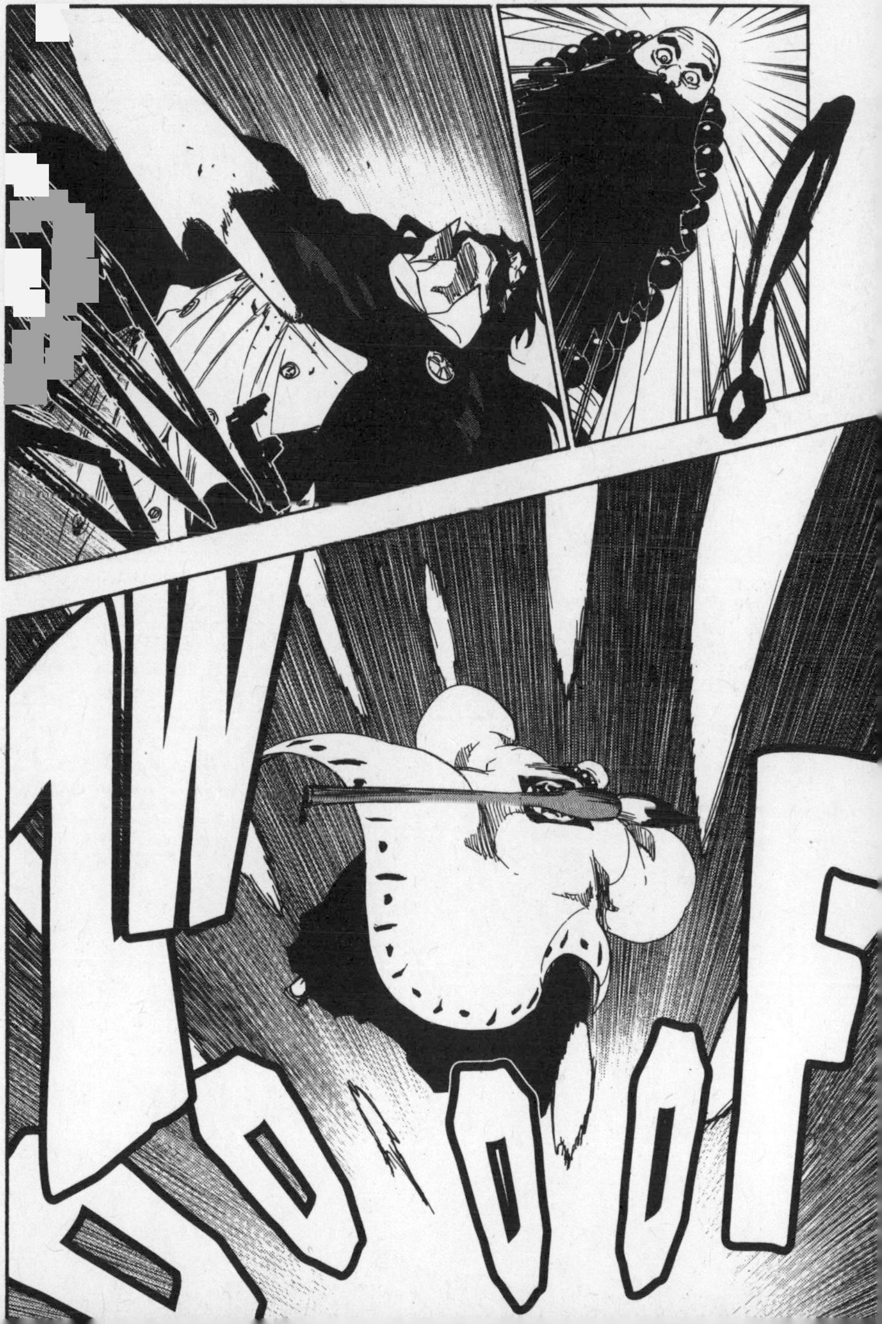

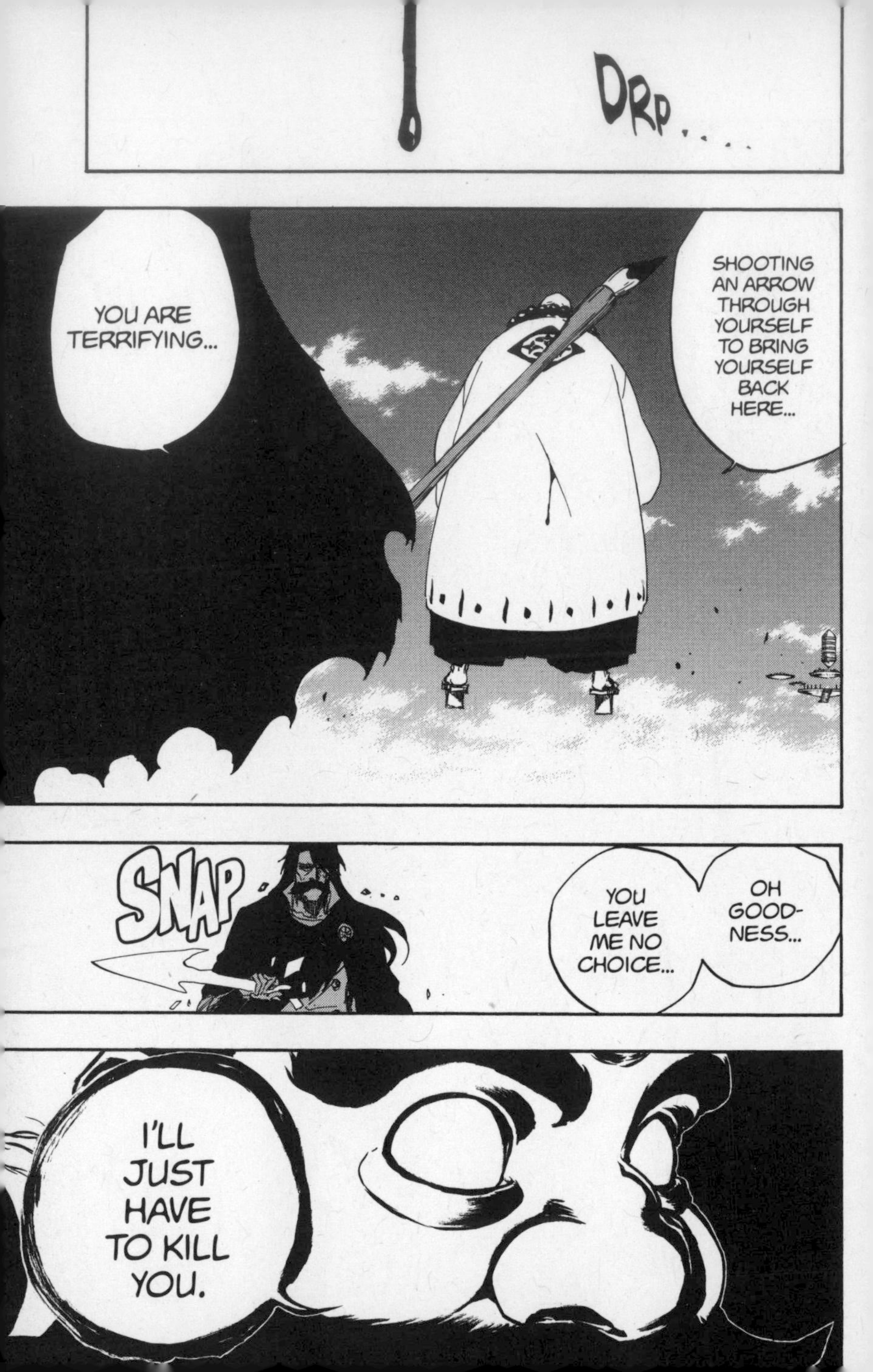
DRP.....
SHOOTING AN ARROW THROUGH YOURSELF TO BRING YOURSELF BACK HERE...
YOU ARE TERRIFYING...
OH GOODNESS...
YOU LEAVE ME NO CHOICE...
SNAP
I'LL JUST HAVE TO KILL YOU.

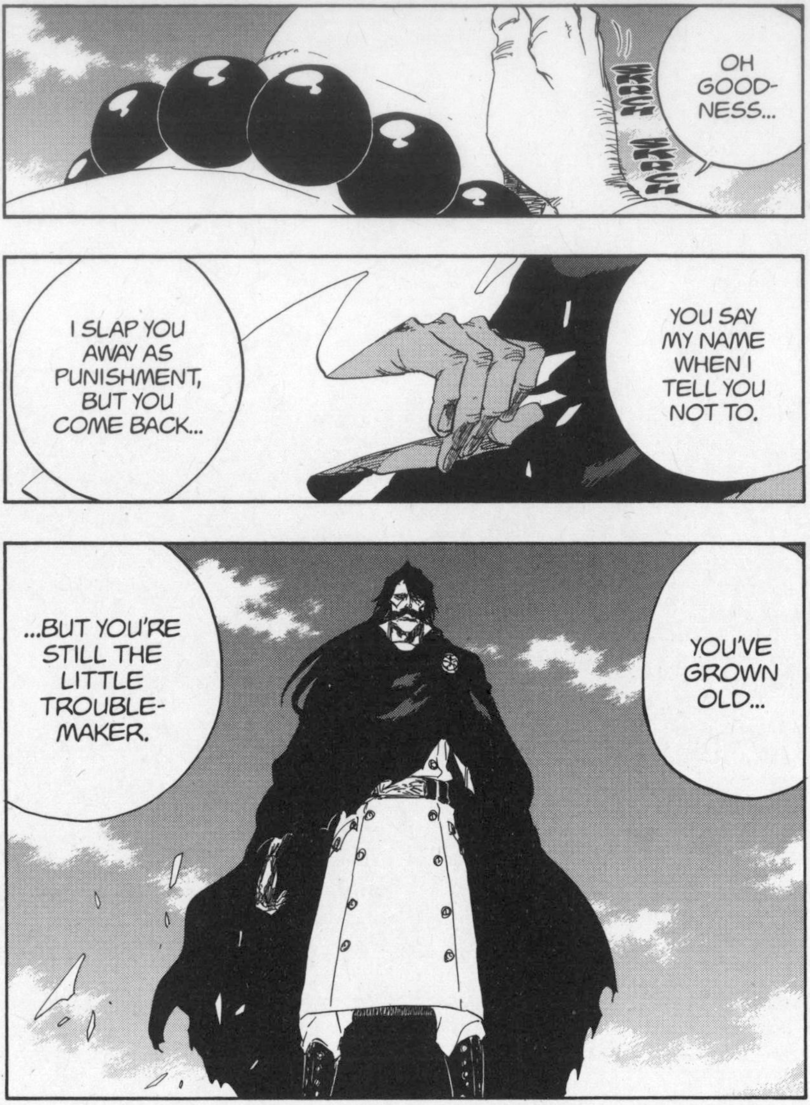
OH GOOD-NESS...
YOU SAY MY NAME WHEN I TELL YOU NOT TO.
I SLAP YOU AWAY AS PUNISHMENT, BUT YOU COME BACK...
YOU'VE GROWN OLD...
...BUT YOU'RE STILL THE LITTLE TROUBLE-MAKER.
IF YOU WON'T LISTEN TO ME...
YOU LEAVE ME NO CHOICE...

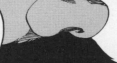

BLEACH 606.

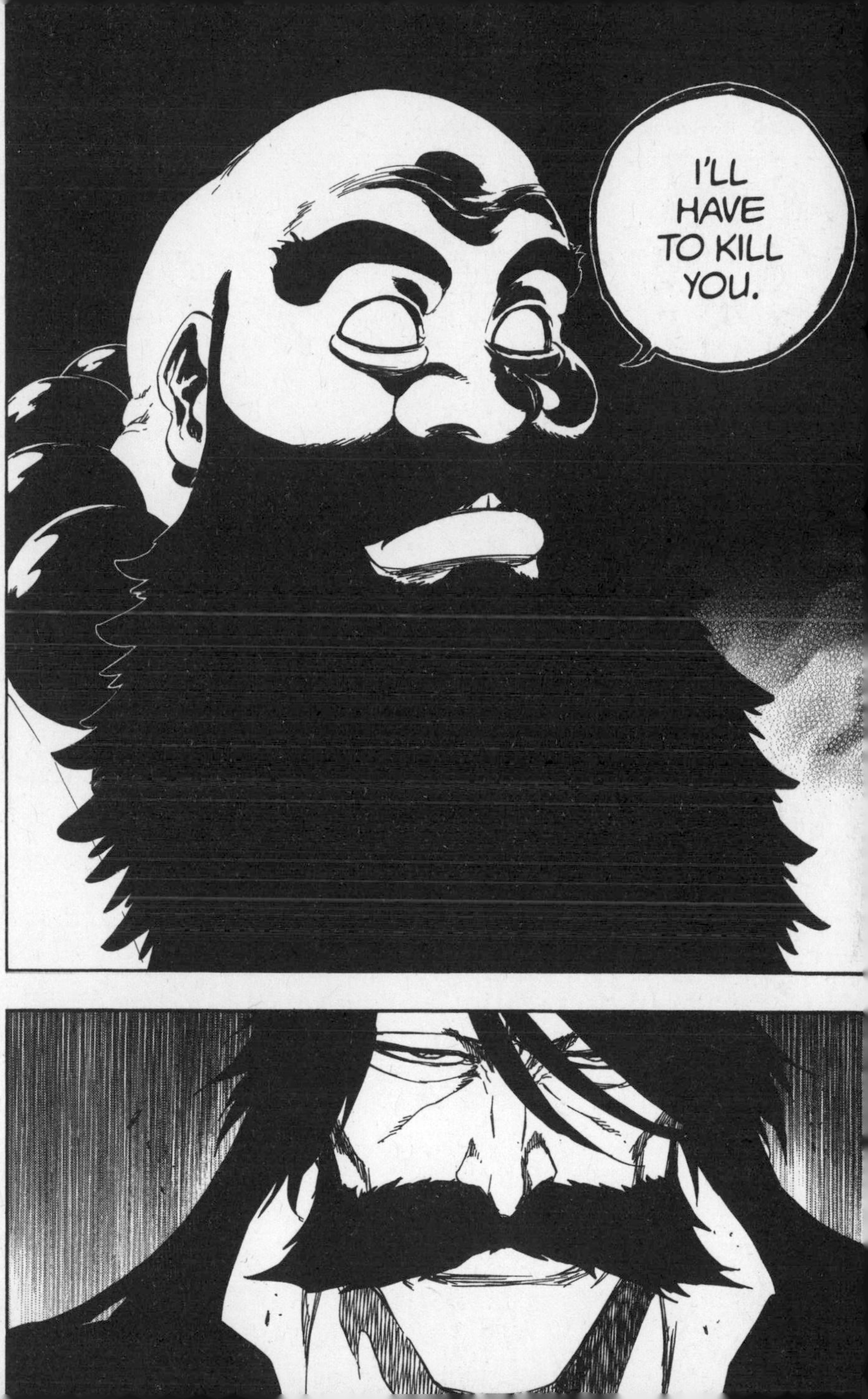
I'LL HAVE TO KILL YOU.

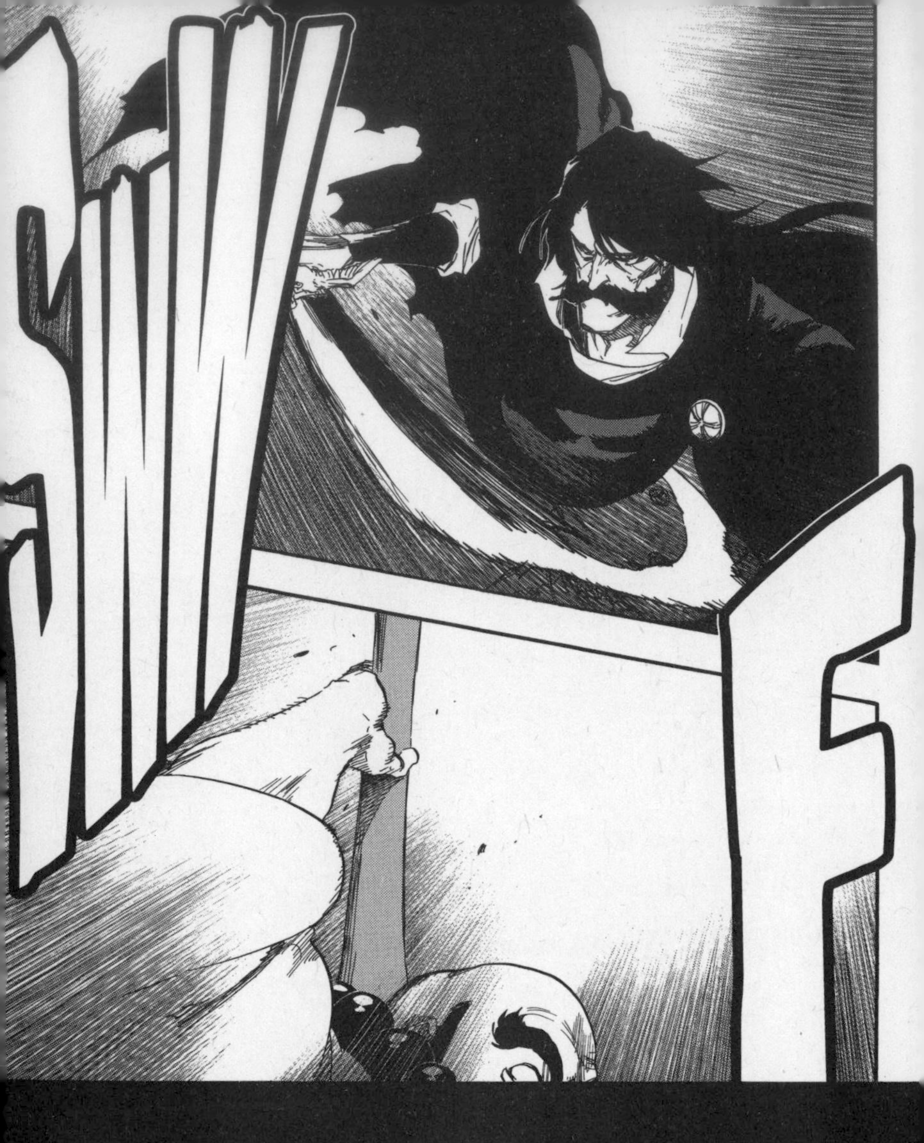

Divine Division

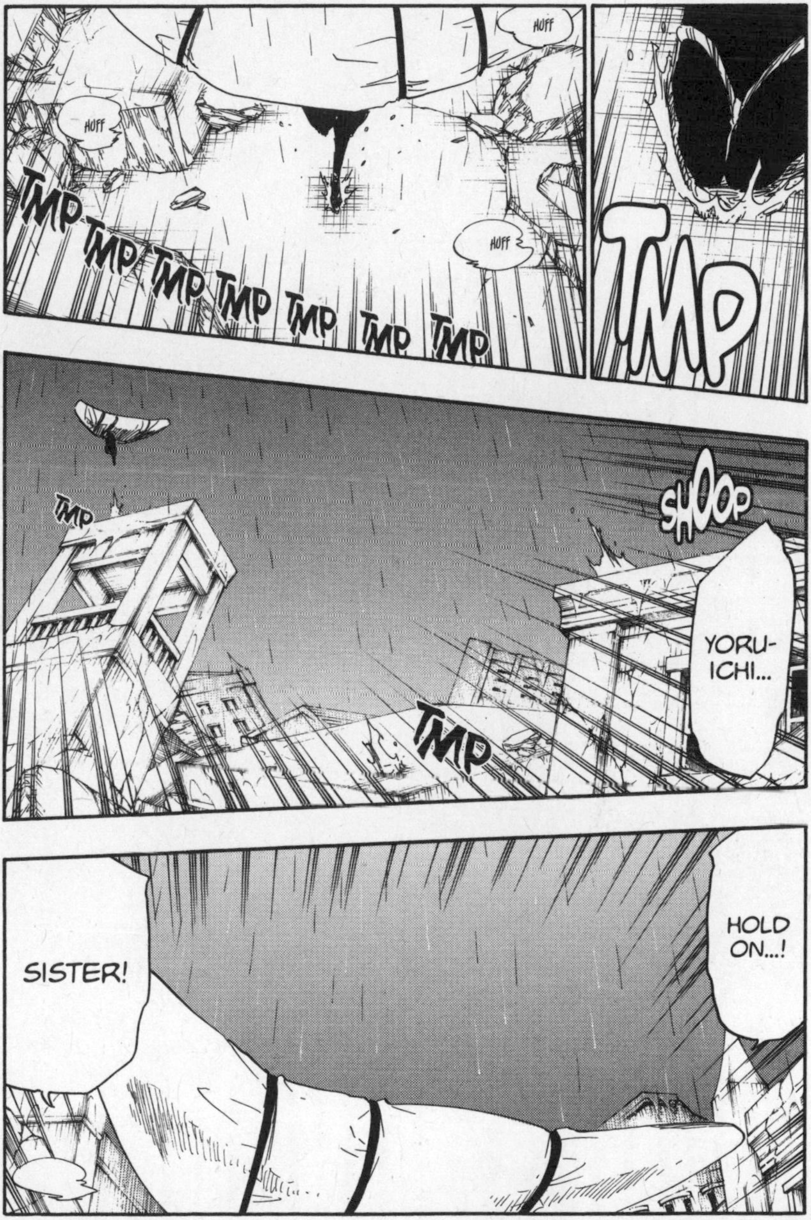
TMP
HUFF
HUFF
HUFF
TMP TMP TMP TMP TMP TMP TMP
SHOOP
YORUICHI...
TMP
TMP
HOLD ON...!
SISTER!

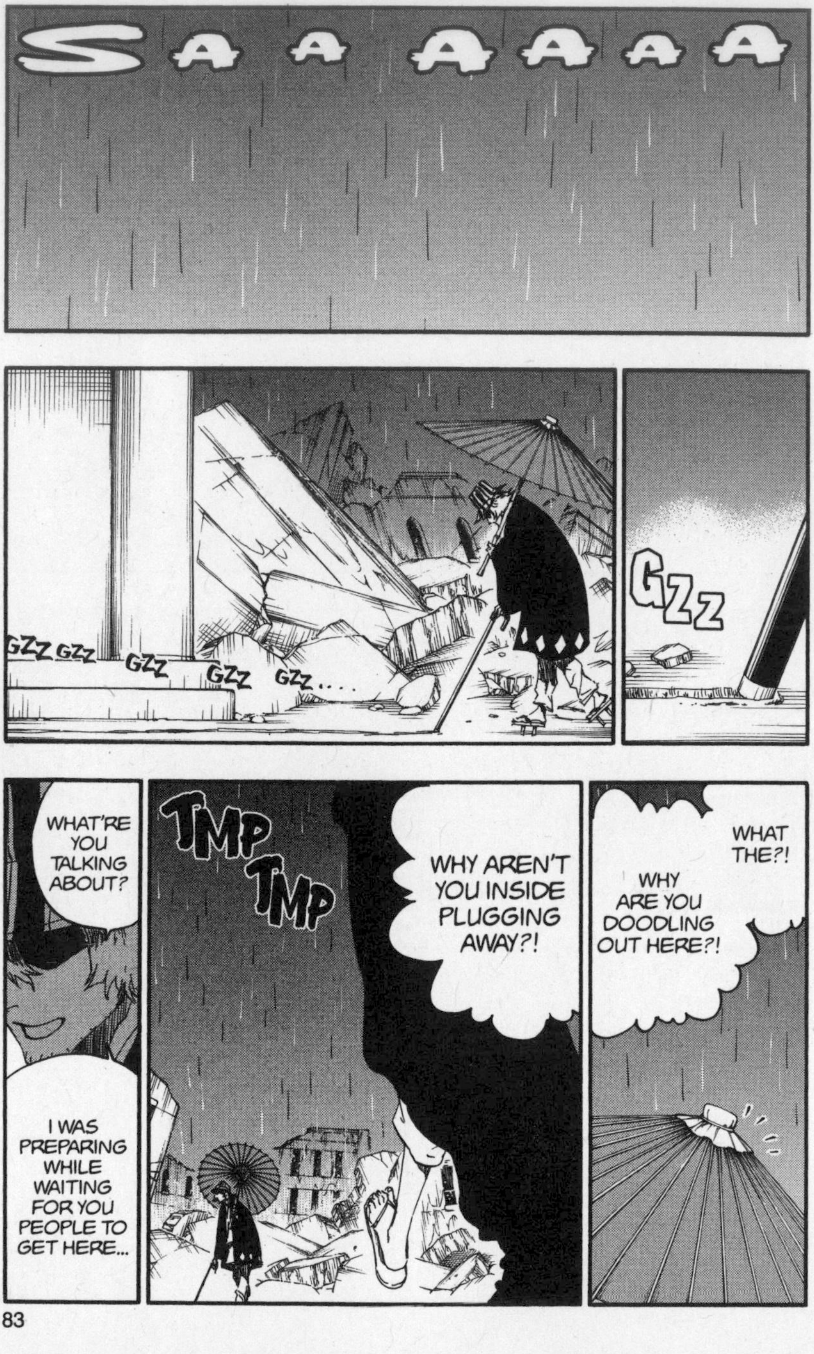
SAAAAAA
GZZ
GZZ GZZ
GZZ
GZZ
GZZ....
WHAT THE?!
WHY ARE YOU DOODLING OUT HERE?!
TMP TMP
WHY AREN'T YOU INSIDE PLUGGING AWAY?!
WHAT'RE YOU TALKING ABOUT?
I WAS PREPARING WHILE WAITING FOR YOU PEOPLE TO GET HERE...

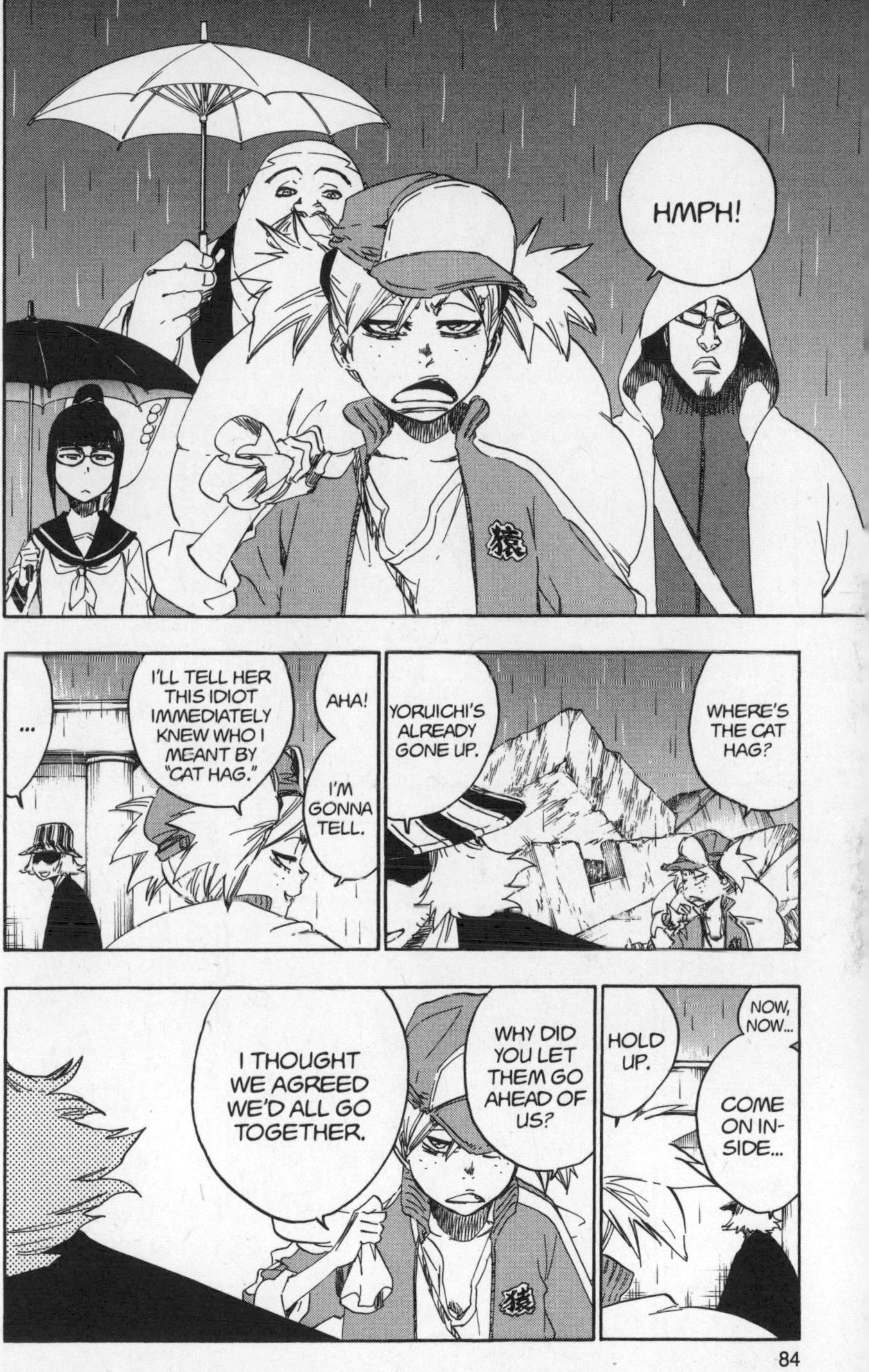
HMPH!
WHERE'S THE CAT HAG?
YORUICHI'S ALREADY GONE UP.
AHA!
I'M GONNA TELL.
I'LL TELL HER THIS IDIOT IMMEDIATELY KNEW WHO I MEANT BY "CAT HAG."
...
NOW, NOW...
HOLD UP.
COME ON IN-SIDE...
WHY DID YOU LET THEM GO AHEAD OF US?
I THOUGHT WE AGREED WE'D ALL GO TOGETHER.

READ THIS WAY

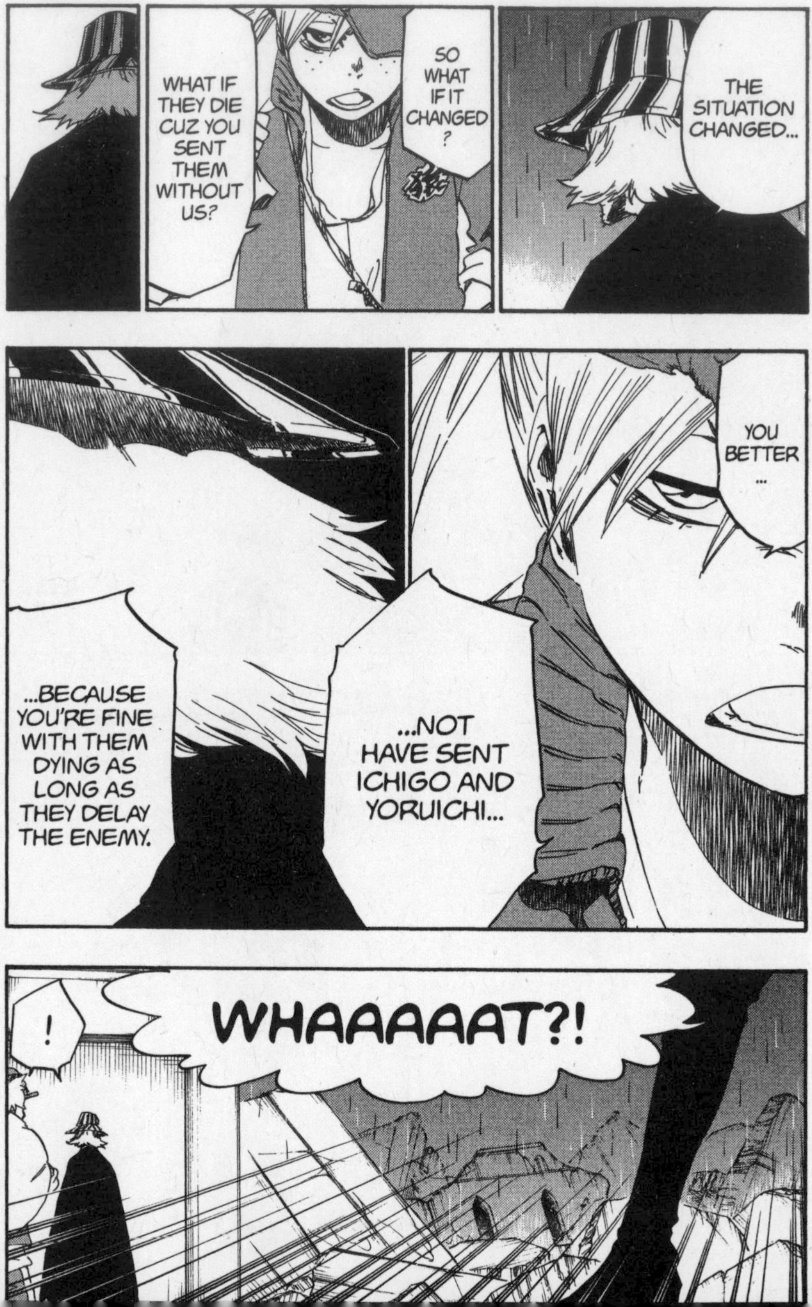
THE SITUATION CHANGED...
SO WHAT IF IT CHANGED?
WHAT IF THEY DIE CUZ YOU SENT THEM WITHOUT US?
YOU BETTER ...
...NOT HAVE SENT ICHIGO AND YORUICHI...
...BECAUSE YOU'RE FINE WITH THEM DYING AS LONG AS THEY DELAY THE ENEMY.
WHAAAAAT?!
!

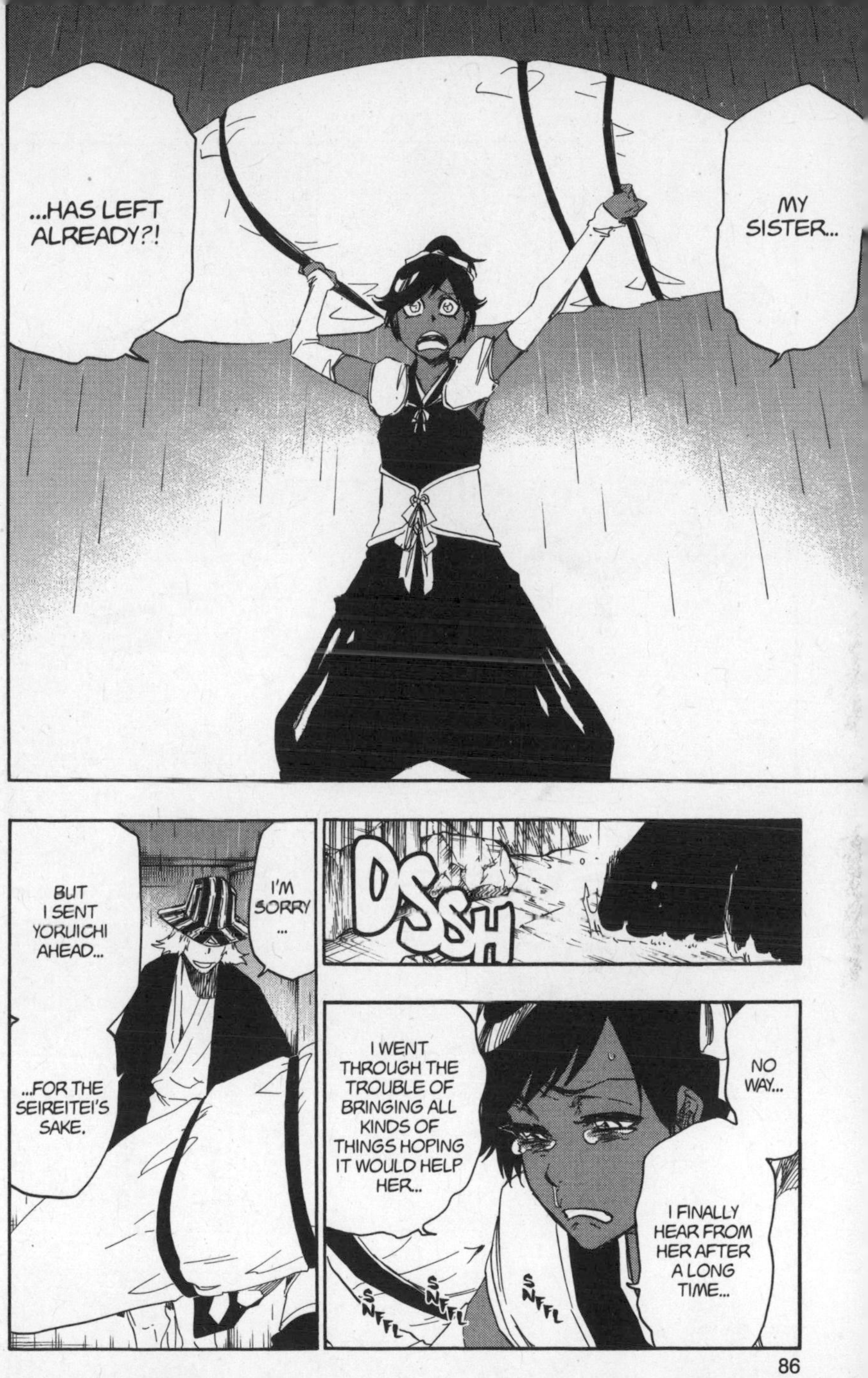
MY SISTER...
...HAS LEFT ALREADY?!
DSSH
NO WAY...
I FINALLY HEAR FROM HER AFTER A LONG TIME...
I WENT THROUGH THE TROUBLE OF BRINGING ALL KINDS OF THINGS HOPING IT WOULD HELP HER...
SNFFL
SNFFL
SNFFL
I'M SORRY ...
BUT I SENT YORUICHI AHEAD...
...FOR THE SEIREITEI'S SAKE.

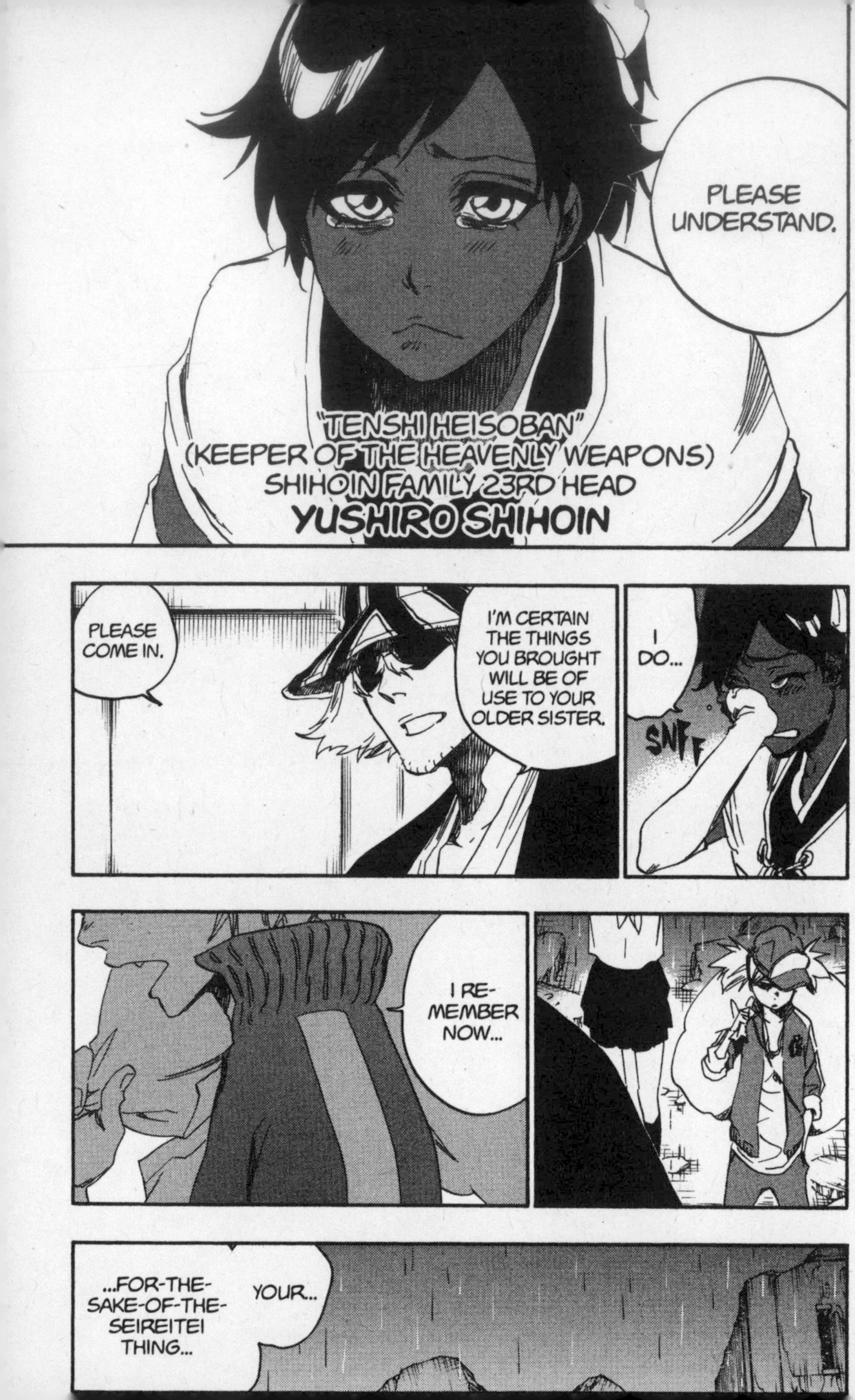
PLEASE UNDERSTAND.
"TENSHI HEISOBAN"
(KEEPER OF THE HEAVENLY WEAPONS)
SHIHOIN FAMILY 23RD HEAD
YUSHIRO SHIHOIN
I DO...
SNFF
I'M CERTAIN THE THINGS YOU BROUGHT WILL BE OF USE TO YOUR OLDER SISTER.
PLEASE COME IN.
I RE-MEMBER NOW...
YOUR...
...FOR-THE-SAKE-OF-THE-SEIREITEI THING...

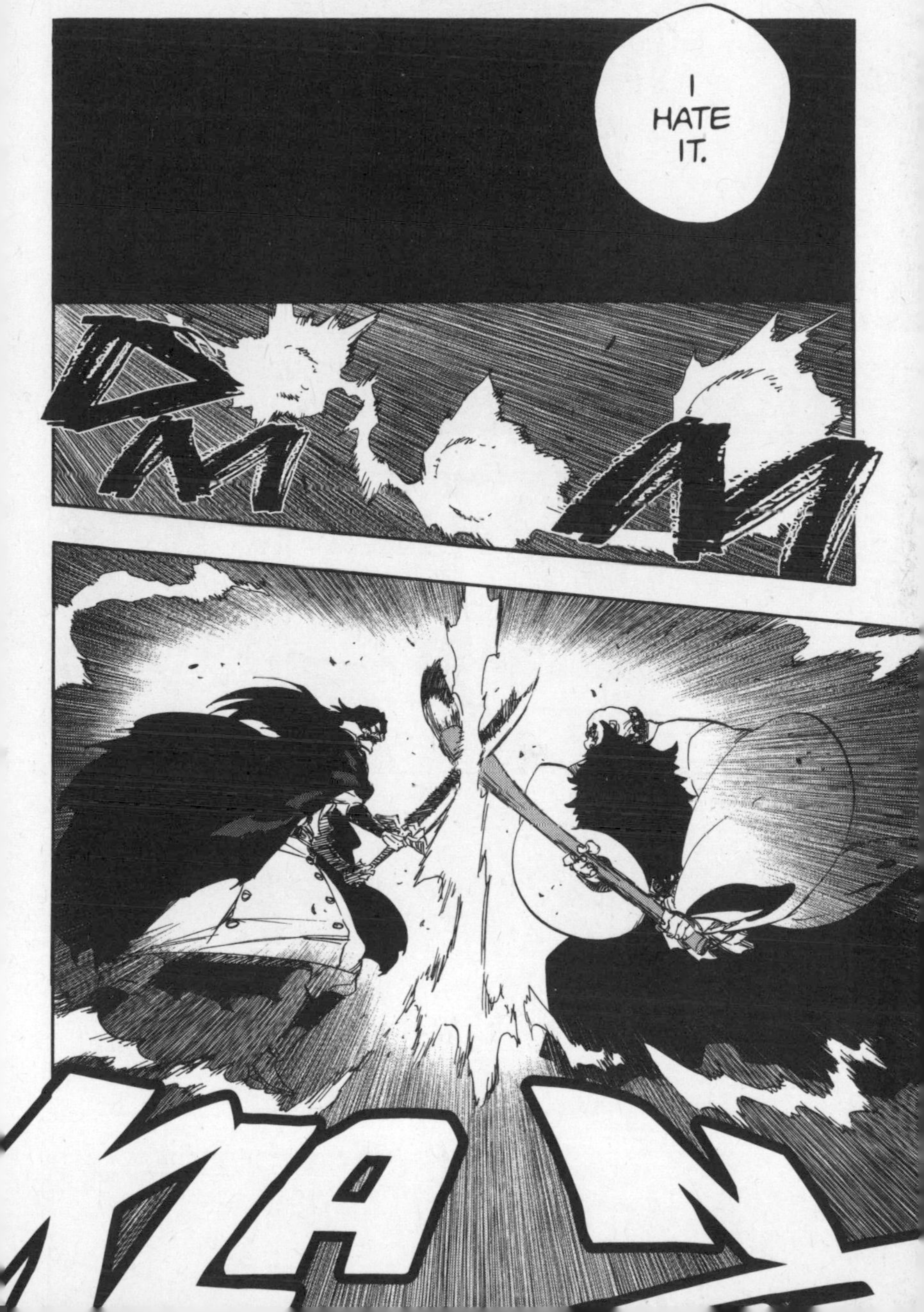
I HATE IT.
DMM
KLAN

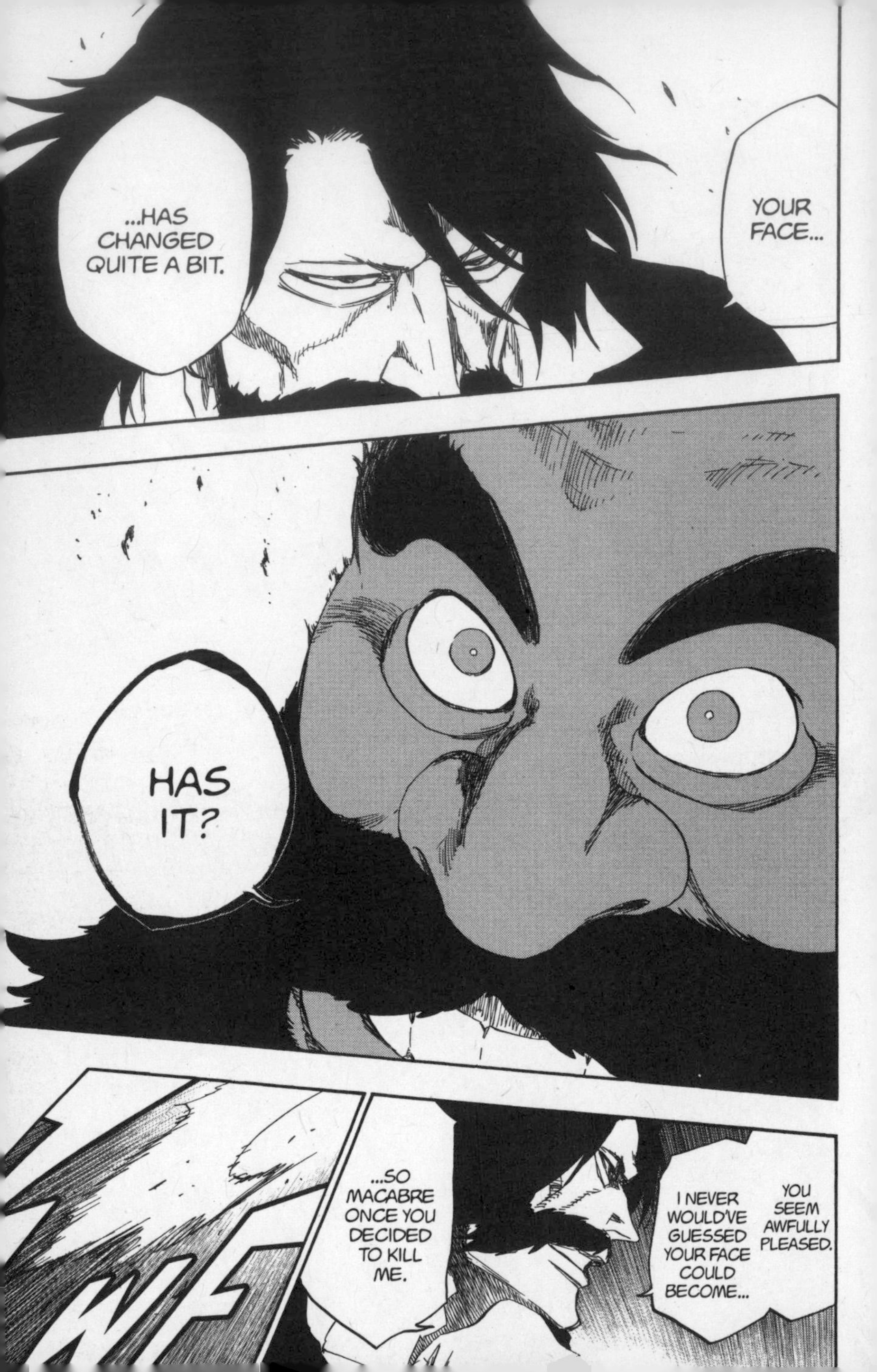
YOUR FACE...
...HAS CHANGED QUITE A BIT.
HAS IT?
YOU SEEM AWFULLY PLEASED.
I NEVER WOULD'VE GUESSED YOUR FACE COULD BECOME...
...SO MACABRE ONCE YOU DECIDED TO KILL ME.

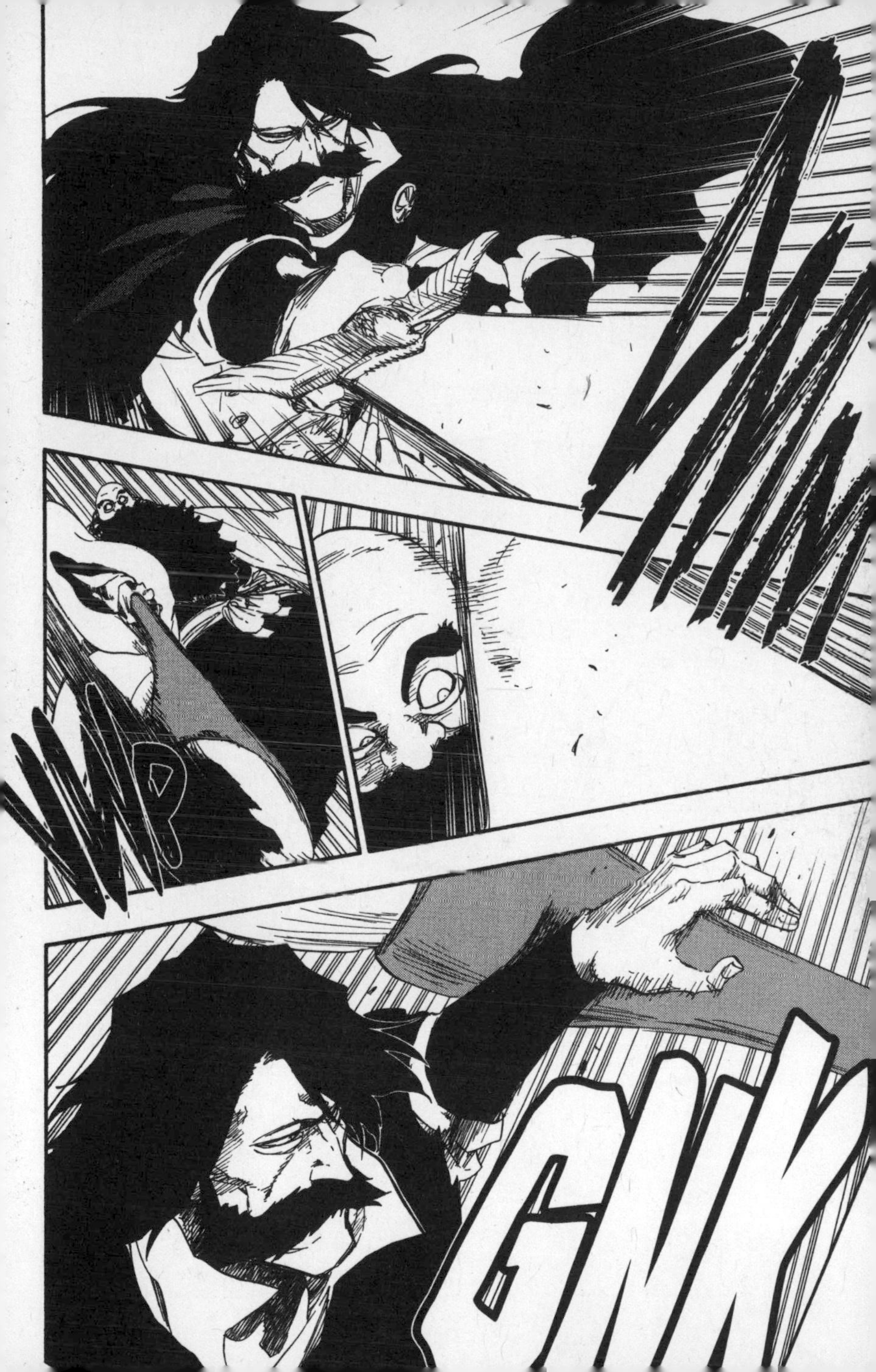
GNK

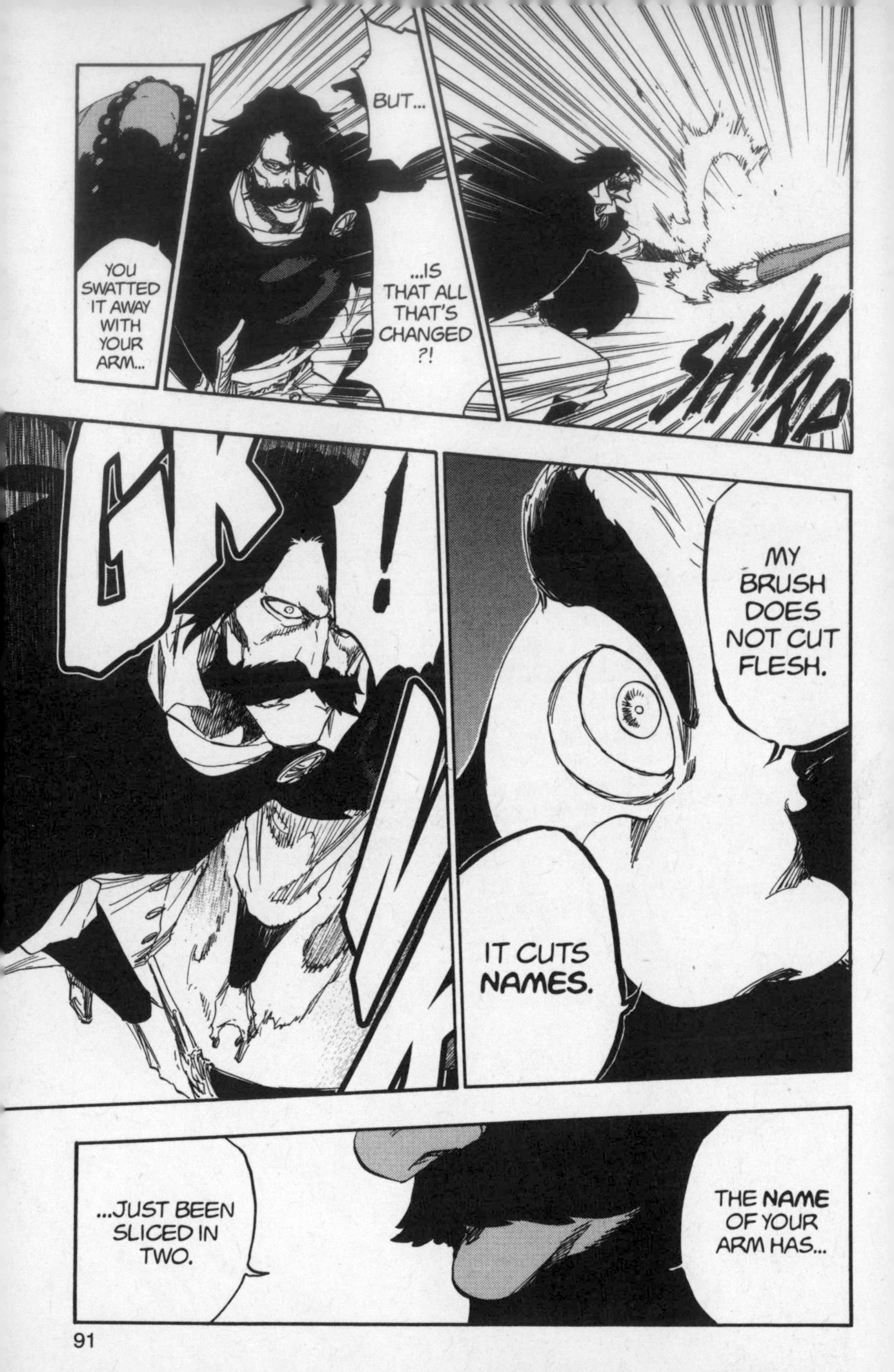
SHWAP
BUT...
...IS THAT ALL THAT'S CHANGED ?!
YOU SWATTED IT AWAY WITH YOUR ARM...
MY BRUSH DOES NOT CUT FLESH.
IT CUTS NAMES.
CK!
THE NAME OF YOUR ARM HAS...
...JUST BEEN SLICED IN TWO.

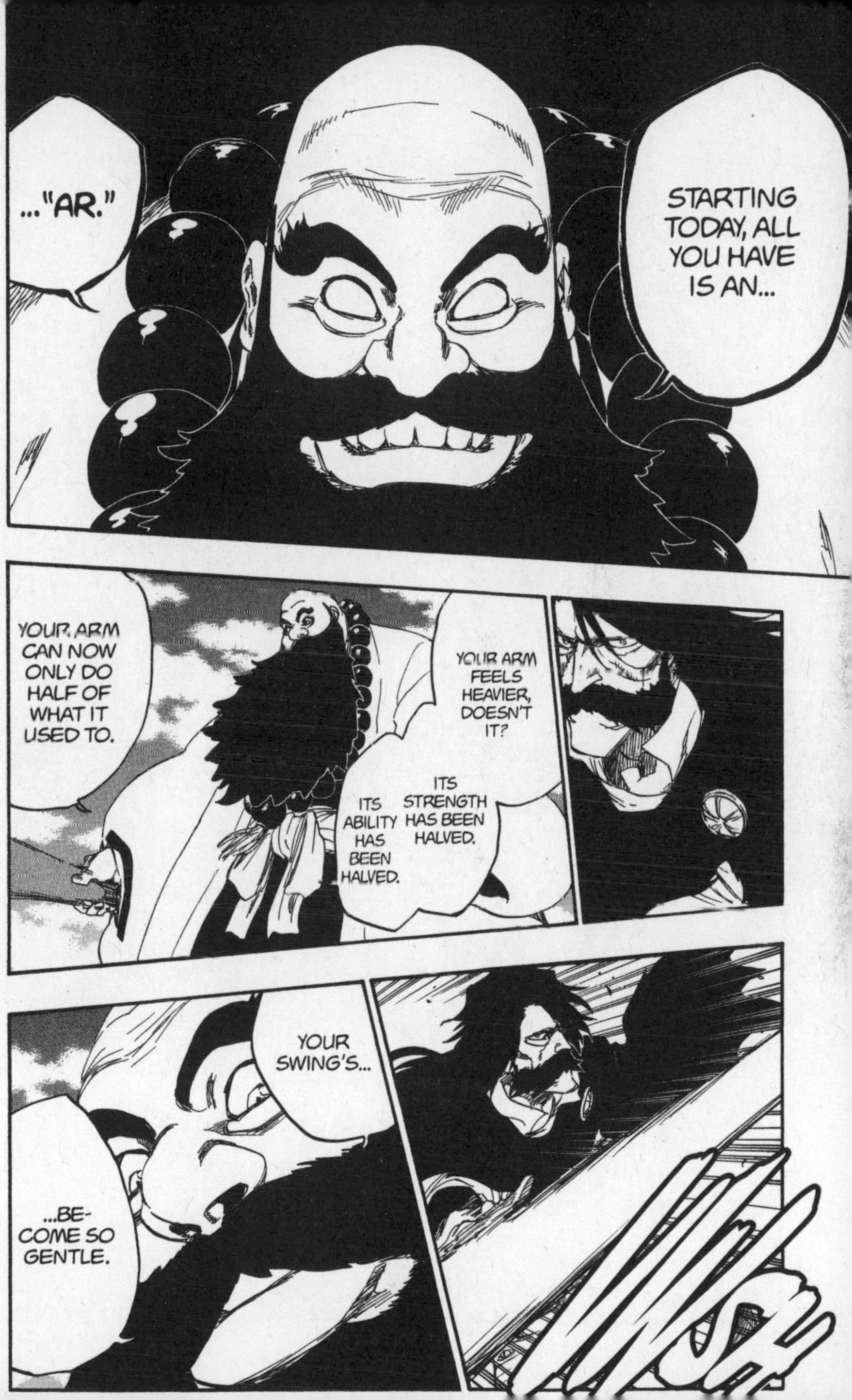
STARTING TODAY, ALL YOU HAVE IS AN...
..."AR."
YOUR ARM FEELS HEAVIER, DOESN'T IT?
ITS STRENGTH HAS BEEN HALVED.
ITS ABILITY HAS BEEN HALVED.
YOUR ARM CAN NOW ONLY DO HALF OF WHAT IT USED TO.
YOUR SWING'S...
...BE-COME SO GENTLE.

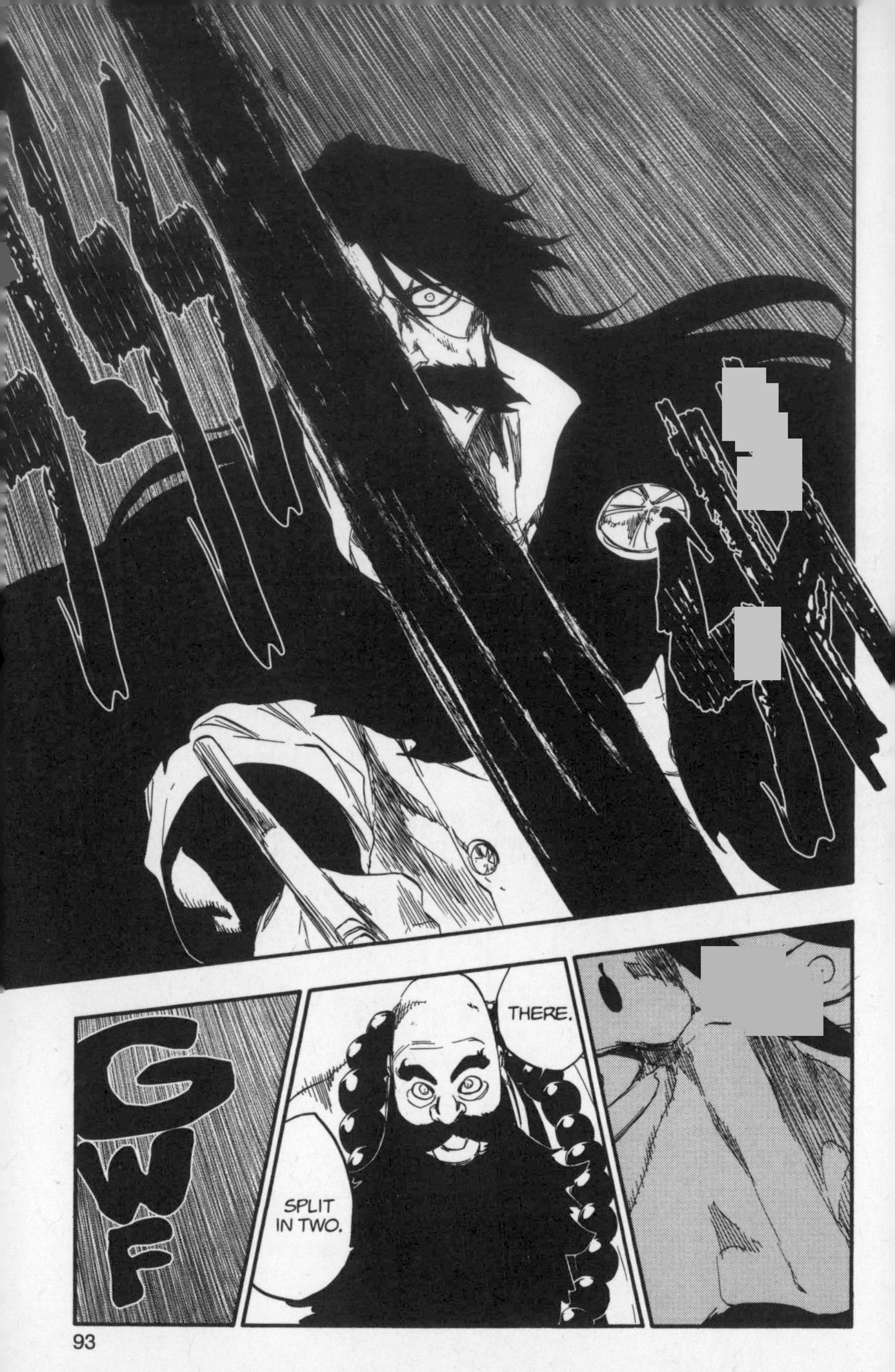
THERE.
SPLIT IN TWO.
GWF

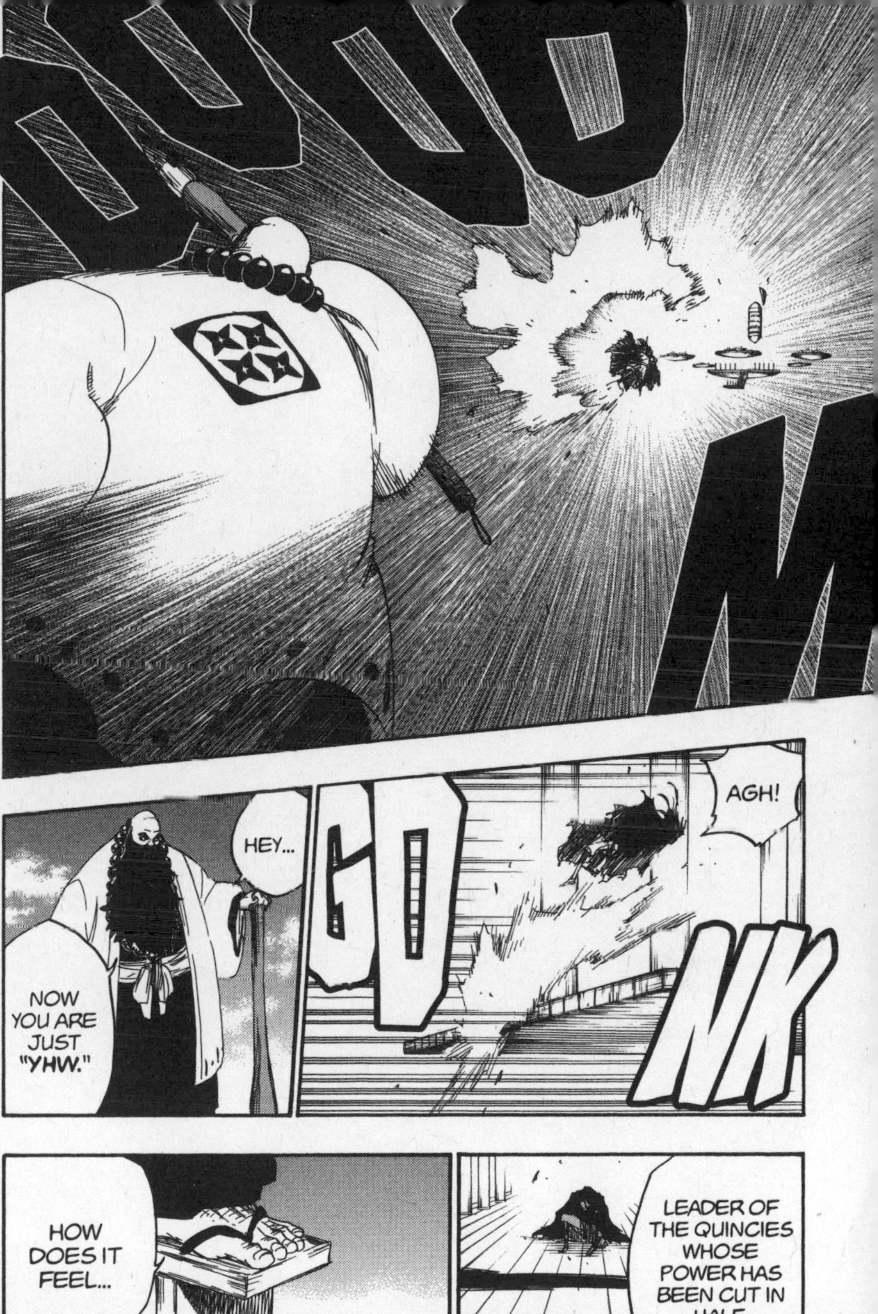
AGH!
GONK
HEY...
NOW YOU ARE JUST "YHW."
LEADER OF THE QUINCIES WHOSE POWER HAS BEEN CUT IN HALF.
HOW DOES IT FEEL...

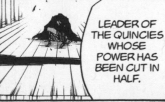

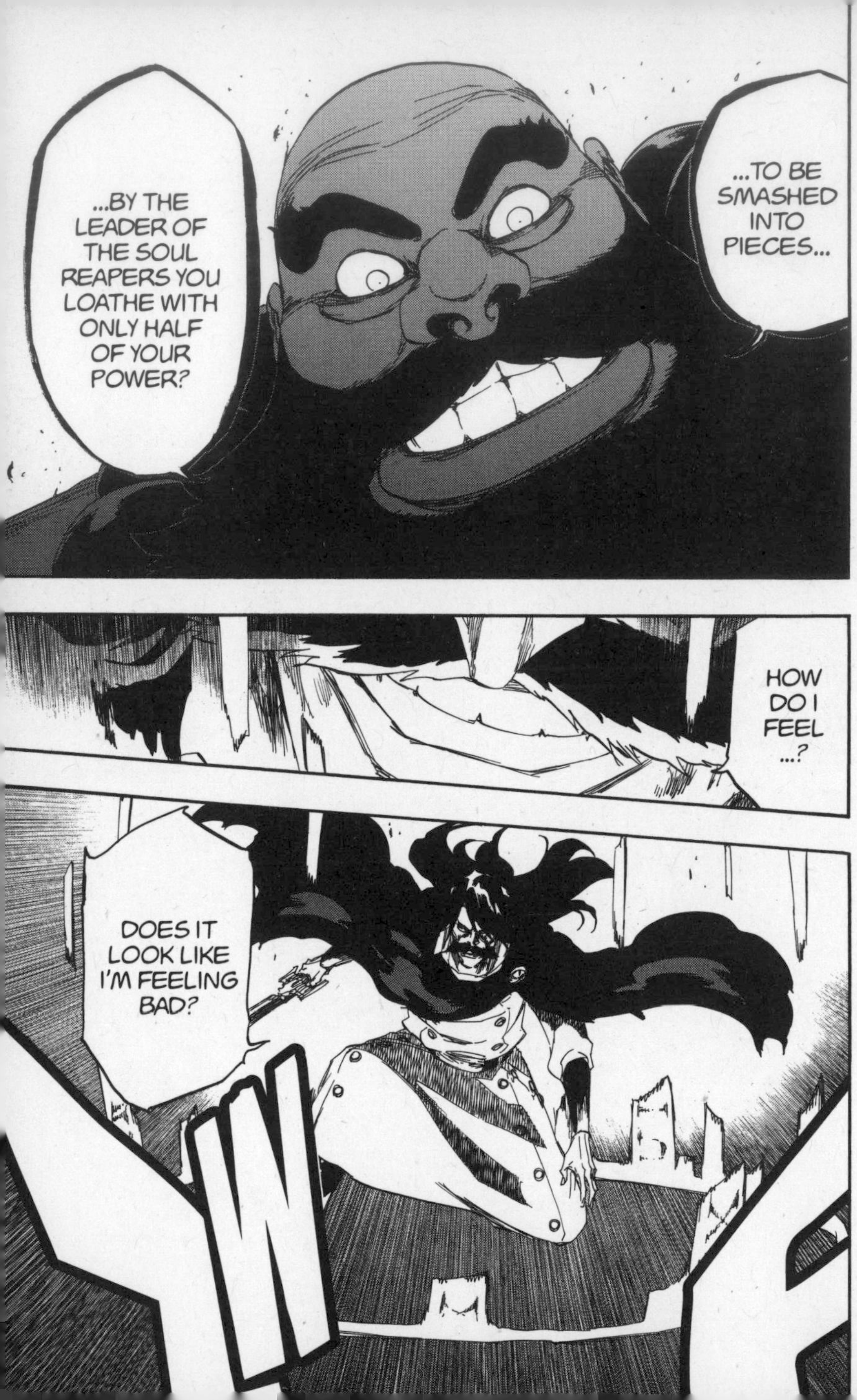
...TO BE SMASHED INTO PIECES...
...BY THE LEADER OF THE SOUL REAPERS YOU LOATHE WITH ONLY HALF OF YOUR POWER?
HOW DO I FEEL ...?
DOES IT LOOK LIKE I'M FEELING BAD?

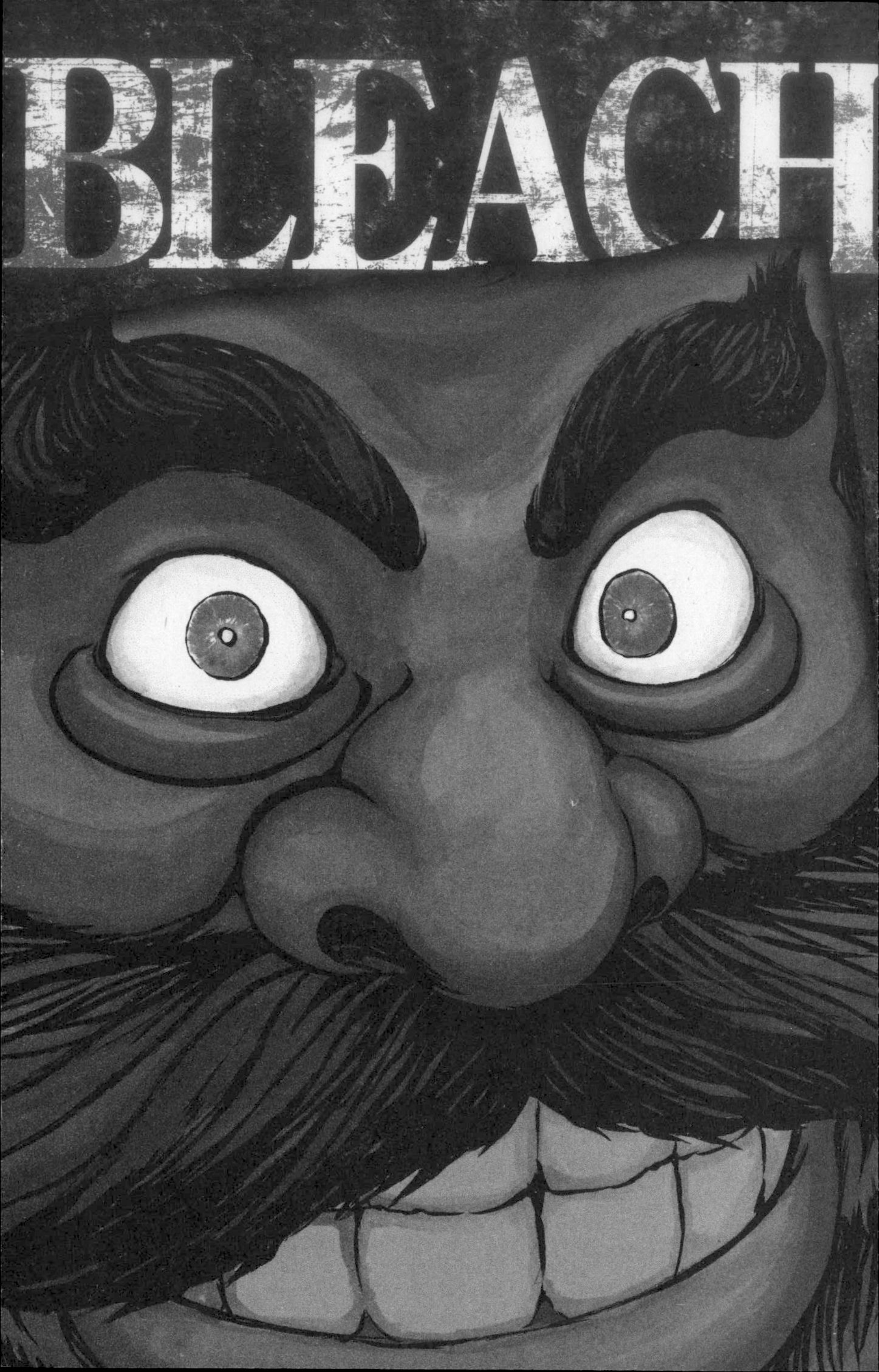
BLEACH

BLEACH ブリーチ

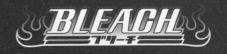

READ THIS WAY

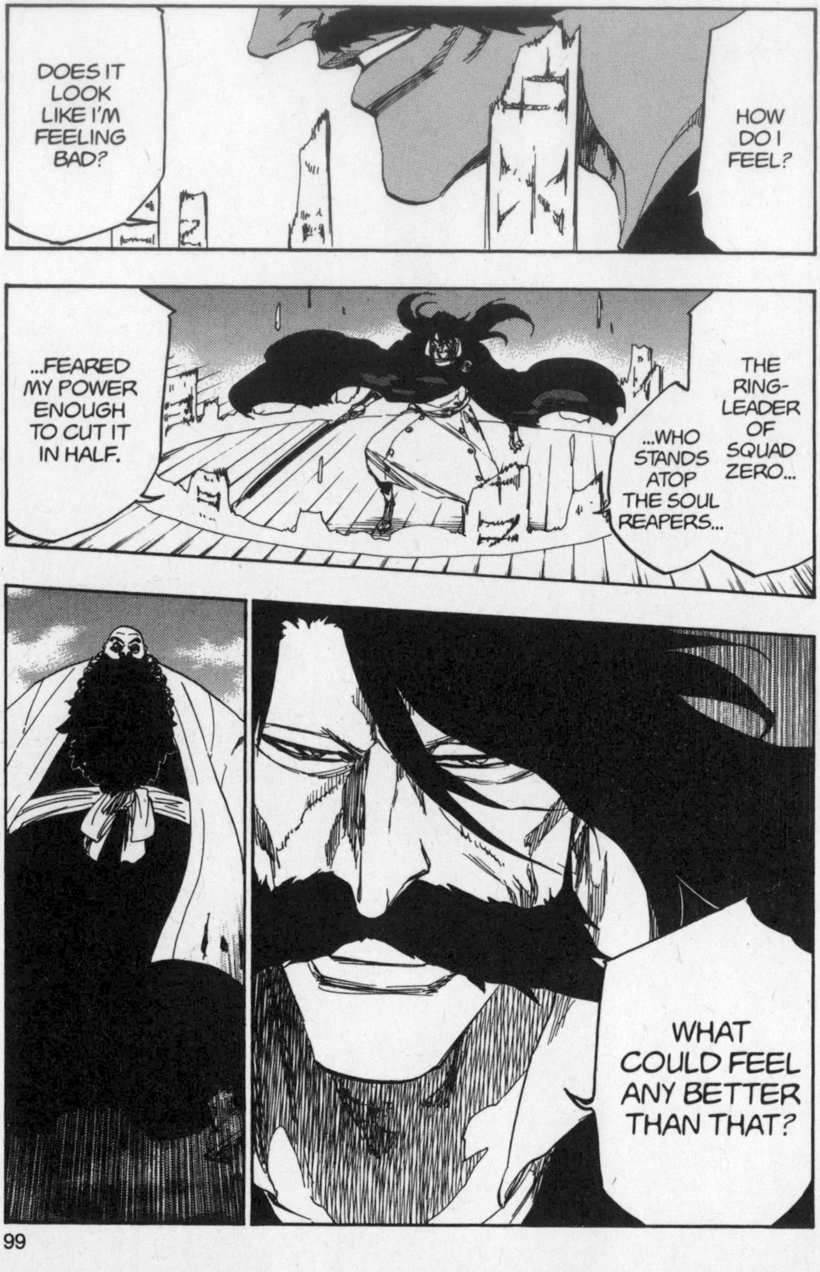
HOW DO I FEEL?
DOES IT LOOK LIKE I'M FEELING BAD?
THE RING-LEADER OF SQUAD ZERO...
...WHO STANDS ATOP THE SOUL REAPERS...
...FEARED MY POWER ENOUGH TO CUT IT IN HALF.
WHAT COULD FEEL ANY BETTER THAN THAT?

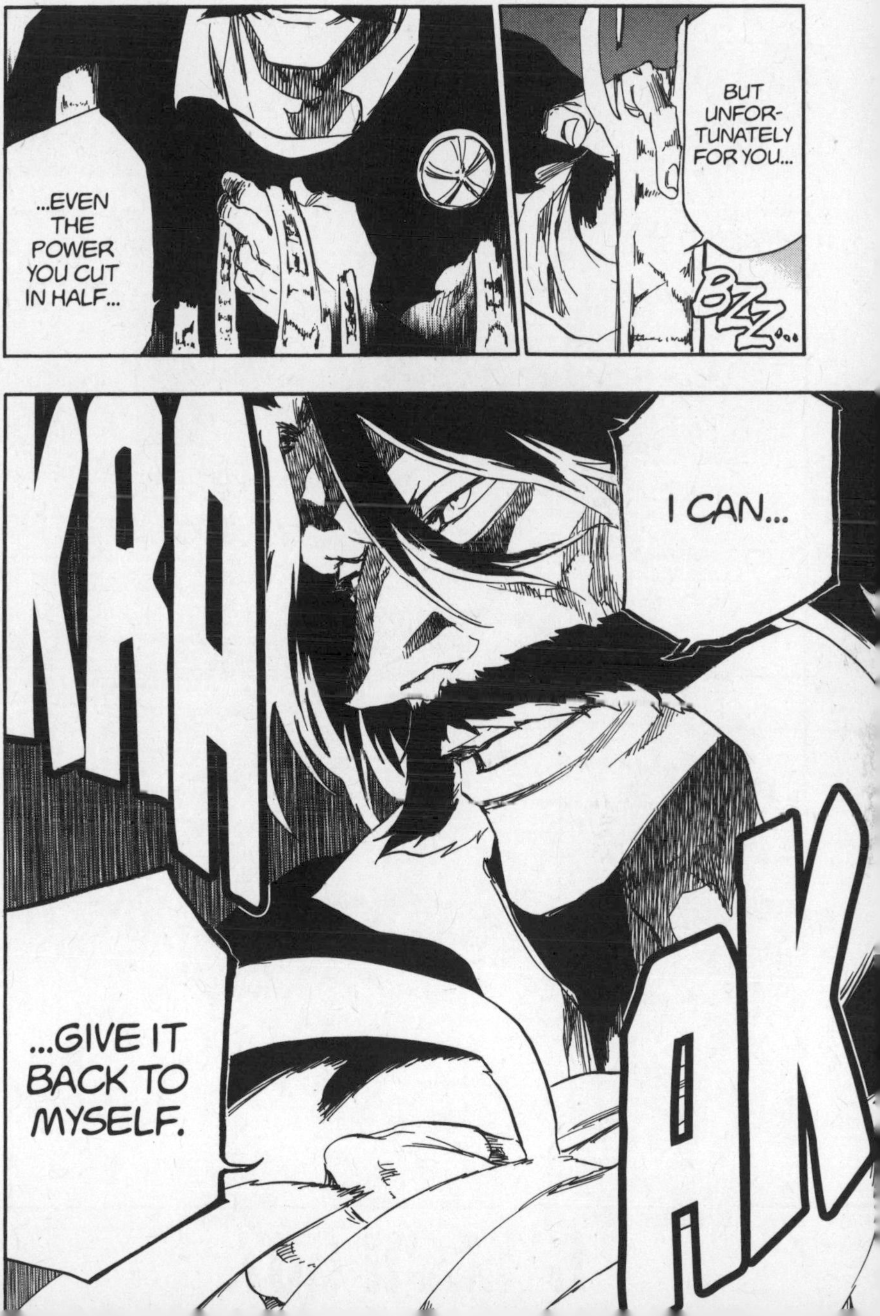
BUT UNFORTUNATELY FOR YOU...
BZZ...
...EVEN THE POWER YOU CUT IN HALF...
I CAN...
...GIVE IT BACK TO MYSELF.
KRAK

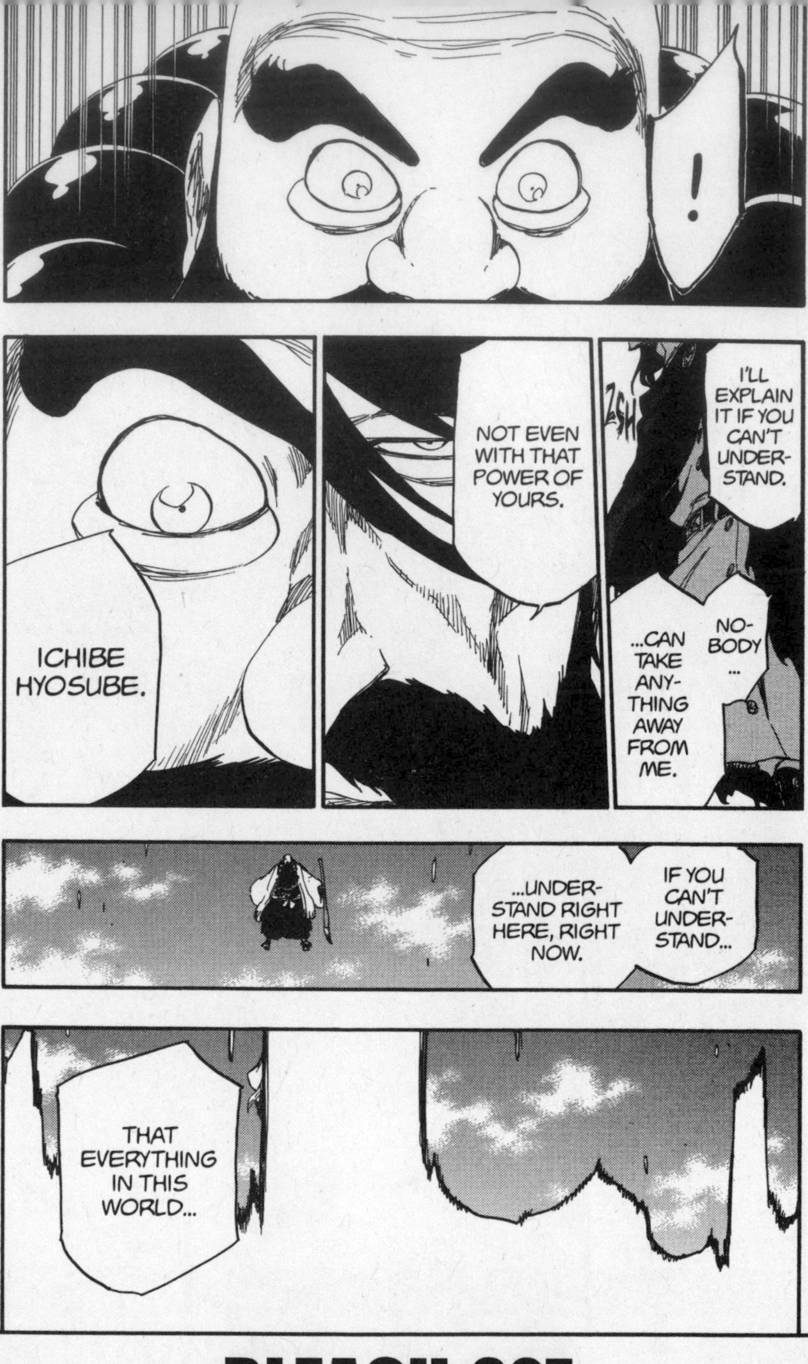
!
ZSH
I'LL EXPLAIN IT IF YOU CAN'T UNDER-STAND.
NO-BODY...
...CAN TAKE ANY-THING AWAY FROM ME.
NOT EVEN WITH THAT POWER OF YOURS.
ICHIBE HYOSUBE.
IF YOU CAN'T UNDER-STAND...
...UNDER-STAND RIGHT HERE, RIGHT NOW.
THAT EVERYTHING IN THIS WORLD...

BLEACH 607.

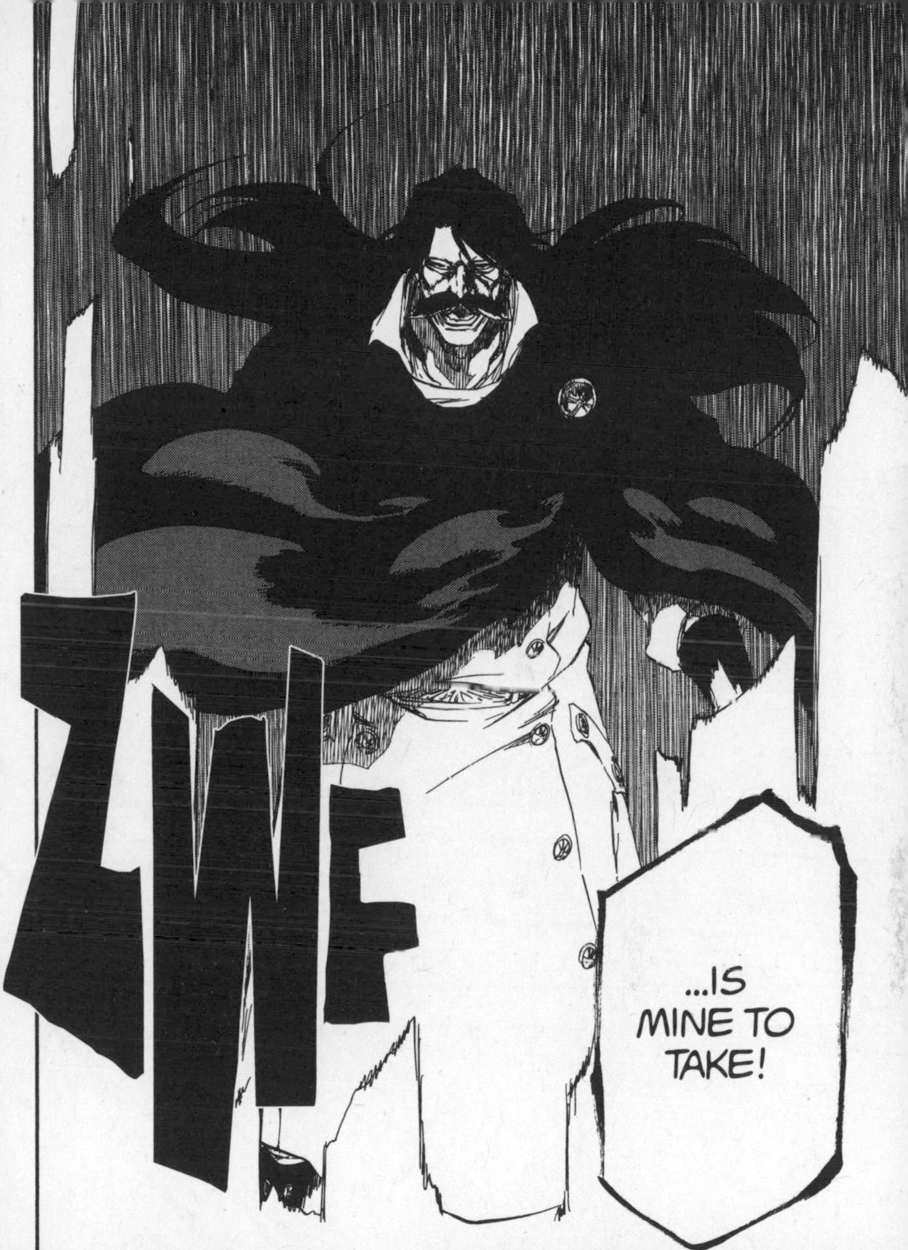
...IS MINE TO TAKE!

THE MASTER

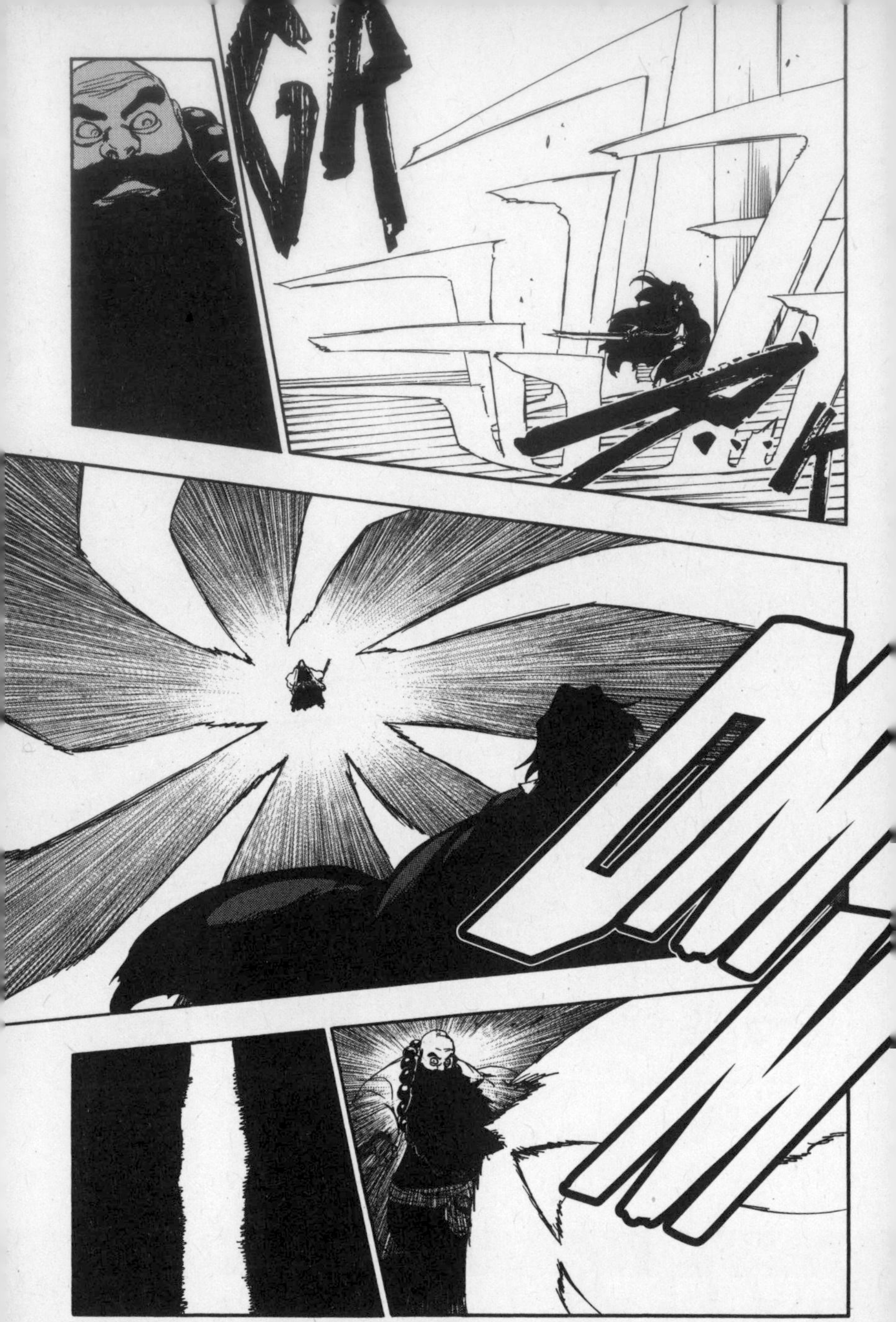
GR

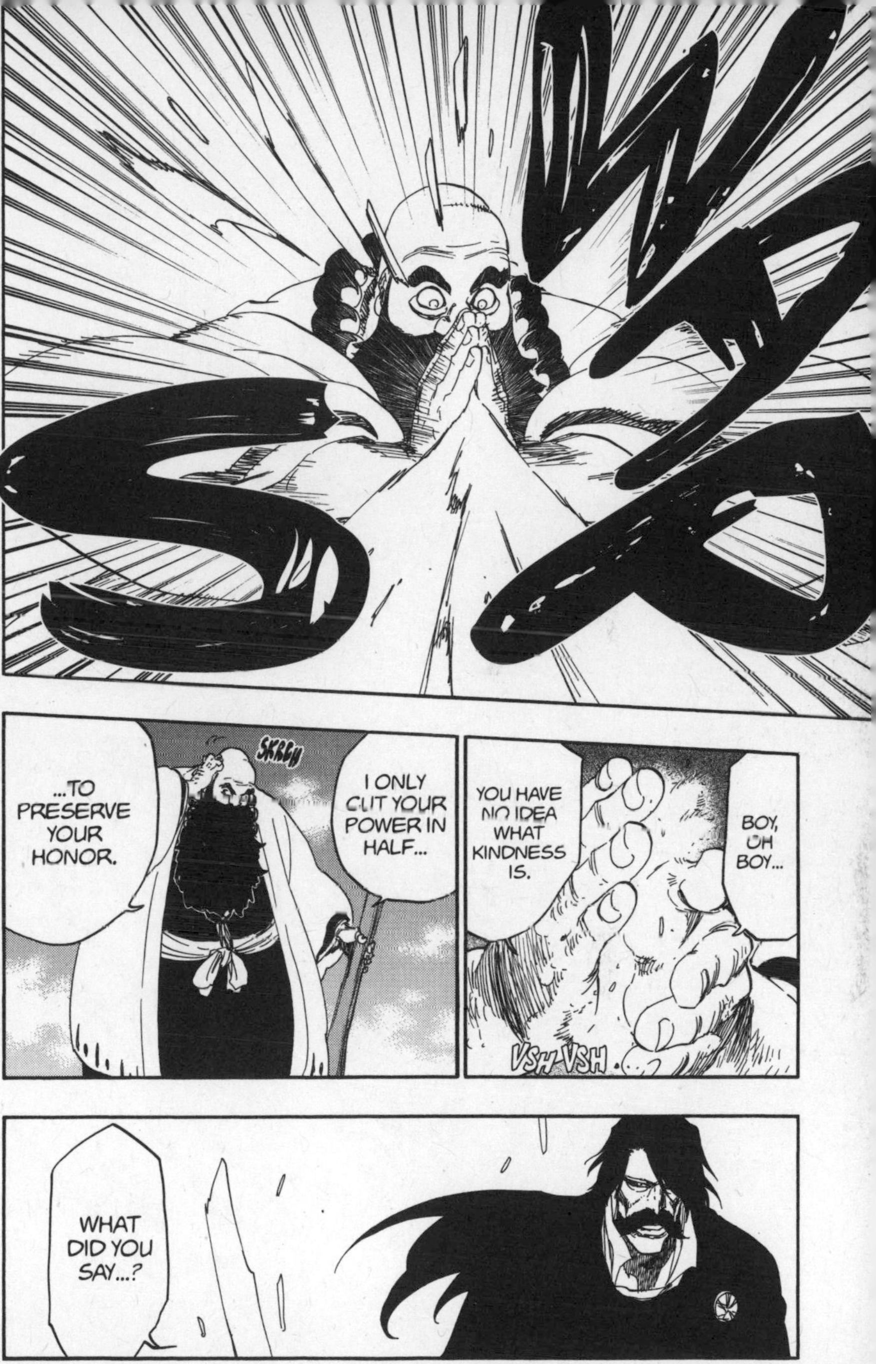
BOY, OH BOY...
YOU HAVE NO IDEA WHAT KINDNESS IS.
VSH VSH
I ONLY CUT YOUR POWER IN HALF...
...TO PRESERVE YOUR HONOR.
WHAT DID YOU SAY...?

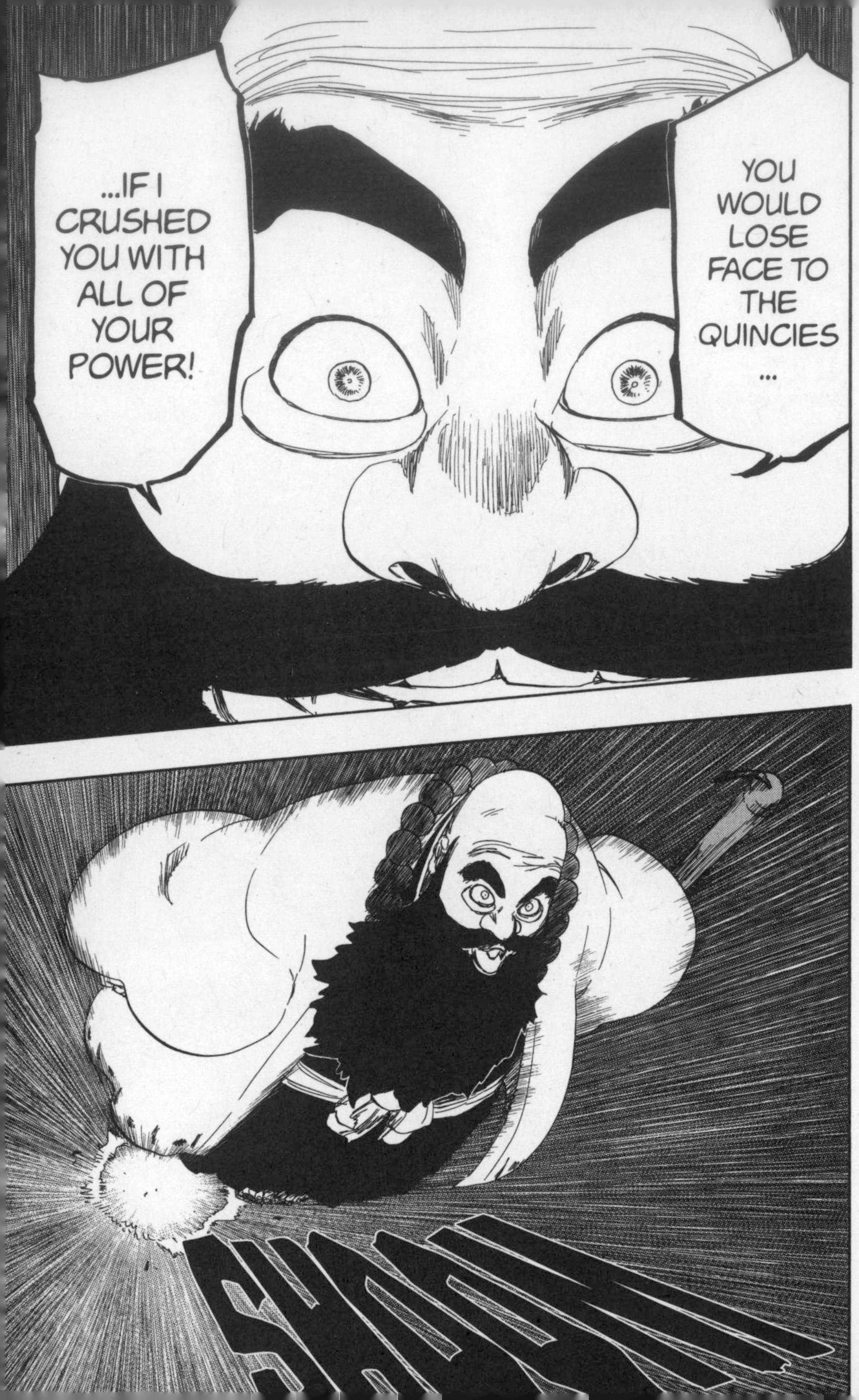
YOU WOULD LOSE FACE TO THE QUINCIES...
...IF I CRUSHED YOU WITH ALL OF YOUR POWER!

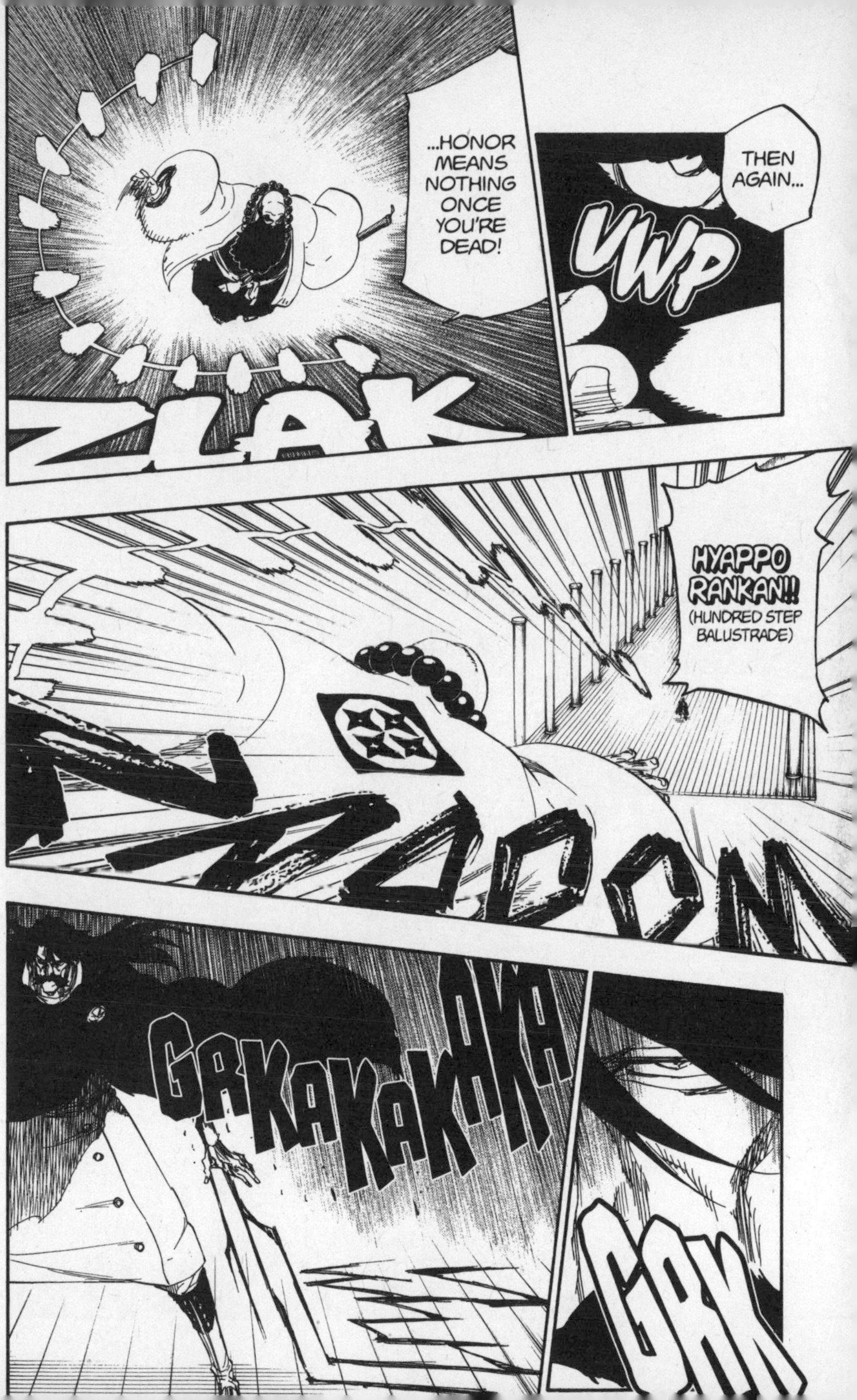
THEN AGAIN...
...HONOR MEANS NOTHING ONCE YOU'RE DEAD!
HYAPPO RANKAN!! (HUNDRED STEP BALUSTRADE)

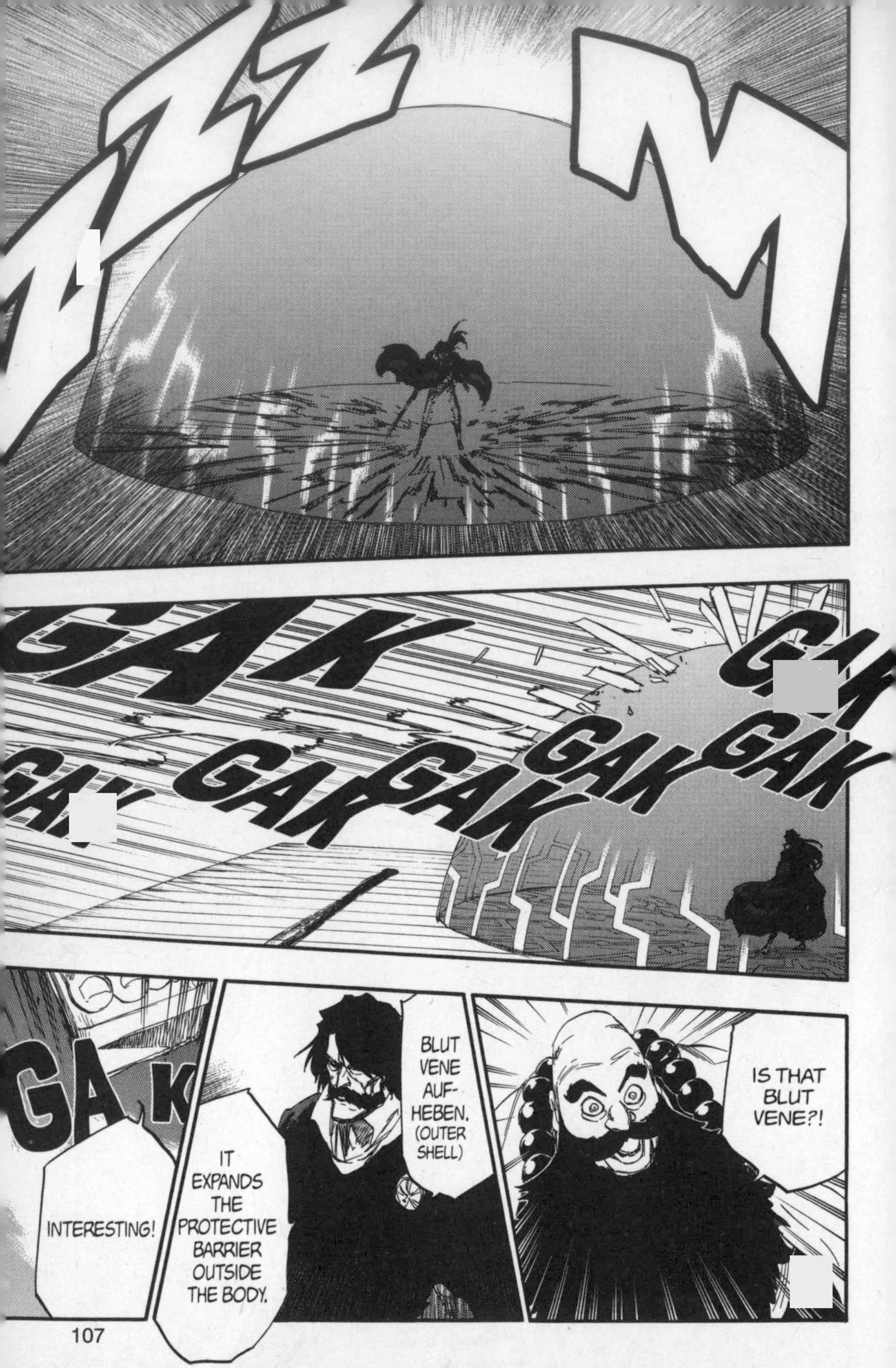
ZZZM
GAK
GAK
GAK
GAK
GAK
GAK
IS THAT BLUT VENE?!
BLUT VENE AUF-HEBEN. (OUTER SHELL)
IT EXPANDS THE PROTECTIVE BARRIER OUTSIDE THE BODY.
GAK
INTERESTING!

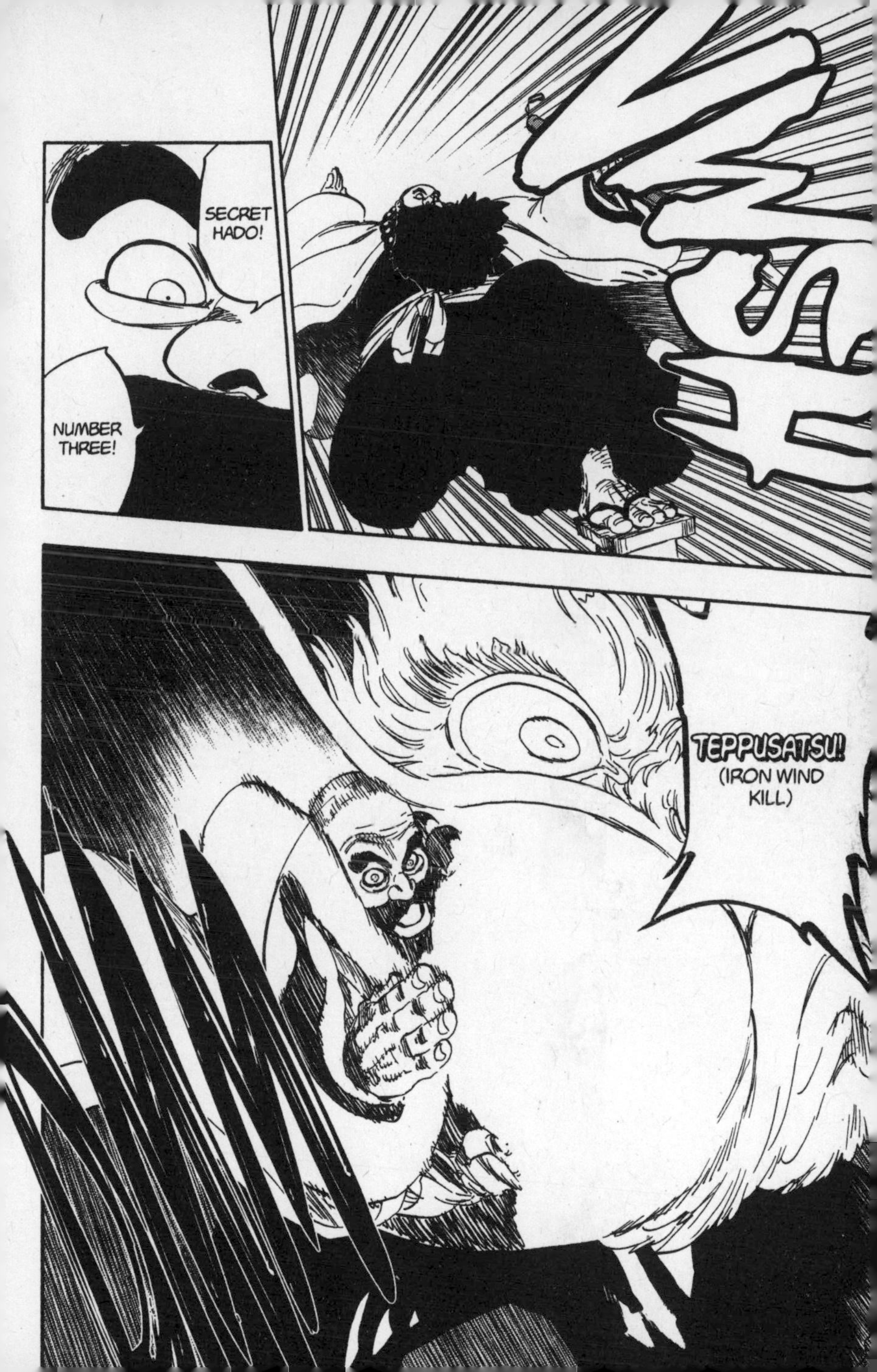
SECRET HADO!
NUMBER THREE!
TEPPUSATSU!
(IRON WIND KILL)

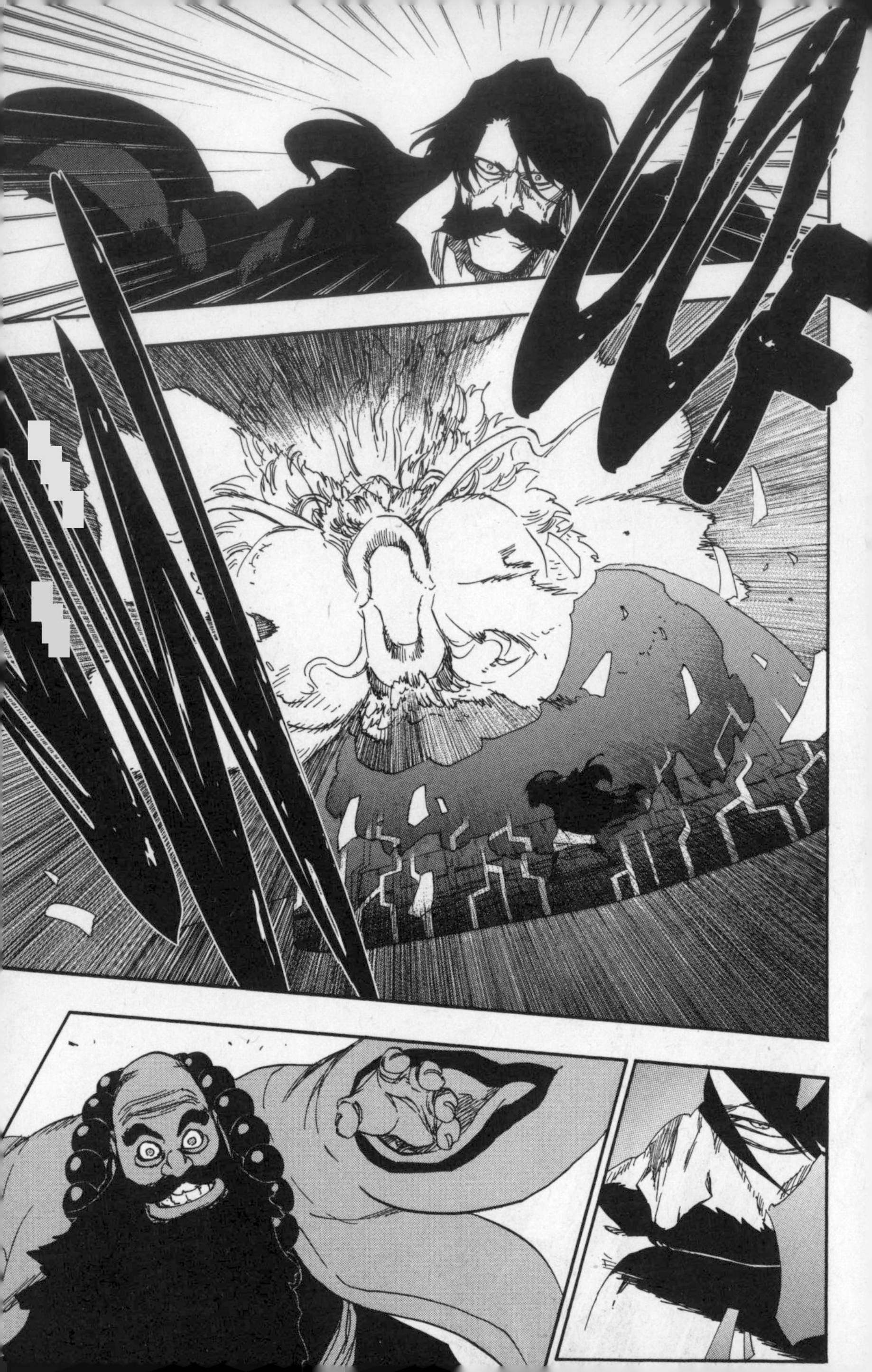

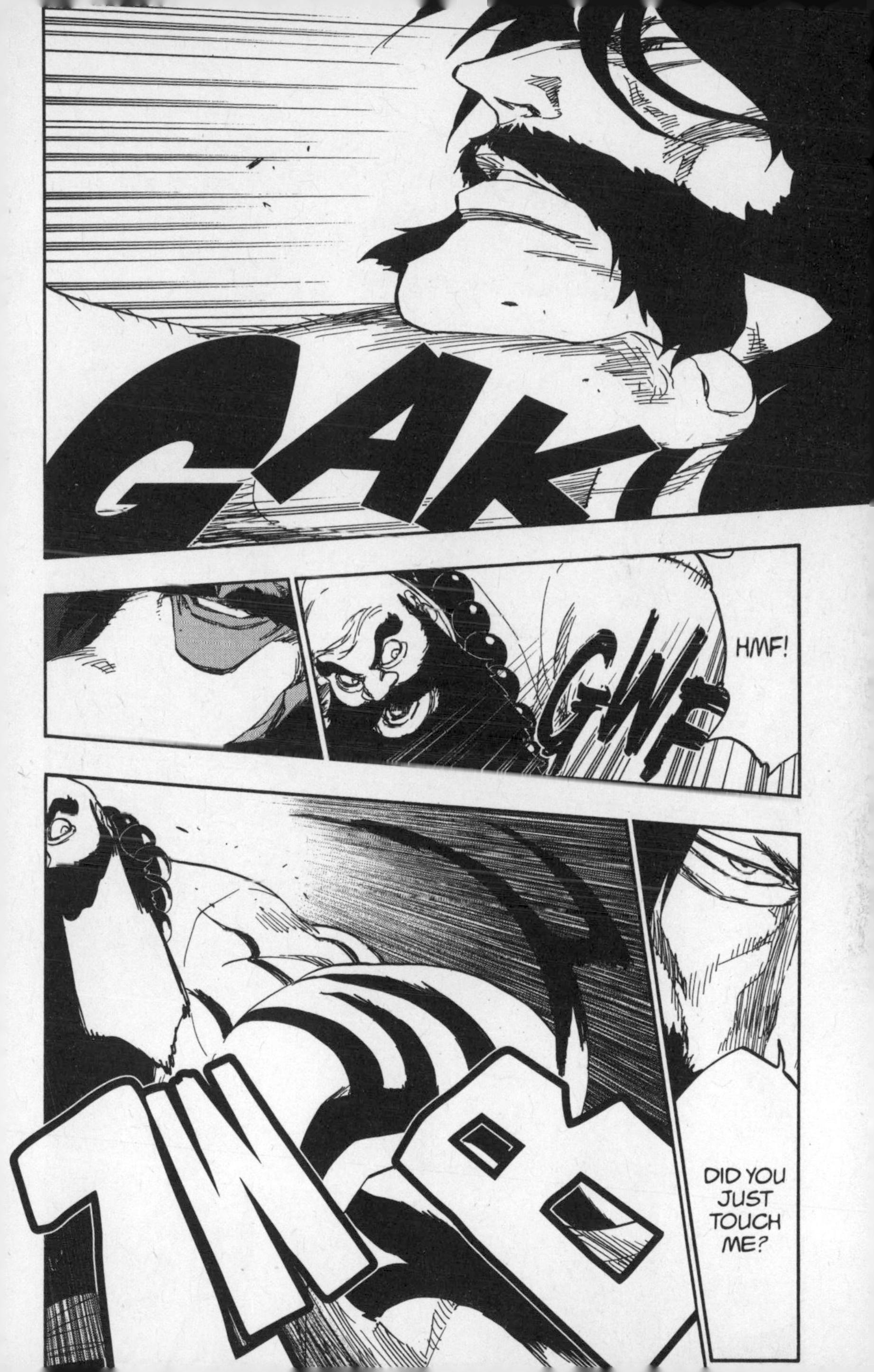
GAK
HMF!
DID YOU JUST TOUCH ME?

READ THIS WAY

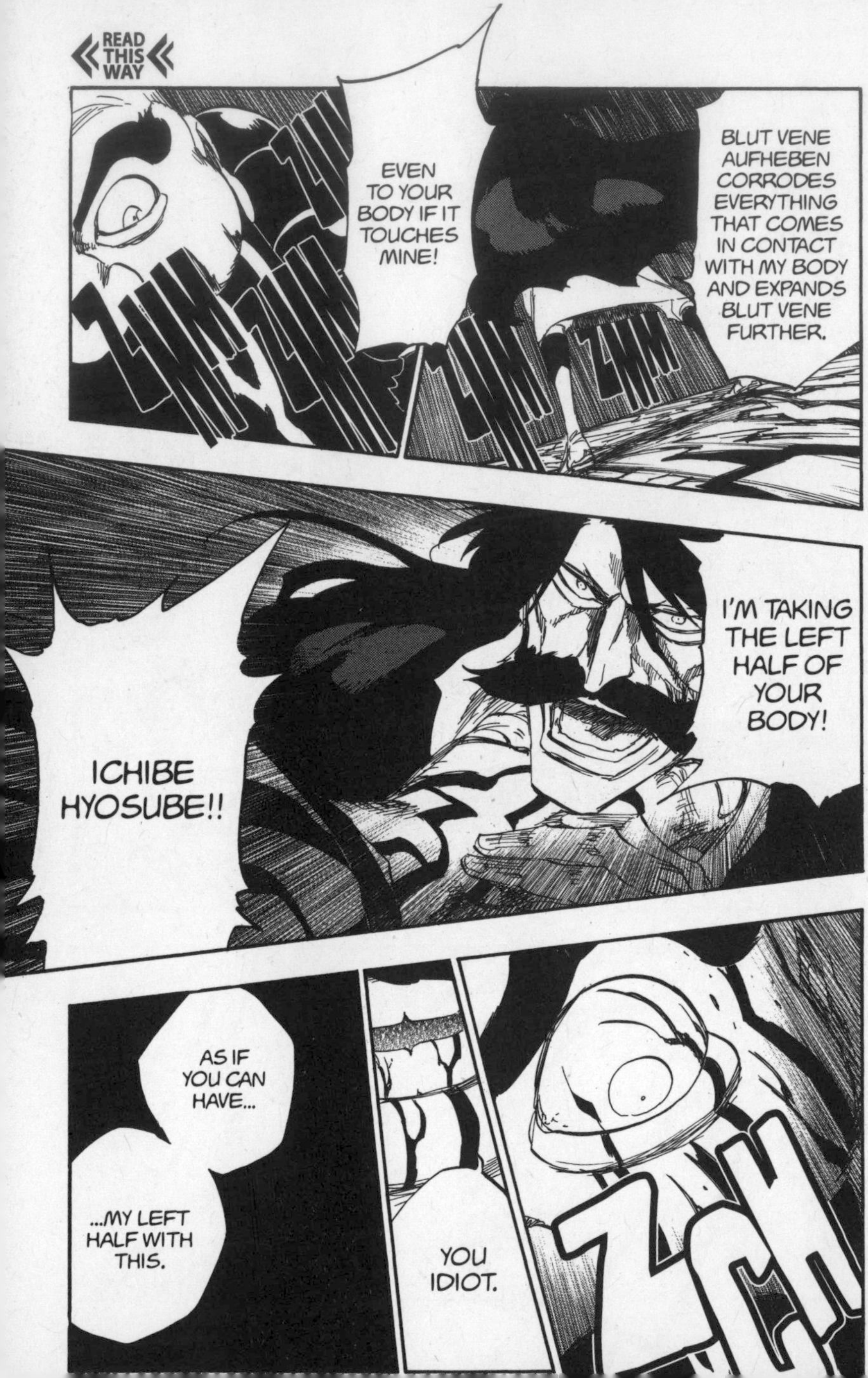
BLUT VENE AUFHEBEN CORRODES EVERYTHING THAT COMES IN CONTACT WITH MY BODY AND EXPANDS BLUT VENE FURTHER.
ZMM
ZMM
EVEN TO YOUR BODY IF IT TOUCHES MINE!
ZMM
ZMM
I'M TAKING THE LEFT HALF OF YOUR BODY!
ICHIBE HYOSUBE!!
ZCH
YOU IDIOT.
AS IF YOU CAN HAVE...
...MY LEFT HALF WITH THIS.

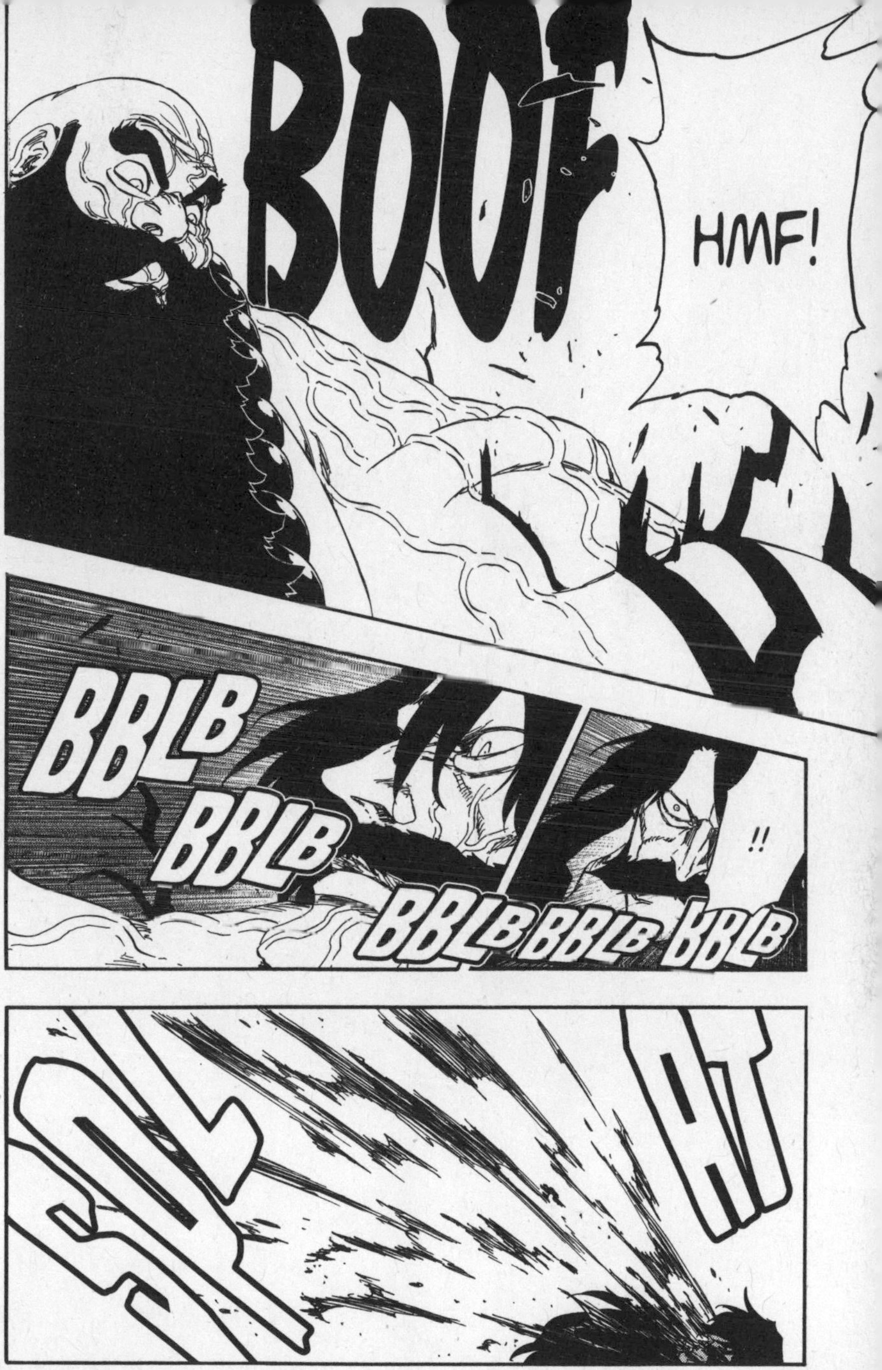
HMF!
BOOF
!!
BBLB BBLB BBLB BBLB BBLB

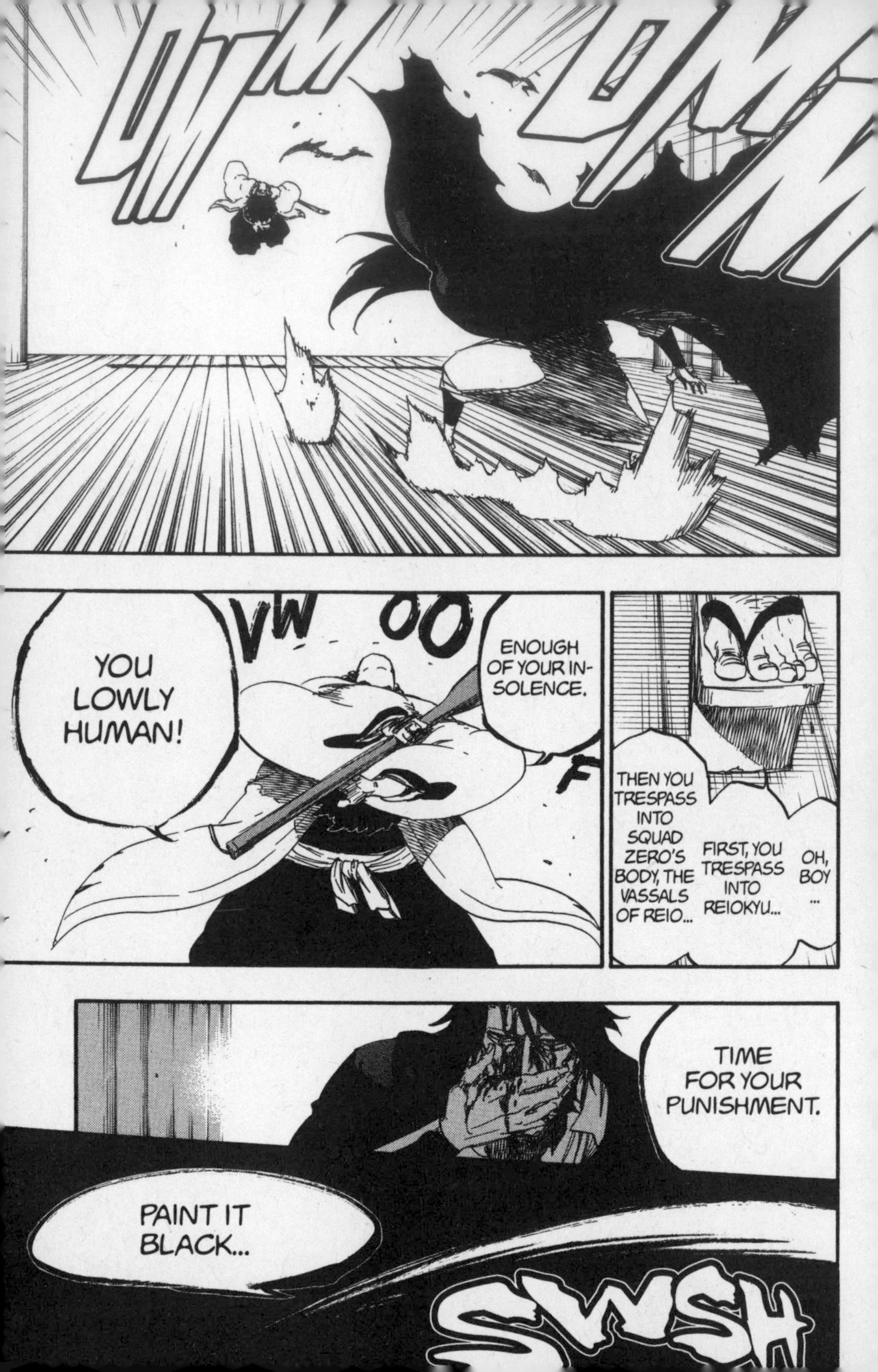

OH, BOY...
FIRST, YOU TRESPASS INTO REIOKYU...
THEN YOU TRESPASS INTO SQUAD ZERO'S BODY, THE VASSALS OF REIO...
ENOUGH OF YOUR IN-SOLENCE.
VWOO
YOU LOWLY HUMAN!
TIME FOR YOUR PUNISHMENT.
PAINT IT BLACK...
SWSH

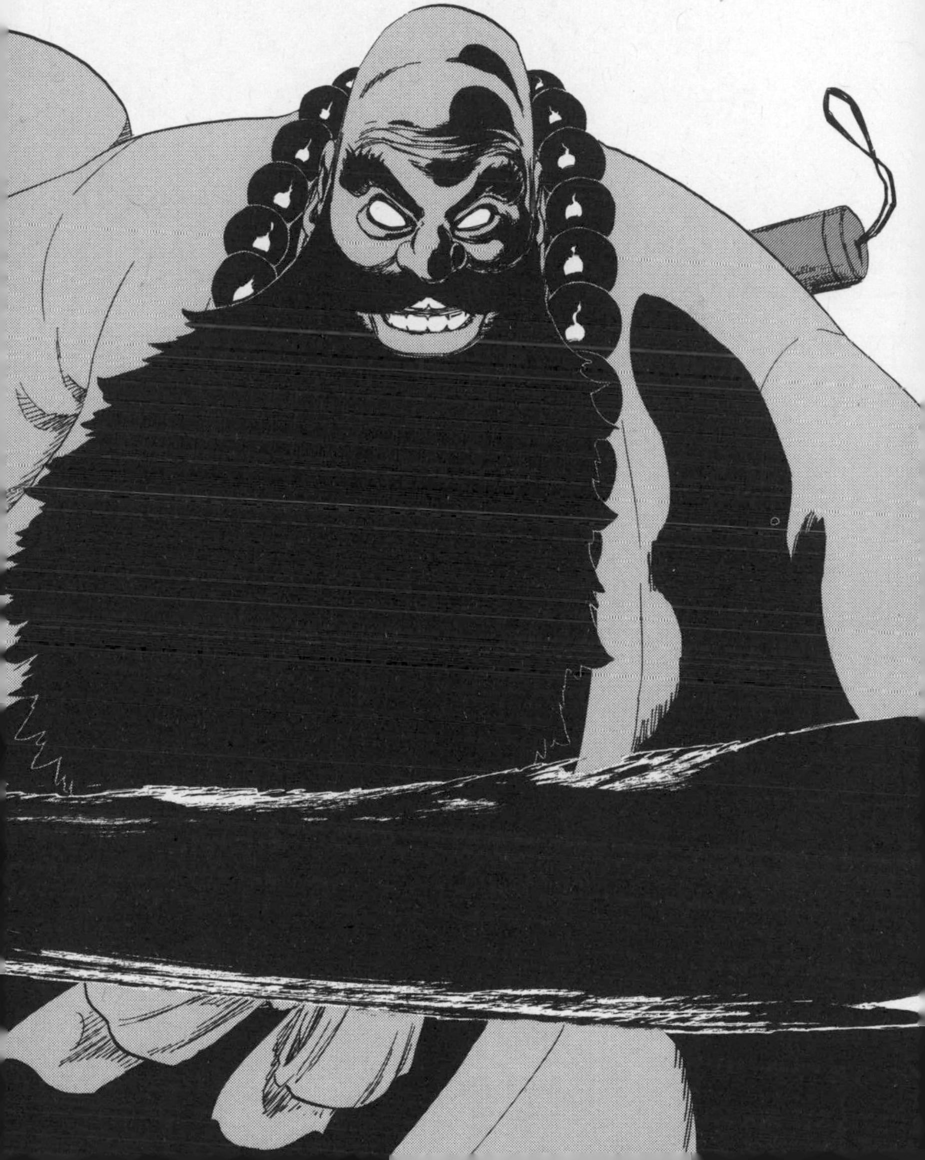

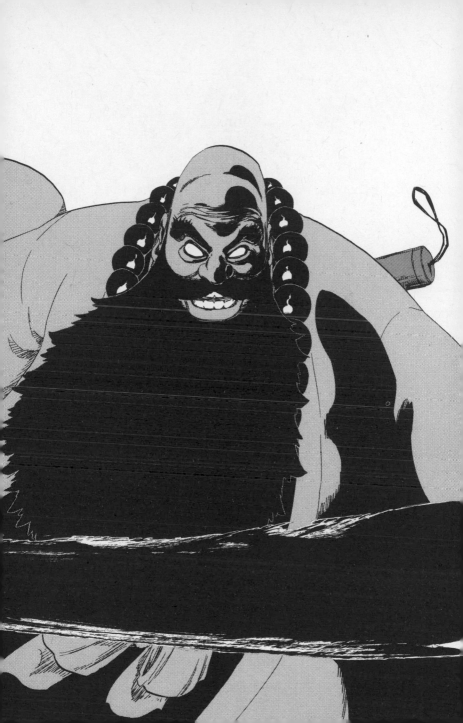

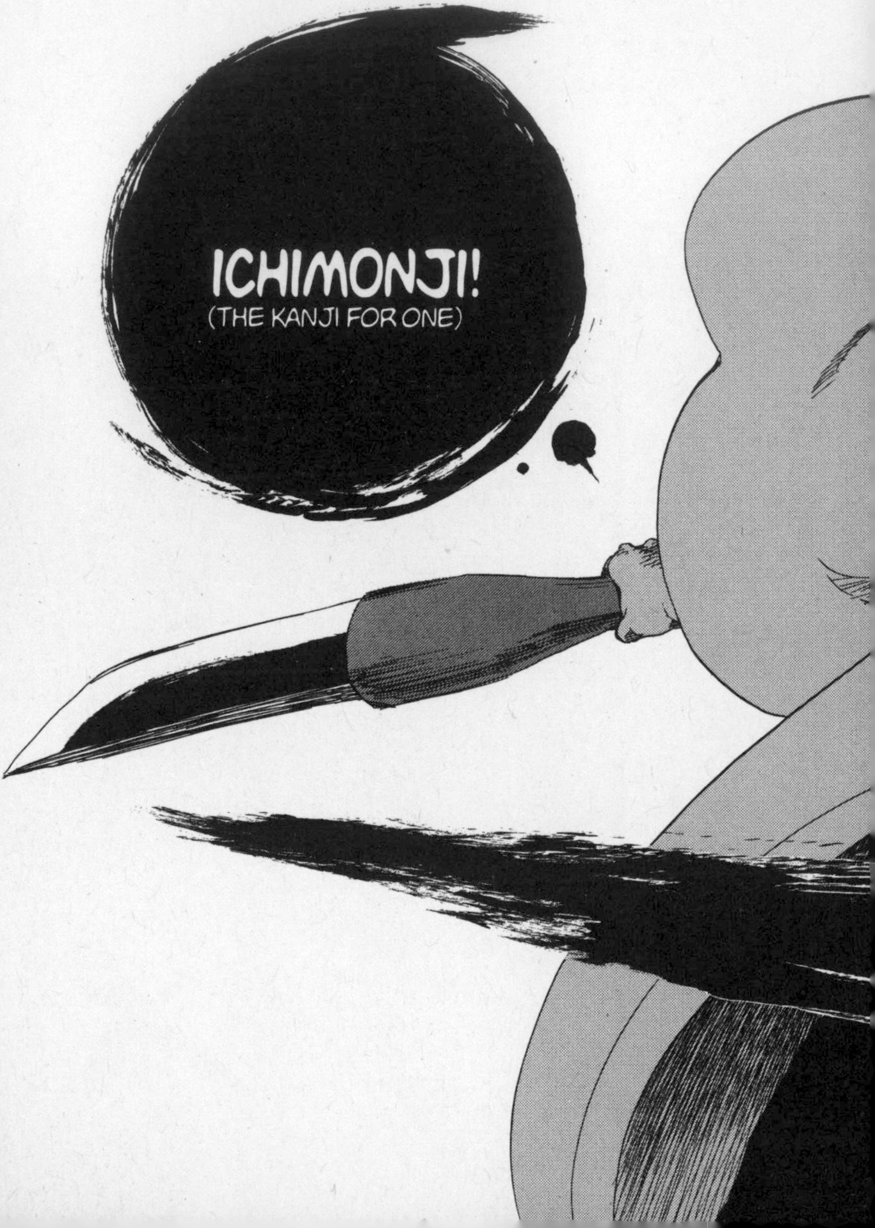
ICHIMONJI!
(THE KANJI FOR ONE)

X

608. BLACKER THAN BLACK

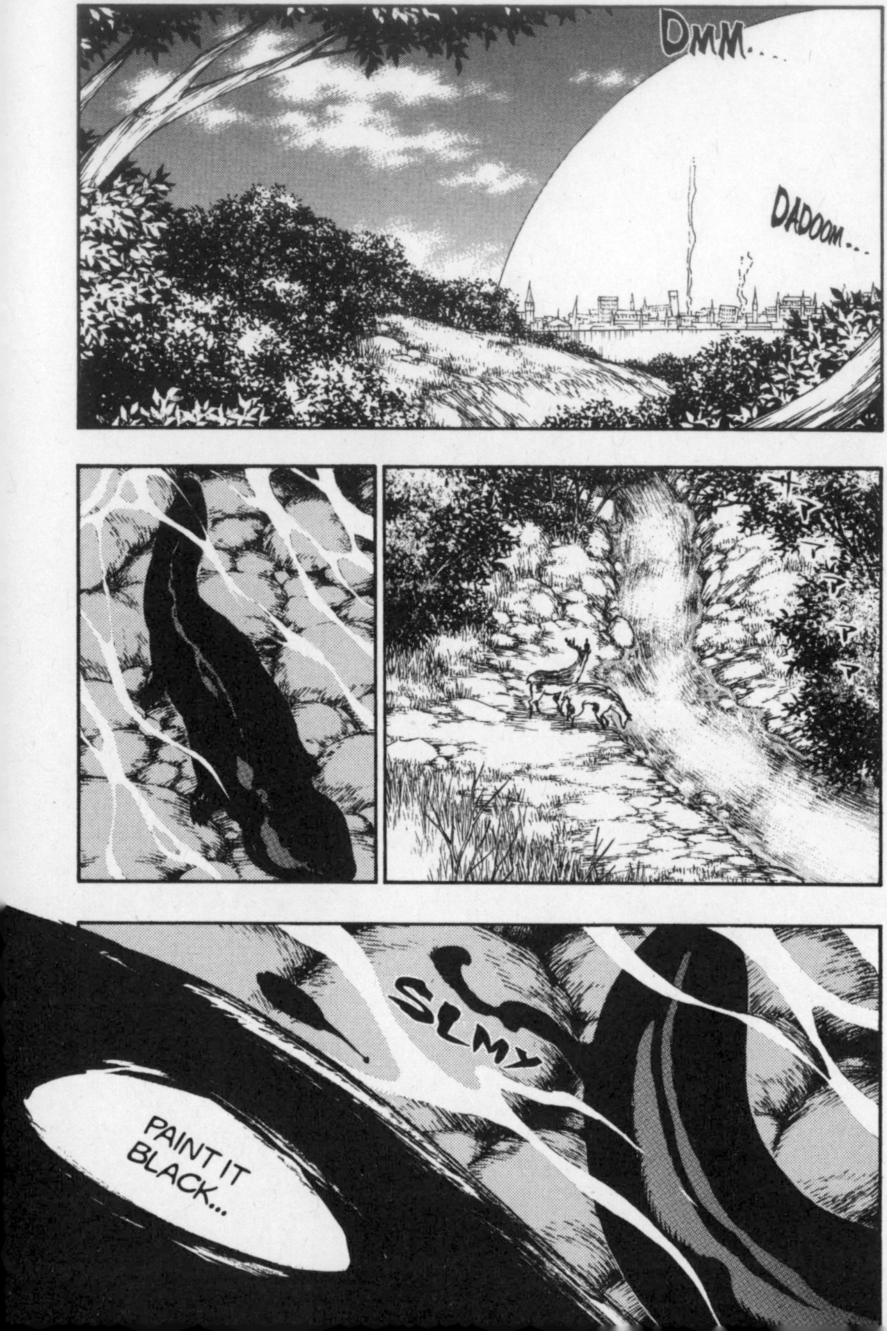
DMM...
DADOOM...
SLMY
PAINT IT BLACK...

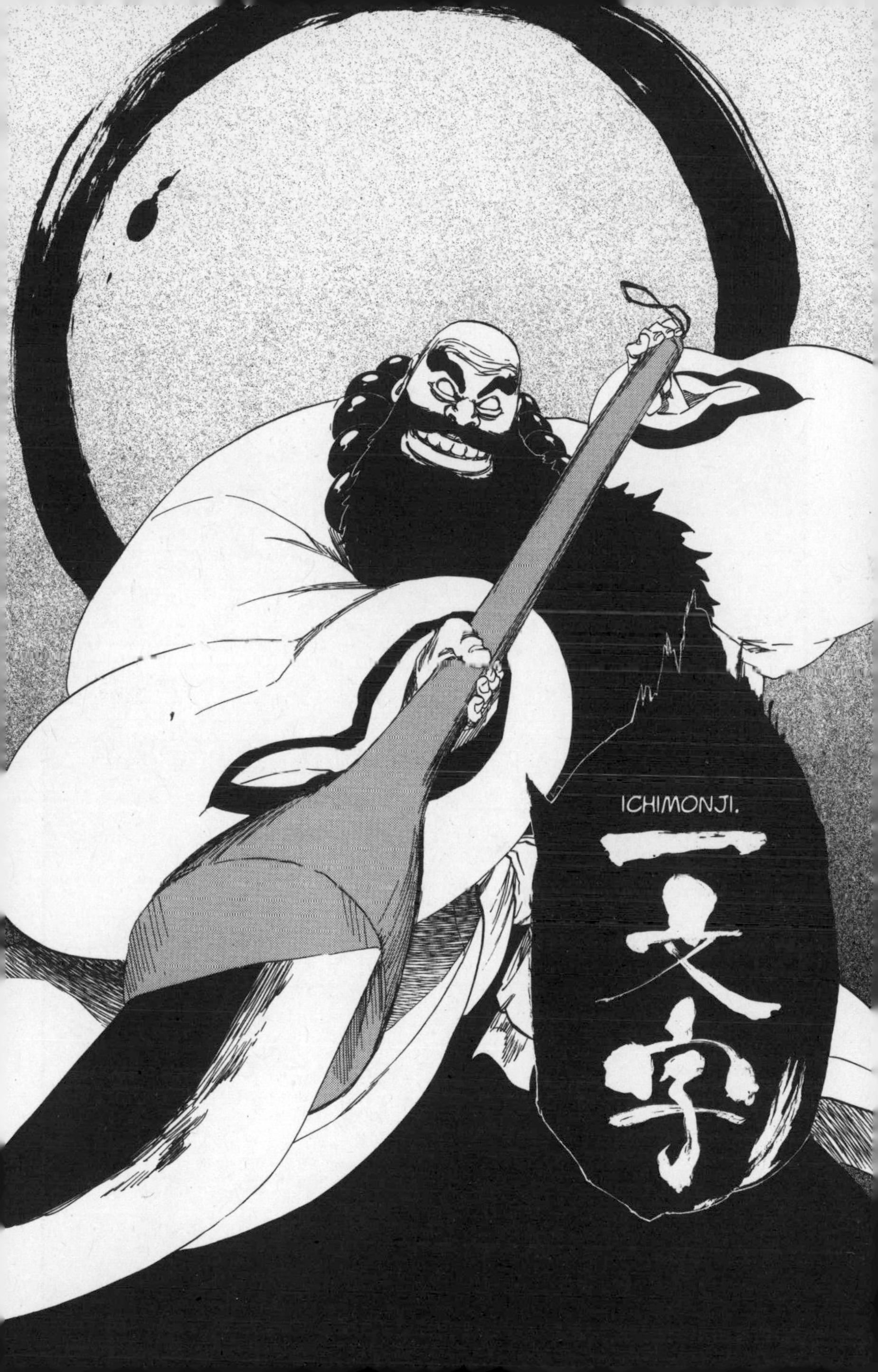
ICHIMONJI.
一文字

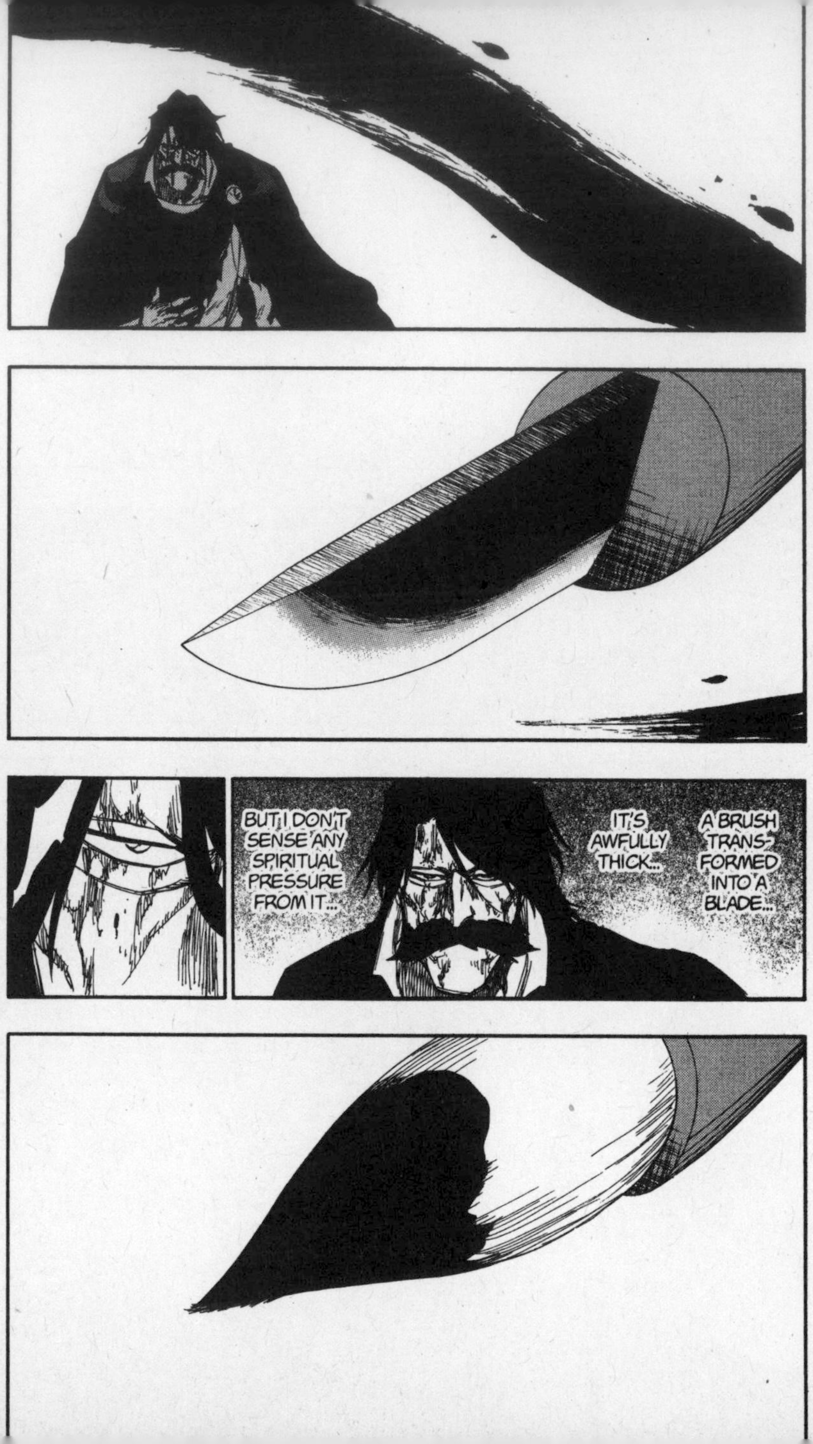
A BRUSH TRANSFORMED INTO A BLADE...
IT'S AWFULLY THICK...
BUT I DON'T SENSE ANY SPIRITUAL PRESSURE FROM IT...

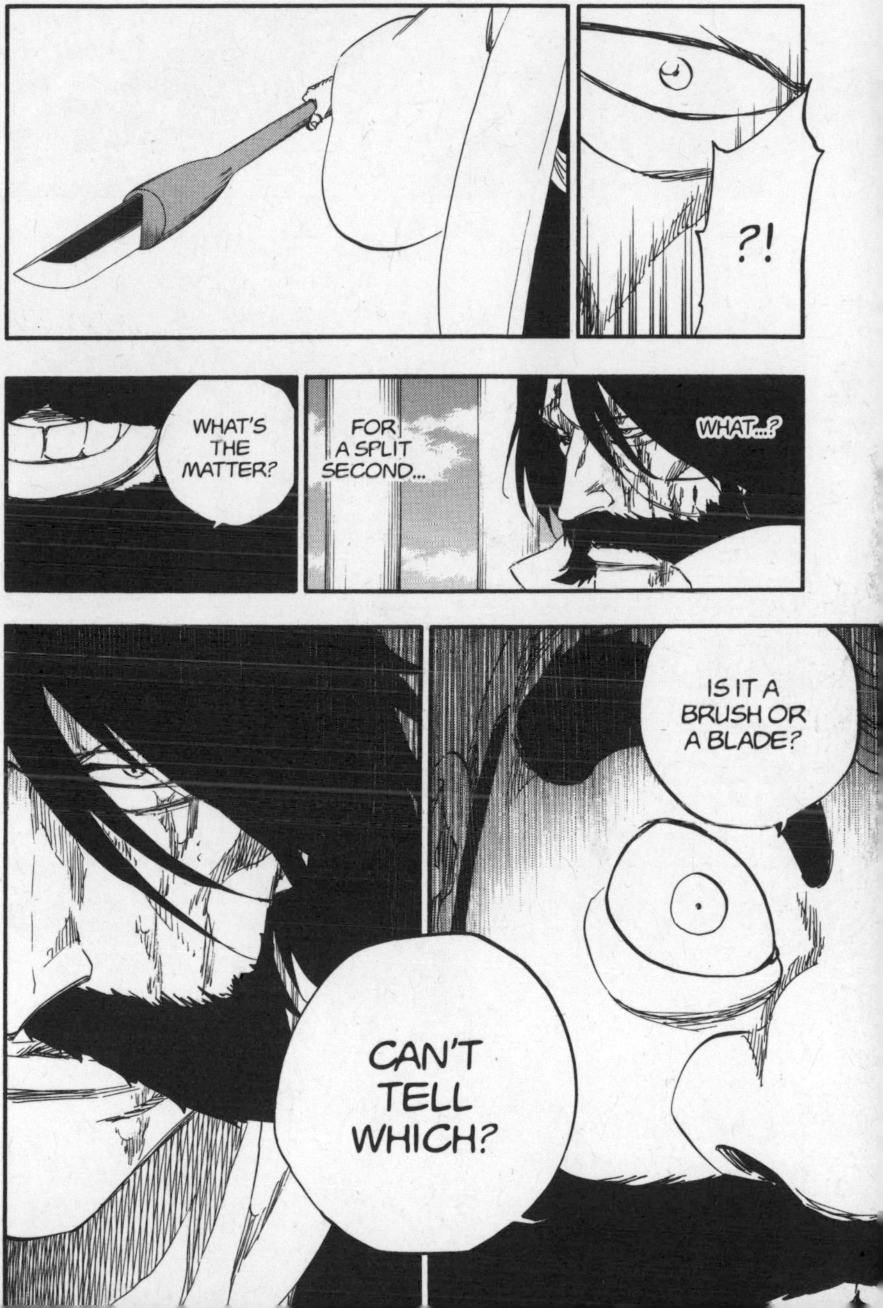
?!
WHAT...?
FOR A SPLIT SECOND...
WHAT'S THE MATTER?
IS IT A BRUSH OR A BLADE?
CAN'T TELL WHICH?

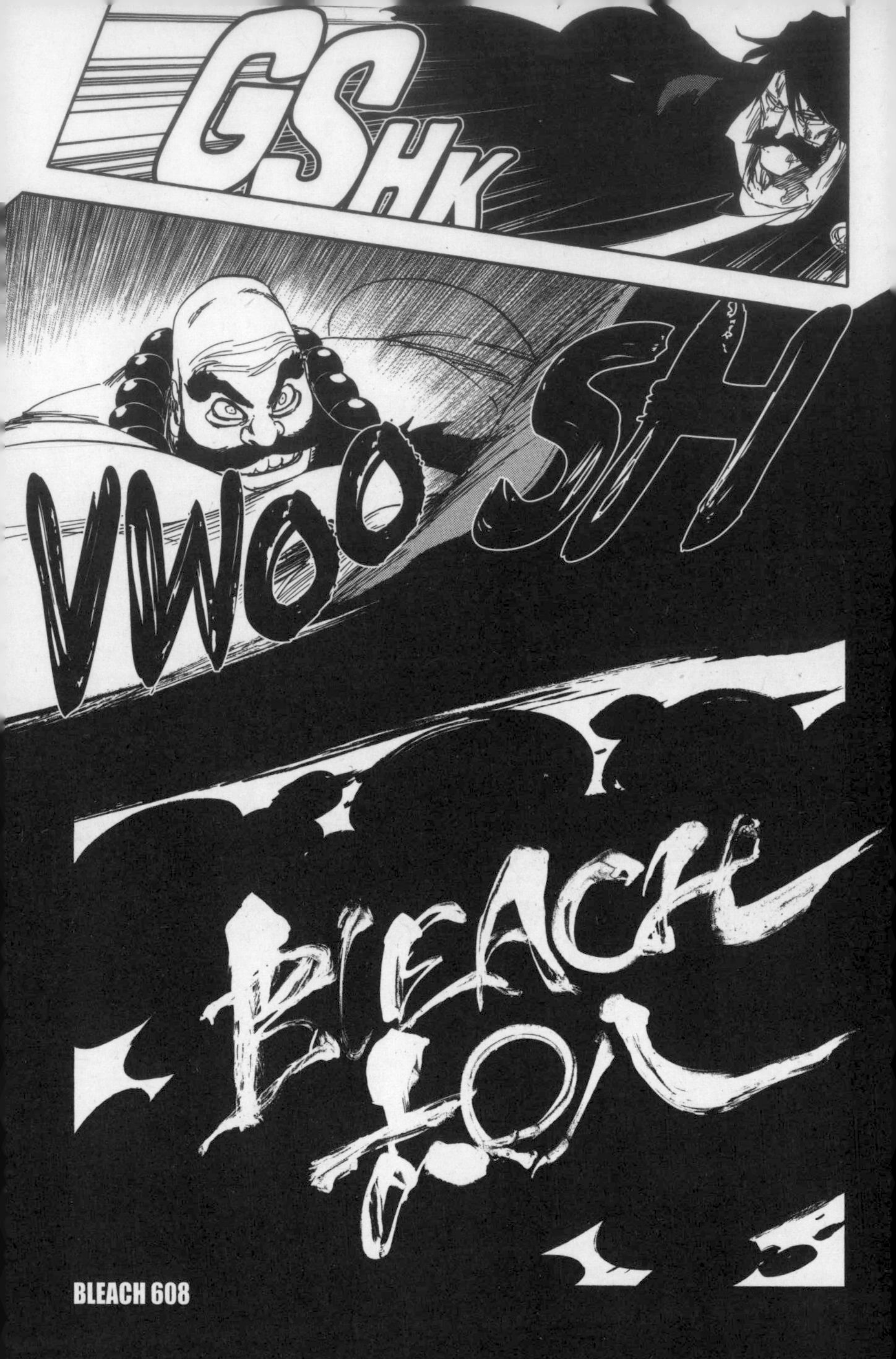
GSHK
VWOOSH
BLEACH 608

BLEACH 608

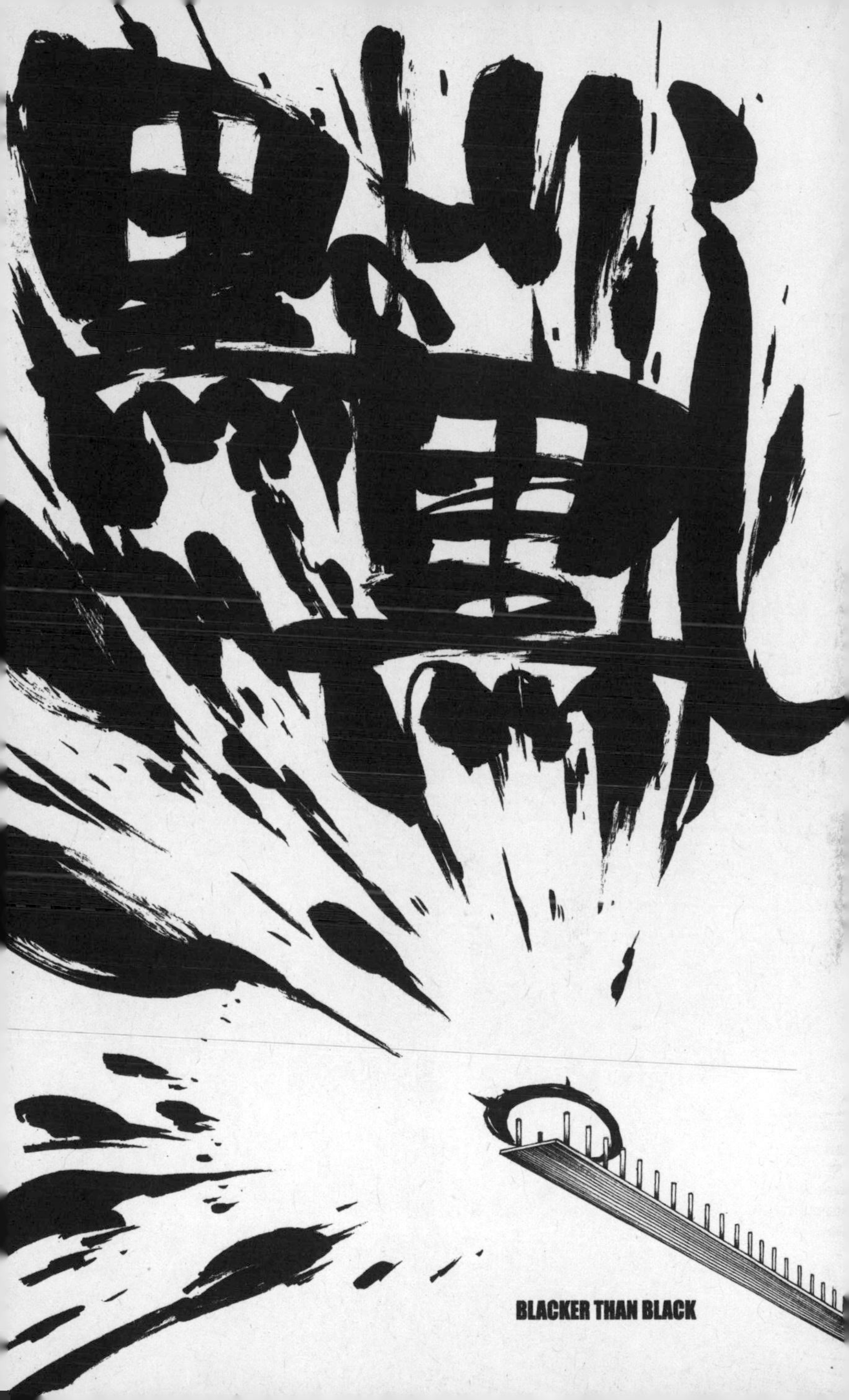
BLACKER THAN BLACK

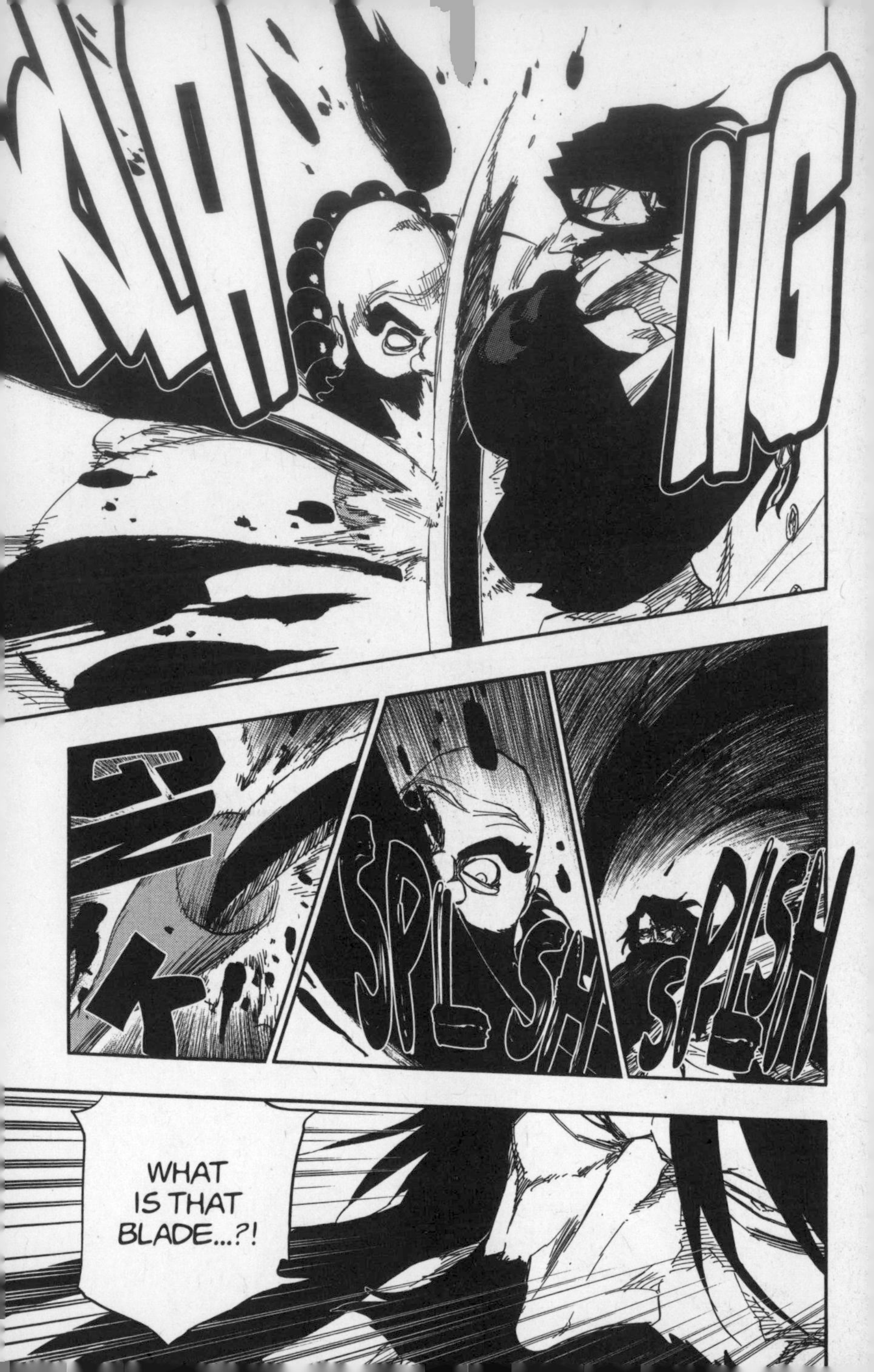
SPLSH
SPLSH
WHAT IS THAT BLADE...?!

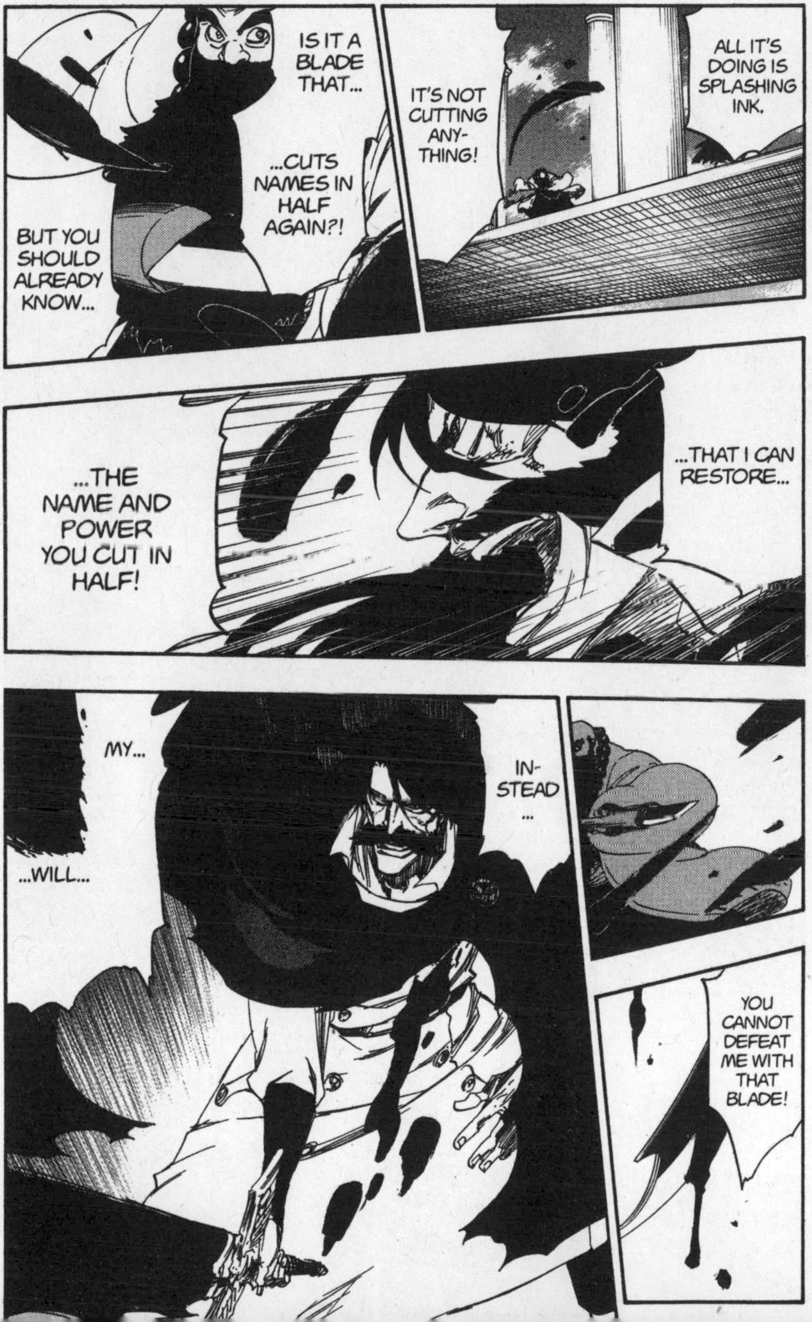
ALL IT'S DOING IS SPLASHING INK.
IT'S NOT CUTTING ANY-THING!
IS IT A BLADE THAT...
...CUTS NAMES IN HALF AGAIN?!
BUT YOU SHOULD ALREADY KNOW...
...THAT I CAN RESTORE...
...THE NAME AND POWER YOU CUT IN HALF!
YOU CANNOT DEFEAT ME WITH THAT BLADE!
IN-STEAD...
MY...
...WILL...

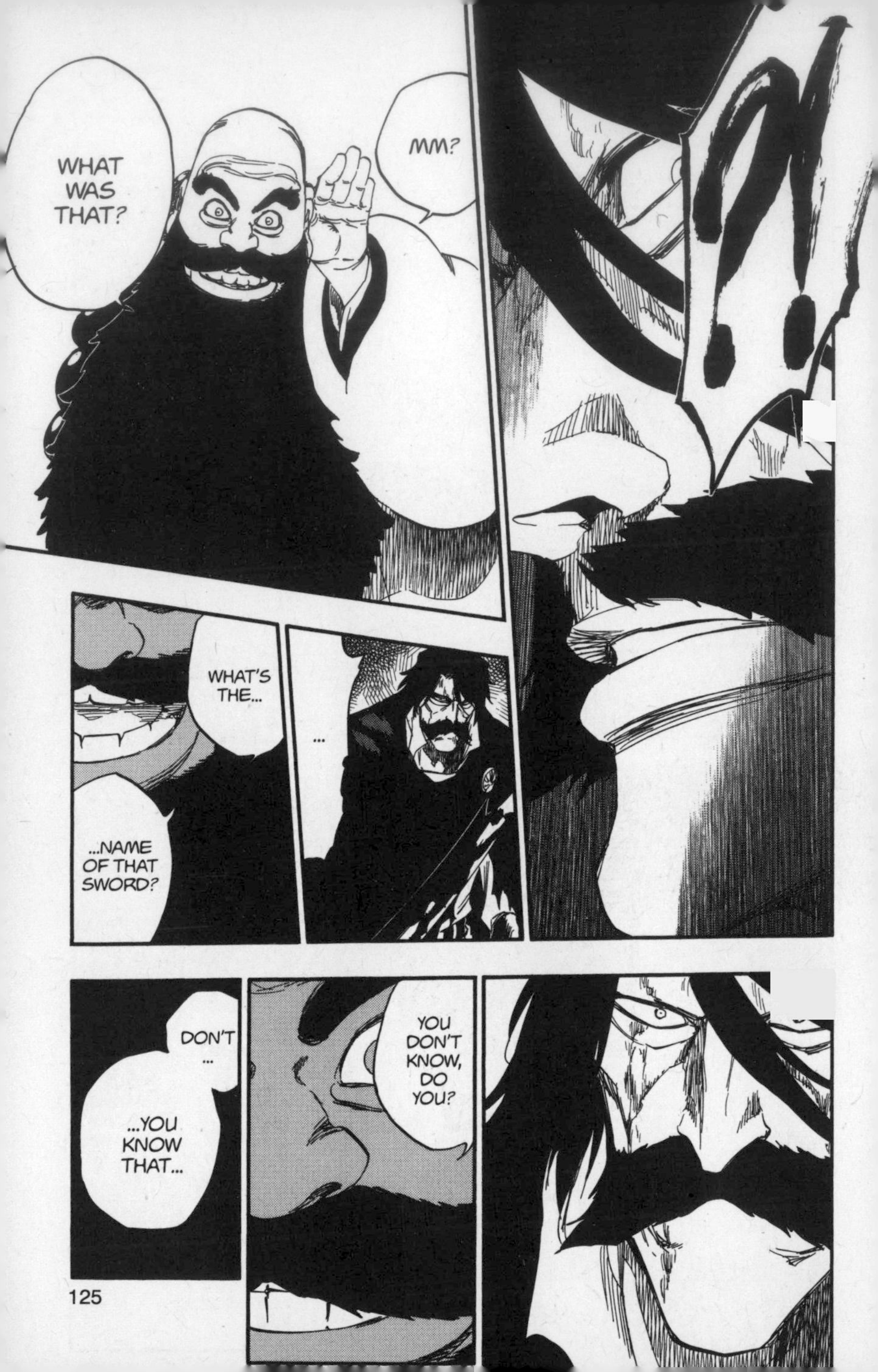
MM?
WHAT WAS THAT?
...
WHAT'S THE...
...NAME OF THAT SWORD?
YOU DON'T KNOW, DO YOU?
DON'T ...
...YOU KNOW THAT...

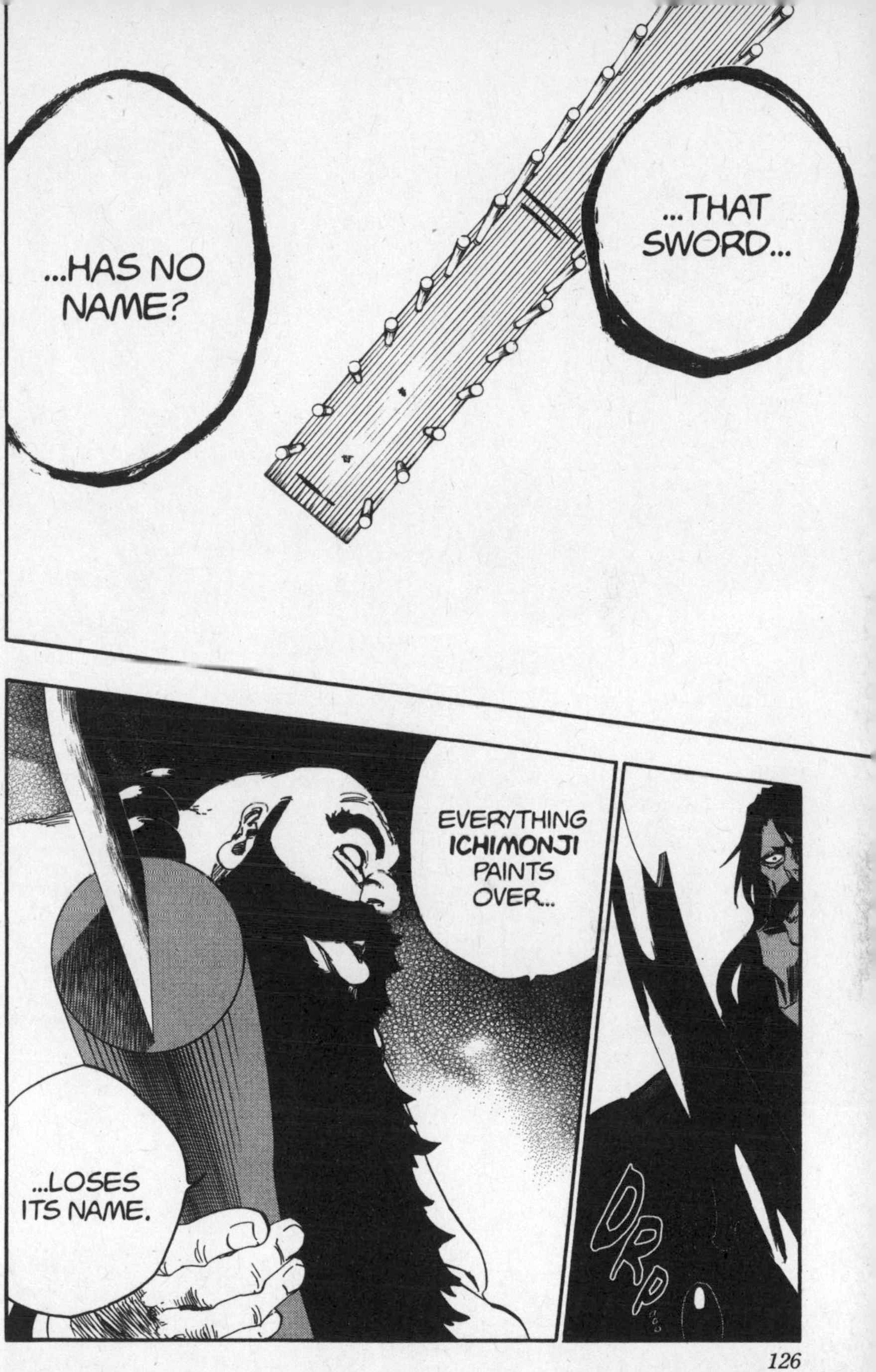
...THAT SWORD...
...HAS NO NAME?
DRP
EVERYTHING ICHIMONJI PAINTS OVER...
...LOSES ITS NAME.

READ THIS WAY

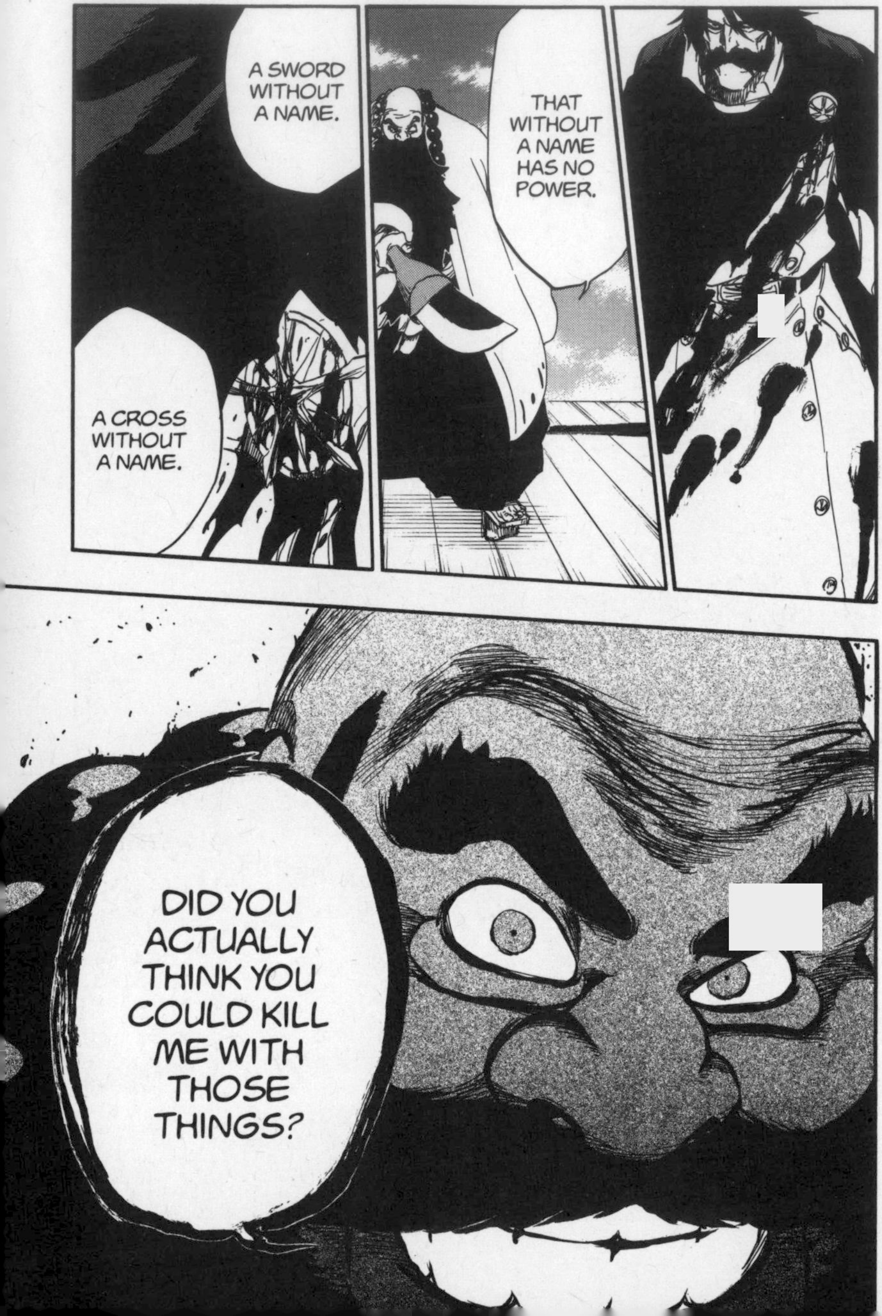
THAT WITHOUT A NAME HAS NO POWER.
A SWORD WITHOUT A NAME.
A CROSS WITHOUT A NAME.
DID YOU ACTUALLY THINK YOU COULD KILL ME WITH THOSE THINGS?

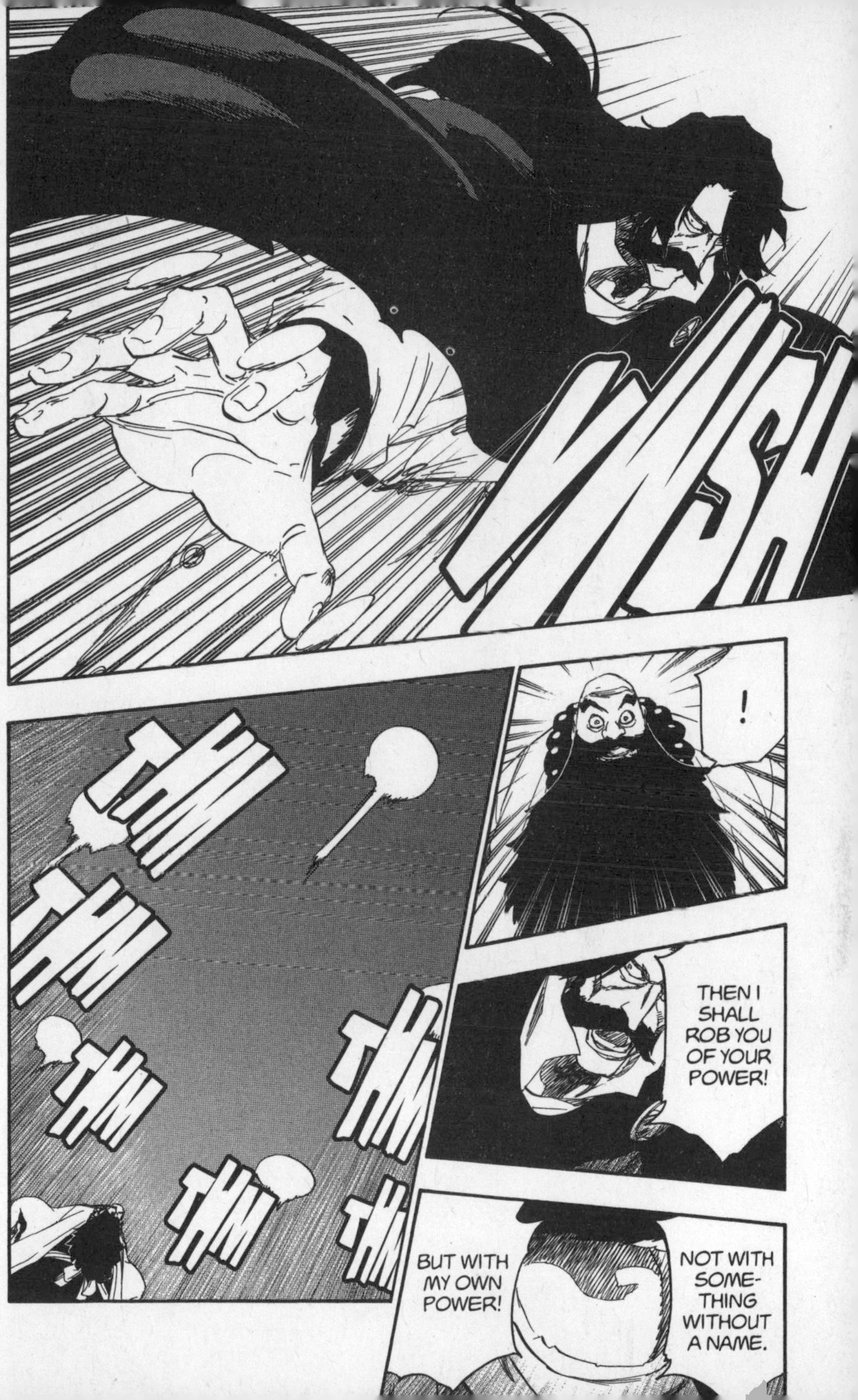
WHSH
!
THEN I SHALL ROB YOU OF YOUR POWER!
NOT WITH SOME-THING WITHOUT A NAME.
BUT WITH MY OWN POWER!
THM
THM
THM
THM
THM
THM

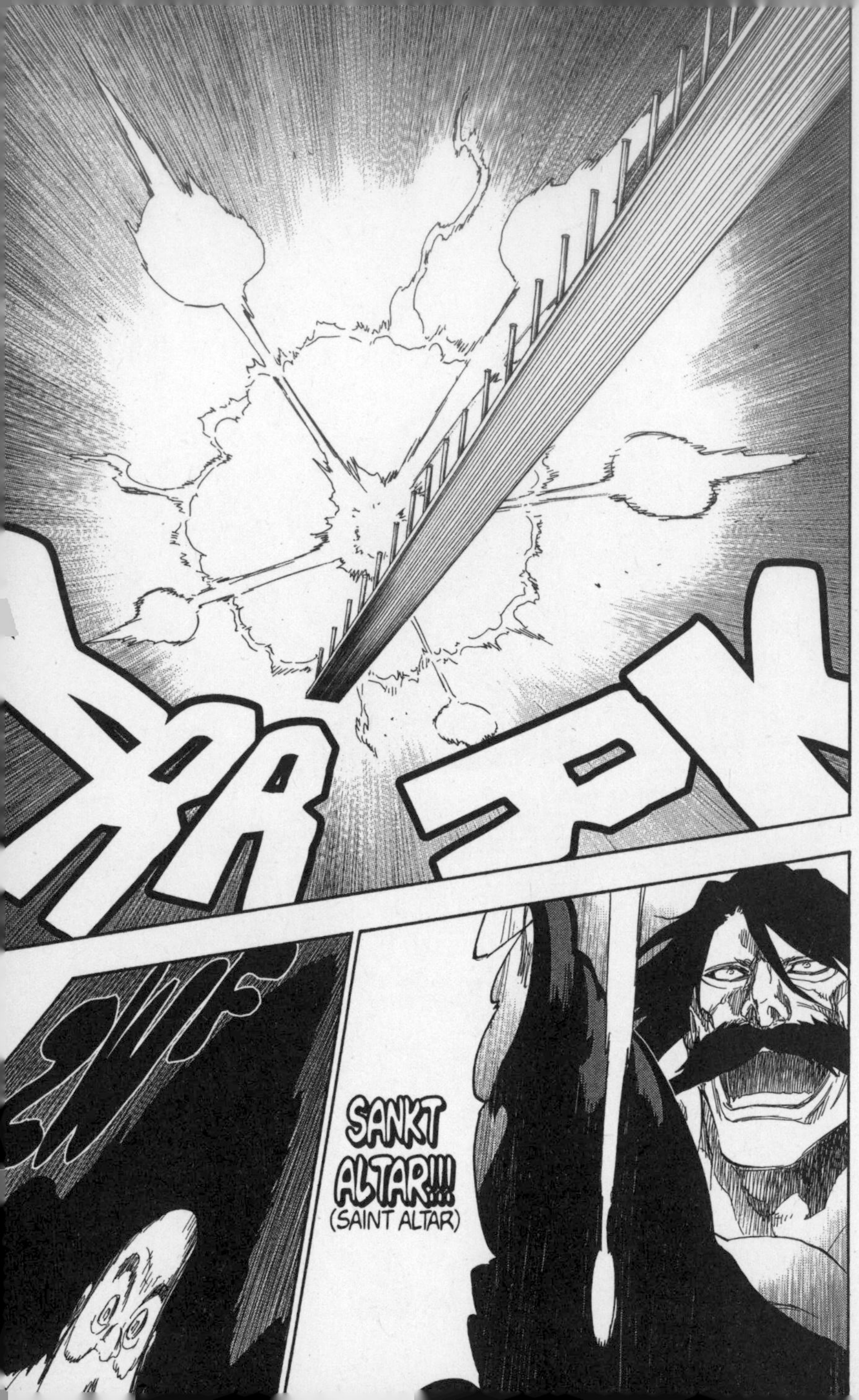
SANKT ALTAR!!!
(SAINT ALTAR)

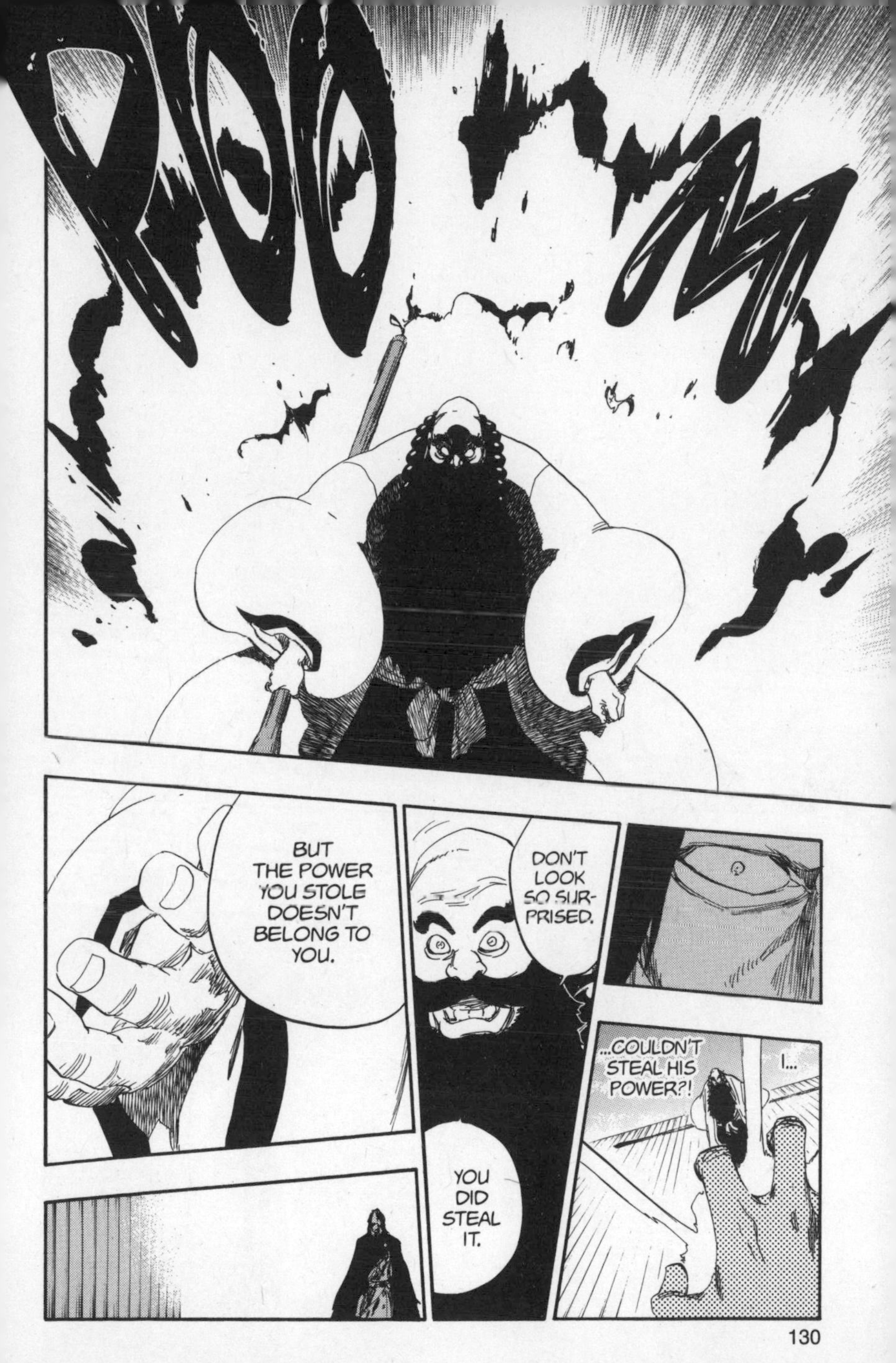
I...
...COULDN'T STEAL HIS POWER?!
DON'T LOOK SO SURPRISED.
YOU DID STEAL IT.
BUT THE POWER YOU STOLE DOESN'T BELONG TO YOU.

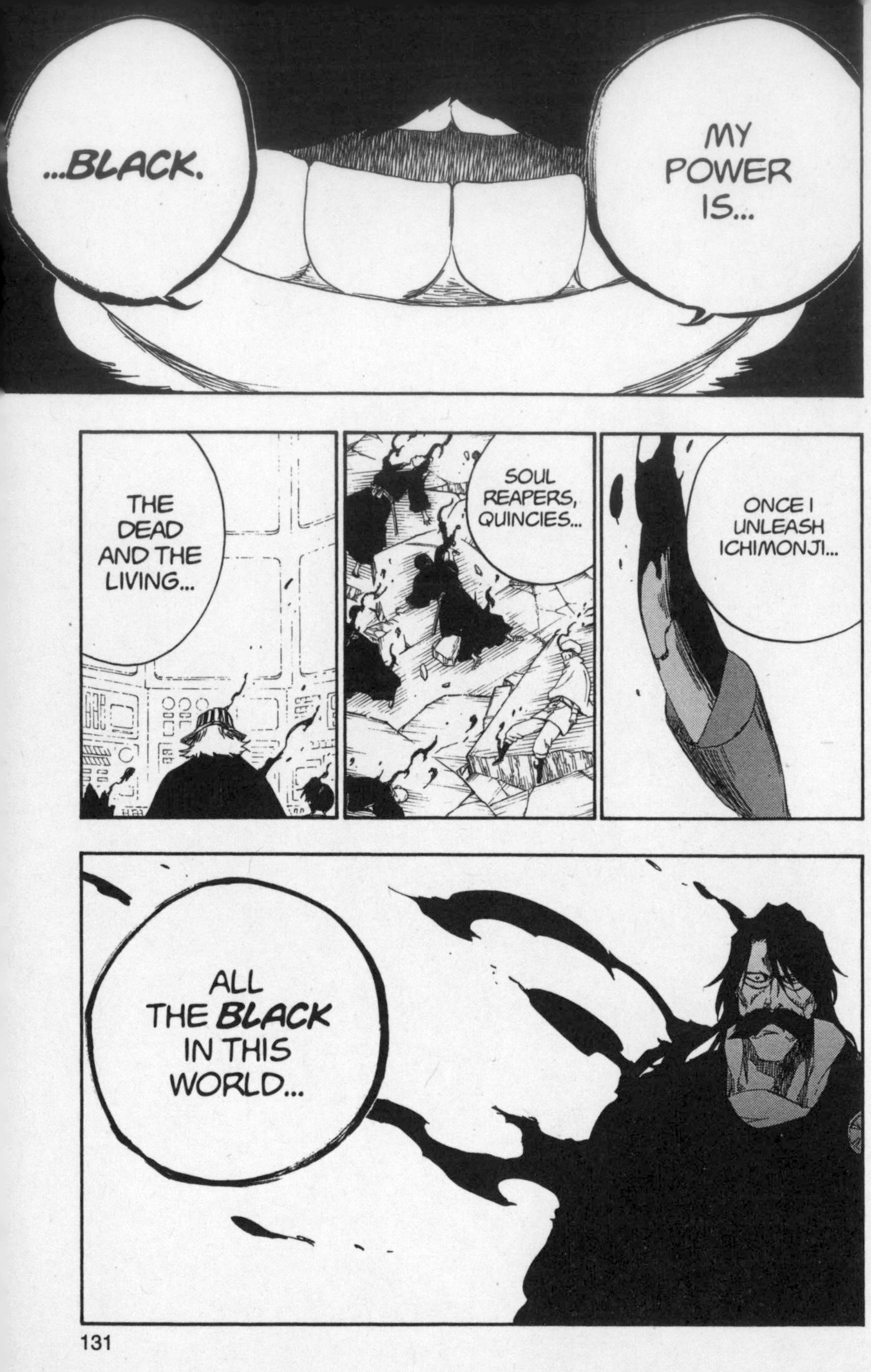
MY POWER IS...
...BLACK.
ONCE I UNLEASH ICHIMONJI...
SOUL REAPERS, QUINCIES...
THE DEAD AND THE LIVING...
ALL THE BLACK IN THIS WORLD...

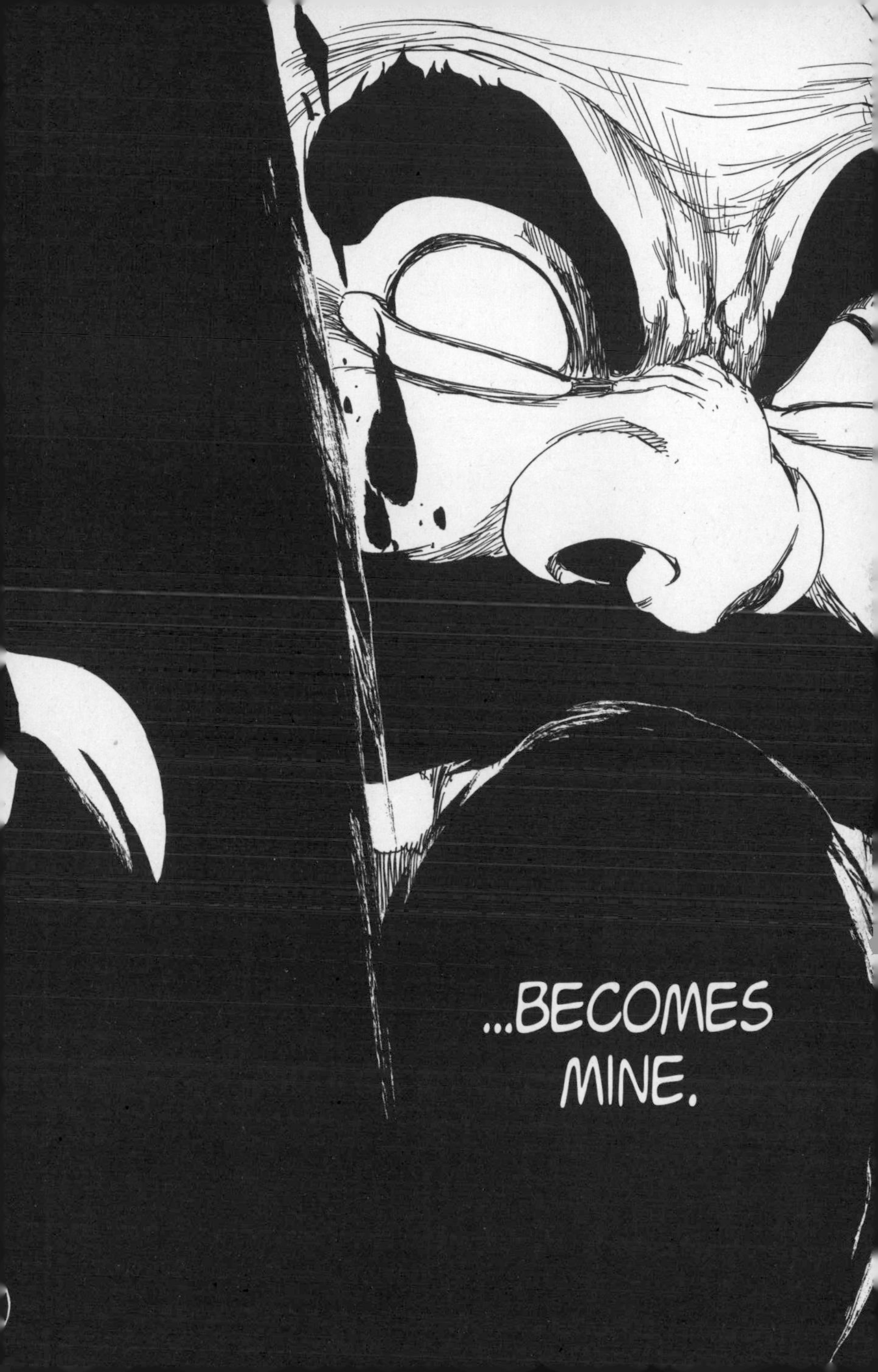
...BECOMES MINE.

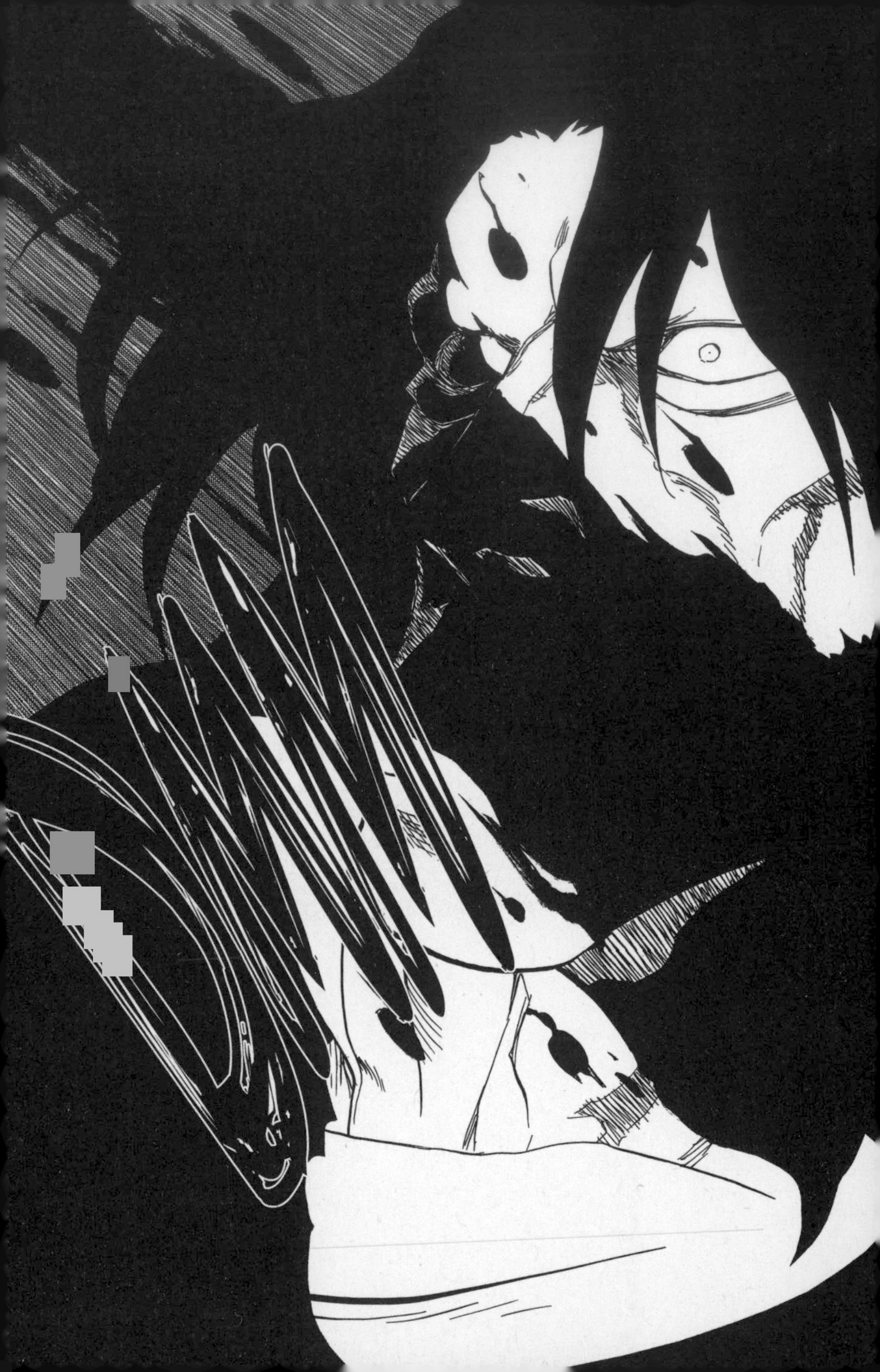

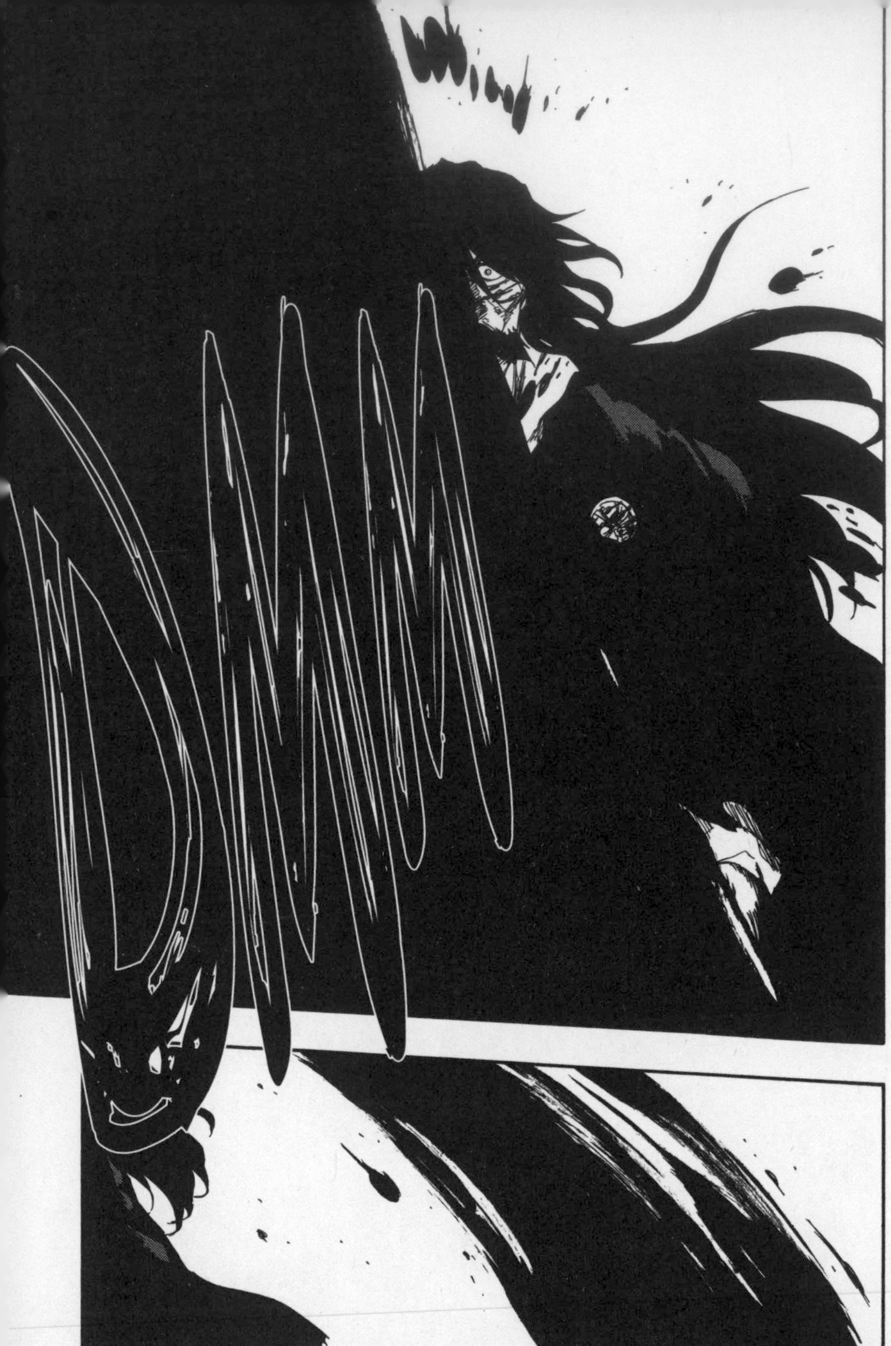

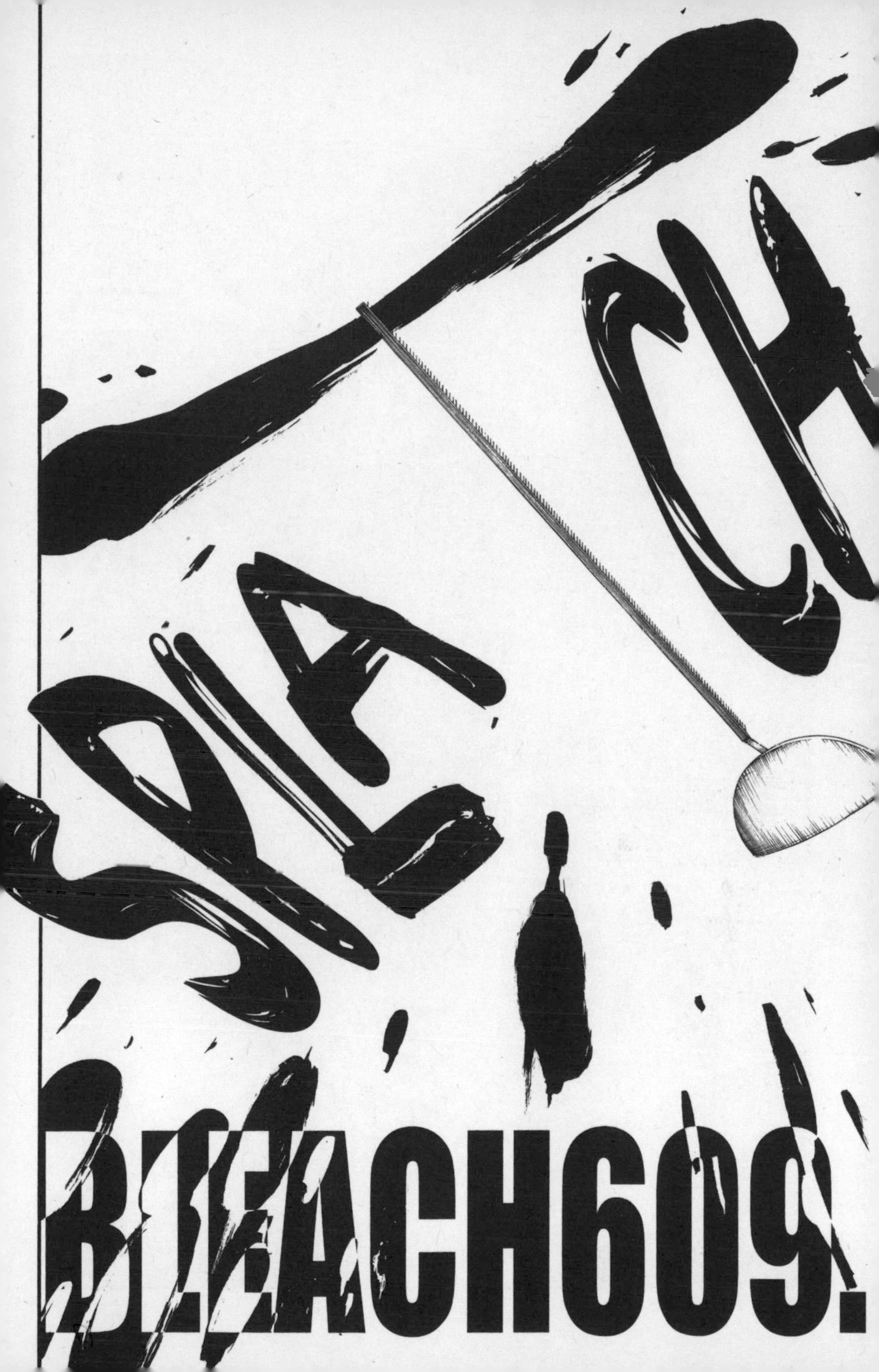
SPLATCH
BLEACH609.

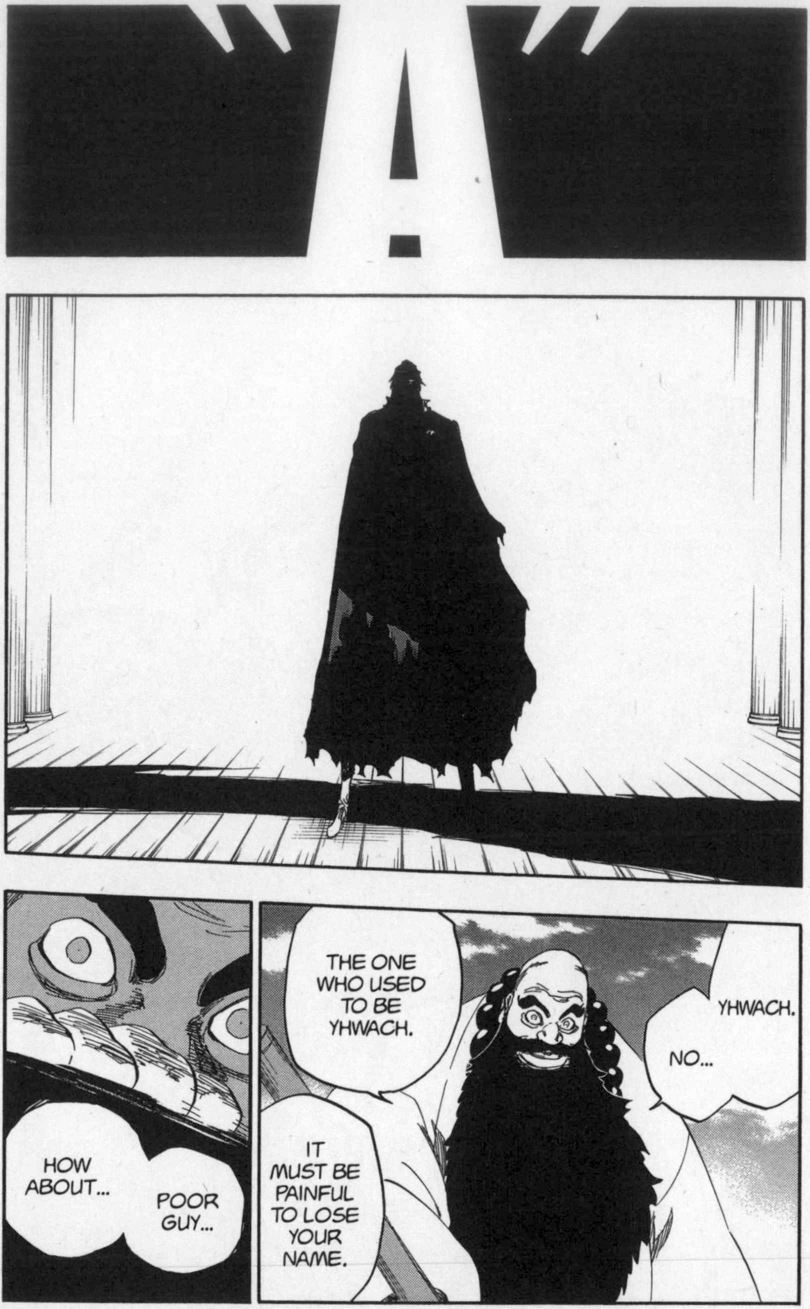
!
YHWACH.
NO...
THE ONE WHO USED TO BE YHWACH.
IT MUST BE PAINFUL TO LOSE YOUR NAME.
POOR GUY...
HOW ABOUT...

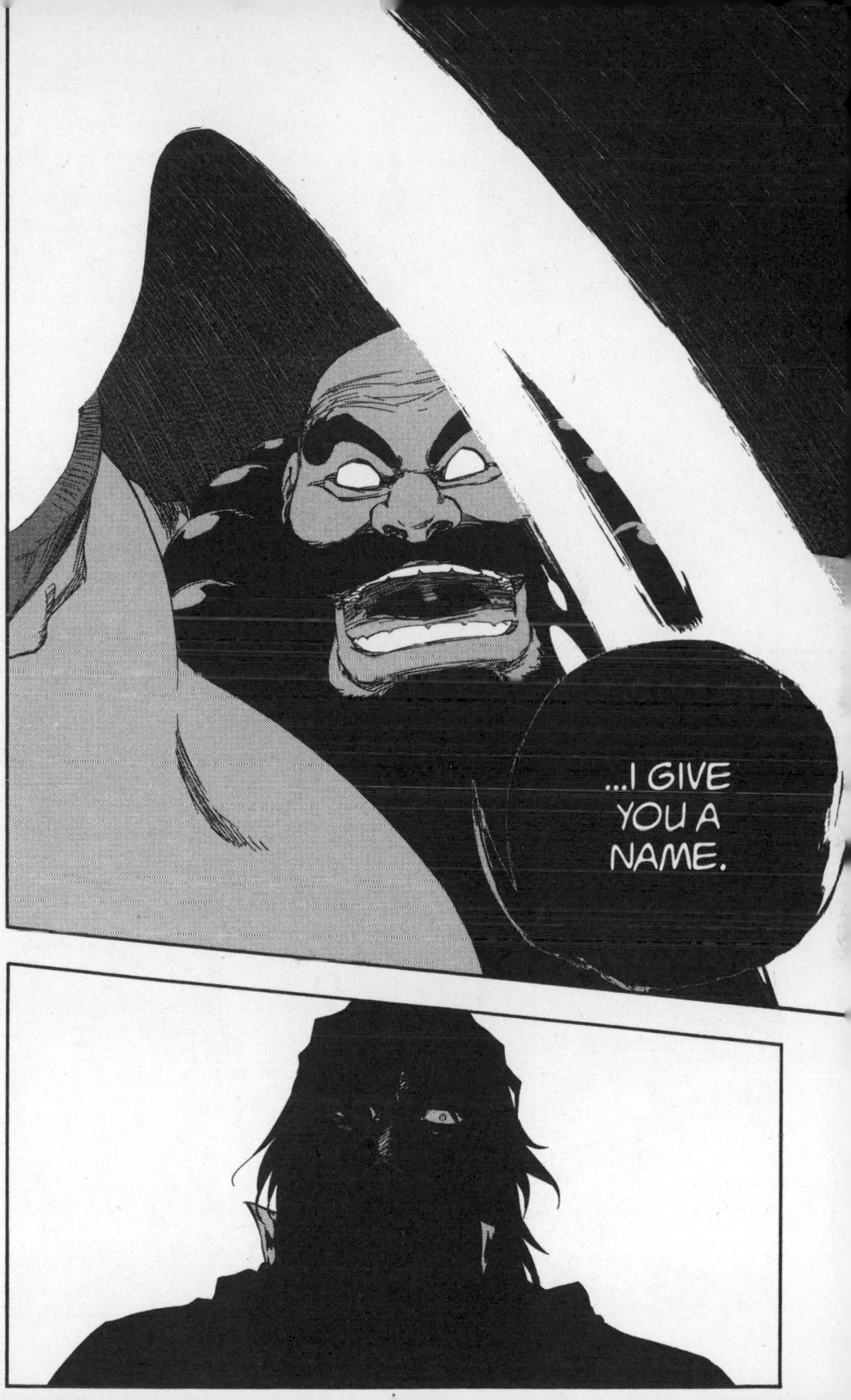
...I GIVE YOU A NAME.

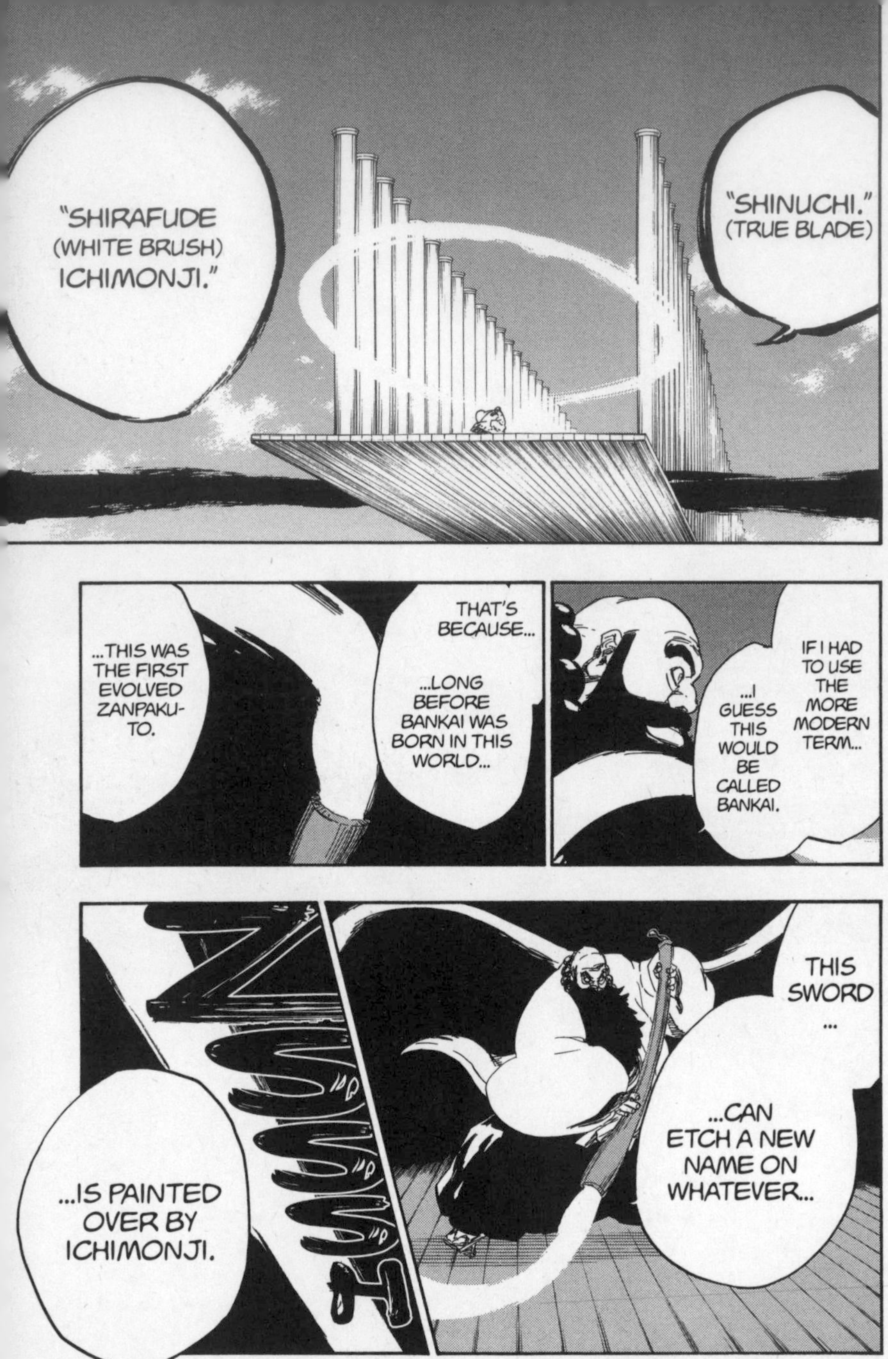
"SHINUCHI." (TRUE BLADE)
"SHIRAFUDE (WHITE BRUSH) ICHIMONJI."
IF I HAD TO USE THE MORE MODERN TERM...
...I GUESS THIS WOULD BE CALLED BANKAI.
THAT'S BECAUSE...
...LONG BEFORE BANKAI WAS BORN IN THIS WORLD...
...THIS WAS THE FIRST EVOLVED ZANPAKU-TO.
THIS SWORD ...
...CAN ETCH A NEW NAME ON WHATEVER...
...IS PAINTED OVER BY ICHIMONJI.

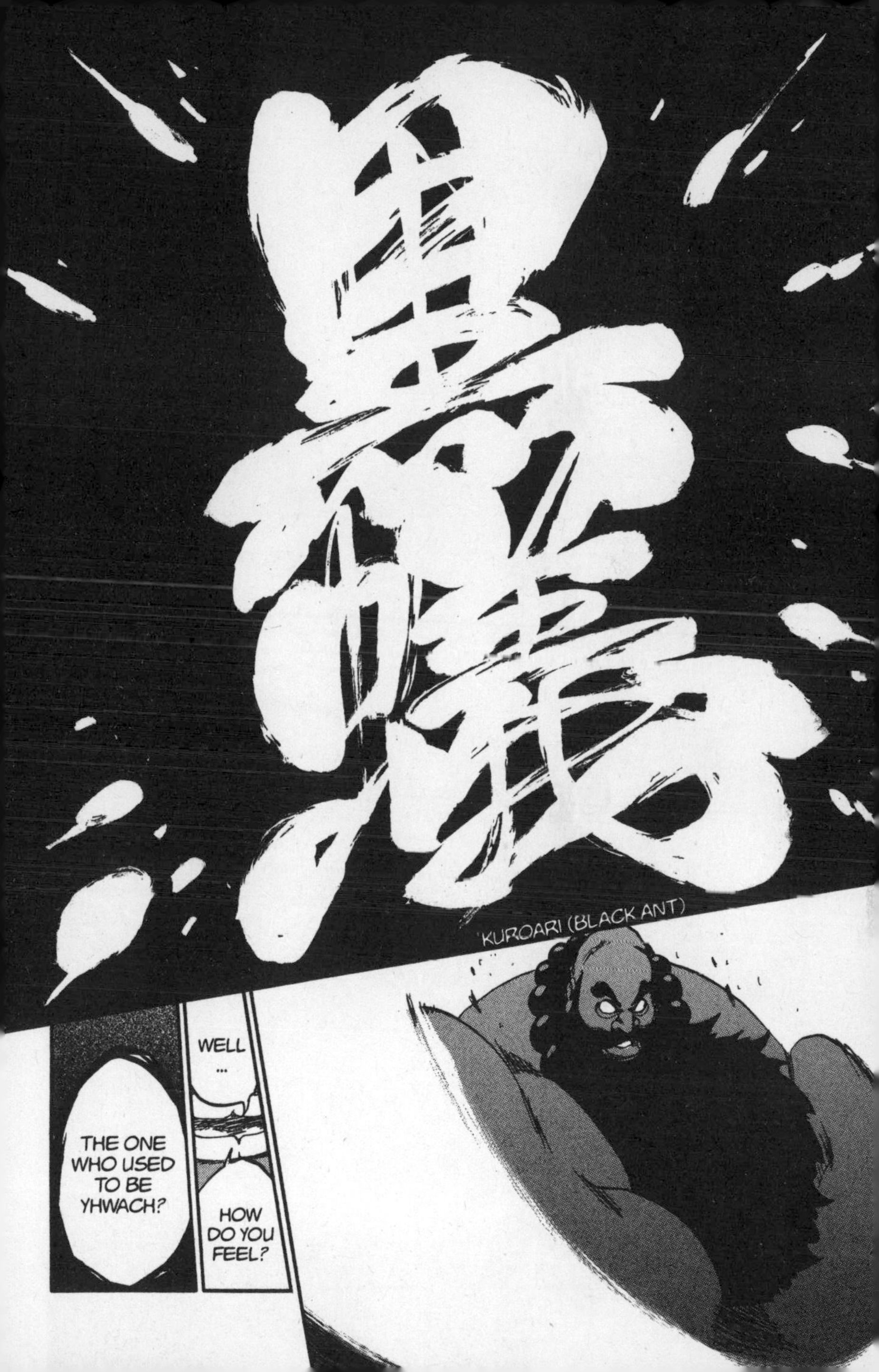

黒蟻
*KUROARI (BLACK ANT)
WELL ...
HOW DO YOU FEEL?
THE ONE WHO USED TO BE YHWACH?

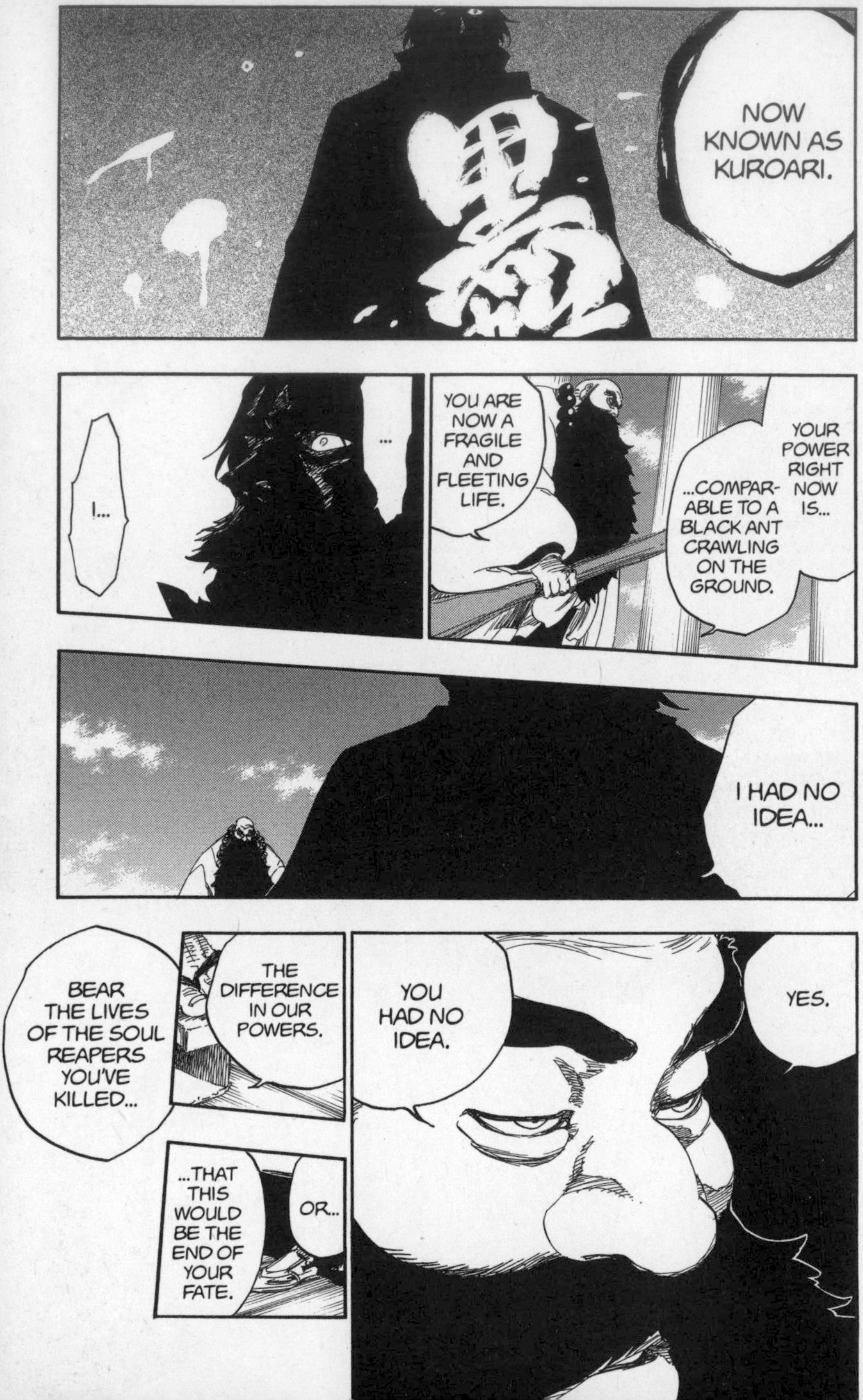
NOW KNOWN AS KUROARI.
YOUR POWER RIGHT NOW IS...
...COMPARABLE TO A BLACK ANT CRAWLING ON THE GROUND.
YOU ARE NOW A FRAGILE AND FLEETING LIFE.
...
I...
I HAD NO IDEA...
YES.
YOU HAD NO IDEA.
THE DIFFERENCE IN OUR POWERS.
BEAR THE LIVES OF THE SOUL REAPERS YOU'VE KILLED...
OR...
...THAT THIS WOULD BE THE END OF YOUR FATE.

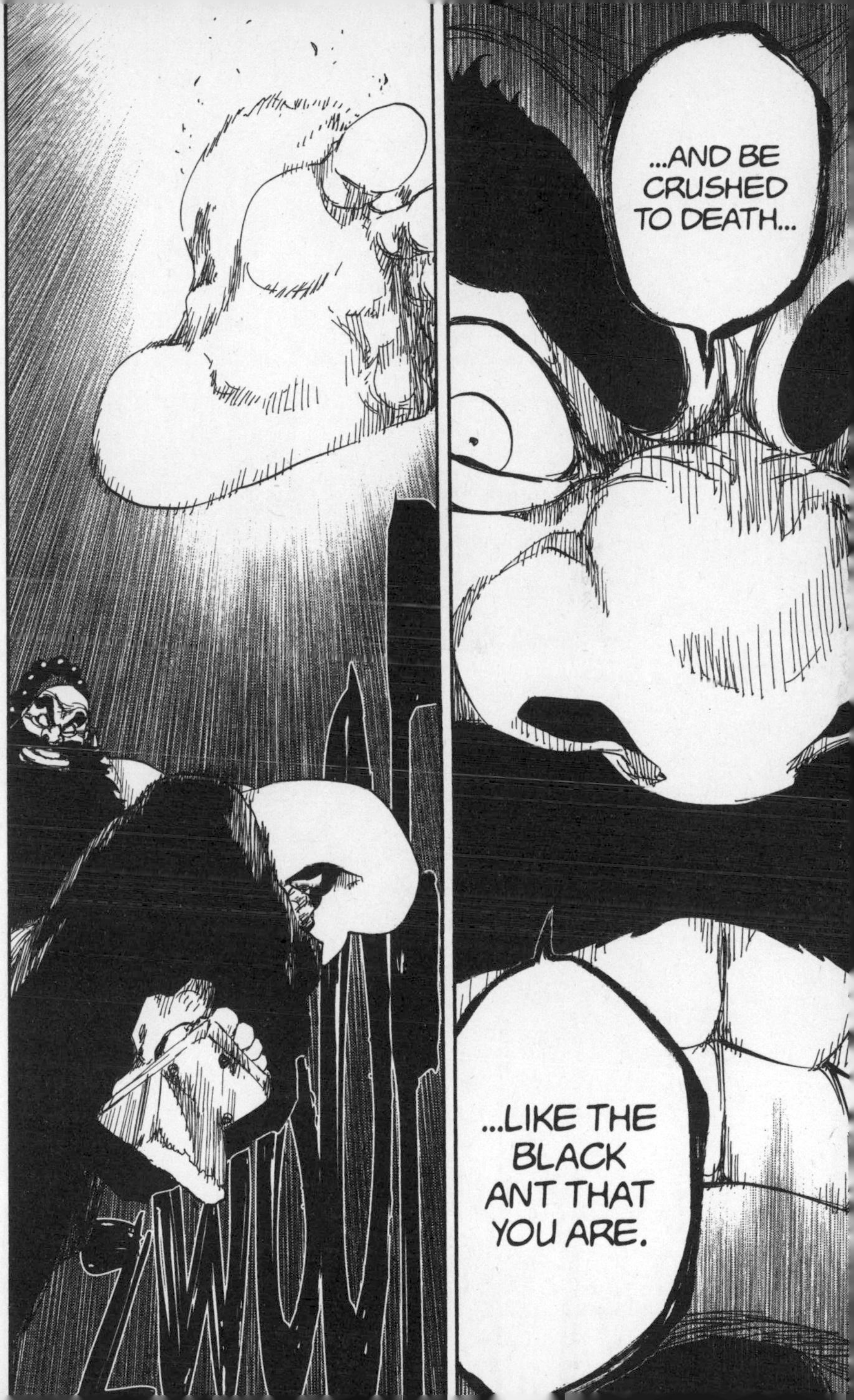
...AND BE CRUSHED TO DEATH...
...LIKE THE BLACK ANT THAT YOU ARE.

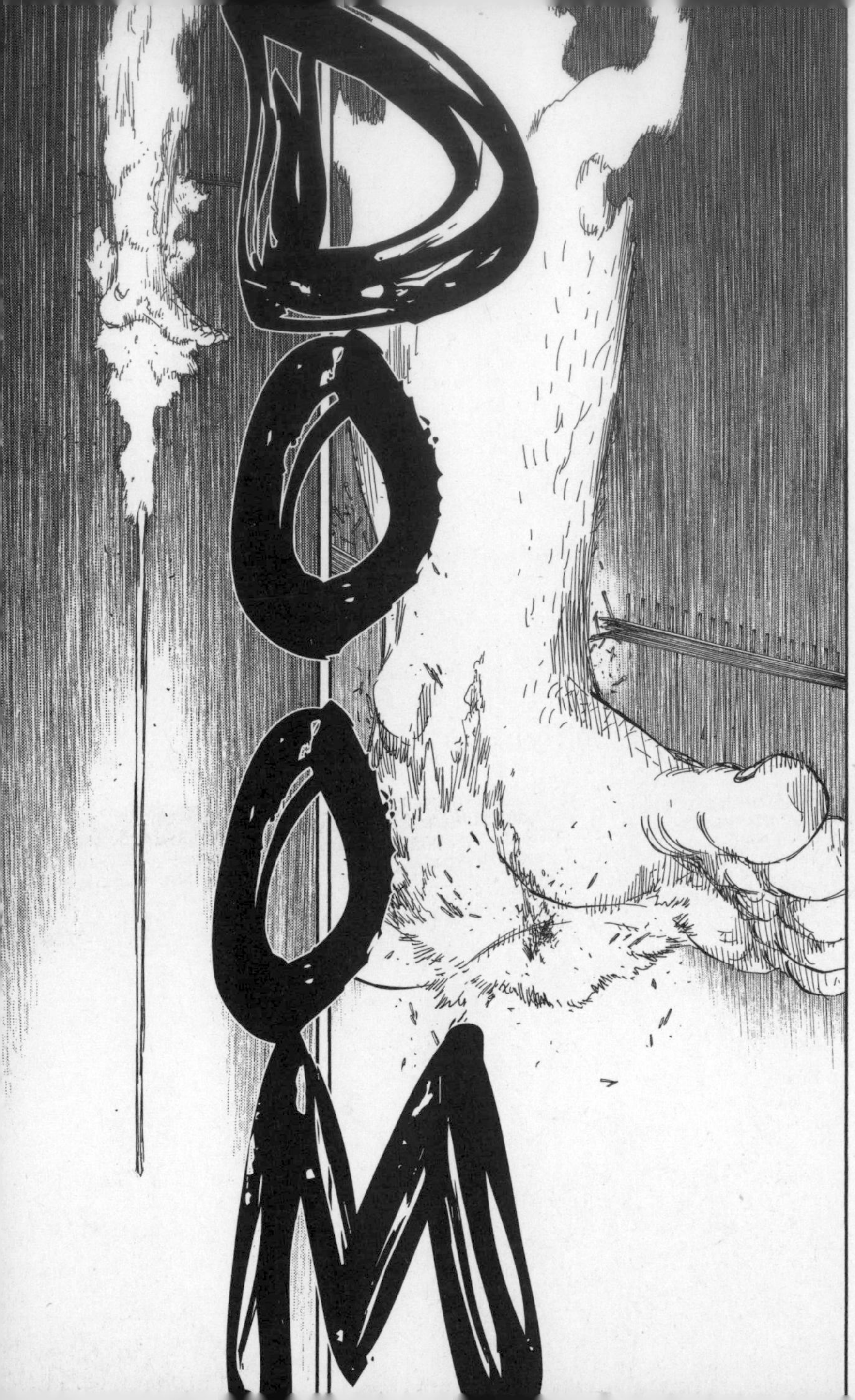
DOOM

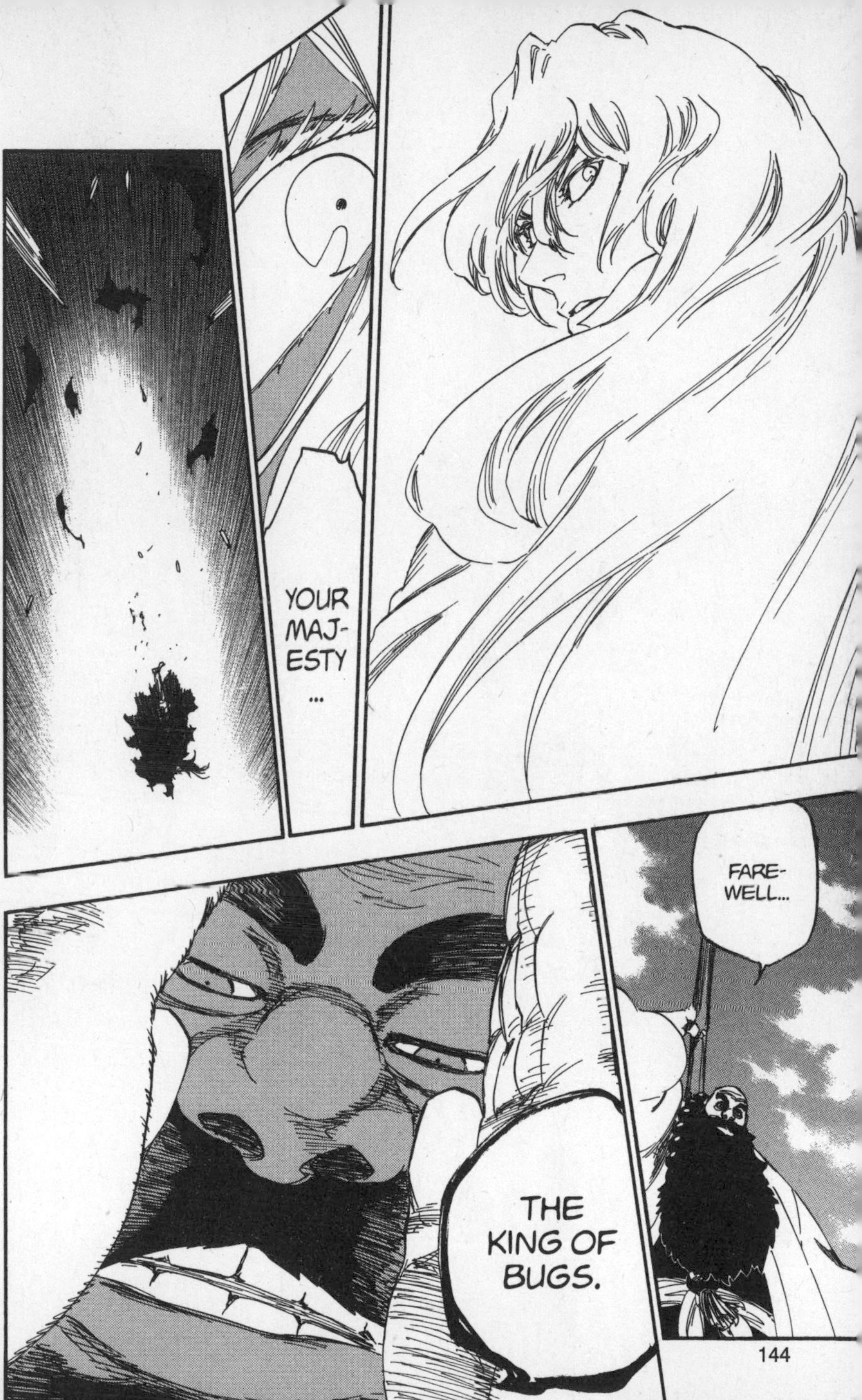
YOUR MAJ-ESTY ...
FARE-WELL...
THE KING OF BUGS.

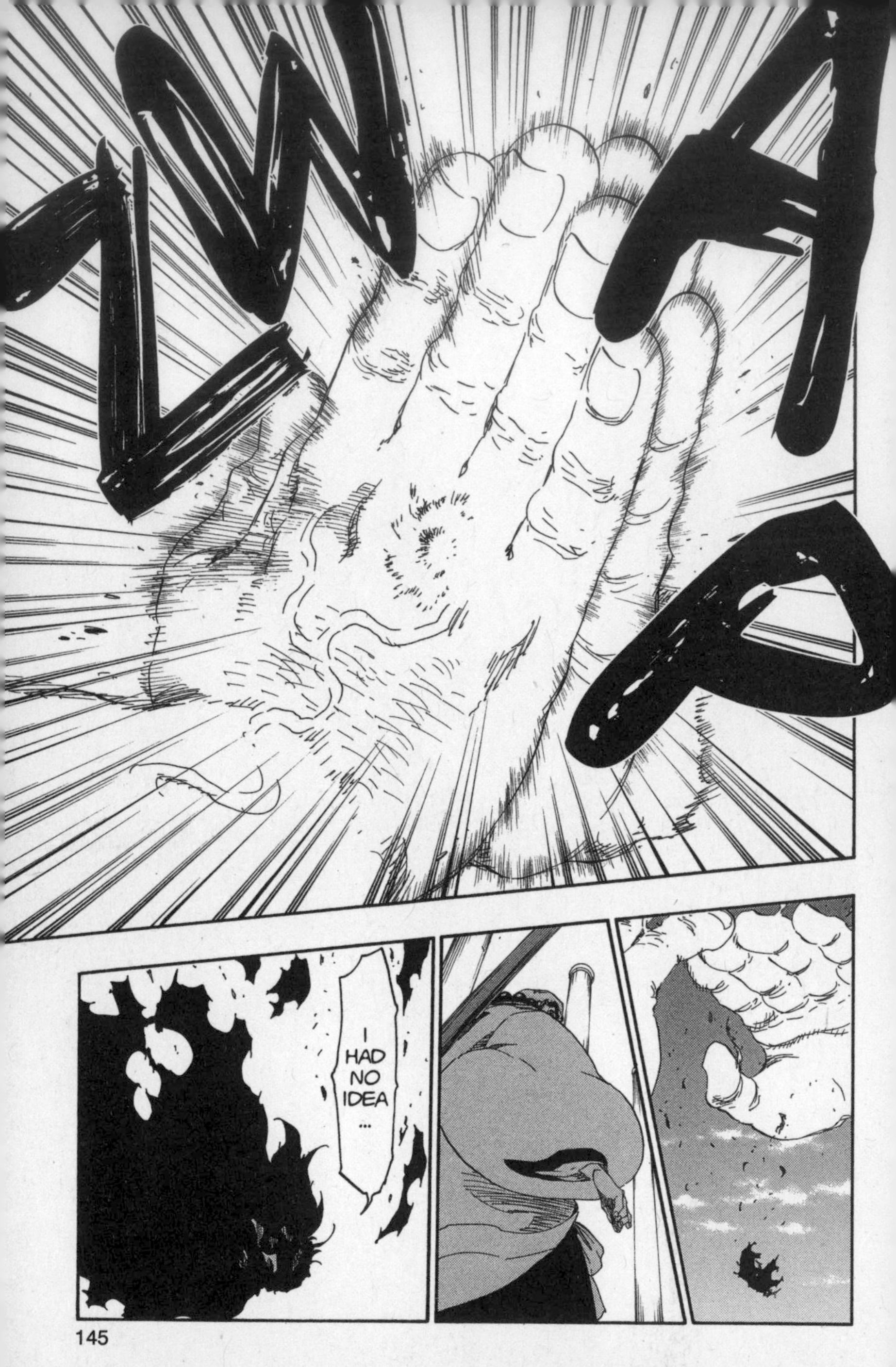
ZWAP
I HAD NO IDEA ...

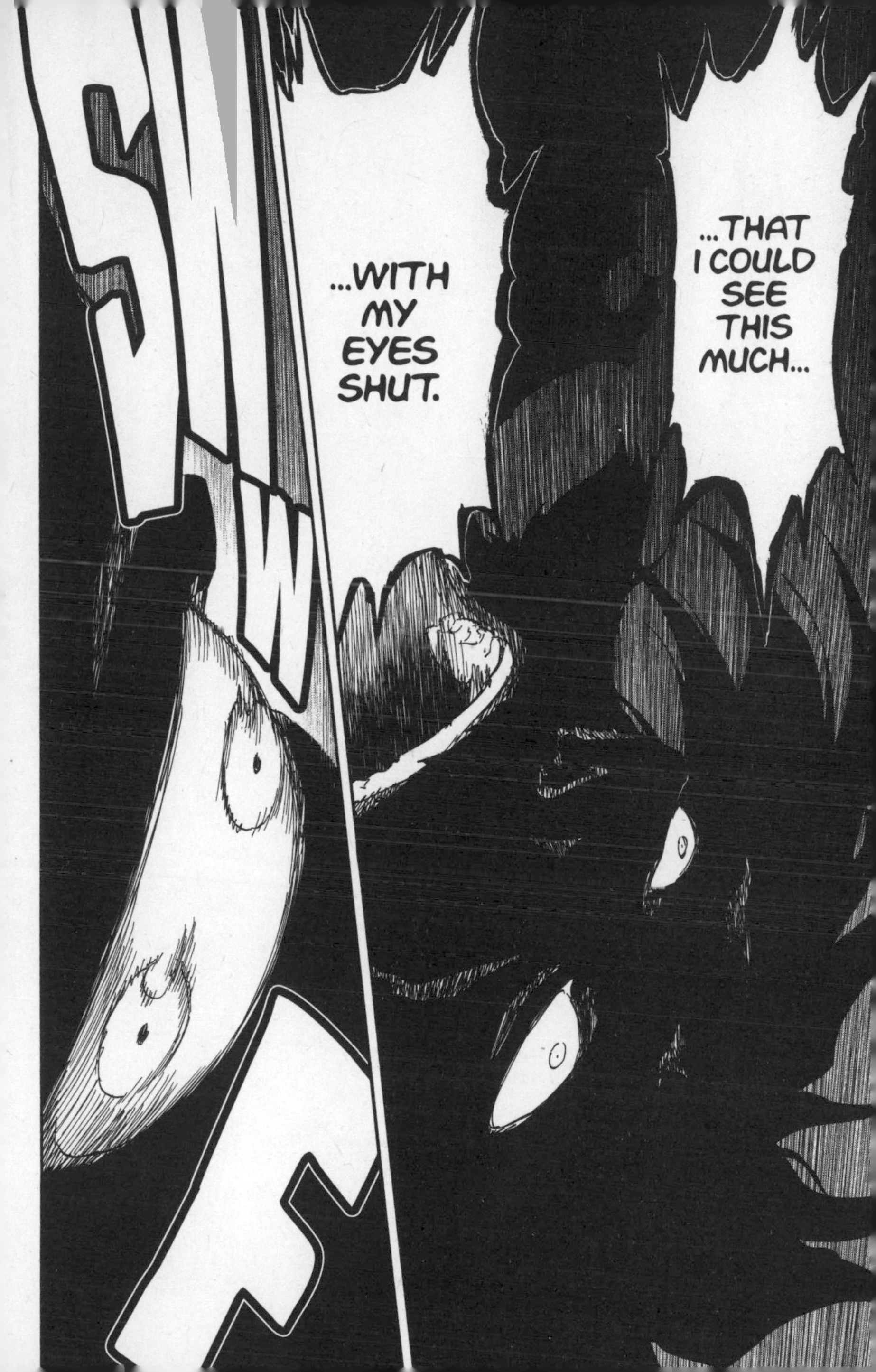
...THAT I COULD SEE THIS MUCH...
...WITH MY EYES SHUT.

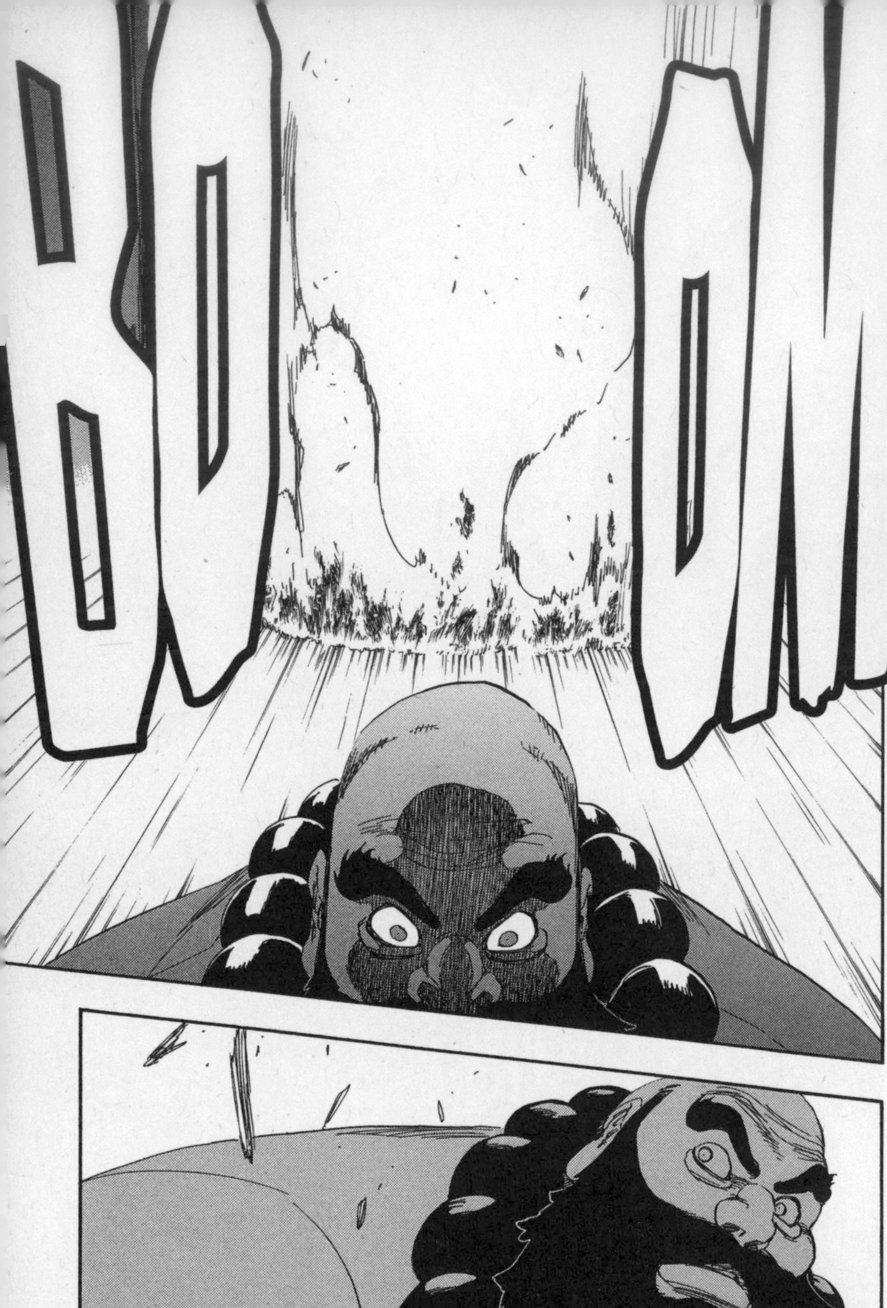
BOOM

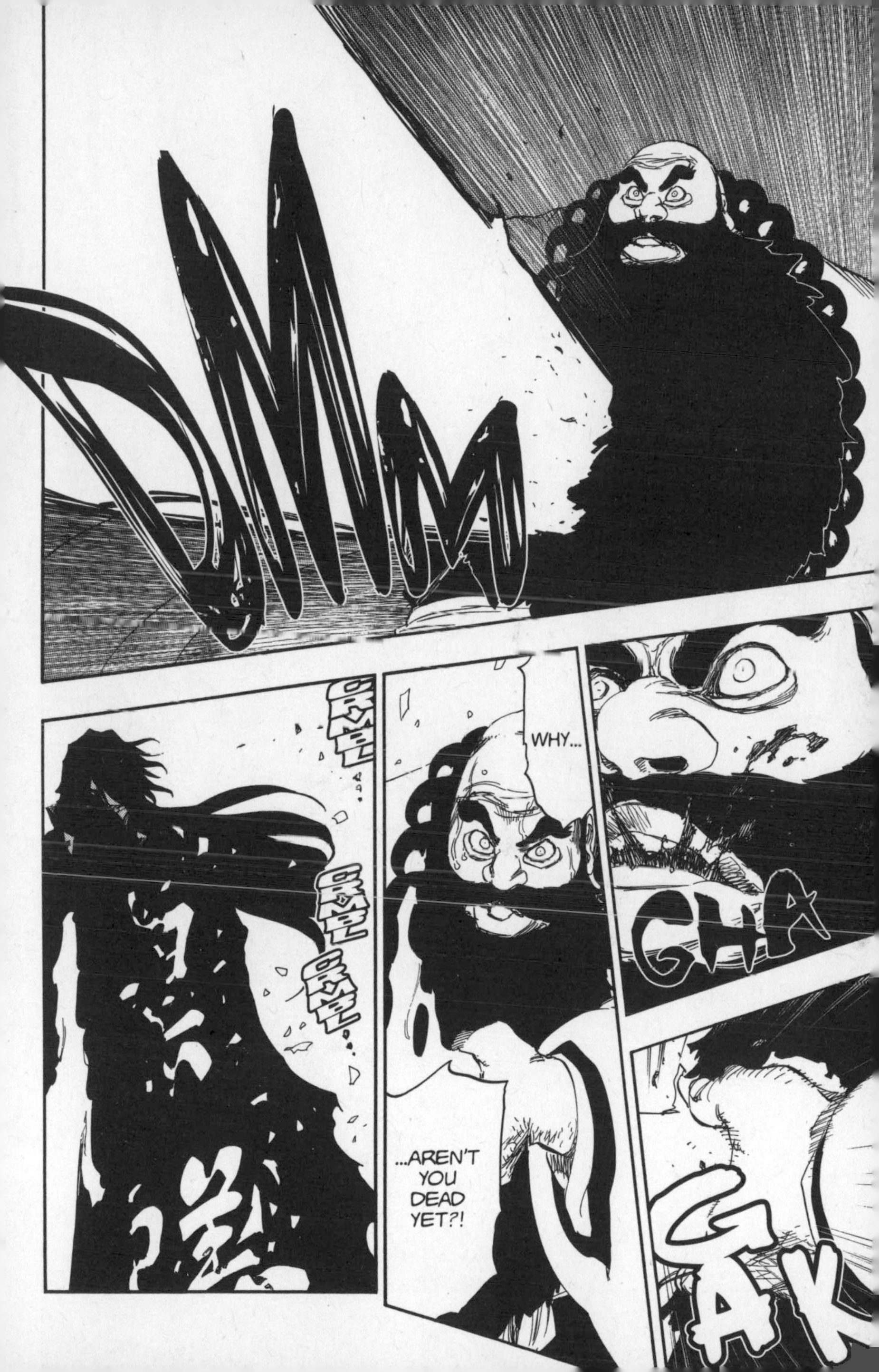
GCHA
GAK
WHY...
...AREN'T YOU DEAD YET?!
CRMBL
CRMBL
CRMBL

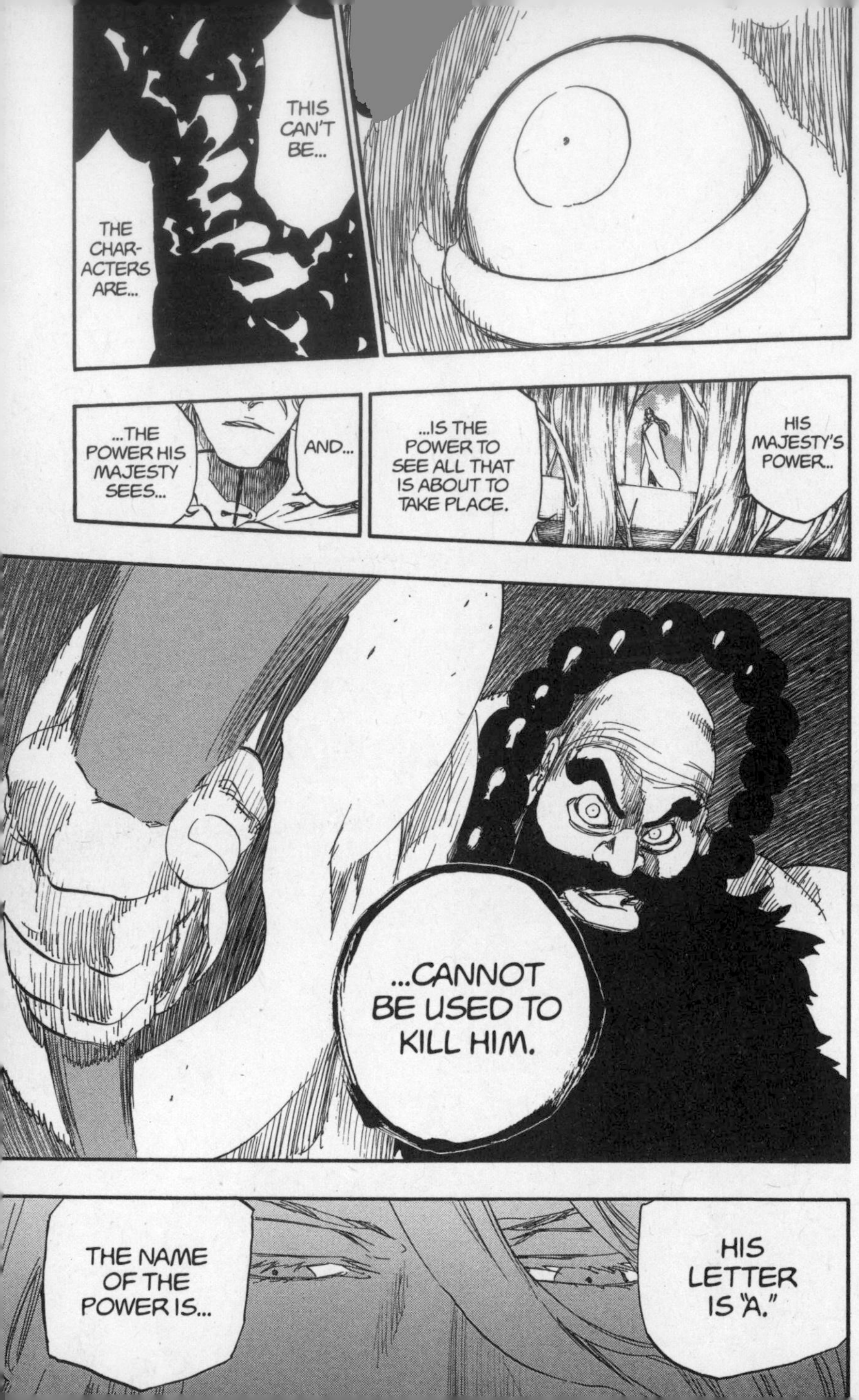
THIS CAN'T BE...
THE CHARACTERS ARE...
HIS MAJESTY'S POWER..
...IS THE POWER TO SEE ALL THAT IS ABOUT TO TAKE PLACE.
AND...
...THE POWER HIS MAJESTY SEES...
...CANNOT BE USED TO KILL HIM.
HIS LETTER IS "A."
THE NAME OF THE POWER IS...

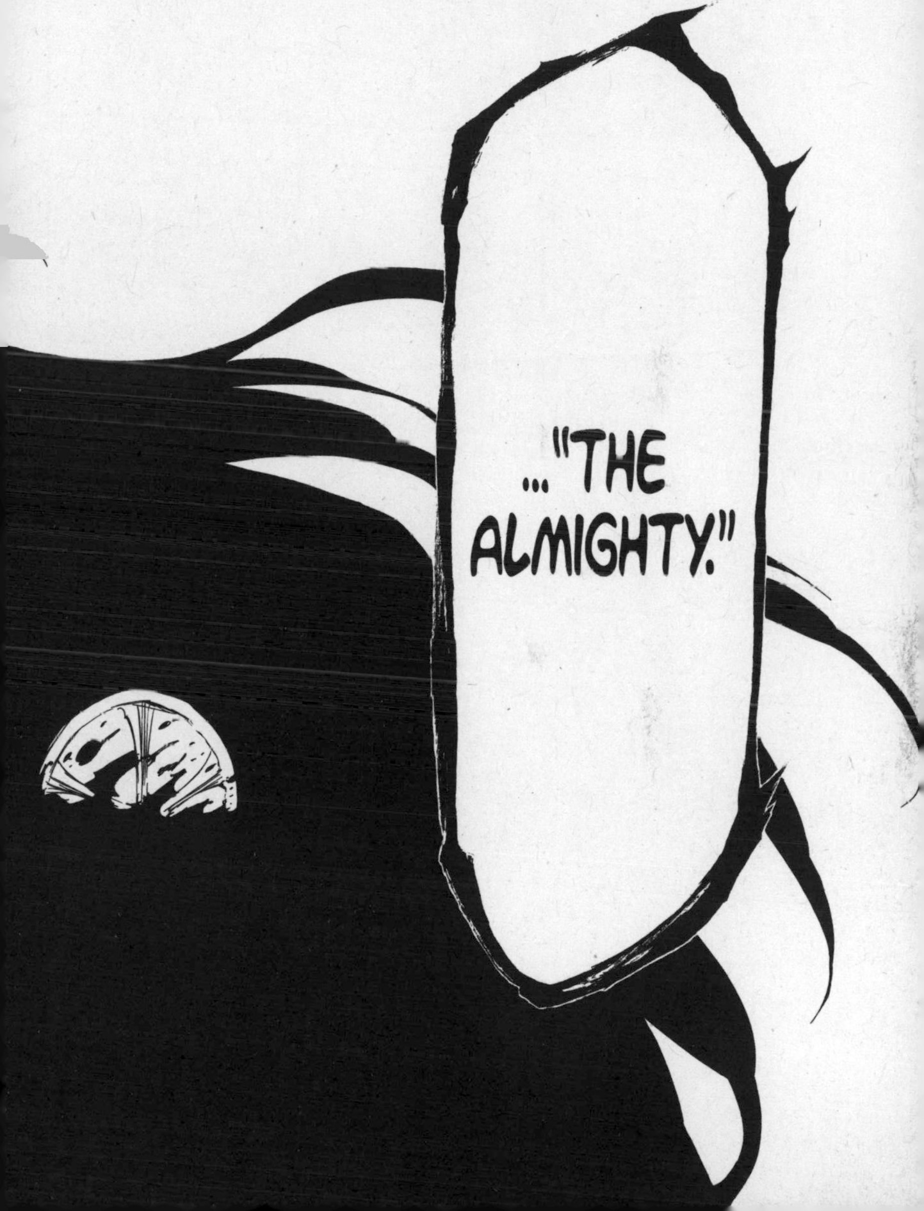
..."THE ALMIGHTY."

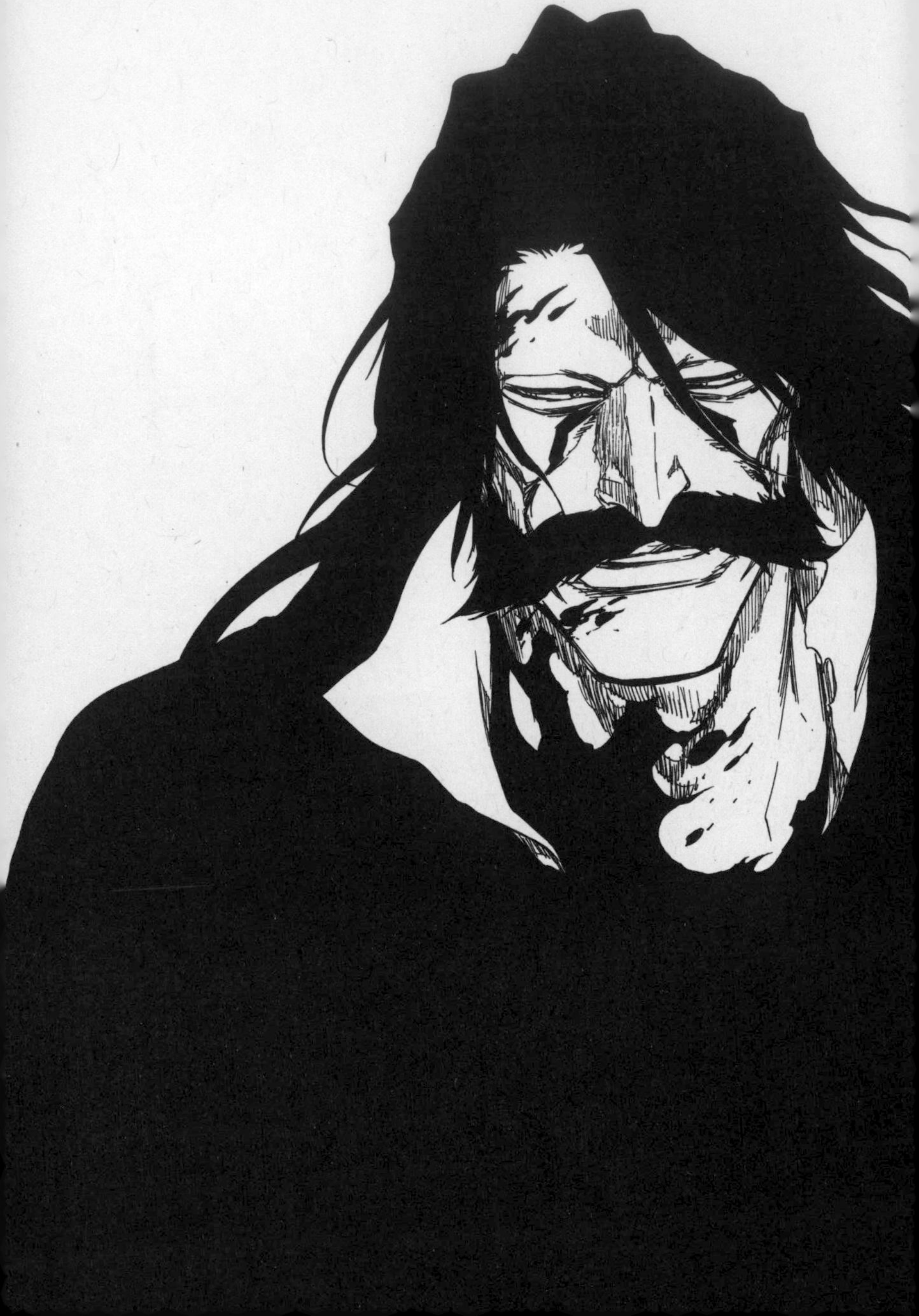

殺

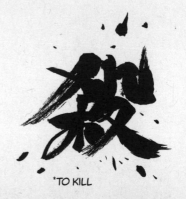

*TO KILL

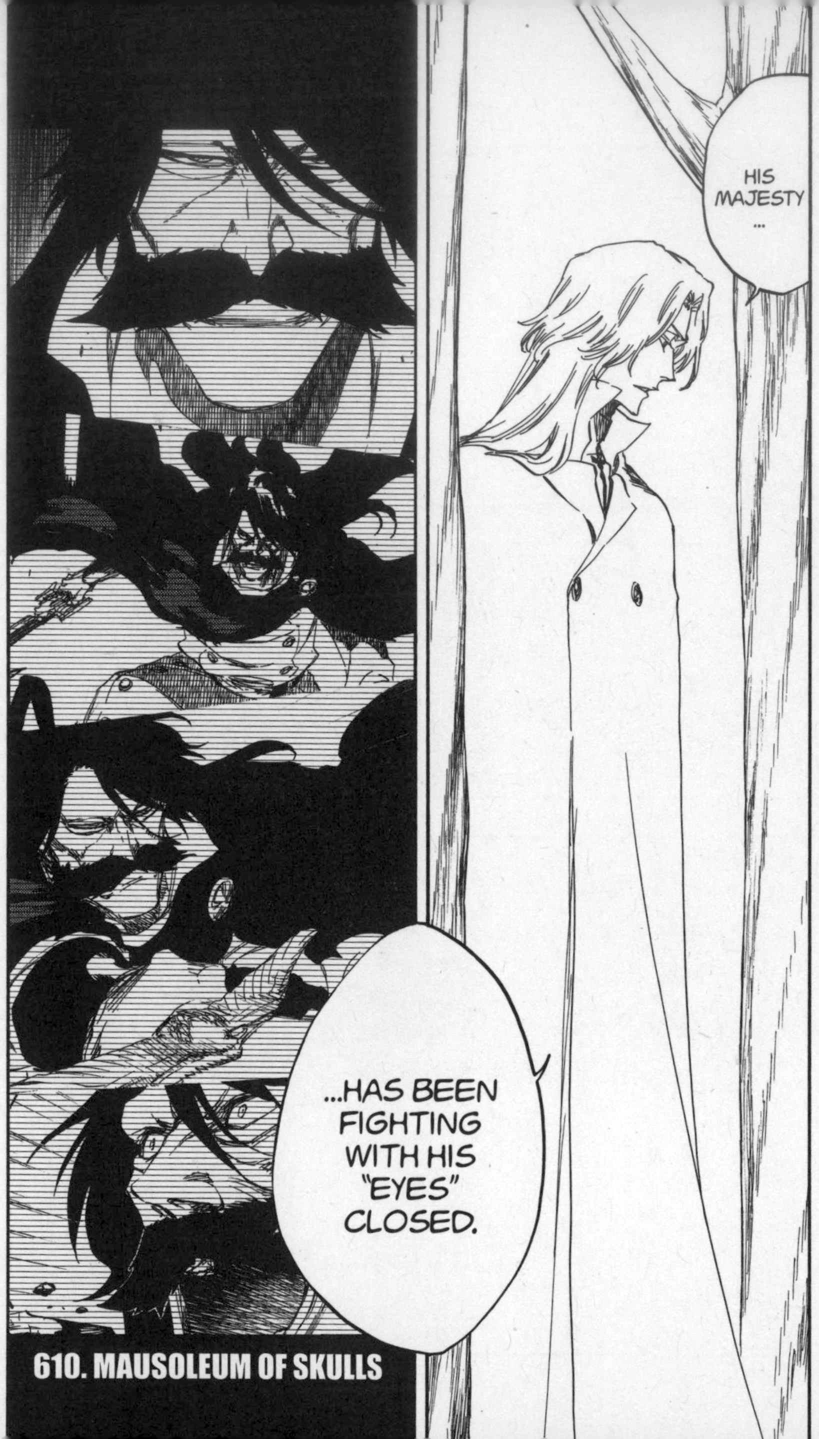
HIS MAJESTY ...
...HAS BEEN FIGHTING WITH HIS "EYES" CLOSED.
610. MAUSOLEUM OF SKULLS

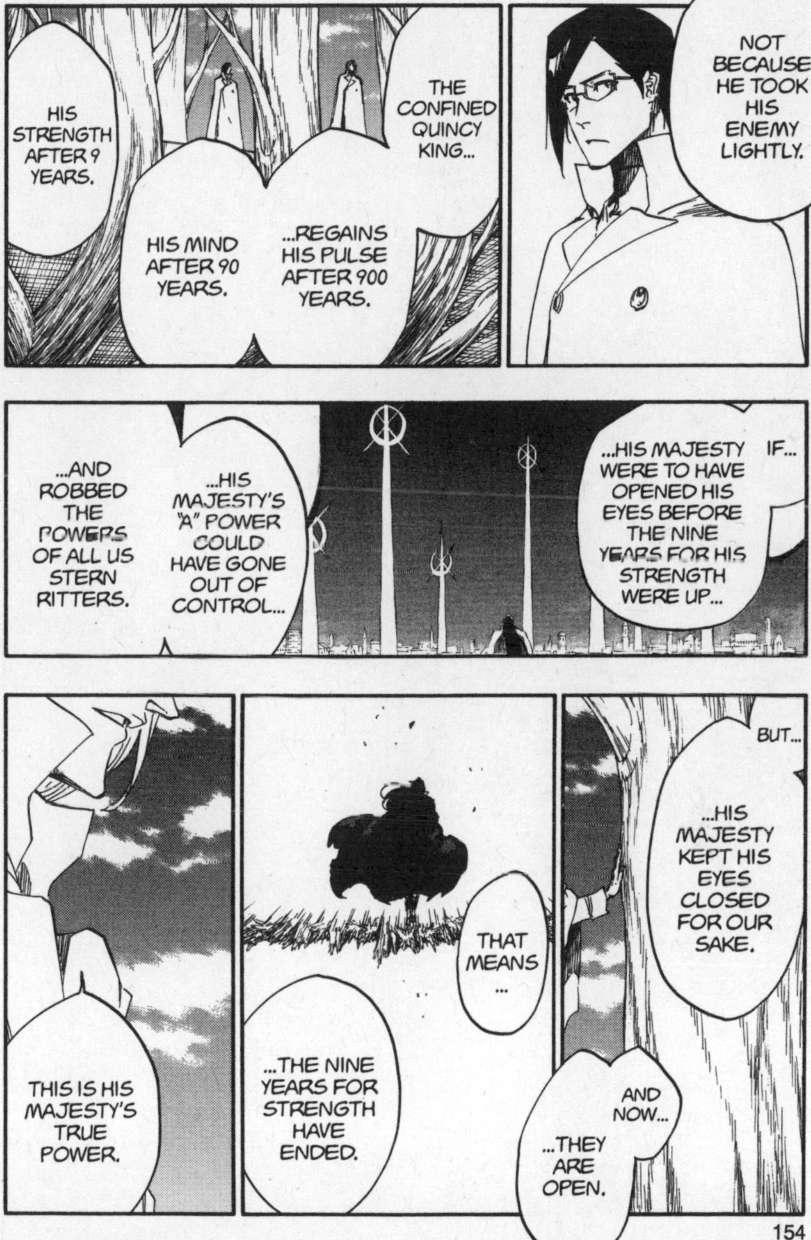
NOT BECAUSE HE TOOK HIS ENEMY LIGHTLY.
THE CONFINED QUINCY KING...
...REGAINS HIS PULSE AFTER 900 YEARS.
HIS MIND AFTER 90 YEARS.
HIS STRENGTH AFTER 9 YEARS.
IF...
...HIS MAJESTY WERE TO HAVE OPENED HIS EYES BEFORE THE NINE YEARS FOR HIS STRENGTH WERE UP...
...HIS MAJESTY'S "A" POWER COULD HAVE GONE OUT OF CONTROL...
...AND ROBBED THE POWERS OF ALL US STERN RITTERS.
BUT...
...HIS MAJESTY KEPT HIS EYES CLOSED FOR OUR SAKE.
AND NOW...
...THEY ARE OPEN.
THAT MEANS...
...THE NINE YEARS FOR STRENGTH HAVE ENDED.
THIS IS HIS MAJESTY'S TRUE POWER.

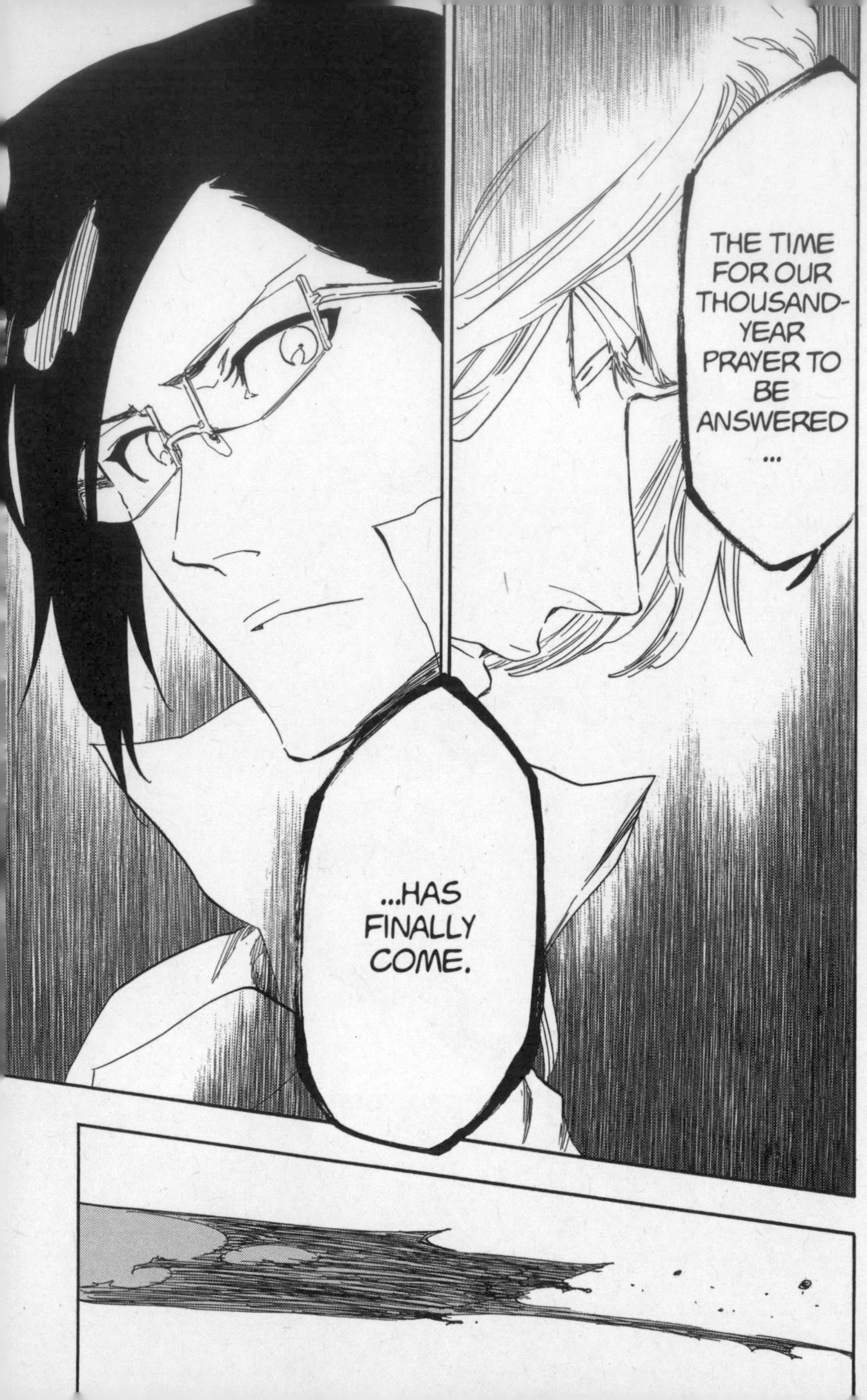
THE TIME FOR OUR THOUSAND-YEAR PRAYER TO BE ANSWERED ...
...HAS FINALLY COME.

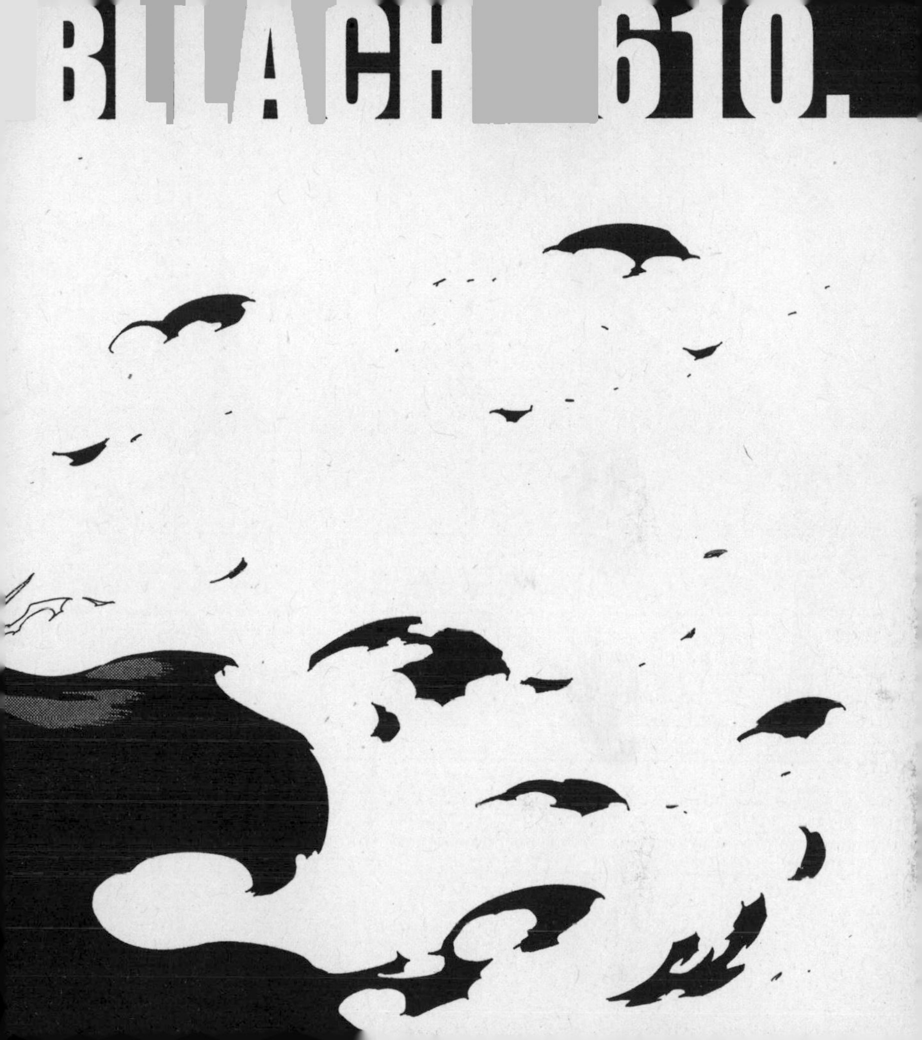
610.

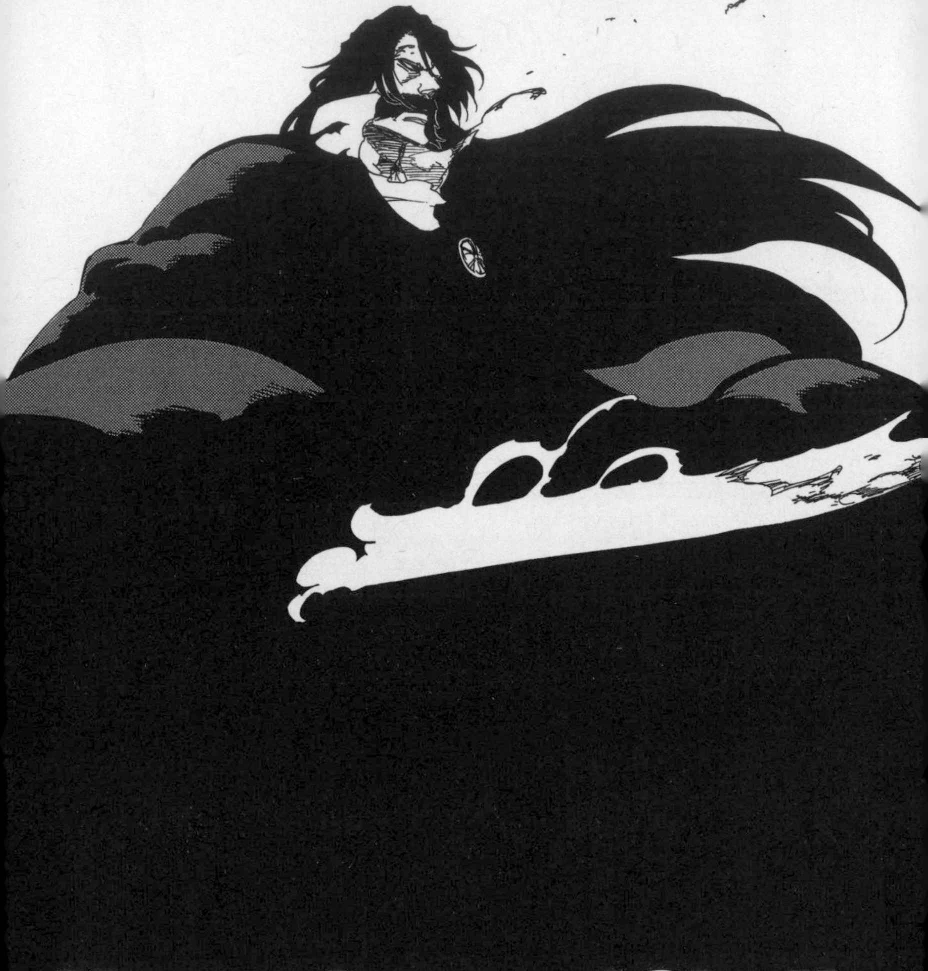

Mausoleum of Skulls

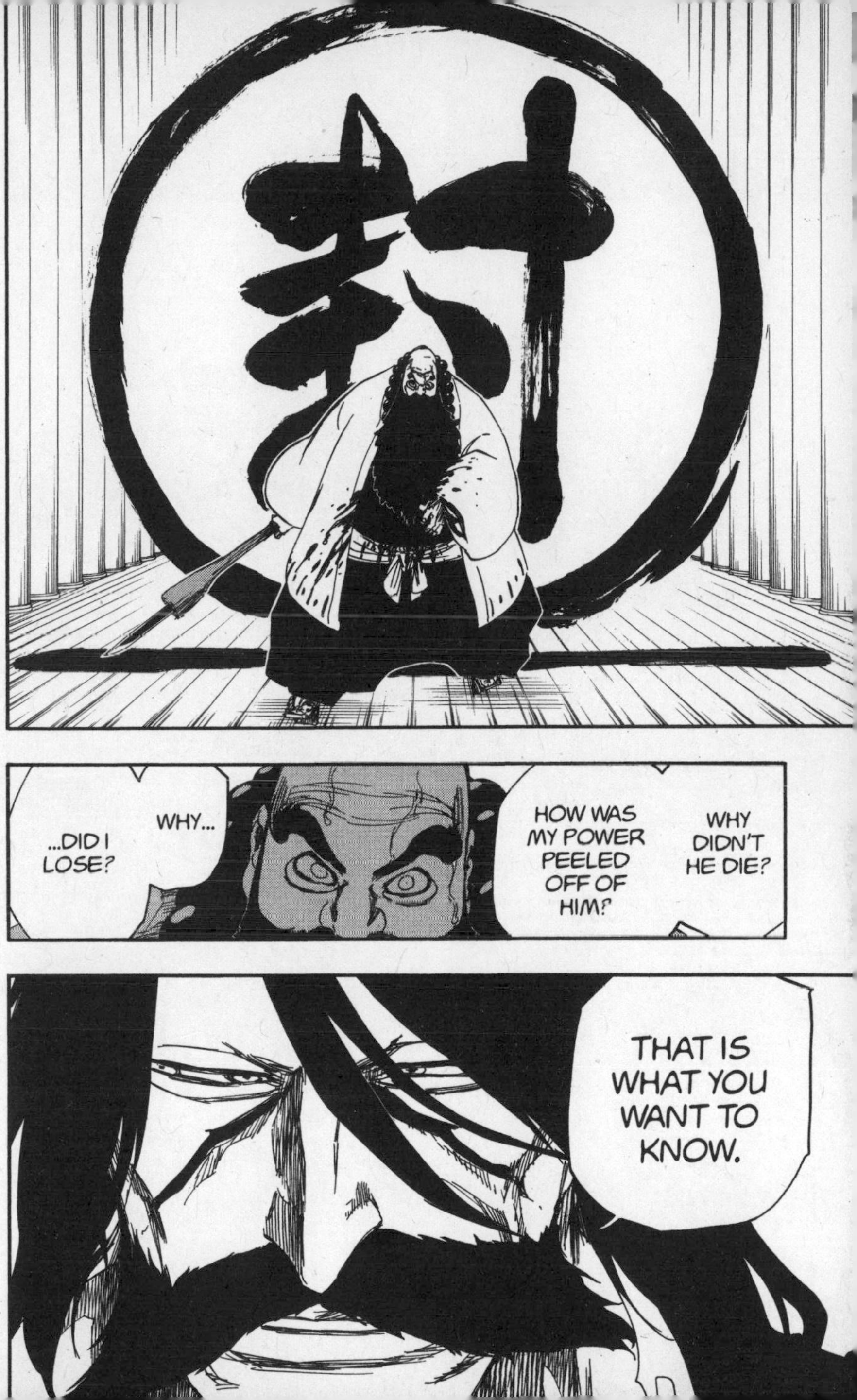
WHY DIDN'T HE DIE?
HOW WAS MY POWER PEELED OFF OF HIM?
WHY...
...DID I LOSE?
THAT IS WHAT YOU WANT TO KNOW.

READ THIS WAY

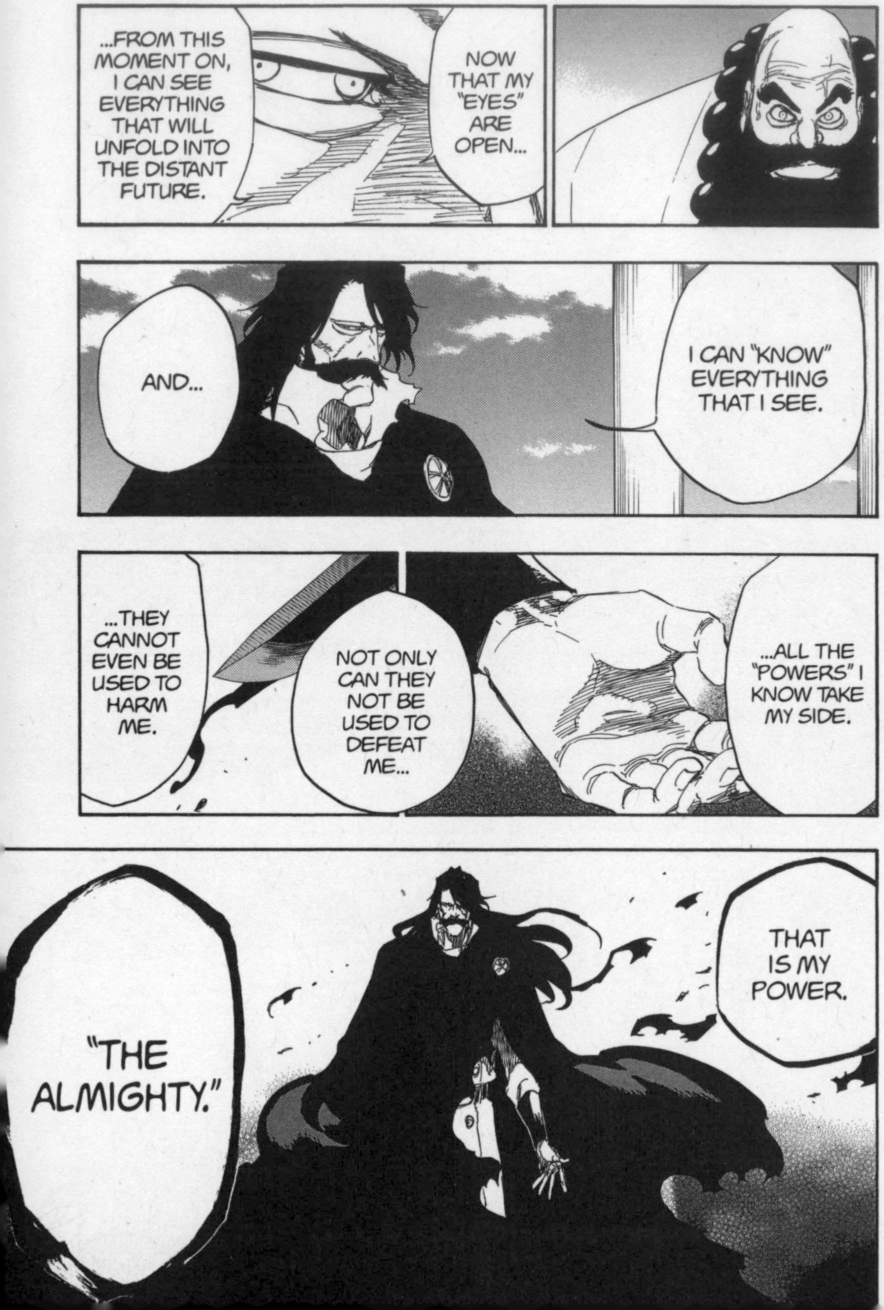
NOW THAT MY "EYES" ARE OPEN...
...FROM THIS MOMENT ON, I CAN SEE EVERYTHING THAT WILL UNFOLD INTO THE DISTANT FUTURE.
I CAN "KNOW" EVERYTHING THAT I SEE.
AND...
...ALL THE "POWERS" I KNOW TAKE MY SIDE.
NOT ONLY CAN THEY NOT BE USED TO DEFEAT ME...
...THEY CANNOT EVEN BE USED TO HARM ME.
THAT IS MY POWER.
"THE ALMIGHTY."

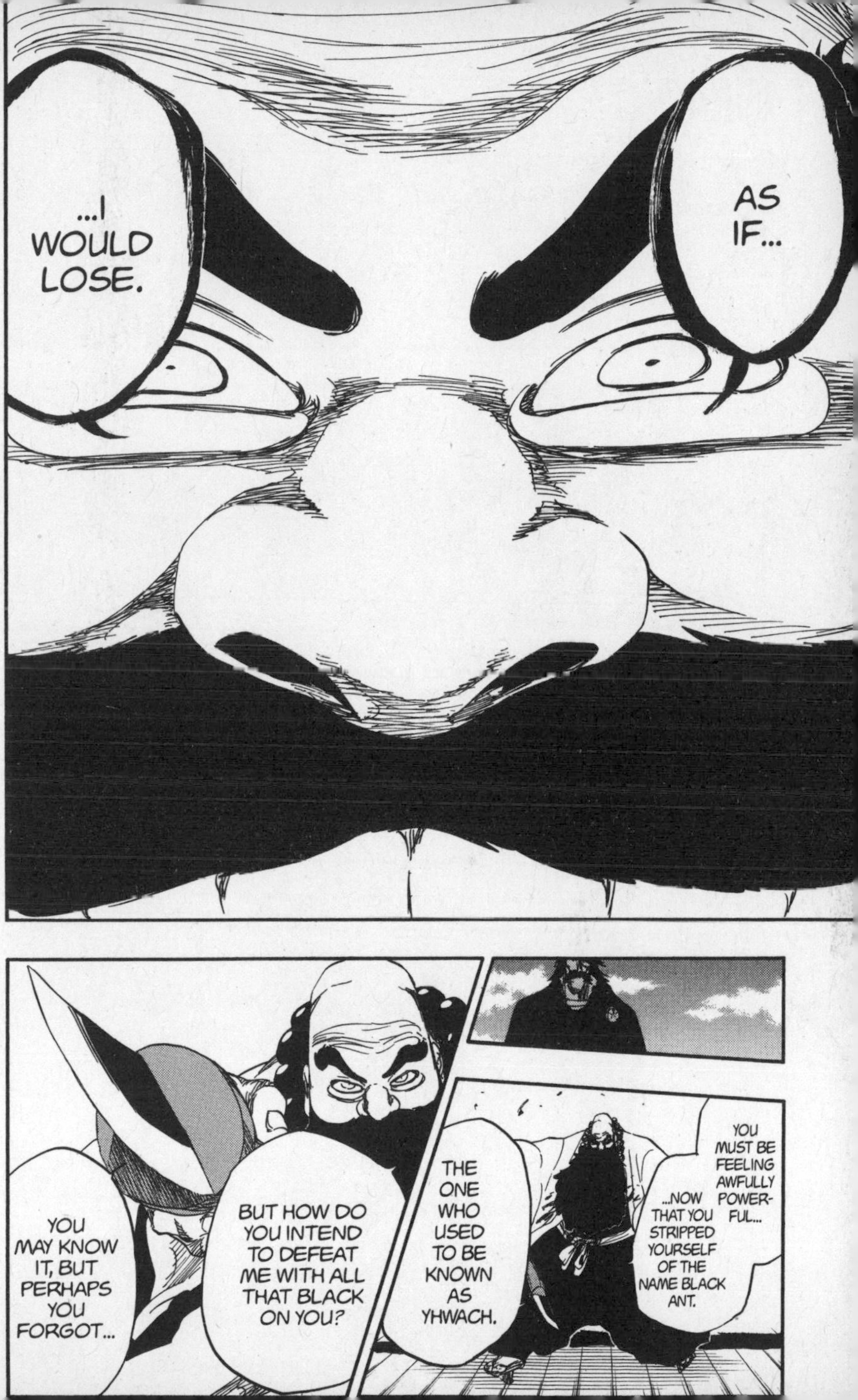
AS IF...
...I WOULD LOSE.
YOU MUST BE FEELING AWFULLY POWERFUL...
...NOW THAT YOU STRIPPED YOURSELF OF THE NAME BLACK ANT.
THE ONE WHO USED TO BE KNOWN AS YHWACH.
BUT HOW DO YOU INTEND TO DEFEAT ME WITH ALL THAT BLACK ON YOU?
YOU MAY KNOW IT, BUT PERHAPS YOU FORGOT...

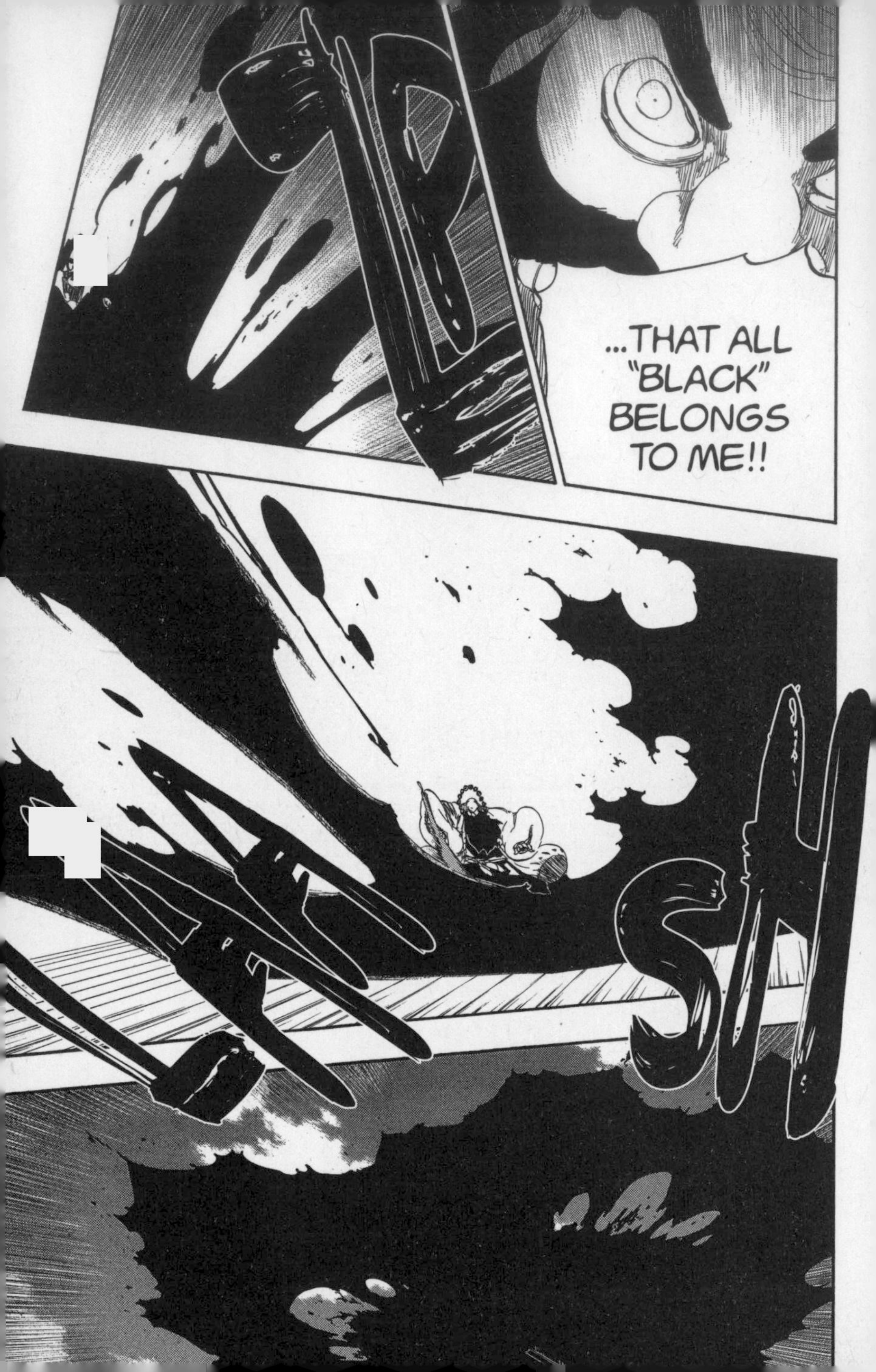
...THAT ALL "BLACK" BELONGS TO ME!!

HEY THERE, DUSK.

HEY THERE, EVERLASTING DARKNESS.

COME ON CLOSER...

SHOW YOURSELF AND HAVE A DRINK...

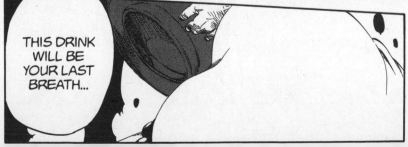

THIS DRINK WILL BE YOUR LAST BREATH...

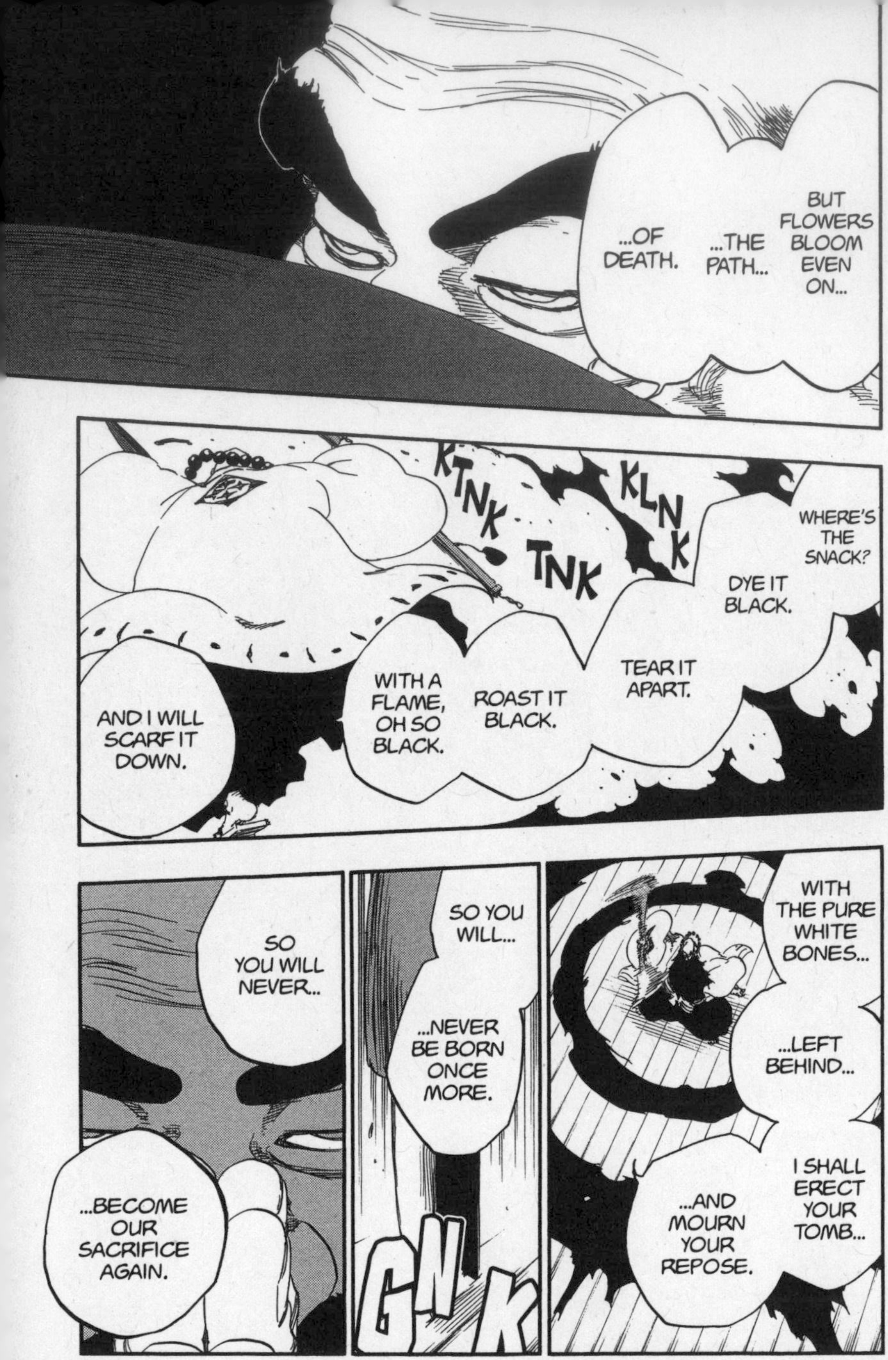
BUT FLOWERS BLOOM EVEN ON...
...THE PATH...
...OF DEATH.
KLNK
KTNK
TNK
WHERE'S THE SNACK?
DYE IT BLACK.
TEAR IT APART.
ROAST IT BLACK.
WITH A FLAME, OH SO BLACK.
AND I WILL SCARF IT DOWN.
WITH THE PURE WHITE BONES...
...LEFT BEHIND...
I SHALL ERECT YOUR TOMB...
...AND MOURN YOUR REPOSE.
SO YOU WILL...
...NEVER BE BORN ONCE MORE.
GNK
SO YOU WILL NEVER...
...BECOME OUR SACRIFICE AGAIN.

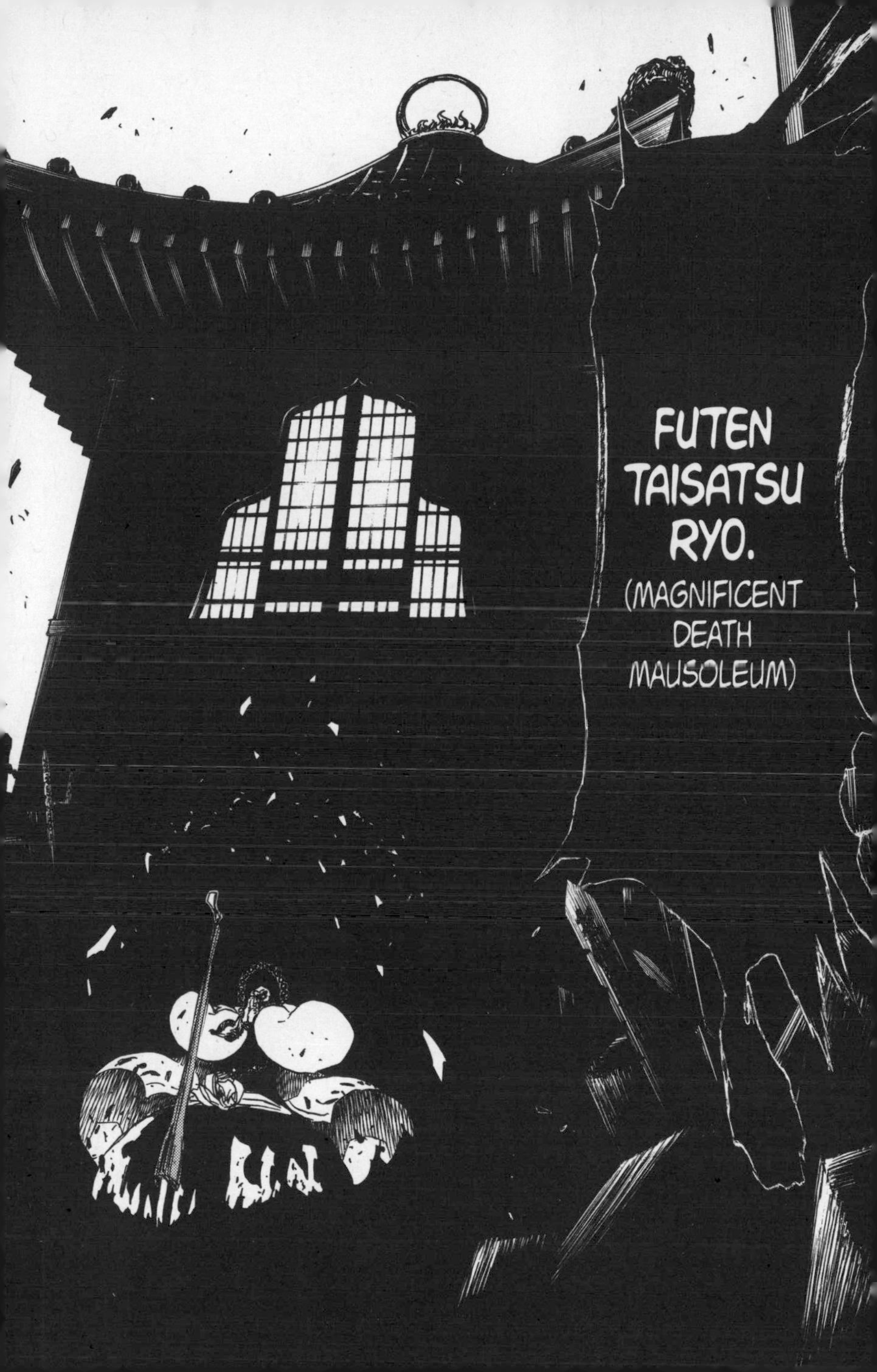
FUTEN TAISATSU RYO.
(MAGNIFICENT DEATH MAUSOLEUM)

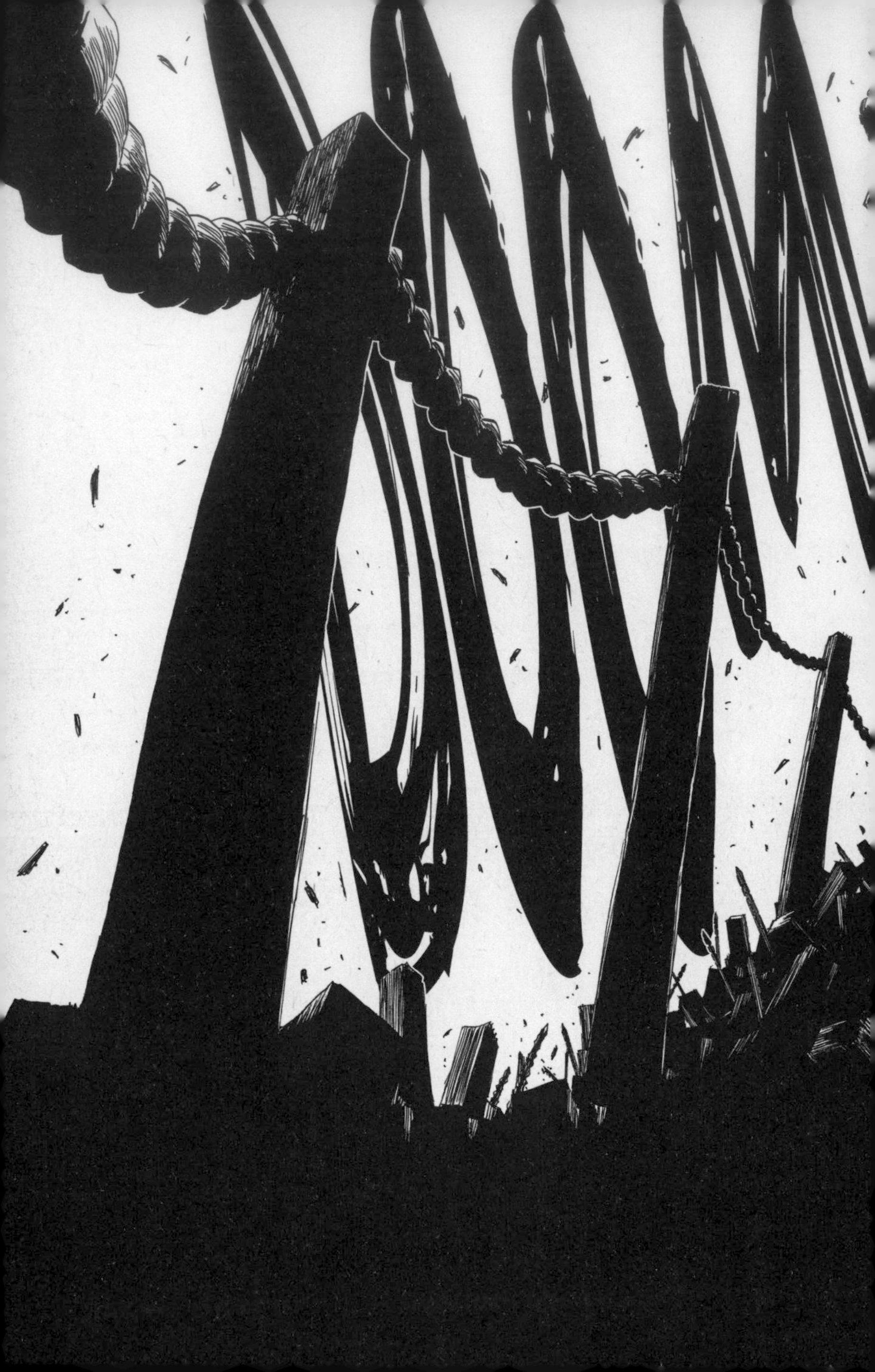

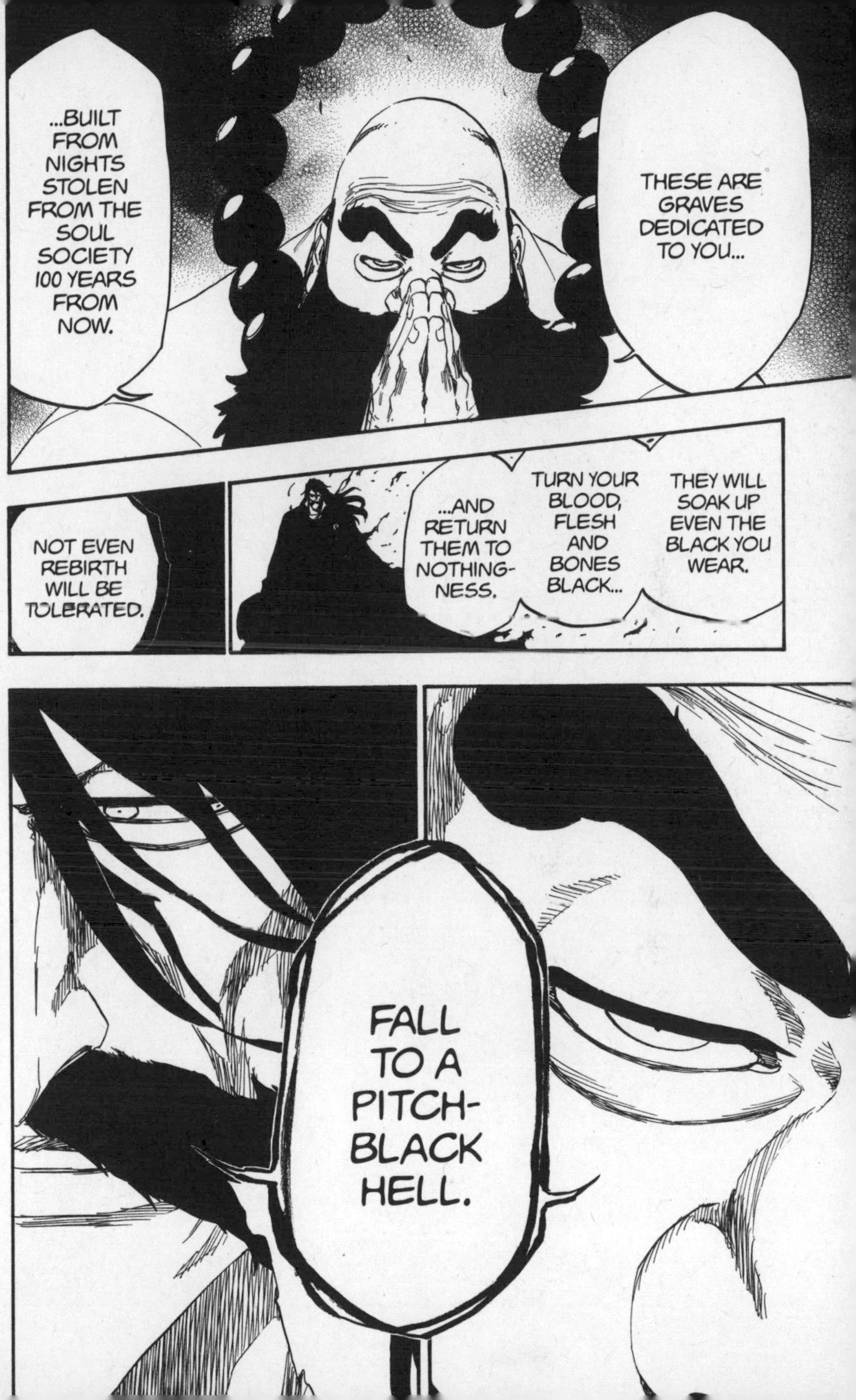
THESE ARE GRAVES DEDICATED TO YOU...
...BUILT FROM NIGHTS STOLEN FROM THE SOUL SOCIETY 100 YEARS FROM NOW.
THEY WILL SOAK UP EVEN THE BLACK YOU WEAR.
TURN YOUR BLOOD, FLESH AND BONES BLACK...
...AND RETURN THEM TO NOTHING-NESS.
NOT EVEN REBIRTH WILL BE TOLERATED.
FALL TO A PITCH-BLACK HELL.

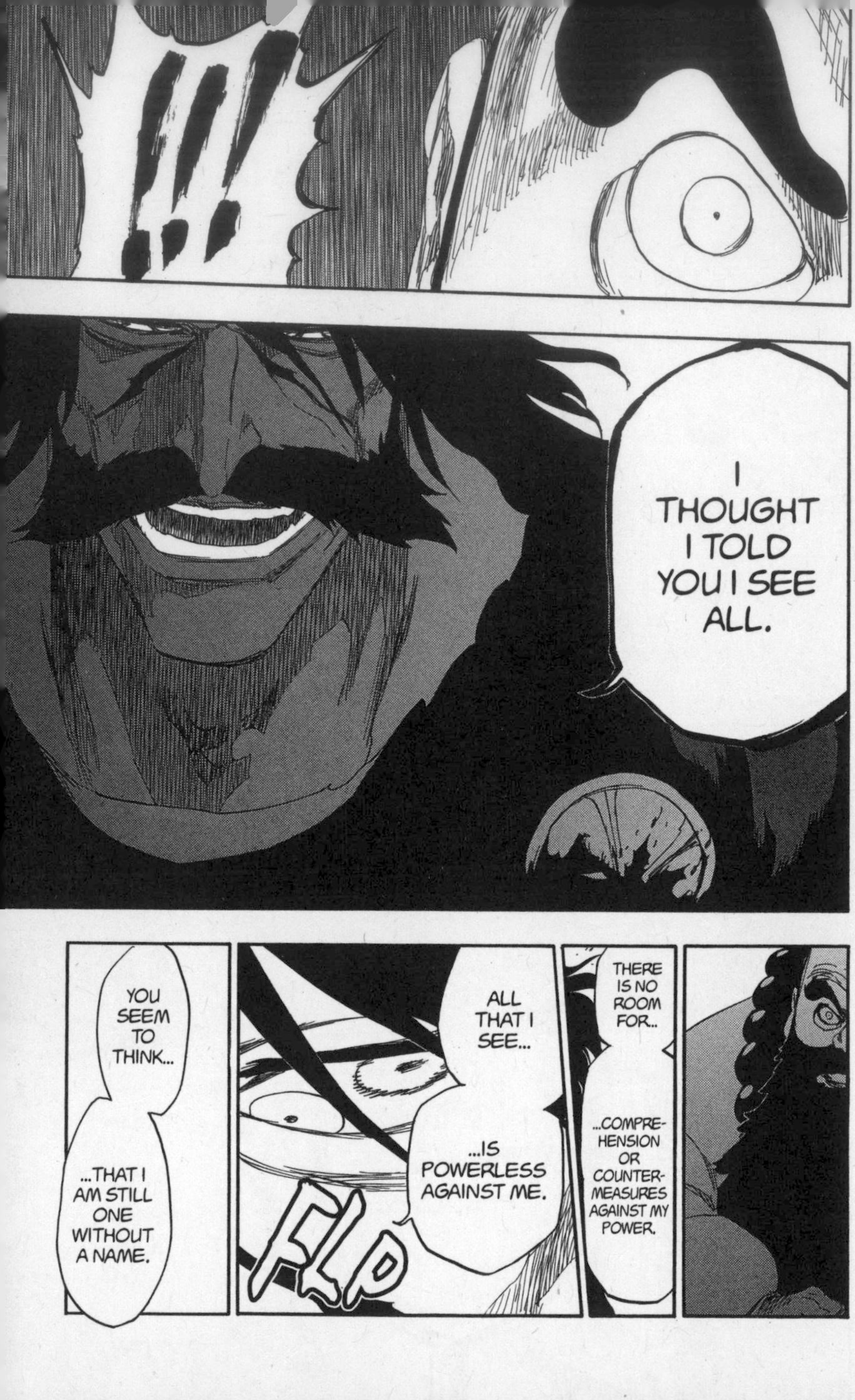
!!
I THOUGHT I TOLD YOU I SEE ALL.
THERE IS NO ROOM FOR...
...COMPRE-HENSION OR COUNTER-MEASURES AGAINST MY POWER.
ALL THAT I SEE...
...IS POWERLESS AGAINST ME.
FLP
YOU SEEM TO THINK...
...THAT I AM STILL ONE WITHOUT A NAME.

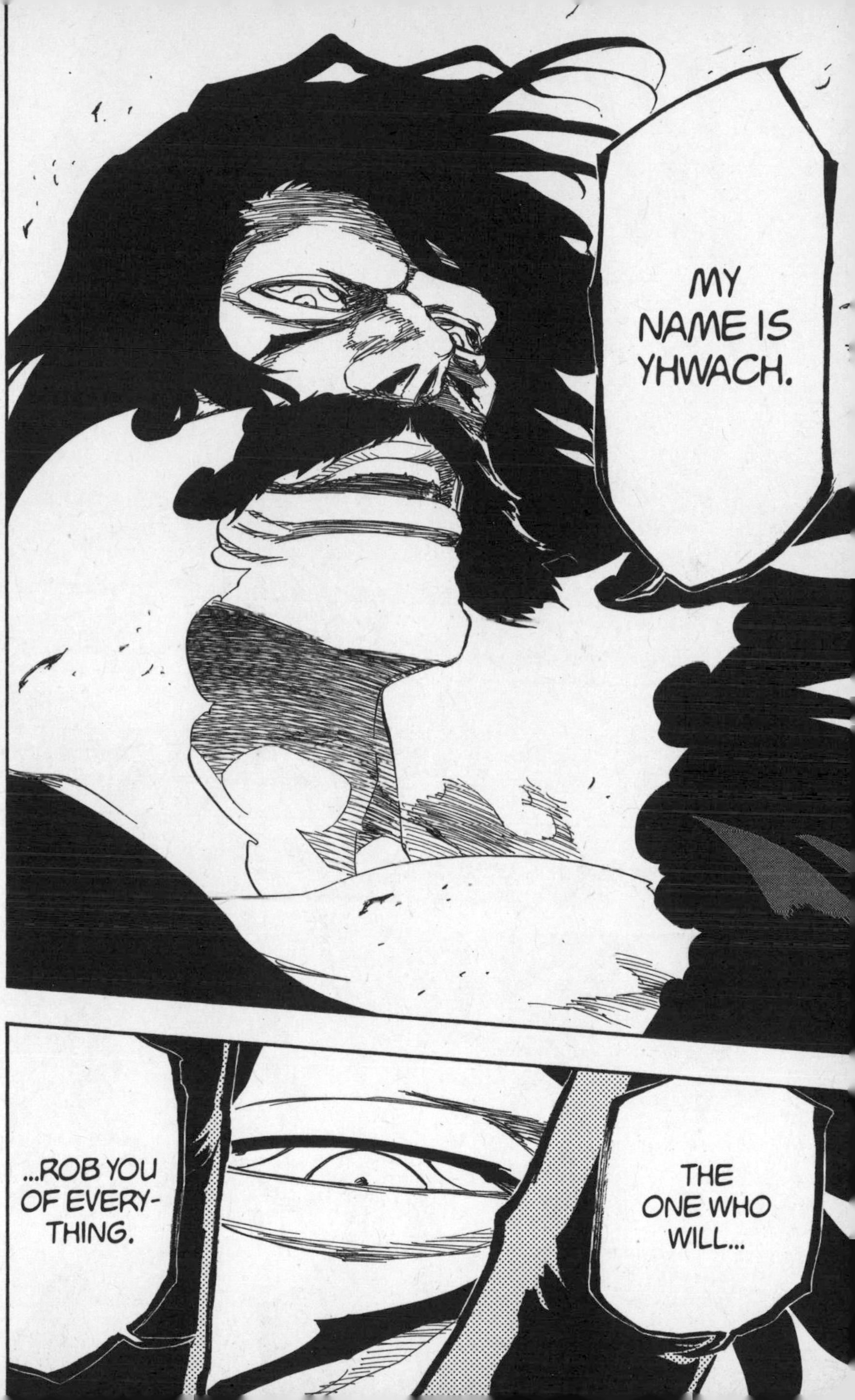
MY NAME IS YHWACH.
THE ONE WHO WILL...
...ROB YOU OF EVERY-THING.

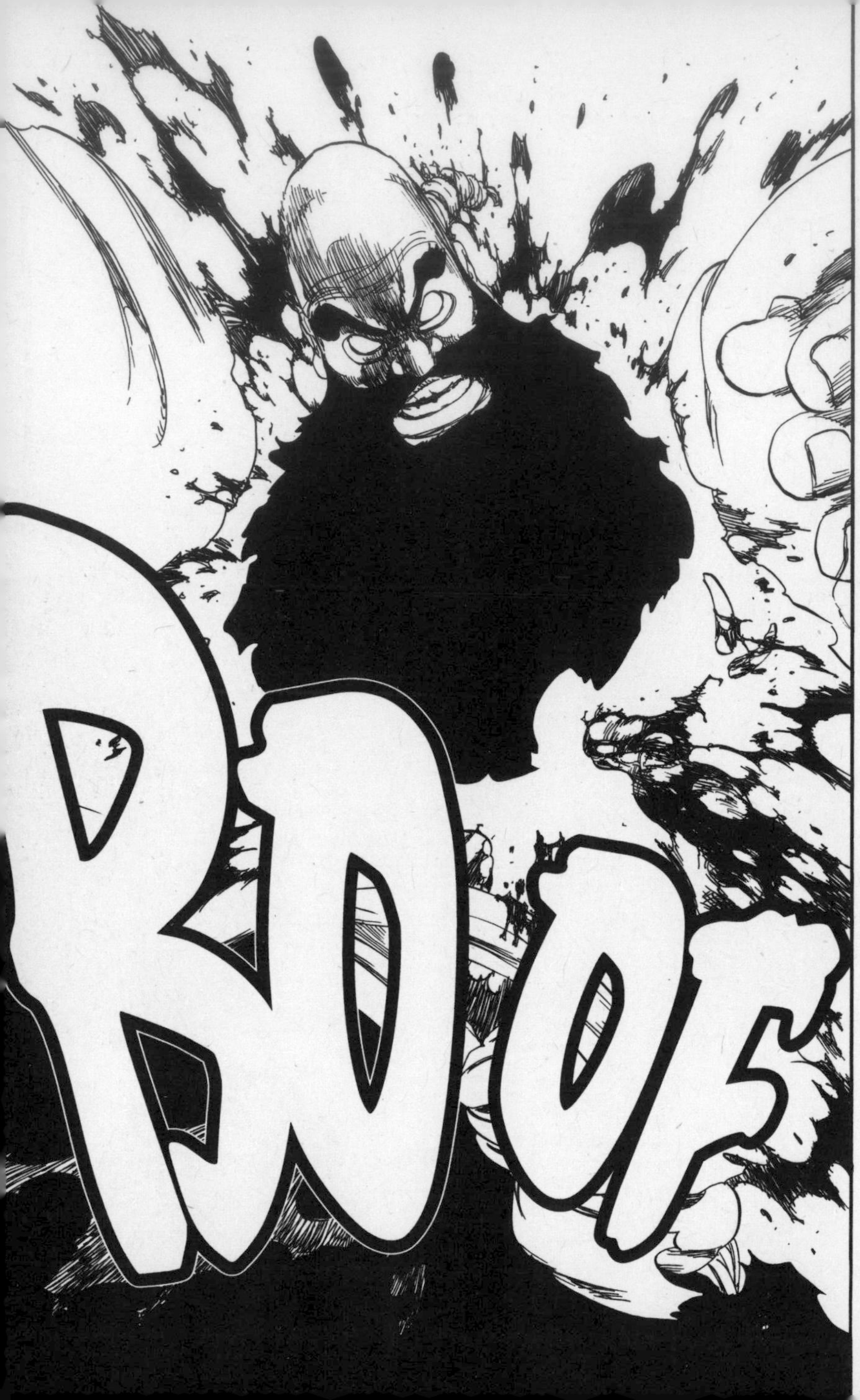

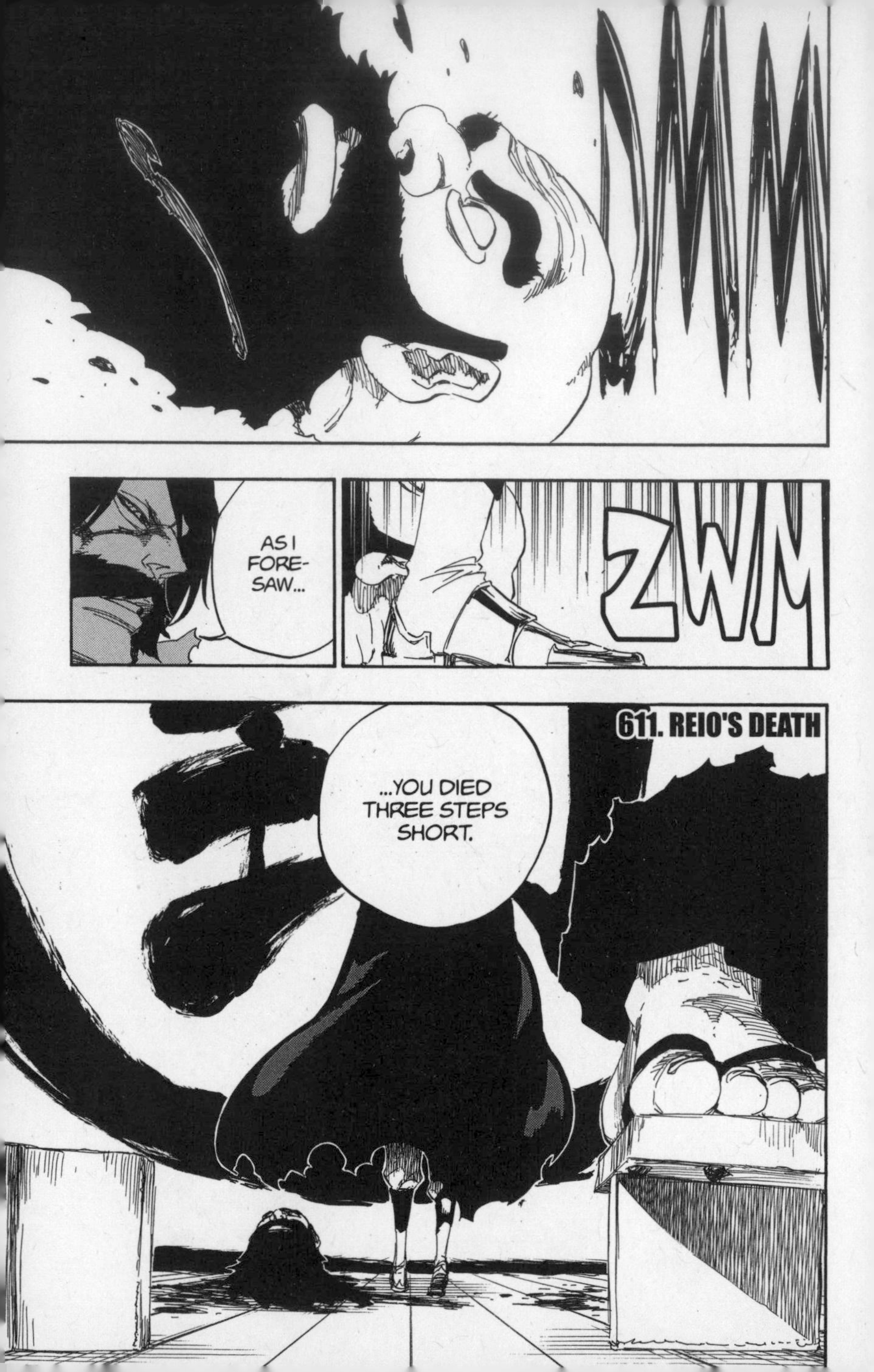
DMMM
ZWM
AS I FORE-SAW...
611. REIO'S DEATH
...YOU DIED THREE STEPS SHORT.

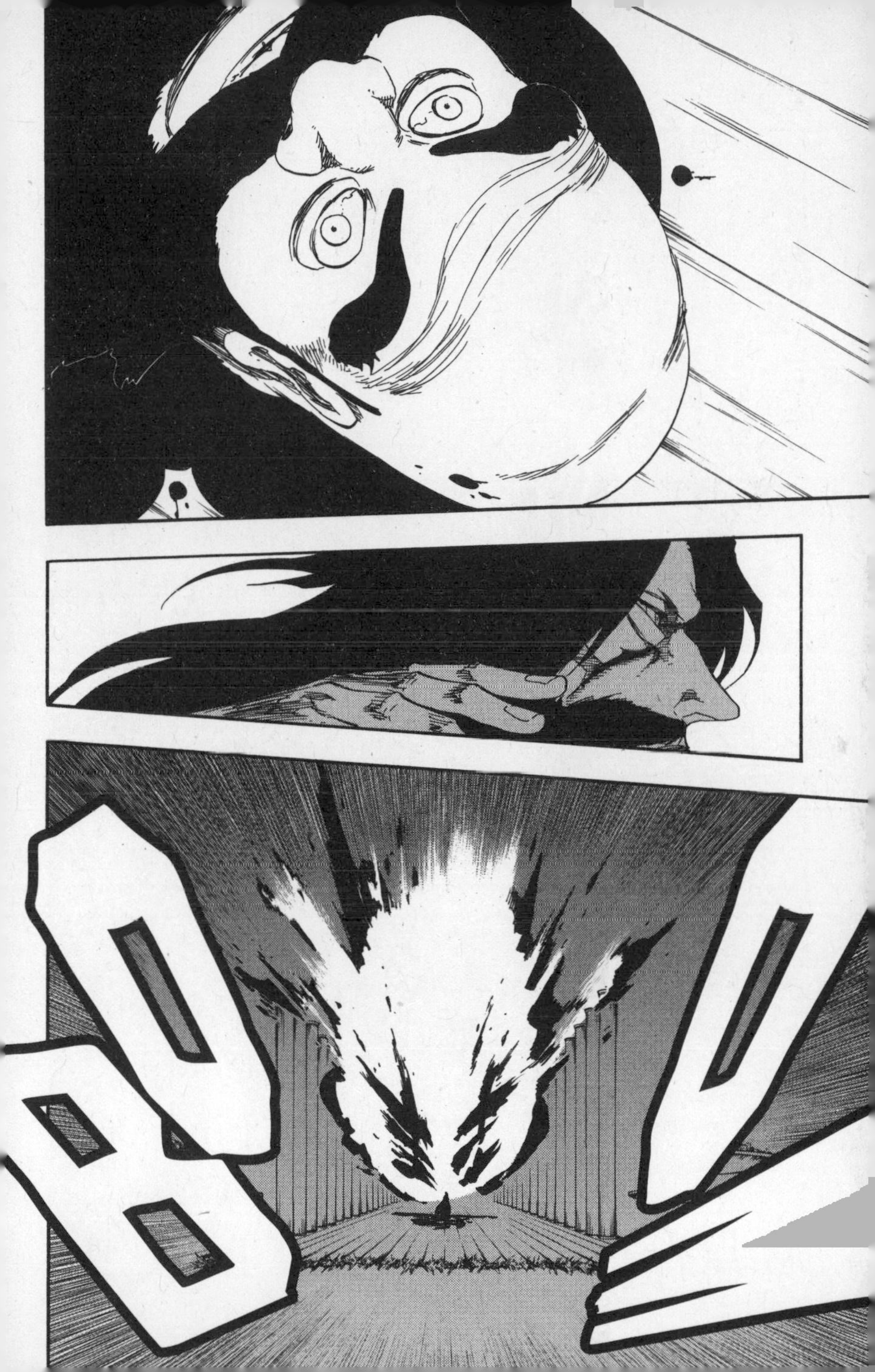
BOOM

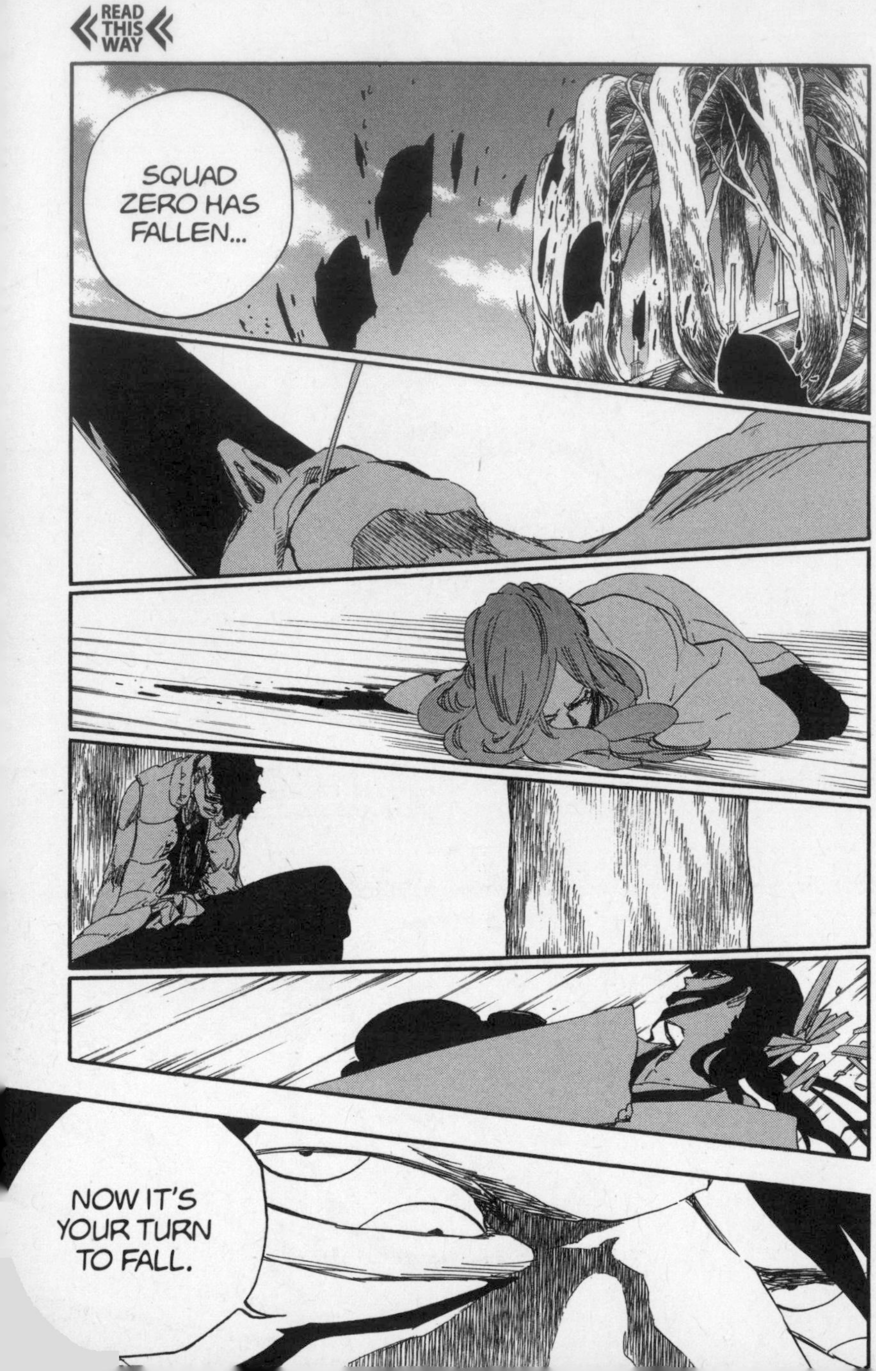
READ THIS WAY
SQUAD ZERO HAS FALLEN...
NOW IT'S YOUR TURN TO FALL.

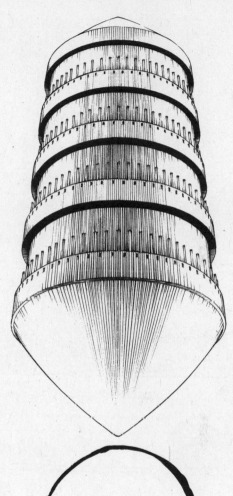

REIO.

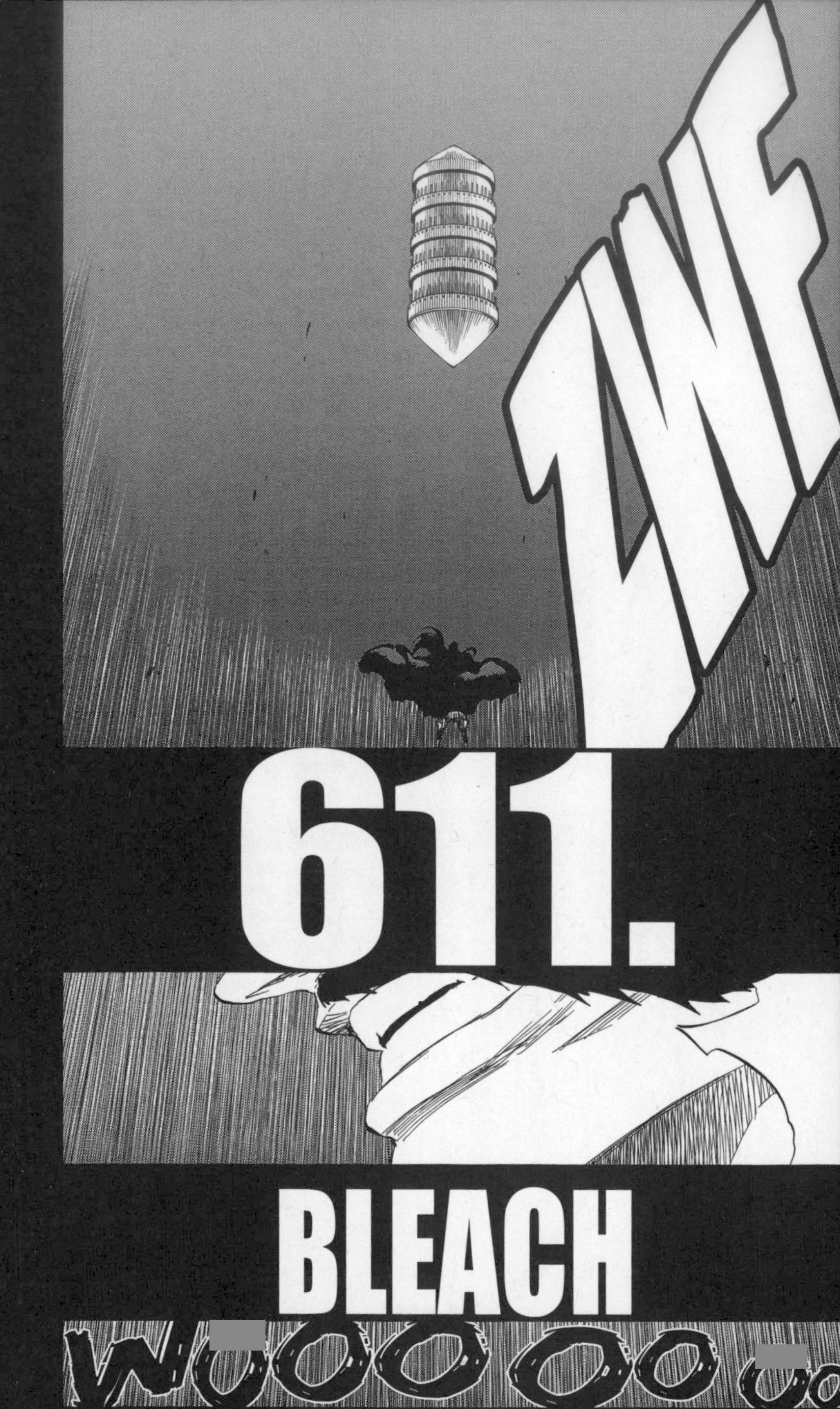
ZWF
611.
BLEACH

REIO'S DEATH

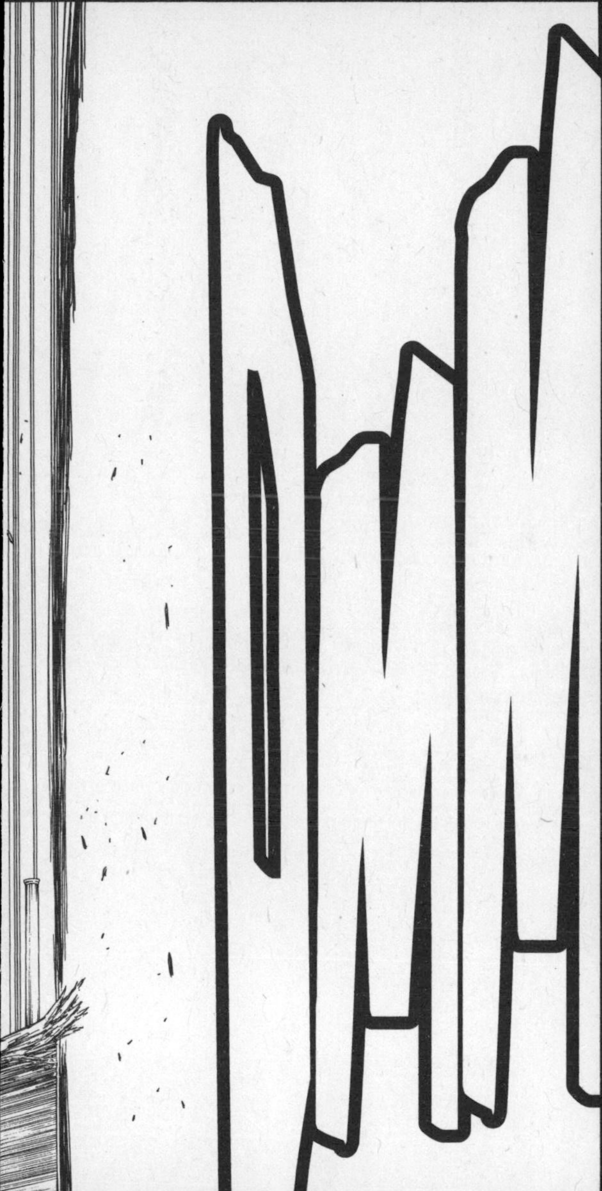

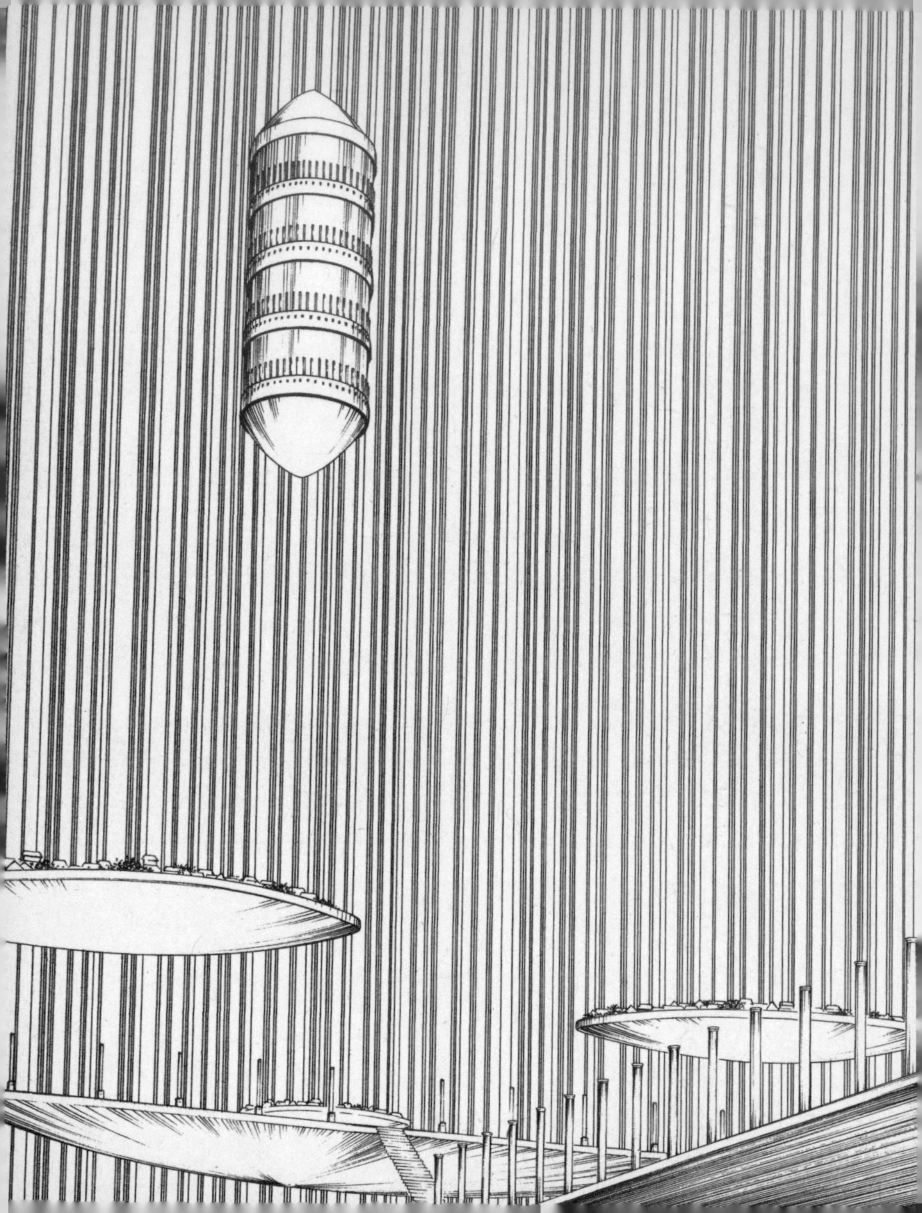

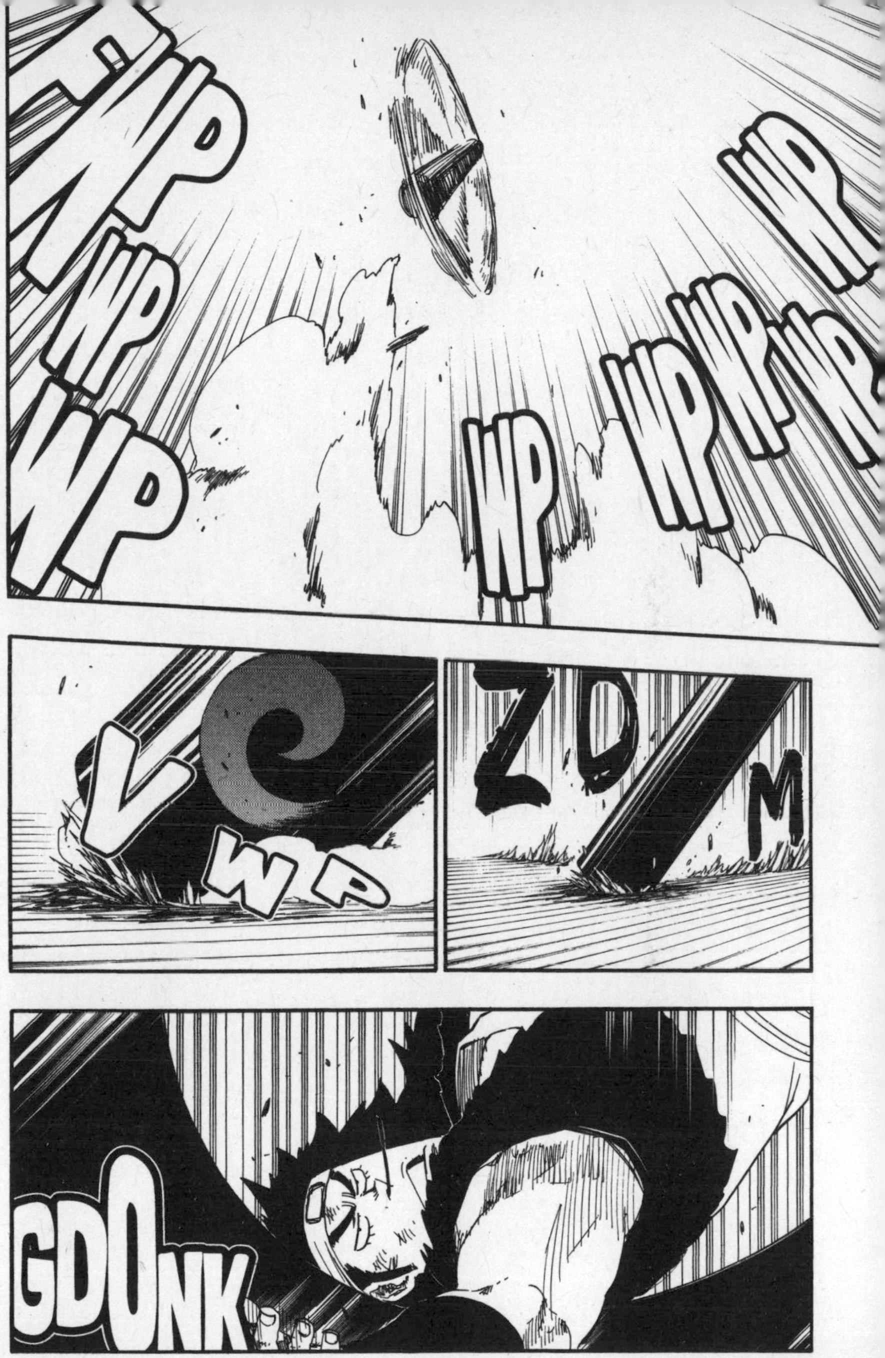
WP
WP
WP
WP
WP WP WP WP
ZDM
VWP
GDONK

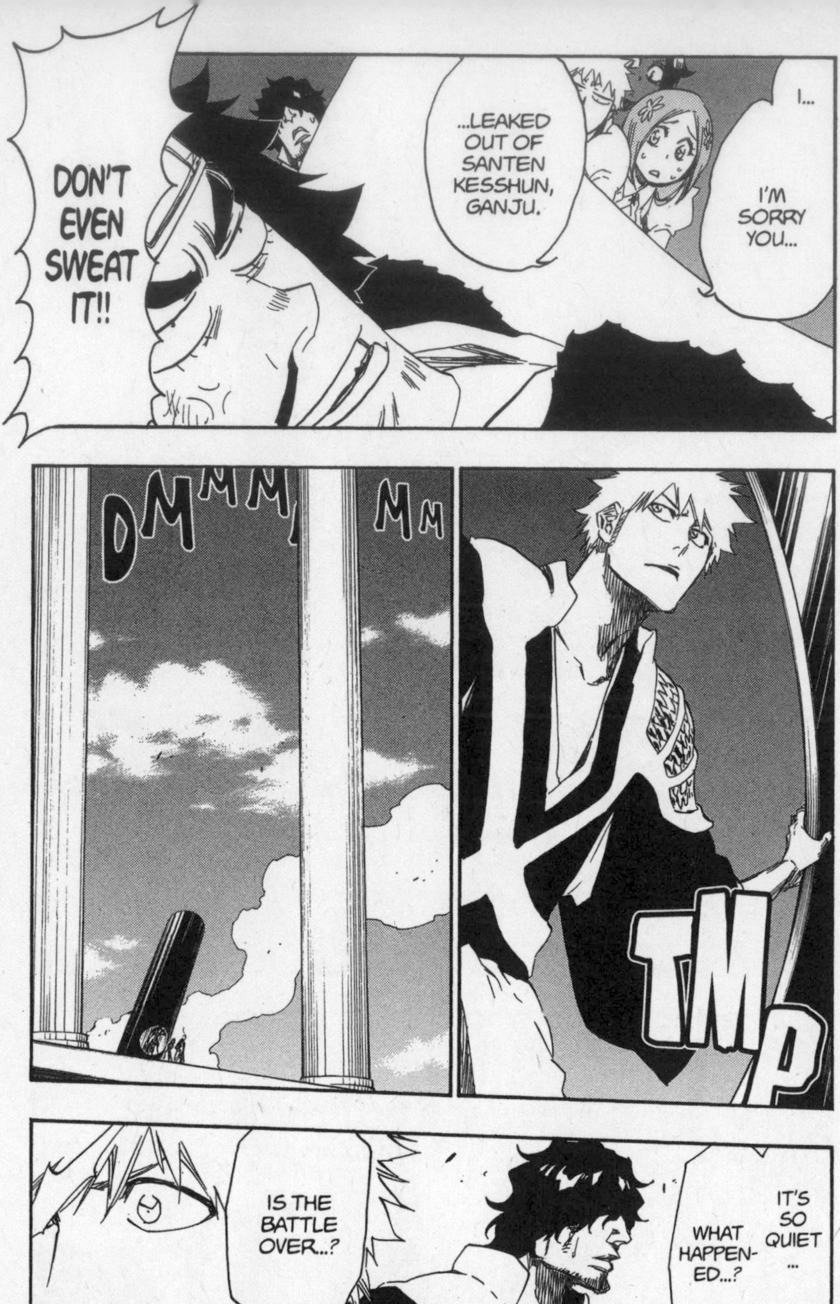
I... I'M SORRY YOU...
...LEAKED OUT OF SANTEN KESSHUN, GANJU.
DON'T EVEN SWEAT IT!!
TMP
DMMMMM
IT'S SO QUIET ...
WHAT HAPPEN-ED...?
IS THE BATTLE OVER...?

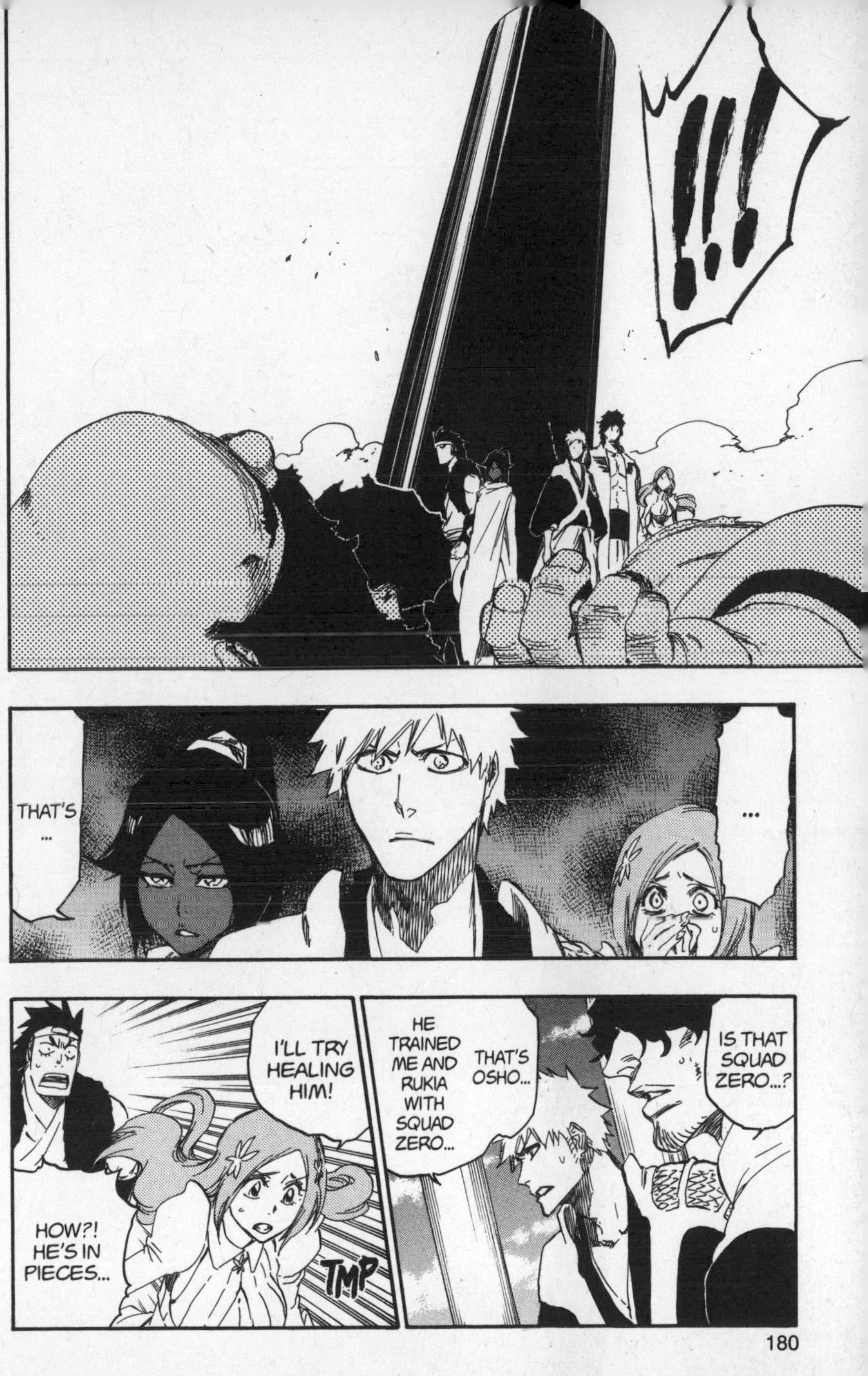
!!
...
THAT'S ...
IS THAT SQUAD ZERO...?
THAT'S OSHO...
HE TRAINED ME AND RUKIA WITH SQUAD ZERO...
I'LL TRY HEALING HIM!
TMP
HOW?! HE'S IN PIECES...

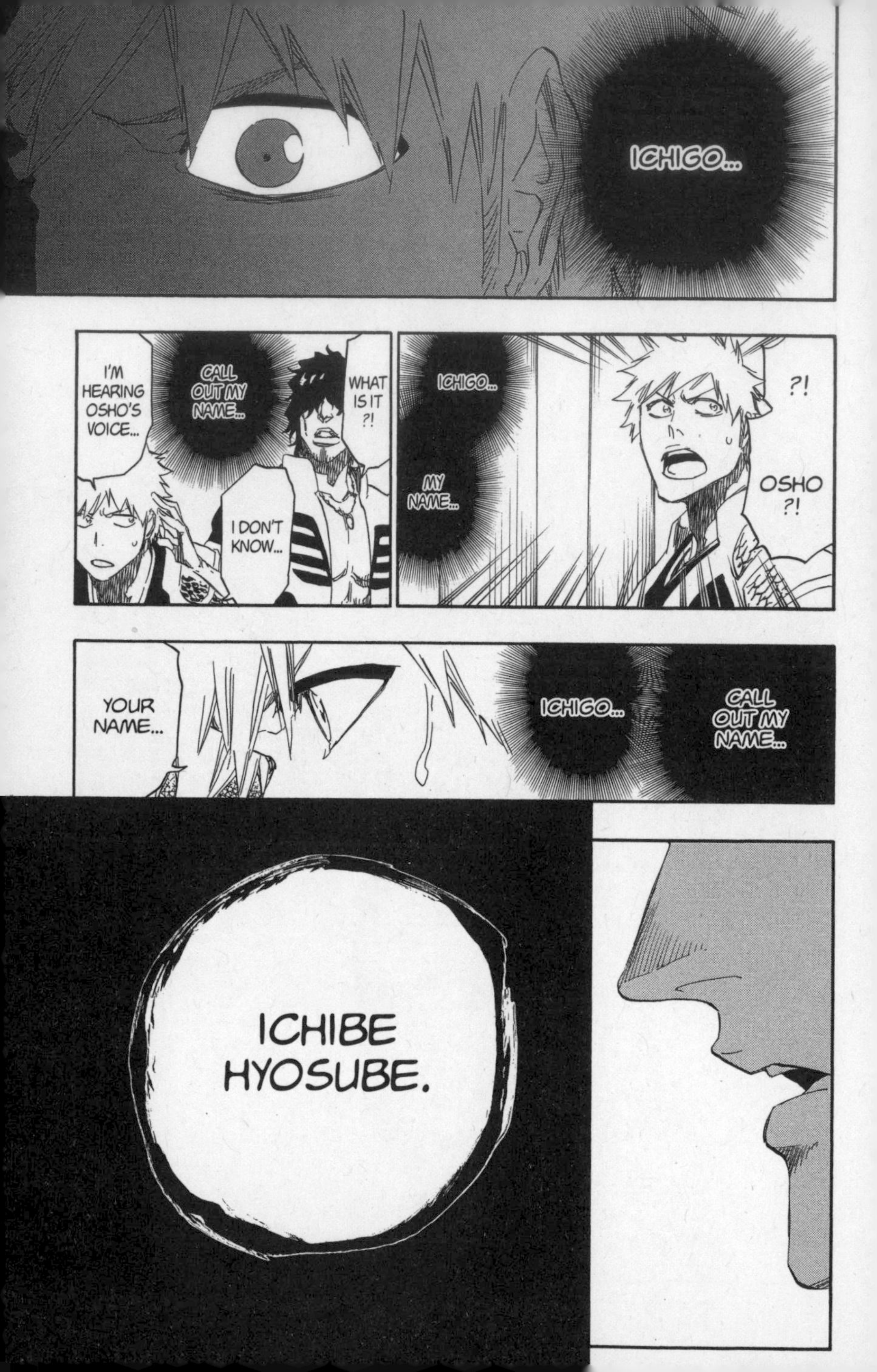
ICHIGO...
?!
ICHIGO...
OSHO ?!
MY NAME...
WHAT IS IT ?!
CALL OUT MY NAME...
I'M HEARING OSHO'S VOICE...
I DON'T KNOW...
CALL OUT MY NAME...
ICHIGO...
YOUR NAME...
ICHIBE HYOSUBE.

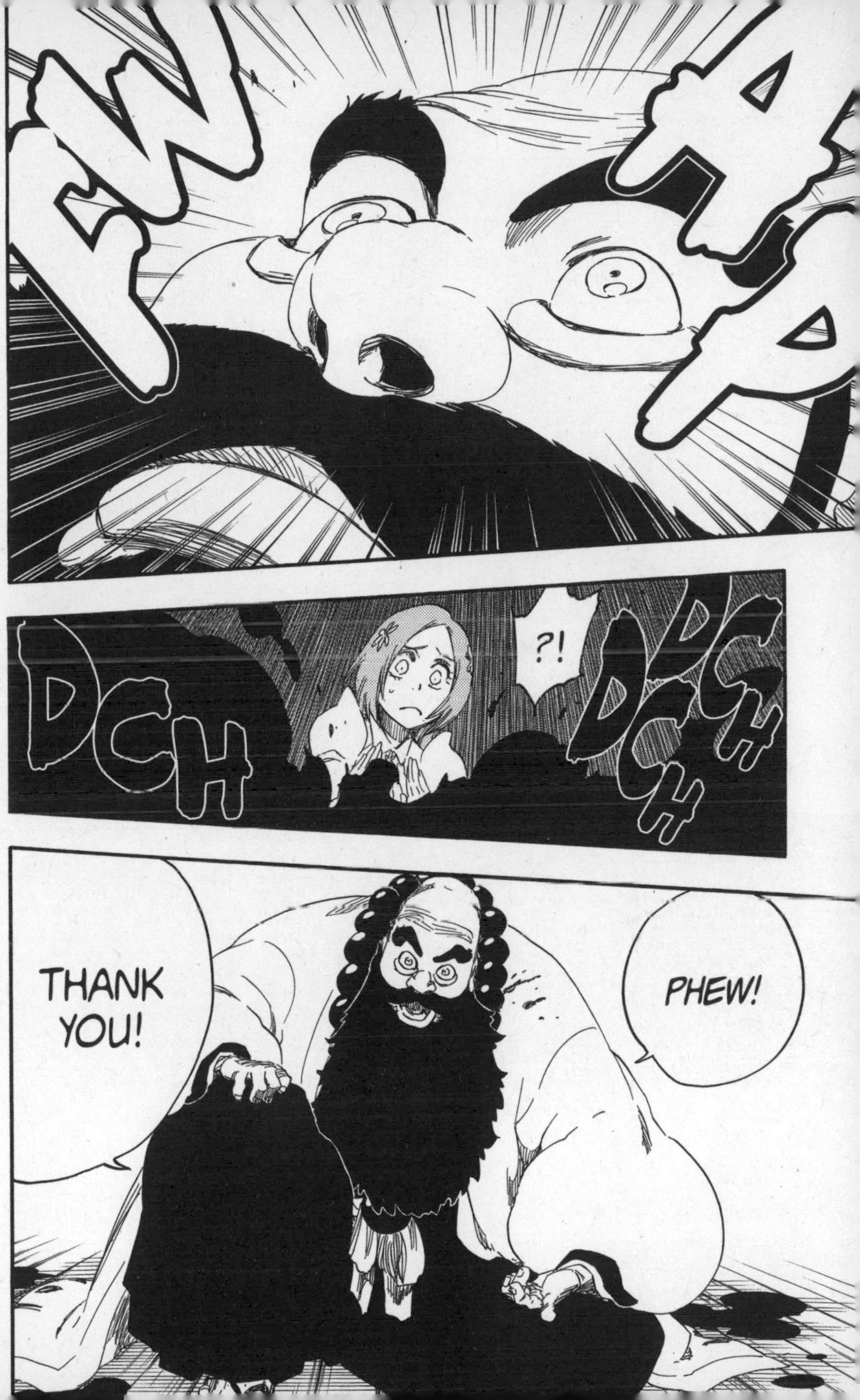
DCH DCH
?!
DCH
PHEW!
THANK YOU!

READ THIS WAY

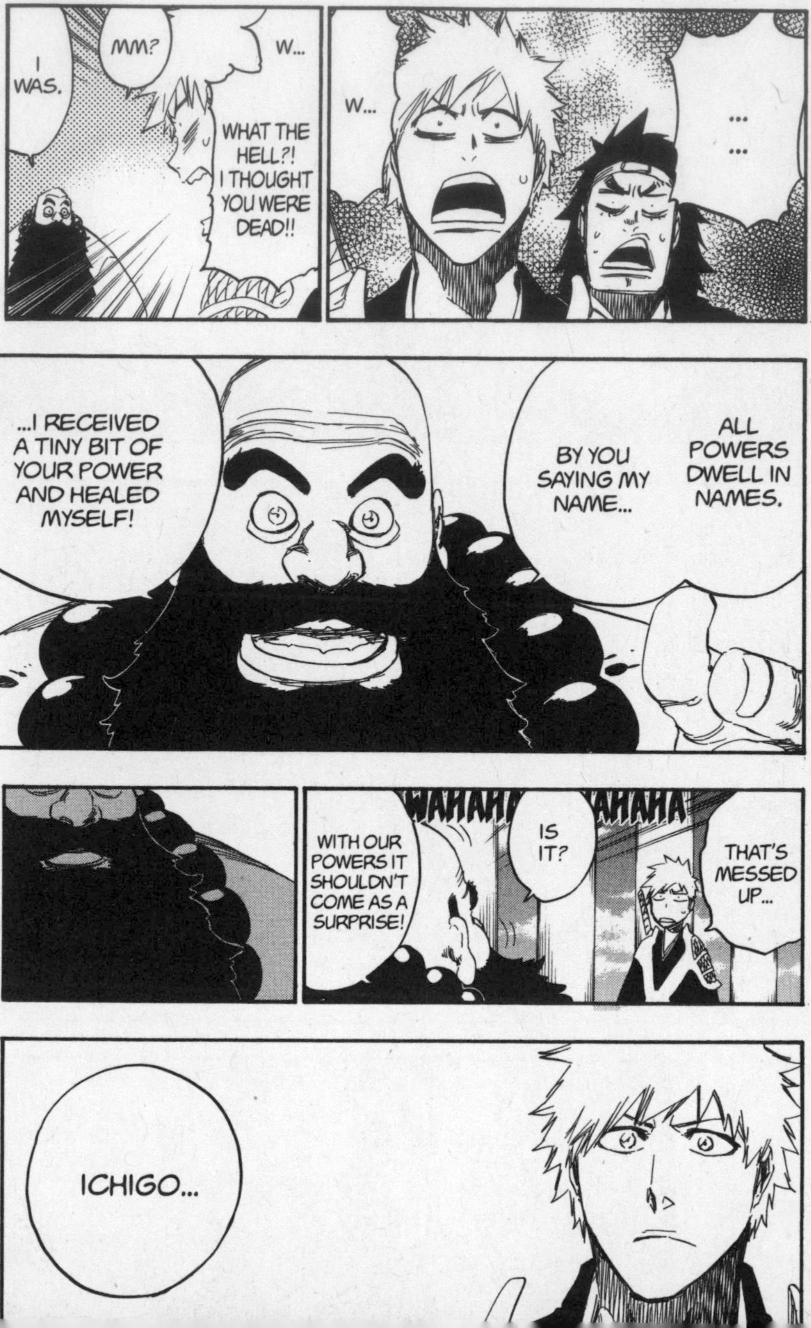
W...
...
...
W...
WHAT THE HELL?! I THOUGHT YOU WERE DEAD!!
MM?
I WAS.
ALL POWERS DWELL IN NAMES.
BY YOU SAYING MY NAME...
...I RECEIVED A TINY BIT OF YOUR POWER AND HEALED MYSELF!
WAHAHA
AHAHA
THAT'S MESSED UP...
IS IT?
WITH OUR POWERS IT SHOULDN'T COME AS A SURPRISE!
ICHIGO...

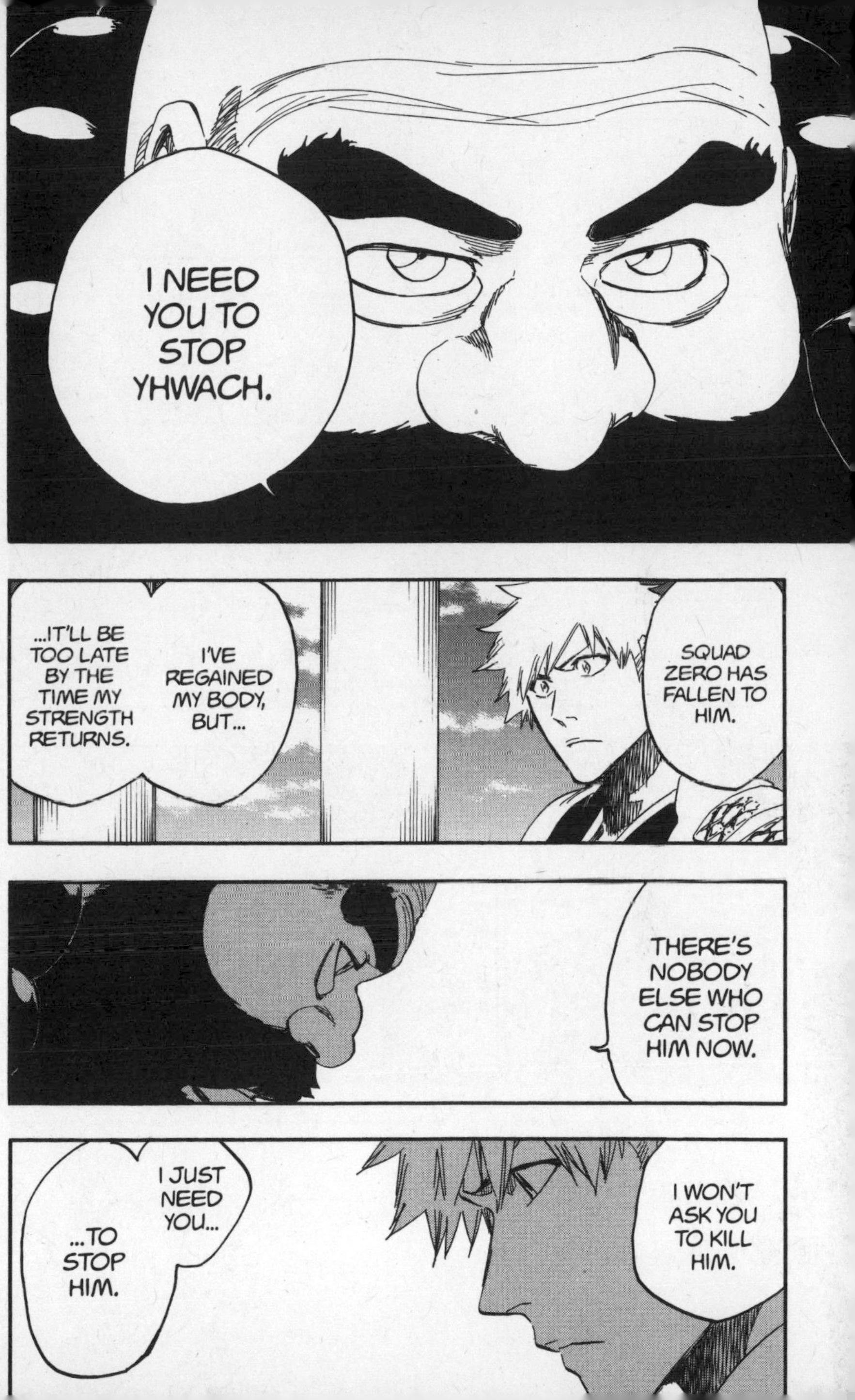
I NEED YOU TO STOP YHWACH.
SQUAD ZERO HAS FALLEN TO HIM.
I'VE REGAINED MY BODY, BUT...
...IT'LL BE TOO LATE BY THE TIME MY STRENGTH RETURNS.
THERE'S NOBODY ELSE WHO CAN STOP HIM NOW.
I WON'T ASK YOU TO KILL HIM.
I JUST NEED YOU...
...TO STOP HIM.

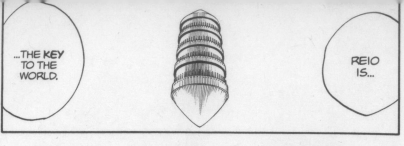

REIO IS...
...THE KEY TO THE WORLD.
IF REIO DIES...
THE SEIREI-TEI...
THE WORLD OF THE LIVING ...
HUECO MUNDO ...
ALL OF IT WILL COLLAPSE AND DIS-APPEAR.
I'M SORRY FOR LAYING...
...SUCH A TASK ON YOU.
ICHIGO...
PROTECT REIO!

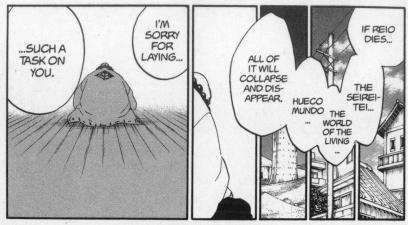

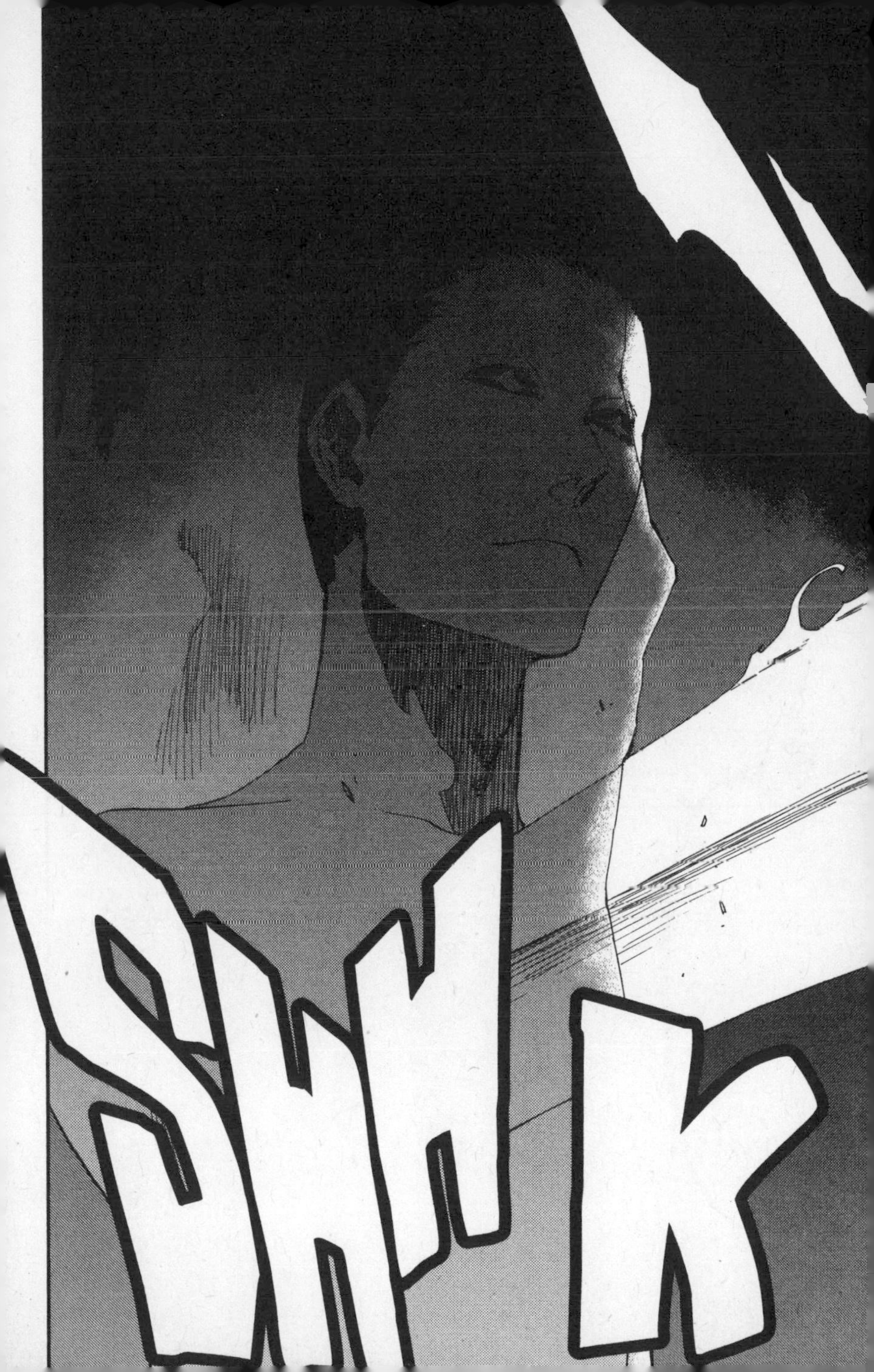
SHUK

FAREWELL, REIO...

MY FATHER WHO HAS...

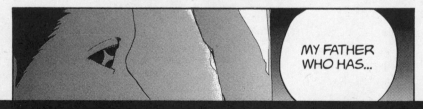

...SEEN THE FUTURE.

CONTI
NUED
IN
BLEACH
68

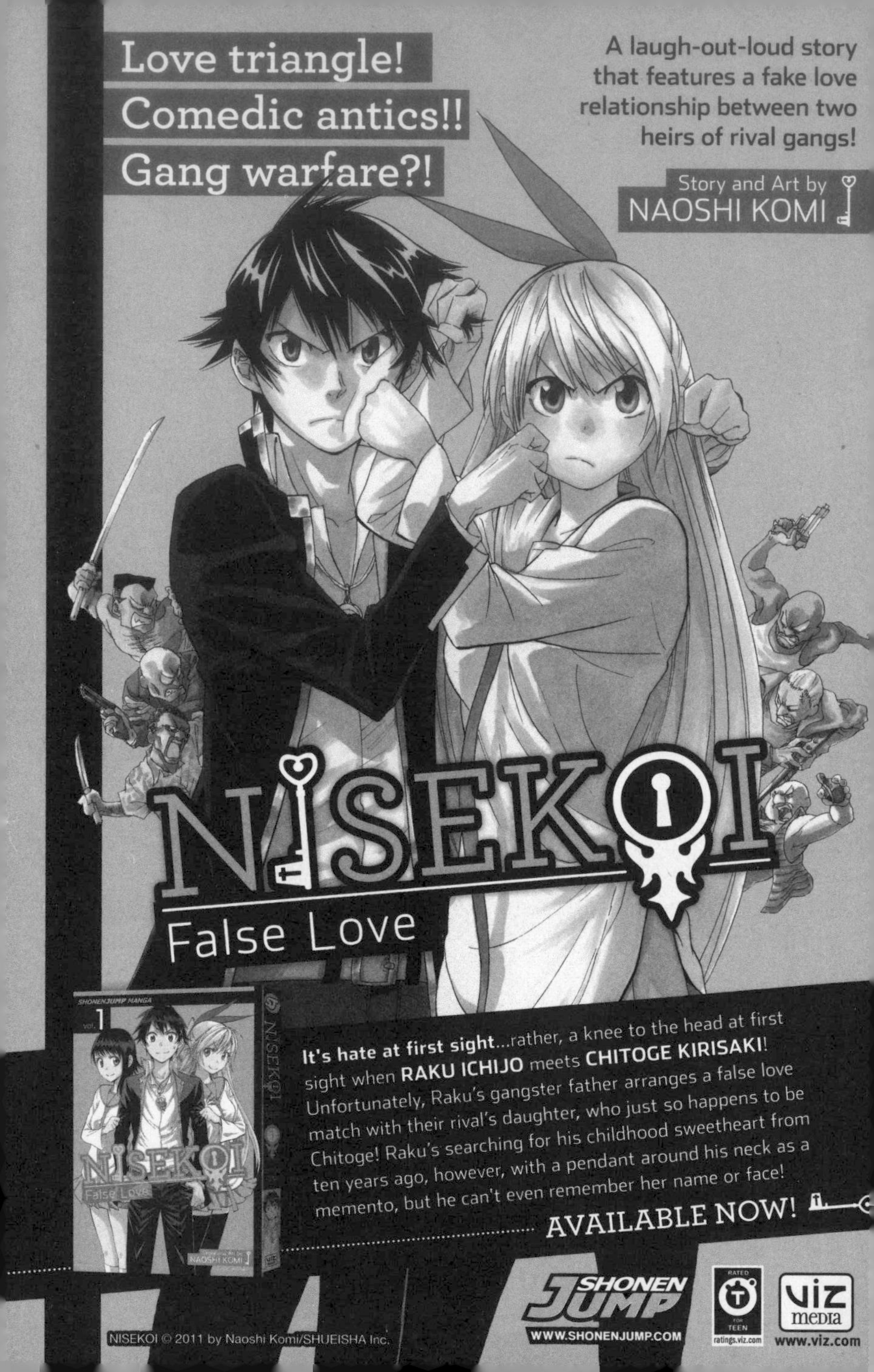
Love triangle!
Comedic antics!!
Gang warfare?!
A laugh-out-loud story that features a fake love relationship between two heirs of rival gangs!
Story and Art by
NAOSHI KOMI
NISEKOI
False Love
SHONENJUMP MANGA
vol. 1
NISEKOI
False Love
NAOSHI KOMI
It's hate at first sight...rather, a knee to the head at first sight when RAKU ICHIJO meets CHITOGE KIRISAKI! Unfortunately, Raku's gangster father arranges a false love match with their rival's daughter, who just so happens to be Chitoge! Raku's searching for his childhood sweetheart from ten years ago, however, with a pendant around his neck as a memento, but he can't even remember her name or face!
AVAILABLE NOW!
SHONEN JUMP
WWW.SHONENJUMP.COM
RATED T FOR TEEN
ratings.viz.com
viz media
www.viz.com
NISEKOI © 2011 by Naoshi Komi/SHUEISHA Inc.

You're Reading in the Wrong Direction!!

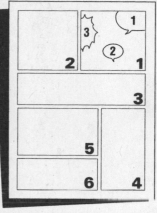

Whoops! Guess what? You're starting at the wrong end of the comic!

…It's true! In keeping with the original Japanese format, **Bleach** is meant to be read from right to left, starting in the upper-right corner.

Unlike English, which is read from left to right, Japanese is read from right to left, meaning that action, sound effects and word-balloon order are completely reversed… something which can make readers unfamiliar with Japanese feel pretty backwards themselves. For this reason, manga or Japanese comics published in the U.S. in English have sometimes been published "flopped"—that is, printed in exact reverse order, as though seen from the other side of a mirror.

By flopping pages, U.S. publishers can avoid confusing readers, but the compromise is not without its downside. For one thing, a character in a flopped manga series who once wore in the original Japanese version a T-shirt emblazoned with "M A Y" (as in "the merry month of") now wears one which reads "Y A M"! Additionally, many manga creators in Japan are themselves unhappy with the process, as some feel the mirror-imaging of their art skews their original intentions.

We are proud to bring you Tite Kubo's **Bleach** in the original unflopped format. For now, though, turn to the other side of the book and let the adventure begin…!

—Editor

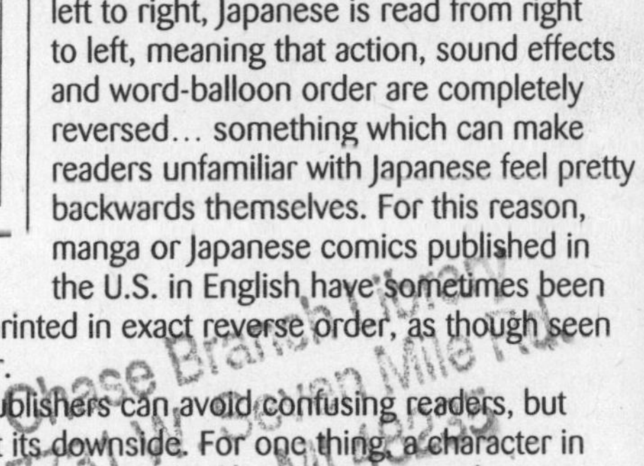